$60

EDUCATION AND CITIZENSHIP
IN LIBERAL-DEMOCRATIC SOCIETIES

EDUCATION AND CITIZENSHIP IN LIBERAL-DEMOCRATIC SOCIETIES

Teaching for Cosmopolitan Values and Collective Identities

Edited by
KEVIN McDONOUGH
and
WALTER FEINBERG

OXFORD
UNIVERSITY PRESS

OXFORD
UNIVERSITY PRESS

Great Clarendon Street, Oxford OX2 6DP

Oxford University Press is a department of the University of Oxford.
It furthers the University's objective of excellence in research, scholarship,
and education by publishing worldwide in

Oxford New York

Auckland Bangkok Buenos Aires Cape Town Chennai
Dar es Salaam Delhi Hong Kong Istanbul Karachi Kolkata
Kuala Lumpur Madrid Melbourne Mexico City Mumbai Nairobi
São Paulo Shanghai Taipei Tokyo Toronto

Oxford is a registered trade mark of Oxford University Press
in the UK and in certain other countries

Published in the United States
by Oxford University Press Inc., New York

British Library Cataloguing in Publication Data
Data available

Library of Congress Cataloging in Publication Data

Education and citizenship in liberal-democratic societies : teaching for cosmopolitan values
and collective identities / edited by Kevin McDonough and Walter Feinberg.
p. cm.
Includes bibliographical references.
1. Citizenship—Study and teaching. 2. Democracy—Study and teaching. 3. Political
science—Study and teaching. 4. Multicultural education. I. McDonough, Kevin, 1963–II.
Feinberg, Walter, 1937–
LC1091 E3843 2003 370.11′5—dc21 2002042555

ISBN 0–19–925366–8(hbk)

1 3 5 7 9 10 8 6 4 2

Typeset by Newgen Imaging Systems (P) Ltd., Chennai, India
Printed in Great Britain
on acid-free paper by
Biddles Ltd., Guildford and King's Lynn

To James Edward and Betty McDonough
To the memory of my grandparents
Jack and Sadie Weisberger

ACKNOWLEDGMENTS

All of the papers in this volume were originally presented at a symposium on "Collective Identities and Cosmopolitan Values: Group Rights and Public Education in Liberal-Democratic Societies", held in Montreal from June 22 to 25, 2000. We gratefully acknowledge The Spencer Foundation and the Social Sciences and Humanities Research Council of Canada for grants that supported this symposium, and without whose support this volume would not have been possible. We also thank the contributing authors, whose participation helped to make the symposium a memorable event, and for the discussion which has valuably enriched the revised essays that make up this volume. At Oxford University Press, we would like to thank Dominic Byatt, our editor, for his steady support for this project since its inception. The two reviewers for Oxford, Daniel Weinstock and Meira Levinson, have waived anonymity, and both deserve special thanks for their constructive and generous criticisms of almost every paper in the volume. Abigail Ostien was extremely helpful in organizing the conference; we thank her, Bryan Parochiniak, and Jane Nicholls for valuable assistance in preparing the typescript. Thanks also to Mercy Isaac for help in preparing the index.

K.McD.
W.F.

My wife, Jane Nicholls, and our son, Owen, deserve a singular note of gratitude. During the completion of this book, they provided enduring love, patience, and strength when it was sometimes difficult to do so. I thank them for this, and for the countless other joys they bring to my life.

K.McD.

CONTENTS

III: Liberal Constraints on Traditionalist Education

ABBREVIATIONS

BISD	Beaumont Independent School District
CIS	Clergy in the Schools
CCG	Comprehensive Conception of the Good
IVCF	InterVarsity Christian Fellowship
SEWA	Self Employed Women's Association

LIST OF CONTRIBUTORS

Anthony Appiah, *Princeton University*
David Blacker, *University of Delaware*
Harry Brighouse, *University of Wisconsin–Madison*
Shelley Burtt, London School of Economics
Joesph Dunne, *St. Patrick's College, Dublin City University*
Walter Feinberg, *The University of Illinois*
Mark Halstead, *University of Plymouth*
Stephen Macedo, *Princeton University*
Kevin McDonough, *McGill University*
Terence H. McLaughlin, *University of Cambridge*
Susan Moller Okin, *Stanford University*
Rob Reich, *Stanford University*
Kenneth A. Strike, *University of Maryland*
Jeremy Waldron, *Columbia University*
Melisse S. Williams, *University of Toronto*

Introduction: Liberalism and the Dilemma of Public Education in Multicultural Societies

WALTER FEINBERG AND KEVIN MCDONOUGH

The Dilemma of Public Education

Public education is at a critical juncture in virtually every liberal-democratic nation in the world. In contemporary liberal societies it was legitimized as the institution that would build a liberal and democratic industrial nation state by developing the surplus loyalty required to cement the particularistic and diverse religious and cultural components of a nation state together.[1] Today it is an object of suspicion among those who view the modern state as the agent, not of freedom and liberty, but of colonialization and oppression. These two views of the modern state set the stage for understanding the issues that are addressed in this book.

If the state is viewed as the agent of enlightenment and liberty, then it is necessary to view the public school as its instrument to bring about the emancipation of enslaved peoples the world over. If a culture oppresses women, then it is the job of the state and the public school to step in and provide a vision of liberation. If gay people are endangered by AIDS or by the violence of others, then the public school must secure their safety through a friendly curriculum and school environment. If a religious community restricts a child's horizons and limits her opportunities, then the public school must open up new vistas and make new opportunities available.

Yet again, if the liberal state is viewed as the instrument of colonialism and internal oppression, then the state supported school is the agent of the hegemonic forces seeking to colonize the life world and to spread the message of consumerism throughout the globe. If the school treats girls and boys equally or normalizes homosexual lifestyles while their local or home culture holds that women should be subordinate to men and homosexuality is sinful, then the school is harming that culture and its norms, as well as disrespecting parents' fundamental beliefs. And if a school teaches the principles of evolution without also teaching the principles of creationism, it is fostering a form of secular humanism on the child and is hostile to religion.[2]

While this debate is not altogether new,[3] at a time when the liberal state is insecure about its own foundations[4] there is an added ideological vulnerability that is not entirely reflected by the present, but possibly fading, dominance of public, state-supported common schools. Given the view, commonly espoused today, that the Enlightenment values that are supposed to underwrite state-supported schools are just one ideology among many,[5] a number of scholars now believe that there is a fundamental fault line in public education and that the very idea of the common school in a liberal society is an oxymoron. To some religious scholars the concept of the "common school" is a performative contradiction with which the state forces autonomy down the throats of children whose parents believe that their children must learn to submit themselves to God's will.[6]

To many, the appearance of such fault lines suggests that we should no longer build our educational superstructure in the same place, and that we should largely give up the idea of compulsory public education.[7] These people argue for vouchers, religious education, and more parental choice. To others the fault lines suggest that public education needs to be strengthened with greater funding, and perhaps with a higher level of accountability and stronger controls.

The primary aim of this volume is to examine some of the fundamental philosophical issues that give rise to these conflicts in order to shed light on questions of educational policy. This volume addresses foundational issues of the crisis in public education in liberal-democratic societies, not in the sense that the essays that comprise it articulate first principles on which the weight of liberal education and the liberal nation must stand or fall, but rather in the sense that the questions they raise cannot be avoided as other critical issues are addressed. Thus, the authors do not discuss choice or vouchers, even though some have written on this topic. With a few exceptions, they do not focus on curriculum issues although curriculum is a critical part of current educational debates. Instead, the focus is on the question of the aim of education in societies which want to advance a liberal-democratic agenda, and how those aims might need to be constrained within the context of religious or cultural groups that have a different agenda. This introductory essay will focus on outlining the educational and philosophical contexts that unify these essays and that together clarify the aims of the volume as a whole.

The Philosophical Context: Classical, Contemporary, and Affiliation Liberalism

It is customary to think of two forms of liberal theory. The first, classical liberalism, is associated with the political writings of John Locke with its emphasis on religious tolerance and individual freedom, and with the economic writings of Adam Smith, with its emphasis on market capitalism and minimum state control. The second, contemporary liberalism, has a more mixed pedigree, but it emphasizes the well-being of the individual and allows that there are times when an activist state may be needed to advance that goal. This form of liberalism is associated with the political writings of John Stuart Mill, John Dewey, and John Rawls, and with the economic writings of John Meynard Keynes. These two forms of liberalism are related because of the priority that they give to securing the conditions of individual liberty; but they differ on the empirical issue of the degree of state intervention which will best serve that goal. The transitional figure here is John Stuart Mill, whose utilitarianism highlights the fact that negative freedom, to use Berlin's term, is not the only goal of liberalism, and is largely the servant of positive freedom.

Classical liberals, such as Smith, argued thus for market capitalism not just on the grounds that negative freedom is a good in its own right, but on the grounds that minimum government controls allow the market to flourish to the benefit of all. Hence when Bentham and Mill articulated the utilitarian formula, they were articulating a principle that was already inherent in classical liberalism itself and were actually disengaging, at least for conceptual purposes, means (state control) and ends (individual well-being). When they made this conceptual move, however, there was still the feeling that minimum government intervention was still the best way to maximize the sum total of happiness. This empirical assumption was most prevalent in Mill's understanding of the principles limiting government authority, allowing it to control only those necessary features of social life that private citizens would not find profitable to undertake. This provision is apparent in Mill's conception of schooling where he feared the homogenizing influence of government schools and argued for a largely private system of education.[8] However, once the conceptual separation between individual well-being and minimum government control was established, other scholars could begin to challenge the empirical connection.

This challenge began to take place on a number of fronts both inside and outside of the liberal framework. Marxism, of course, was the major challenge that arose from outside the liberal tradition, because Marxists argued that the capitalist state itself was a causal factor in the continuation of human misery and needed to be overthrown. However, within the liberal tradition philosophers such as John Dewey argued that the state needed to take a more controlling role in advancing the public interest,[9] and economists such as Keynes[10] described some of the mechanisms that governments could use to direct and control the economy so that it more consistently served the general good. Later, John Rawls used liberal contract theory to argue for an interventionist liberal state that is justified by the benefits that it provides to its least advantaged citizens.[11]

Contemporary liberalism also had a profound impact on the way in which society viewed the role of government-controlled education, providing the philosophical foundation for the expansion of compulsory public schooling. The expansion was justified on a number of grounds; utilitarianism and nationalism being among the most prominent. However, there was also a concern, especially in the context of growing immigration, that children must be protected from the worst forms of child labor and that the state had the obligation to extend their opportunities and horizons beyond the limitations set by their parents and their affiliations. Hence, contemporary liberalism provided the state with a more active educational role, and provided a rationale that enabled schools to go beyond the authority of the parents.

The ideal of freedom of association was supposed to govern collective relationships, and this ultimately included the freedom to associate or to disassociate with the affiliations of one's own parents. Both classical and contemporary forms of liberalism were intended to lift the individual above the constraints of family or cultural background and education was expected to be the device for realizing this vision. As such, the ideal liberal teacher was the one who was blind to racial, ethnic, religious, or gender differences and was able to treat all children alike.

Both classical and contemporary forms of liberalism have been attacked by communitarian critics[12] who emphasize the fact that we do not choose all of our associations as the liberal would have it, but that we are embedded in certain relationships more than in others, and that our very physical and psychological development is dependent on some more than others. The communitarian concludes from this factual basis that there are certain duties and obligations that we have that are not dependent on free choice or a right to associate with whomever we wish, and that our very character is a matter of how well or how poorly we execute these duties.

Whereas contemporary liberalism has often been seen in conflict with classical liberalism because of the different emphasis given to negative and positive freedom,[13] there is now emerging a third form of liberalism that is in tension with both because of the emphasis that it gives to cultural collectivities. The newest phase of liberalism—what we call here affiliation liberalism—takes a page out of the communitarian critique but turns it in a different direction. Affiliation liberals acknowledge the culturally embedded self, but reject the communitarian conclusion that individual flourishing depends on permanent loyalty to one's primary group. Rather, affiliation liberals allow that individual flourishing takes place within a cultural context, and they conclude that when such support is threatened the state may have a responsibility to provide special protection to certain collective formations, be they cultural, religious, or national, from temptations that the larger society allows individual members to choose in ways that weaken solidarity. For example, Charles Taylor argues that the expressive authenticity that liberals seek is to be found not just within individual persons but also within cultural formations, and that states may have obligations to shape individuals who will choose in ways that will strengthen culture. Similarly, Will Kymlicka argues that because individual flourishing depends on a congruent culture, the modern liberal state has special obligations to threatened minority societal cultures to help them maintain their cultural and linguistic heritage. Thus affiliation liberals accept as a primary value the idea of freedom of association, but they allow that in certain cases state support for collective formations may be a precondition which individuals require if this and other liberal values are to be fully exercised. When fragile cultural groups are allowed to disappear it both detracts from the number of alternatives available within a society and provides additional pressures to individuals born into that culture to exit it. Thus, while affiliation liberals accept the communitarian idea that individuals are embedded in a collective identity that nourishes them and provides them with the means for flourishing, it uses this insight to press the larger society for certain cultural dispensations or supports.

The educational model for the affiliation liberal then is not the colorblind teacher of the classical or the contemporary liberal, but the culturally sensitive or aware teacher. It is the teacher who understands the character of the culture of her children, can speak their language, discuss their literature, respect their values, and engage with their expressive cultural forms. It is the teacher who, while empowering her students to negotiate the practices and institutions of the larger society, allows them the self-confidence to carry their culture with them when doing so.[14]

Affiliation liberalism draws from a number of traditions outside of philosophy. While it has not yet developed the systematic economic framework of the classical or contemporary strains, the work of Amartya Sen and his attempt to develop an economic standard of human flourishing that can be applied comparatively across different groups has a certain affinity with the concerns of the affiliation liberal.[15] On a practical basis, the work of the Grumeen bank in Bangladesh, as well as the South Shore Community Bank in Chicago, provide models whereby traditional economic institutions can be employed to advance communal goals.

Unlike the earlier forms of liberalism, economics has taken a back seat to other disciplines, especially anthropology, as the ally of affiliation liberalism. The anthropologist has taught the liberal the significance of culture and the multiple forms that human flourishing can take. Thus instead of condemning alternative cultural forms as inferior to those thought best to support liberal ideas, some affiliation liberals now allow for a plurality of cultures, generally of equal worth.[16] These liberals must also consider the likelihood that those cultural forms that support liberalism are themselves just one among this plurality.

This turn, however, is not a comfortable one for every brand of liberalism. There is some tension even within affiliation liberalism itself, a tension that has contributed to weakening liberalism's confidence in itself. Affiliation liberalism largely subscribes to the major values of previous forms of liberalism, but it differs with them over the conditions that their fulfillment requires. One of the reasons for this weakened confidence can be seen if we examine the question of the limits of individual freedom, especially the freedom of parents to educate their children, in light of the problems that affiliation liberalism introduces. In classical and contemporary liberalism, individual freedom ended when someone else's rights were trespassed upon. However, this assumed a reasonable consensus about what to count as a right and what to judge as a trespass, a consensus that is not clear for affiliation liberalism. Freedom had its limits and one of the critical places where these limits were most visible was in the education of young children. It was the obligation of the liberal state to minimize the opportunity that parents and teachers had to indoctrinate children, and in turn to make them into reflective critical thinkers. Just how to set the standard for determining whether or not indoctrination was taking place and how to develop the pedagogy to minimize its occurrence occupied the attention of the most prominent philosophers of education for a few decades.[17]

The question of limits is considerably complicated by affiliation liberalism. On the one hand, liberalism requires a commitment to basic individual rights while affiliation liberalism's sensitivity to cultural differences informs it that different cultures understand such rights differently, and that not all cultures are committed to respecting human rights; or at least they are not committed to respecting the same package of rights in exactly the same ways.

Contemporary liberalism also assumed that individual freedom was a necessary condition of human flourishing. While individuals could exercise their right to choice poorly and hence choose alternatives in which their well-being was not well served, there were few who would allow that free choice was not at least a necessary condition of human well-being. This was the point of John Stuart Mill's quip that he would rather be Socrates dissatisfied than a pig satisfied.

Thus some liberals say that children have a right to an autonomous future in which they can choose to live their own lives according to their own conception of the good.[18] Other liberals hold that the state has an obligation to honor the references of local cultural groups and religious affiliations and to allow parents to direct the education of their children, even if that education advances illiberal values.[19] Some hold that this contradiction can be resolved as long as we read it not as rejecting individual rights altogether, but as a presumption of cultural worth, a presumption that could prove to be false if individual rights are systematically violated.[20] Yet others argue that the greater danger is the trigger-happy response of some contemporary liberals who insist that every cultural deviation is a threat to national coherence.[21] According to some of these critics, the only requirement that liberals need to make is that cultural and religious groups provide their members with a right of exit. Beyond that, the state should have little concern with the inner workings of a group and the way it treats its own members.[22]

The crucial issue here is how to determine the limits to parents' educational rights when two aspects of affiliation liberalism conflict—a concern to promote children's autonomy conflicts with maintaining group integrity. This issue has been tested in the courts, and the direction has been uncertain and inconsistent. In Yoder, for example, the US Supreme Court asserted the right of a cultural/ religious group, the Amish, to limit the opportunities of their own children in order that the coherence and solidarity of the culture could be maintained. Many liberals applauded this decision. In the Mozert case, a Court refused this same right to a religious group that wished to remove their children from a reading unit when the parents claimed that by participating in the program the students would be sinning against God's will as this group understood it. Here too liberals applauded. The problem is that in these, and in more mundane instances, two aspects of liberalism come into conflict, and the distinctions, exceptions, and priorities that are needed to anticipate and resolve these cases are in the process of being created, and remain to be refined by affiliation liberals. Public education in virtually every Western country is in the cross hairs of this internal conflict within liberalism. Furthermore, because populations are migrating from many different parts of the globe, challenging previously taken-for-granted cultural assumptions, almost every country in the Western world is confronted with this issue.

Educational Context: Beyond Governance

The chapters in this book address the requirements of citizenship education in liberal-democratic political theory as it has evolved in recent years, in order to take into account claims for cultural recognition through education.[23] Education presents a unique problem for such theories, because young children as yet have no culture of their own. As Anthony Appiah observes in Chapter 2 of this volume, children are not born into the world with a full-blown set of attachments or loyalties. The phrase "their culture" should thus be followed by a question mark. We normally use the phrase without quotation or question marks only because we assume that there is some agent—parent, community, or state—that is marked as a part of a cultural formation to which the child should automatically have an affiliation. However, what is to count as "their culture" is sometimes a matter of contention. They do not have a culture until their parents, their parents' community, the state, or some other agent "give" them a culture.

Given this insight, whatever school the children attend it will contribute to the shaping of their future allegiances. While recently parents have gained a more sympathetic hearing,[24] in the earlier part of the nineteenth century it was assumed, at least for immigrant children in the United States, that the schools were there to shift the child's loyalty away from the parents' cultural community toward the national one.[25] Thus, there is no single ready-made answer to the question, "Who should control and govern the education of the child?" During some periods the state has asserted a stronger claim than during others. However, even in cases where parents have been given a presumptive right over their children's education, it is because of the assumption that they have a stronger interest in the child's future well-being and that they have greater knowledge about the child's interests than any other person. Importantly, this presumptive right is conditional and can be withdrawn if the child's interests are not being served in a reasonable way,[26] and the state usually reserves for itself and its agents the role of determining the limits of an education that meet those interests. Thus the questions of school governance, control, and accountability entail questions about educational aims and the legitimate claims that different groups can make on a child's developing attachments. What is the state to count as a reasonable educational interest, and how far can a cultural or a religious group go in shaping a child's loyalty?

The answer to this question is not fixed once and for all, but undergoes changes. When liberalism was secure in its own Enlightenment foundation, few educators doubted that the school had an important role in developing citizens committed to the nation state. Given this unquestioned goal, some educators claimed that they had an obligation to erase the remnants of the parents' immigrant culture and to reproduce in the child an emotional attachment to the nation state. Today, few educators would voice their commitment in such absolute terms. In the United States a series of Supreme Court cases have provided parents with some preemptory rights in determining the education of their children.[27] In Canada, indigenous groups have attained greater authority over their children's education, and in Denmark and the Netherlands state funds are available to religious groups who wish to establish schools.

The present debate pulls public schools in different directions. On the one hand many subgroups within the state—racial, religious, or ethnic groups, or the disabled—lay claim to cultural rights and, as an extension of those rights, to greater authority over their children's education. On the other hand, some people believe that both local cultural allegiance and national loyalty are outdated ideals, dating back to a time before the high-tech revolution and before we knew much about the threat to our environment arising from overpopulation and overconsumption. According to this cosmopolitan view the greatest need is to establish global objects of loyalty that supersede local and national ones.

All objects of identity are constructed in one sense or another. Before people became attached to the modern nation state as we know it, there was no nation state.[28] Even "primary" cultural groups are, as Waldron points out in this volume, constructed out of the historical encounters of different people moving in and out of different regions. This construction continues to happen, and one of the most interesting things about educational practices, including those that occur in schools, is that they are involved in the process of creating and then maintaining the very object of attachment that will, turned around now as supporting structures, continue to sustain them. For example, there is a growing precipitous movement toward a European identity that is reshaping the form of affiliation education and broadening children's sense of community. As Dunne points out in Chapter 4, in cases such as Northern Ireland this wider community may then provide the healing tissue required to close the open wounds of nationality and enable religious conflicts to mend.

We cannot anticipate with absolute certainty the way in which any of these movements will eventually work out. From the organic community of Plato to the working class of Marx, history is replete with vain predictions about future affiliations. Nevertheless, we can try to understand the nature of the concerns people have when they press for different forms of affiliation and the possible responses that the liberal state might make to them.

At present, the issues involved in affiliation education have been papered over by a state level discourse that focuses on the utilitarian side of education. This discourse would have us evaluate schools and nations in terms of scores on standardized tests, scores that are intended to serve as a proxy for evaluating the quality of the nation's future workforce. Yet this focus is both partial and distorting.

It is partial because it already assumes, by asserting that the nation is the ultimate unit of competition, that the nation is also the appropriate object of the attachments that should be developed in the school.[29] Yet by failing to make this assumption explicit, this discourse dissembles a robust discussion of affiliation education, one that is able to take into account the fact that much of labor, and a great deal of capital, is becoming more global in nature. (At the conference at which the papers in this volume originated, at least eight of the participants were teaching in a country that was different than the one in which they held primary citizenship.) Thus when we project a nation's future work force, we should realize that students and workers are not coextensive. Many students presently in schools in Canada, for example, will be a part of the work force of another country and many now being educated in other countries will become part of the Canadian work force. And what is true for Canada is also true for most other Western nations.

The focus on the vocational aspects of education is distorting because it incorrectly assumes that the vocational side of schooling should be the exclusive side of schooling. Yet every vocation is supported by a vast network of relationships—functional, conceptual, and emotional— that tie people with different skills together into mutual service. When it was assumed that the nation state was the ultimate and exclusive agent of such attachments, citizenship education was understood to be an essential component of the school experience. Vocationalizing the discourse about schooling does not eliminate citizenship education. Rather it makes labor and consumption the most significant features of citizenship while overwhelming other possibilities. It intensifies the competition between nations by teaching every student that they are employees in the nation's efforts to produce and market its goods, and it overwhelms conceptions of citizenship that may require different skills and different affiliations.

Overview of the Book

The essays that follow were presented for the first time at a conference held in Montreal in June 2000 entitled "Collective Identities and Cosmopolitan Values: Group Rights and Public Education in Liberal-Democratic Societies." They focus on elaborating and critically evaluating the expectations for citizenship education in liberal-democratic societies, and explore the extent to which schools should be concerned about cultural, as well as national, identity. In doing so, they address the problems and also some of the promises that arise when national, subnational, and/or supranational affiliations compete. The six essays in Part I articulate aspects of the major themes which preoccupy the authors in the volume as a whole— examining and applying the themes of cosmopolitanism, cultural identity, and common education. Jeremy Waldron's essay suggests that the title of this volume should not be taken to assume that there is an inevitable divide between the local and the cosmopolitan and that the local is inevitably cut off from the cosmopolitan. If Waldron is correct, that such an assumption is inaccurate, at least in terms of its historical context, then we may find that there are promising responses to some of the modern educational conflicts. Thus, part of the task of this volume is conceptual. Just what is a local culture? How is it related to other cultural groups? Is it reasonable to see the local and the cosmopolitan as distinct entities?

Anthony Appiah's essay begins by identifying a distinctive feature of classical liberalism—namely, that the state must respect substantial limits with respect to its authority to impose restrictions on individuals, even for their own good. Nevertheless, Appiah points out, the primary aim of liberal education is to "maximize autonomy not to minimize government involvement." Most of the essays in this volume, including Appiah's, are attempts to address the question of what the liberal commitment to maximize personal autonomy means when it comes to the teaching of what Appiah refers to as "identity-related claims."

Kenneth Strike's essay takes up the concept of identity and contrasts cultural and religious pluralism. He argues that the issues of affiliational obligation and recognition are often different in these two cases, and that religious groups are often asking for something very different from cultural groups. Strike argues for a more fluid conception of the idea of identity and against its essentialist form. He holds, for example, that some of his affiliations are stronger than others and more tied to his sense of a larger self, but it is questionable, he argues, whether any of these affiliations could not be reevaluated without loss of the larger idea of the self. Strike does allow that members of groups more oppressed than his might certainly rally around the attributes that they hold in common, and he is sympathetic to this strategic function of identity. Nevertheless, he wants to hold onto the individualized and phenomenological conception of identity. Identity is whatever the agent feels it to be.

Joseph Dunne's essay begins by examining the ways in which schooling in modern liberal-democratic societies tends to function as the agent of cultural homogenization and alienation, and thus blocks liberal-democratic efforts to offer meaningful recognition of local cultures and to promote the skills and dispositions required for participatory democratic citizenship. The danger here, as Dunne points out, is that when the homogenizing elements of modern schooling become dominant, they might serve to encourage an "insouciant cosmopolitanism that may fail to meet people's needs for identity (and by this failure help to open the door to the very xenophobic nationalism it wishes to repudiate)." Dunne's chapter concludes by reflecting on some possible educational responses that might offer some hopeful ways of addressing such dismal extremes. In particular, Dunne is interested in the educational possibilities offered by a reconfiguration of national identities and state institutions in the emerging European community in the context of national, cultural, and religious strife that currently besets Northern Ireland. Thus, like Waldron, Dunne sees local cultural identities—be they national, religious, or cultural—as complexly related to, but potentially compatible with, cosmopolitan historical forces.

Terence McLaughlin's chapter addresses the conceptual and practical complexities involved in identifying and evaluating the nature, status, and institutional context of common education in pluralist societies. McLaughlin points out that the relationship between common schools and common education is a contingent one—the adequacy of a particular institutional arrangement, such as the common school, depends critically on the extent to which it embodies an adequate conception of common education. Thus, while there might be a presumption in favor of common schools as the most suitable arrangement for advancing common education, the presumption cannot be made decisive without bringing other considerations into play. McLaughlin's chapter is especially helpful in identifying a number of the most important of these considerations and his essay maps quite intricately the conceptual, curricular, pedagogical, and policy issues that must be addressed in clarifying and defending the role of common schools and common education in liberal-democratic societies.

Harry Brighouse's essay concludes Part I by taking up one aspect of the task of clarifying the role of common education, by applying it to the teaching of patriotism in public schools. Are liberal and cosmopolitan values compatible with a common education aimed at fostering patriotic attachment to the nation? Brighouse carefully examines numerous arguments recently developed to justify fostering patriotism in public schools from a liberal-democratic perspective and finds them all wanting. However, even if liberal-democratic arguments for teaching patriotism could be found which withstand the criticisms he advances, Brighouse argues that public schools should avoid using history as the vehicle for fostering patriotic loyalty. Even the most honest, clear-sighted, unsentimental attempts to teach national history "warts and all," Brighouse argues, is likely to degrade and undermine other purposes that teaching history properly has.

Many traditionalists would reject the permeable and fluid conception of identity defended or assumed by many of the papers in Part I. According to the orthodox tradition, Jews can fall away from God but if they do so they are lapsed or fallen Jews. Their identity has not changed; they still have it but are just not living up to it. Although none of the authors in this book argue for this conception of identity, there are some who would like to find ways for the liberal state to honor the self-definitions of traditional cultures and to find ways of avoiding a confrontation with differences. The chapters in Part II by Shelley Burtt, Melissa Williams, David Blacker, and Mark Halstead fall into this category. For example, Burtt argues that the liberal state has good reason to be far more accommodating of traditional groups than liberals commonly recognize. She argues that liberal autonomy, properly understood, is not threatened in any special way by traditional religious or cultural groups, and that traditional cultures are as capable of fostering autonomy as their more cosmopolitan counterparts. Most strikingly, she argues that it is a good thing *from the perspective of liberal autonomy* to be encumbered by unchosen attachments and loyalties such as those that we might expect to be most fully developed within religious communities.

Williams argues the other side of the same coin. According to Williams, the liberal state often demands too much in the way of loyalty from traditional groups, and when it does it runs a strong risk of becoming oppressive and illiberal. Moreover, she holds that there is no need for a single shared identity among citizens of the liberal state. Her conception of people tied together by a shared fate is to this extent compatible with Burtt's attempt to make liberalism's commitment to autonomy more hospitable to groups of individuals encumbered by unchosen attachments; but Williams's notion of citizenship as shared fate also goes further than, and possibly stands in some tension with, Burtt's view since it allows and even encourages people to develop primary affiliation to all kind of groups—traditional as well as global.

Blacker's essay develops a Rawlsian conception of civic friendship, the scaffolding of which is necessarily provided by the wide range of comprehensive conceptions of the good that characterize democratic societies. Thus, Blacker argues, a democratic civic education "allows citizens to embrace democracy on their own terms, drawing support for democracy's requisite political conceptions from the perspectives of citizens' many different secular and/or religious comprehensive doctrines." For Blacker, a conception of civic friendship which is friendly to citizens' multiple comprehensive doctrines also entails a substantial lowering of the "wall of separation" between church and state so that courts might be more willing than they currently are to allow the use of state funds to support religious groups, in particular where these groups perform functions within public schools that converge with public interests. Blacker's essay concludes by proposing and defending two policy initiatives that are consistent with his politically liberal ideal of civic friendship—the revival of a "school stamps" plan first proposed in the 1970s and a modified version of a "clergy in the schools" program recently struck down by a federal circuit court in Texas.

Another task of this volume is to separate out different kinds of affiliation and the extent to which the arguments made about cultural recognition can be extended to other objects of affiliation. Mark Halstead's chapter provides a very useful catalogue of the different types of groups which are to be found in liberal societies, and the different kinds of cultural and educational claims that are typically attached to each of them. His definition of minority group is especially useful in conceptualizing many of the papers in the volume.

The essays in Part III by Susan Okin, Rob Reich, Walter Feinberg, Stephen Macedo, and Kevin McDonough argue for a more regulatory conception of liberal education and emphasize the need for some controls over cultural and religious educational authority. Okin is mostly concerned, not with the oppression of traditional groups by the liberal state, but with the oppression of individuals, and especially girls and women, by the traditional community. She is critical of those liberal theorists who argue that a right of exit is sufficient to qualify a cultural or religious group for special recognition in liberal societies. To counter these views she notes that the unequal treatment of girls and women can mean that even though they may have a formal right to exit a group, their actual opportunities for doing so are far less adequate than their male counterparts. She holds then that the right of exit is not sufficient and that the liberal state should have a higher requirement, namely that girls and women should be treated fairly within the group and thus be able to take advantage of any formal right of exit. Reich's essay extends this view beyond the treatment of women and proposes that the liberal state needs to rethink its commitment to cultural groups whose educational agendas advance the integrity of the group over and against the freedom and equality of its members, and that thus educate in ways that place strict limits on the autonomy and critical thinking skills of their members.

What sorts of educational constraints can liberalism legitimately impose on minority national groups within multinational societies? Assuming, *pace* Williams, for example, that liberal-democratic principles of justice can best be supported and sustained within a national context in which individuals evince a loyalty to the nation and to one another, which national identity should take precedence? McDonough's essay develops a conception of multinational civic education which allows for both federal and minority national groups to reinforce conditional civic attachments. This "conditionalist" view of civic education is necessary in multinational federal societies, he argues, because appeals to one set of national attachments may exacerbate rather than alleviate particular injustices in particular circumstances. For example, McDonough argues that when aboriginal women and children are the victims of injustice at the hands of tribal institutions and leaders, they must be able to appeal to their fellow non-aboriginal citizens and federal institutions for assistance. This is not possible unless citizens—aboriginal and otherwise—have come to regard attachments to the minority nation as conditional rather than absolute. Similarly, citizens whose primary identification is to the federal society must be able to recognize that some of their fellow citizens legitimately have a minority nation as the object of their primary loyalty. Otherwise, efforts to support federal intervention in minority national affairs will be vulnerable to forces of cultural insensitivity and arrogance, rather than of liberal justice.

Feinberg's essay takes up the issue of educational constraints with respect to religious schools in liberal democratic societies. While he allows that religious education need not be inconsistent with liberal goals, and can find reasons why some liberal societies feel it appropriate to provide public support for religious schools, he argues that certain conditions can render such support tyrannical and unwise. He concludes that if the conditions are appropriate for public support of religious schools, then there should also be significant public control.

Finally, according to Macedo, while liberalism's commitment to individual freedom and equality is far more easily reconciled with group-based remedies for group-based inequalities than liberalism's critics allow, the liberal commitment to freedom of association imposes limits on group recognition by insisting on intragroup openness and diversity. For example, in discussing a recent case at Tufts University in which a student Christian group sought to ban one of its members from running for office because that member had recently revealed her homosexuality, Macedo argues that groups should not be allowed to enact such bans simply because some members express dissenting views (or, more specifically, express views which dissent with respect to the message preferred by the most powerful members of that group).

Conclusion

Ultimately, one of the most important contributions of the volume is to highlight the problems that emerge when one passes from abstract philosophical principle to educational policy. The authors in this volume are sensitive to the complexities of moving from abstract ideals of schooling and education, on the one hand, to the task of achieving those ideals in educational practice and policy. However, it's worth pointing out one way in which the authors in this volume take divergent approaches in addressing practical problems of education.

To take just one example for the purposes of illustration, consider the practical implications of the liberal commitment to personal autonomy. On the one hand, some essays emphasize a relatively linear and direct connection between liberal principles and liberal educational policies. For example, Reich, Feinberg, and Macedo interpret this principle as supporting policies of common schooling and common education which provide children with a rich and sustained cross-cultural, interreligious educational experience. However, some essays suggest that the standard goals of liberal education are best pursued indirectly. For example, Blacker and Burtt either reject the standard liberal assumption that autonomy demands educational policies that privilege exposure to cultural diversity (Burtt), or else, less strongly, they stress the point that particular conceptions of the good do important motivational work in reconciling citizens of diverse horizons to the strictures of a liberal political order (e.g. Blacker).[30] Once one takes such practical considerations on board, they argue, the ideal outcome for liberals might not be an educational strategy of exposing children to as much cultural and religious diversity as possible. Rather, it might be one which seeks to reinforce and buttress children's immersion in a particular religious or cultural conception of the good. For example, it might shelter them from the corrosive forces of diversity characteristic of common schools or include a protected space for particular conceptions of the good within common schools.

The essays in this volume provide a heightened sense of the issues, both theoretical and practical, at stake in the debate between nationalists, multiculturalists, and cosmopolitans in the field of education. It is our hope that the genuine dialogue between political and legal philosophers and educational theorists represented in this volume illustrates how productive the debate between scholars from these areas can be.

NOTES

1. See for example, H. Mann, "1796–1859," in Lawrence A. Cremin (ed.), *The Republic and the School: The Education of Free Men* (New York: Teachers College Press, 1957); E. Durkheim, *Education and Sociology*. Sherwood D. Fox

trans. (Glencoe, Ill.: Free Press, 1956); J. Dewey, *Democracy and Education* (New York: The Free Press, 1916).

2. W. A. Nord, *Religion and American Education: Rethinking a National Dilemma* (Chapel Hill: The University of North Carolina Press, 1995).

3. For example, the foundation of Catholic Parochial Schools in the last century arose out of similar concerns. See J. W. Fraser, *Between Church and State: Religion and Public Education in a Multicultural America* (New York: St. Martin's Press, 1999).

4. R. Rorty, "The Priority of Democracy to Philosophy" in *Contingency, Irony, and Solidarity* (New York: Cambridge University Press, 1989); John Rawls, *Political Liberalism* (New York: Columbia University Press, 1993); see Blacker's essay in this volume.

5. A. C. MacIntyre, *Whose Justice? Which Rationality?* (Notre Dame, Ind.: University of Notre Dame Press, 1988).

6. Nord, ibid.; E. J. Thiessen, *Teaching for Commitment: Liberal Education, Indoctrination, and Christian Nurture* (Montreal: McGill-Queen's University Press, 1993).

7. J. Chubb and T. Moe, *Politics, Markets and America's Schools* (Washington, DC: Brookings Institution, 1990); M. Friedman, *Capitalism and Freedom* (Chicago: University of Chicago Press, 1963); C. E. Finn, *Charter Schools in Action: Renewing Public Education* (Princeton, NJ: Princeton University Press, 2000); M. Holmes, *The Reformation of Canada's Schools: Breaking the Barriers to Parental Choice* (Montreal: McGill-Queen's University Press, 1998).

8. J. S. Mill, *On Liberty*, Gertrude Himmelfarb (ed.) (London: Penguin Books, 1974).

9. J. Dewey, *The Public and its Problems* (Denver, A. Swallow, 1954).

10. J. M. Keynes, *The General Theory of Employment, Interest and Money* (London: Macmillan for the Royal Economic Society, 1974).

11. J. Rawls, *A Theory of Justice* (Cambridge: Harvard University Press, 1972).

12. M. J. Sandel, *Democracy's Discontent: America in Search of a Public Philosophy* (Cambridge: Harvard University Press, 1996); A. MacIntyre, *After Virtue*, 2nd edn (South Bend, Ind.: Notre Dame University Press, 1984).

13. I. Berlin, "Two Concepts of Liberty" in *Four Essays on Liberty* (London: Oxford University Press, 1969).

14. The educational model for the affiliation liberal as described here is also, arguably, completely compatible with the commitments of contemporary liberalism, and should thus be embraced by teachers with contemporary liberal commitments. Nevertheless, the point being stressed here is not about the alleged conceptual links between different forms of liberalism and their respective normative ideals of teaching; rather, the point is historical with respect to the development of liberal political and educational theory. In this latter sense, the colorblind teacher has been associated with the rise of contemporary liberalism and the model of the culturally sensitive teacher has only become prominent with the rise of affiliation liberalism.

15. A. K. Sen, *Development as Freedom* (New York: Knopf, 1999).

16. C. Taylor, *Multiculturalism and the "Politics of Recognition"* (Princeton, NJ: Princeton University Press, 1992); Y. Tamir, "Two Concepts of Multiculturalism" in *The Journal of Philosophy of Education* (1995).

17. I. A. Snook, *Indoctrination and Education* (London: Routledge and K. Paul, 1972). See also M. Levinson, *The Demands of Liberal Education* (Oxford: Oxford University Press, 1999).

18. A. Gutmann, *Democratic Education* (Princeton, NJ: Princeton University Press, 1987).
19. Tamir, "Two Concepts of Multiculturalism."
20. Taylor, *Multiculturalism and the "Politics of Recognition."*
21. A. Schlesinger, Jr, *The Disuniting of America: Reflections on a Multicultural Society*, 2nd edn (New York: W.W. Norton, 1998).
22. C. Kukathas, "Are There any Cultural Rights?" in *Political Theory*, 20(1) (1992), 105–39; W. Galston, *Liberal Purposes: Goods, Virtues, and Diversity in the Liberal State* (Cambridge: Cambridge University Press, 1991).
23. W. Kymlicka, *Multicultural Citizenship: A Liberal Theory of Minority Rights* (Oxford: Oxford University Press, 1995); E. Callan, *Creating Citizens: Political Education and Liberal Democracy* (Oxford: Oxford University Press, 1997); W. Feinberg, *Common Schools/Uncommon Identities: National Unity and Cultural Difference* (New Haven, CT: Yale University Press, 1999); M. Levinson, *The Demands of Liberal Education*; S. Macedo, *Diversity and Distrust: Civic Education in a Multicultural Society* (Cambridge, MA: Harvard University Press, 2000).
24. S. G. Gilles, "On Educating Children: A Parentalist Manifesto" in *University of Chicago Law Review*, 63(3) (1996), 937–1034.
25. D. Tyack, *The One Best System: A History of American Urban Education* (Cambridge, MA: Harvard University Press, 1974).
26. H. Brighouse, *School Choice and Social Justice* (Oxford: Oxford University Press, 2000).
27. *Wisconsin v. Yoder*, 406 U.S. 205 (1972).
28. B. Anderson, *Imagined Communities: Reflections on the Origins and Spread of Nationalism* (London: Verso, 1983).
29. E. D. Hirsch, *Cultural Literacy: What Every American Needs to Know.*
30. Thanks to Daniel Weinstock for helping us to articulate this point.

PART I

COSMOPOLITANISM, LIBERALISM, AND COMMON EDUCATION

CHAPTER 1

Teaching Cosmopolitan Right

JEREMY WALDRON

The idea of cosmopolitan education was put on the agenda recently
by Martha Nussbaum in an article written for the *Boston Review*
and published subsequently as a book (together with responses by
various other scholars interested in moral education).[1] Taking her
lead from the Stoic tradition that,

each of us dwells...in two communities—the local community of our birth
and in the community of human argument and aspiration... 'in which we
look neither to this corner nor to that, but measure the boundaries of our
nation by the sun.'[2]

Nussbaum argued that we should make "world citizenship, rather
than democratic or national citizenship, the focus for civic education."[3] Civic education should not be conceived only in terms of love
of one's own country and its traditions, or concern only for fellow
members of one's society. The moral concern we should be teaching
our children is equal concern for all humans in the world; and the
identity we should encourage young people to recognize is an identity that involves "recognizing humanity in the stranger and the other"
and responding humanely to the human in every cultural form.[4]

   Against this generous vision, Nussbaum's respondents scrambled
to defend the importance of the parochial and the particular claims
of kin and culture. They said they were afraid that cosmopolitan
concern would "rob us of our concreteness and our immediacy."[5]

What cosmopolitanism obscures, even denies, are the givens of life: parents,
ancestors, family, race, religion, heritage, history, culture, tradition, community—and nationality. These are not "accidental" attributes of the individual. They are essential attributes... To pledge one's fundamental
allegiance to cosmopolitanism is to try to transcend not only nationality but

all the actualities, particularities, and realities of life that constitute one's natural identity.[6]

One critic worried that if we "[t]each children...to be 'citizens of the world,'...in all likelihood they will become neither patriots nor cosmopolitans, but lovers of abstraction and ideology, intolerant of the flaw-ridden individuals and cultures that actually exist..."[7] Another was alarmed at the prospect of children being taught to take seriously no "allegiances other than those to human beings in general", children who when faced with a choice between rescuing two drowning people might choose to rescue a stranger rather than someone of their own nationality.[8]

In general, Nussbaum's respondents were repelled by what they thought was the colorlessness and insubstantiality of a cosmopolitan morality.[9] They feared that unless children learned first to love their kin, their culture, and their nation, they would not be able to develop any allegiances at all, let alone a love of humanity.[10] Morality, they said, draws its nourishment in the first instance from the particular close-knit group, not from the abstractions of Kantian universalism: "We come to the larger only through the smaller, and it is the moral emotions connected with the smaller that can be expected to have the most force."[11]

For Nussbaum and her opponents in this debate, the important opposition is between a moral education centered around universal human norms, undifferentiated by culture, and a moral education oriented more specifically to the particular society in which the education is taking place. Now, if we have to stick with *that* opposition, then it seems to me that Nussbaum has the better case. Indeed most of what is morally valuable in the particularity of a given society is just that society's particular take on ideals that present themselves as moral universals—I mean things like the commitment to human rights that one might learn from one's own constitution, or the commandment to love all men that one might learn in a particular church. We must remember, too, that even if the practice of universalist moral reflection is abstract in its content and its reference, it is not itself an abstraction: it has a particular history;[12] it sustains itself through various traditions and activities, including traditions of argument and the activity of listening; and it represents the concrete endeavor of flesh-and-blood people to build a community of a certain sort.[13] Nor, finally, is there anything offensively distant or passionless about such universalism: a simple humane response to human suffering, for instance, is likely to be much more immediate than the response of someone who, when they see a person suffering, must first run their finger down a checklist to see where the sufferer fits in their scheme of blood, kin, and country.[14]

Perhaps a more accurate observation is that both communitarian and universalistic formulations are artificial: for the purposes of critical reflection, both of them represent people's moral response in terms of an abstract model. This is evident and familiar in the case of the utilitarian calculus or the Kantian kingdom of ends; we *know* these are models, not recordings of how ordinary morality works. But it is equally true of nationalism and communitarianism. Those theories take as their paradigm something like a Midwesterner's view of the moral difference between a job opportunity being lost to a Texan family (whom he has never met) and the same job opportunity being lost to a Mexican family (whom he has never met). The analytic contortions that one has to go through to explain—in an intellectually satisfying way—why the *American's* unemployment should be of greater concern than the Mexican's unemployment to a fellow American (who lives a thousand miles away) are no less daunting, no less twisted—certainly no more "natural"—than those required to sustain the abstract categories of universalistic humanism.

That said, however, the opposition between universalism and particularism may be misleading in a couple of ways. First, it neglects the importance of multicultural citizenship.[15] Children in the modern world are being brought up in a milieu where many cultures rub shoulders, and where it is important for people to know something about and reflect upon cultures other than those that are present in their immediate surroundings (e.g. their family, their church, or their circle of friends). Even to be a good citizen of a particular country—a good citizen of England, for example—one has to know something more than the particular history, traditions, and folkways embodied in English culture. To be a good citizen, an Englishman must also know something of the culture of the other nations in the United Kingdom—the Scots, the Welsh, the Irish (including both the Unionist and Nationalist traditions)—and he must have some grasp also of Islamic culture (for there are several million Muslims in England), Carribean culture, and various cultures (Sikh, Hindu, Pakistani) originating in the Indian subcontinent. For all these—and to understand why it all matters (to him)—he will also need some understanding of the history of the British empire, from a subaltern as well as a metropolitan point of view. Beyond that, since the citizen of England is also a citizen of the European Union, he must know something of the distinctive cultures and traditions of the other societies with which his nation cooperates in that overarching institution. Also, he must also know something of England's place in the world: its affinities, alliances, the extent of its openness to visitors, immigrants, and refugees, its historic faults and responsibilities, the influence of its laws and institutions, its trade, the pervasiveness of its language, and its role in international life. One can bring all this into the picture—one can *insist* on bringing all this into the picture—without going anywhere near universalism or cosmopolitanism. Anything less than this multicultural awareness is simply an inauthentic response to the particularity of the society which the person we are imagining inhabits.[16]

The second respect in which one may be misled by the opposition that emerged in the Nussbaum debate is one that I want particularly to highlight in this chapter. Cosmopolitan moral education is not just an education in moral ideals. It is—or it ought to be—also an education in the *particular* ways in which people have inhabited the world (as opposed to purely local aspects of their inhabiting particular territories). One's life in the world—that is, the worldly or global aspect of one's life, the impact on it of global events and relationships—is not something abstract to be opposed to the immediacy of one's life in, say, a particular village. The one is as concrete as the other, with a particular history (the actual history of interaction—war, trade, marriage, migration, dispersion, influence, conquest, etc.—among peoples), a particular infrastructure (trade routes, ocean currents, airlines, telecommunications, extradition treaties), and a particular location (which is why Immanuel Kant found it necessary to emphasize in his "Cosmopolitan Right" the fact that nature has enclosed the nations of the earth "within determinate limits by the spherical shape of the place they live in, a *globus terraqueus*")[17].

The two points are connected of course. It is no accident that most people live in multicultural societies. Their prevalence is witness to the history—the *particular* history—of human movement and resettlement around the globe. It is witness to the fact that most human lives are not led within the confines of a particular culture but are framed and formed both by the movements of people among cultures and by the movements of culture among peoples. Indeed the beginning of wisdom in multicultural education is the rejection of any simple correlation along the lines of "one person–one culture." Each of us is the embodiment of fragments from a great many cultural traditions,[18] and the modes in which they have managed to impinge on us, despite their seeming oppositions and the evident difference in their provenance, tell us as much about what respect for persons is like in a multicultural society as a study of the contents of the various cultures themselves.

A

Let me begin the detailed discussion by asking: how does a society become multicultural? How does it come to pass that members of different traditions and ethnicities find themselves living in the same territory—in Kant's phrase, "unavoidably side-by-side?"[19]

In one sense, of course the question is impossible to answer, on account of the vagueness and ambiguity of words like "culture" (not to mention the contestability of the rules for the individuating of cultures, i.e. the rules that determine where one culture stops and another may be said to begin). Before I am done, I hope to be able to *aggravate* this definitional indeterminacy. But if we want to proceed in a loose sort of way,[20] then the usual account goes something like this.

Once upon a time humans lived stably in separate communities, each group inhabiting its own territory, and practicing its distinctive way of life (with its own economy, kinship structure, customs, religion, etc.) The arrangement was tidy, because each community had its own culture and its own domain in which to practice it. On this account, there was initially no mixing, no conquest, no imperialism, no Kantian universalism: just several societies enjoying their distinct ways of life. Then—according to the usual story—various things happened to upset the tidiness of this arrangement, things of the following nature.[21]

1. A single culture split into separate cultures as the community it characterized grew and became differentiated. An example of this process is religious differentiation in European communities in and after the sixteenth century; despite the split, often the resultant (sub)cultures continued to inhabit the same territory, with only loose spatial differentiation.
2. An organized society with one culture conquered the territory of a society with another culture, or in some other way "muscled in" on its domain—either by moving wholesale into the latter's territory, or by planting colonies, or simply expanding its own domain to annex new lands (and their inhabitants) to its old lands. The subjugation of the aboriginal communities of North America and Australasia by European colonists is a clear instance of this.

3. Either incidentally to (2) or independently, the members of one society may drive another people out of a territory that the latter have immemorially inhabited, forcing them to relocate somewhere else, as white Americans drove many Indian groups out of the lands they had traditionally inhabited. In southeastern Europe, this sort of ethnic cleansing has once again become characteristic of conflict in multicultural societies.

4. The overlords of one community began importing captive or subject peoples as slaves or indentured workers, like the slave trade out of Africa to the Americas, or the importation of ethnic Indians to Fiji.[22]

5. Two or more communities with distinct cultures confederated for political or security reasons, coming sufficiently to terms with one another to constitute a common polity or state. The Act of Union between England and Scotland in 1707 is one of the best known examples of this.

6. The overlords of one society transferred that society and its territory to another, as France and Spain ceded and retroceded the territory in the Americas known as Louisiana in the eighteenth century back and forth between themselves, until eventually it was sold to the United States in 1803 (by France).

7. Some members of a given community migrated—one-by-one or family-by-family, in waves perhaps, but not as an organized mass—to another country, and when they arrived and settled there, they joined with other migrants to preserve what they could of the culture of their provenance. This is typical of many communities in the United States: Chinese, Italian, Jewish, Amish, Korean, Irish, and so on. Such migration has often been the consequence of an oppressive response to the process mentioned in (1), as members of a dissident sect seek refuge abroad from domestic persecution.

There are doubtless many other ways in which cultures may end up in odd and even offensive juxtaposition—many other stories to be told of war, refugees, and colonial conquest—and countless combinations and variations on these themes. But these seven types will do to begin with. Between them, they seem to explain a great deal of the multiculturalism of modern societies. The diversity of cultures in the United States, for example, represents the legacy of (1) with regard to modern pluralism and sectarianism, (2) and (3) with regard to the ethnic cleansing of Native Americans, (4) with regard to the Union of former British colonies, (5) with regard to African-Americans,

(6) with regard to the acquisition of California, Texas, and Louisiana, and (7) with regard to the mass immigration of the late-nineteenth and twentieth centuries. Likewise, the diversity of the United Kingdom represents the legacy of all the many ways in which the British Empire has impacted upon the peoples of the world and the reflux of that in Britain, not to mention the effects of English hegemony within the British Isles and the impact on the British Isles itself of incursions by Romans, Angles, Saxons, Danes, Normans, etc. And for Canada, South Africa, Australia, New Zealand, Brazil, Russia, Poland, Germany, France, Spain, Israel, and on and on, the same or similar stories can be told.

These are grim stories, and with the possible exceptions of (7) and (5), they associate the mingling of cultures with some of the most hideous forms of human wrongdoing—war, racism, imperial conquest, ethnic cleansing, and exploitation. The juxtaposition of different cultures in a single society may not a priori be a subject of moral concern. But as a matter of fact where different cultures coexist, there usually *has* been great injustice; and where the injustice is less than a few hundred years old, there are lingering grievances, demands for reparation and apology, and even aspirations (more or less realistic, mostly less) for some sort of return to the local *status quo ante*, so far as the tidy separation of cultures and territories is concerned.[23]

Also, the effect of these processes in most real-world situations is that the integrity of various cultures has been compromised, particularly the integrity of those cultures subordinate in the encounter, as people who are conquered, sold, transported, and enslaved are forced to adapt themselves to the ways of their overlords. For this reason, there always seems to be something heroic about a subordinated culture sticking up for itself—a victim people clinging gamely to the integrity of their traditions, in spite of everything. And by the same token, the ongoing impact of a dominant culture upon a subordinate culture—even what is now an apparently benign impact taking place well in the aftermath of one of these encounters—can easily seem to those involved like a continuation of conquest by other means. In my other writings on this issue, I have argued that the identity of most persons is composed of many fragments, from disparate cultures.[24] But if an individual in one of the multicultural societies we have just been talking about—England in the aftermath of empire, or the United States in the aftermath of racist slavery and the ethnic cleansing of aboriginal peoples—finds fragments of many cultures in his identity, that will probably seem to him like the relic of a tragedy that has befallen his people. Or worse: if he is a member of a dominant group, the *mélange* of his identity may seem to others a flaunted display of conquest, like the exhibition of shrunken heads, feather cloaks, and Beninese ivories in General Pitt Rivers' museum.[25]

I said this is the account that is commonly given; and saying that is usually a prelude to explaining why it is wrong. In fact there is nothing wrong at all in emphasizing the seven stories of the origins of multicultural societies that I have just set out. Migration; conquest, colonization, and expropriation; slavery and migrant labor; union, cession, fission—this is the history of the real world, most of it shameful. What is wrong, however, with what I have called the usual account is the tidy premise it begins with: the premise which holds that, apart from all this wickedness, apart from these seven sources of convulsion and oppression, distinct societies would live (and *did* live, historically) in distinct territories, apart from one another, each with its own culture and way of life. As soon as we subject that premise to examination, its falsity is evident.

So let me count the ways in which the tidy picture is false, over and above the seven ways we have already noticed in which history has messed it up.

First, we should remember that at all stages of their evolution human groups have been migratory. Moving initially out of Africa, into Asia and then into Europe, the Americas, and the Pacific, human prehistory is a history of movement, not a history of the eternal association of each separate people with a given patch of land. (Indeed, in several of the cases in which the bond of a people to its land is the most celebrated and is felt with the most intense yearning—the people of Israel and *Eretz Yisra'el*; the Maori and their relation to *Aotearoa*—the arrival of the people in question on their land is no more than a couple of thousand years old.)[26] Moreover, the trajectory of these movements has not necessarily been conducive to anything approaching cultural integrity. The paths of different human groups have crossed. Over a millennium or more, a given society— to the extent that its own identity has remained intact to the point of traceability—may have coexisted with several others, including others that are not currently on its horizon. The Neapolitans used to have to deal with the Normans; the Indians with the Greeks; and the current inhabitants of Spain with peoples erupting out of the Russian steppes into Central Europe. (And since we are not talking about movement for movement's sake, but a standing disposition to respond to various events—such as famine, climate change, etc.—with migration, we must remember, too, that the movement of one group is often a stimulus to the movements of others.)[27]

Second, in almost every human society there are people—often among the more powerful and creative—who take an intense interest in the ways of life of other societies in the vicinity of their own. This is not just a precaution or a prelude to depredation. It is partly innate curiosity, and partly a matter of vindicating or reinforcing some trend in local development (or local politics). Mostly it is born of a sense that there are useful and profitable things to learn. Of the practices, traditions, and technology that we call *culture* in any society, an enormous proportion of it is shared or transmitted or imitated. From patterns on the sides of pots, to metallurgy, to monotheism—cultures learn from one another and adapt one another's ways.

Jared Diamond's description of the dissemination of alphabetic writing provides a good example.[28] Left to their own devices, in time probably many cultures would have developed alphabetic writing. Writing solves a number of problems; it makes a number of other practices possible and more efficient; it is almost always to the advantage of the power-bearing strata of a society; and though its invention is certainly very difficult, there are no particular obstacles that present themselves as much more of a problem for some cultures than for others, at least above a certain level of prosperity.[29] In fact, we know that writing was invented independently in no more than four, perhaps in as few as two, distinct societies; and that alphabetic writing was invented only once.[30] Human curiosity and a pragmatic eagerness to learn from other cultures and adopt or adapt their ways meant that the invention of alphabetic writing in one place simply preempted its invention anywhere else.

In the case of other practices and technologies, the proliferation of culture is not always so straightforward. The wheel makes sense only for societies that have domesticated animals, and domesticable animals are not distributed evenly throughout the world.[31] Metallurgy may be dispersed only to the loci of base metals, otherwise it is the finished products of metallurgy that will be dispersed, by trade. And many technologies will spread partly by association with the more vicious forms of interaction between societies mentioned earlier (war, colonization, etc.), where the ability to learn from one's adversaries may be a matter of life and death.[32]

The interest taken by the members of one society in the ways of another need not be only for the purposes of cultural appropriation. It can also be cultural proselytism—the deliberate enterprise of actively spreading elements of one's culture beyond the given borders of one's society. This is most familiar to us in the spreading of ideas, particularly religious ideas, by missionary activity.[33]

The New Testament *Acts of the Apostles* provides an excellent example of this: the dissemination of the radical ideas of a particular Jewish sect into the Greco-Roman world. Initially the early Christian proselytes "made their way to Phoenicia, Cyprus, and Antioch, bringing the message to Jews only." But gradually they began preaching also to Greeks,[34] exciting incidentally a huge controversy among members of the original sect in Jerusalem as to whether it was even permissible for Christians to associate with "the uncircumcised,"[35] and whether Gentile converts to Christianity were to be required to submit to circumcision.[36] The account given of Judaeo-Christian proselytism in Athens is particularly fascinating:

Now while Paul was waiting for [*his companions*] at Athens, his spirit was provoked within him as he saw that the city was full of idols. So he argued in the synagogue with the Jews and the devout persons [*i.e. Gentile worshipers*], and in the market place every day with those who chanced to be there. Some also of the Epicurean and Stoic philosophers met him. And some said, 'What would this babbler say?' Others said, 'He seems to be a preacher of foreign divinities'—because he preached Jesus and the resurrection. And they took hold of him and brought him to the Are-op'agus, saying, 'May we know what this new teaching is which you present? For you bring some strange things to our ears; we wish to know therefore what these things mean.' Now all the Athenians and the foreigners who lived there spent their time in nothing except telling or hearing something new.

So Paul, standing in the middle of the Are-op'agus, said: 'Men of Athens, I perceive that in every way you are very religious. For as I passed along, and observed the objects of your worship, I found also an altar with this inscription, "To an unknown god." What therefore you worship as unknown, this I proclaim to you.'

'The God who made the world and everything in it, being Lord of heaven and earth, does not live in shrines made by man, nor is he served by human hands, as though he needed anything, since he himself gives to all men life and breath and everything. And he made from one [*person – i.e. Adam*] every nation of men to live on all the face of the earth, having determined allotted periods and the boundaries of their habitation, that they should seek God, in the hope that they might feel after him and find him ... The times of ignorance God overlooked, but now he commands all men everywhere to repent, because he has fixed a day on which he will judge the world in righteousness by a man whom he has appointed, and of this he has given assurance to all men by raising him from the dead.'

Now when they heard of the resurrection of the dead, some mocked; but others said, 'We will hear you again about this.' So Paul went out from among them. But some men joined him and believed, among them Dionys'ius the Are-op'agite and a woman named Dam'aris and others with them.[37]

Notice that although Paul himself invokes the tidy picture of various nations with "allotted... boundaries of their habitation,"[38] in fact we are presented in this story with a very complicated account of cultural interaction. Paul, a Jew from Asia Minor, is waiting in Athens for his fellow evangelists (mostly from the Jerusalem community) to join him. He engages in conversation and debate with Jewish Athenians, non-Jewish worshipers at the Jewish synagogue, and Greek philosophers. Although the latter half-heartedly complain about his propaganda for foreign deities, they are mostly curious to hear what he has to say, "for all the Athenians and the resident foreigners had time for nothing except talking or hearing about the latest novelty." Their curiosity is evidently matched by Paul's, for when he is not preaching and debating, he is examining inscriptions on local shrines and altars. One inscription actually indicates the Athenians' openness to foreign religious ideas, and Paul takes this as the starting point of his address in the Areopagus, an address that is met with a predictable, though still fascinating, mixture of mockery, enhanced curiosity, and—at least among a few men and women—acceptance and conversion.

This, I submit, is how existing cultures ordinarily live and relate to one another. They do show some half-hearted self-protectiveness for the integrity of their own traditions and practices. But it is almost always alloyed with intense mutual curiosity, with various people on all sides going out of their way to engage in active and inquisitive intercultural arbitrage.[39]

Third, the human appetite for foreign ideas is matched by the ability of people in most societies to figure out how to trade and exchange goods with people in other societies, even societies initially quite alien to them. Trade seems as old as civilization; and it has long been the case that a substantial part of the material basis of culture in any country is derived from social and economic activities taking place well outside its borders. Wool is grown in England and worn in Lombardy. Vineyards are cultivated in Provence and the wine consumed in Denmark. Malachite is mined and smelted in Asia Minor and alloyed with tin to make weapons that are wielded in the Aegean. Kiwi fruits, initially from China,[40] are cultivated in New Zealand and served in salads in New York. Trade establishes real connections between local economies that are often so pervasive that they are simply taken for granted—or even ignored, as we continue to imagine societies as self-sufficient despite the fact that real autarchy has been out of the question for thousands of years. Connections of trade are connections of other cultural elements as well, for they represent ways in which the culture of production and supply in one society affects patterns of consumption in another, and cultural practices affecting demand in one society make a difference to what is possible and profitable in the way of cultures of production in another.

These three factors—migration, intercultural transmission of ideas, and intersocietal trade—make an immense difference to our understanding of the separateness of cultures. They draw our attention to fluidity, movement, mixture of peoples; they remind us of the porousness of boundaries and the daily infiltrations and transfusions across them; and they explain the confusion, juxtaposition, and pastiche of cultural elements that one finds in all actually existing ways of life. They ruin the tidy picture that we began with—distinct societies, distinct cultures, distinct territories—except for its application to a very few societies that by accidents of history or geography have been until recently isolated from these processes. And they diminish any confidence we might have had in our ability to define and individuate particular cultures as such, as a presupposition of valuing their identity or integrity, even their diversity.

What is more: these processes were not waiting around for a philosopher to discover them. They are self-conscious and already reasonably well understood; and anything that is said in the world affirming the separateness of cultures needs to be heard as a more or less deliberate reaction to them. Thus, a fourth point worth emphasizing is that the world we inhabit is not just a world of given or immemorially existent things called "cultures." As practices, technologies, and ideas change and proliferate, their organization into sociological *wholes* that may be referred to (proudly or taxonomically) as distinct cultures is itself a matter of historical contingency and often quite deliberate creativity. The division of the world into nation-states is one of the most powerful stimuli in this process, as those who wield political power within a given territory (even one inhabited by disparate cultures) felt obliged to *come up with* some sense of "the officially designated culture of the people of this country." Or, if the members of some concentrated ethnic minority conceive a reasonable aspiration to political independence, then it may be worthwhile for them to exaggerate the homogeneity of their culture and even to remake it in a way that lends credence to the exaggeration. In addition, there are the more general stories told by Benedict Anderson about the cultural imagination of nationhood in the shadow of the provincial boundaries of empire and of the administrative infrastructure of each province or colony,[41] and by Eric

Hobsbawm and others about the creation of national languages and popular identities to answer various social and political needs in the nineteenth century.[42] Since such a culture is never created out of whole cloth, since it involves the reorganization of existing cultural materials not initially given as parts of this whole, as well as the invention of new ones, the result is often a "multicultural culture", with disparate and sometimes quite shallow traditions crammed together under a thin veneer of intellectual or political rationalization. Or else it is something which is not so much a distinct culture as an organized response to some (real or, more usually, imagined) threat to the integrity of a set of cultural traditions that has been cobbled together precisely to head off that threat. (*Québécois* "culture" seems to be the leading example of this in the modern world.)[43]

At the other extreme, these processes have led some to doubt whether it makes sense to even attempt to individuate social reality at the level of cultures and communities.[44] Maybe "civilization" is the better category,[45] though the boundaries of a civilization are no less porous and their differentiation from one another no less artificial and question begging. What civilizations do India, South Africa, Brazil, and Japan respectively, belong to? Even to ask the question, in the case of any of these countries, is to feel the need to explode the traditional tidy taxonomy. So civilization is hardly a satisfactory substitute. Even so—and to return for a moment to our main theme—if one had to choose a concrete social entity as a particular source of morality and a particular locus of moral upbringing—as opposed to the Kantian abstractions that Nussbaum's critics associate with her cosmopolitan thesis—I suspect one would be on firmer, certainly more sociologically credible ground mentioning the particularity of a whole civilization, or a particular one of the great worldwide religions (Islam, say, or Christianity), than the particularity of even a national, let alone a local community of, affection and kinship.

B

All the processes referred to and discussed in the previous section of this chapter are matters of fact, in the sense that they refer to the contingency of actual events (though often dense patterns of events, repeated over millennia) that have taken place on this planet. They are not concoctions of the Kantian a priori,[46] and so they are not to be contrasted—as in abstract vs. concrete—with what we fancy as the concrete particularity of the small-scale community. They are particular facts about the wider world: actually existing cosmopolitanism, in Scott Malcolmson's phrase.[47] I believe they provide a perfectly respectable grounding for something like Martha Nussbaum's cosmopolitan morality and her ideas about educating children as citizens of the world.

I want to begin my argument to that effect now, by examining what we may refer to (pompously) as the *infrastructure* of cultural interaction: the actually existing traditions, institutions, and practices that result from this mixing but also make this mixing possible. We can understand that infrastructure in two ways: (a) in terms of the outward-looking characteristics of particular communities and cultures in a multicultural world, or (b) in terms of the web of relations and connections that characterize the *in–between* of global community. Both modes of understanding are valuable. Let us begin with (a).

(a) In the circumstances of continuous interaction that we have been discussing, the cultures of distinct societies will quickly come to include practices and traditions oriented specifically toward that interaction. Those that spring most readily to mind involve preparation for war (whether defensive or offensive) and various practices associated with it—like politics and strategy, heraldry, diplomacy and espionage, and perhaps also warrior cults such as chivalry and some sense of the laws and usages of war. Many of these practices will have a role in the local peacetime culture as well: politics, for example, may begin as something like a Homeric practice of bellicose deliberation about threats and opportunities for war, but evolve into a more general and established mode of collective decision on all matters of community concern.[48]

Other outward-looking practices may have little or nothing to do with military matters. There will be cultures of hospitality, asylum, and more general traditions for regulating emigration and immigration. There will be rules about exogamy. If a society benefits (as most do) from the importation of foreign goods, there will be rules about the sojourn of merchants, rules about prices, contracts, and exchange, and the local economy will have to develop structures that make trade permanently possible. The presence of merchants, migrants, and refugees will raise issues about the practice of foreign cults and customs in a given locality. Practices of cultural accommodation—ranging from a strictly patrolled *millet*[49] to some looser version, such as everyone worshiping his own Gods in his own way—are by no means an invention of the modern world (as our earlier example from *Acts of the Apostles* illustrates).

Finally, the members of a society that has anything to do with other cultures will likely develop as part of their own culture *a view about outsiders*, an ideology of foreignness: they are devils (or gods), or barbarians, or infidels, or potential converts, or coexistent parts in a great and variegated tapestry. Every culture has, in a sense, a foreign policy—a stance in the world, looking out to other cultures—so that even the particular communities that Martha Nussbaum's critics oppose to her cosmopolitan vision do in fact position themselves in the wider world, as a part of what they are. No one can be a member of a particular culture without having an obligation to understand what that positioning involves; and one's responsibility as a member of a particular culture includes the responsibility to nourish and care for—and that may well include talking about, reflecting upon, even criticizing and proposing changes in—these outward-looking practices. Moreover, the outward-looking side of a culture cannot plausibly be regarded as merely derivative or secondary to its inward-looking side, something one comes to grips with *after* one has learned the local culture wholly on its own terms. One does not learn *first* how to be a pure Athenian or Judean or Zimbabwean, and *then* learn about trade goods, exogamy, and hospitality. Given what we said in Section A about inter-cultural influence, we must accept that a given culture *is*, in part, what it makes of such foreign ideas as come across its horizon, and also what it makes of foreignness as such.

(b) We must now consider the prospect that the world we have been discussing (the real world) also has practices and traditions in it which are not rooted in sedentary cultures at all, but are practiced among those who move back and forth between cultures or who mediate cultural relations in various ways. I have in mind the practices of merchants and missionaries, seafarers, and sightseers. These practices may add up to cultures which are either intersocietal or interstitial in character.

Some global cultures have existed interstitially for all or most of their lifetimes. Catholic Christianity is an example. Though we call it "Roman," it can hardly be regarded as an off-shoot or projection of a culture that grew up on the banks of the Tiber. If Catholic Christianity once had a home, it was the Jerusalem community described at the beginning of the *Acts of the Apostles*, or the Galilean villages from which its figurehead sprang. Gradually it came to exist simply in the work of its evangelists traveling around the Roman Empire, and in the sense of connection with that work felt by settled communities in Corinth, Antioch, Thessalonika, and so on. Its establishment of itself in Rome was not a matter of putting down cultural roots, but rather a base of operations for a cosmopolitan enterprise in the most cosmopolitan city in the contemporary world. And so it exists today, exercising pastoral leadership over a billion people, most of whom regard their involvement in this vast global enterprise as the most profoundly important feature of their lives and local culture.[50] Other cultures with this sort of interstitial aspect include not only the other great world religions (Islam, in particular), but also things like the scientific community, the arts, the sporting community, and even (what's left of) the Socialist International. These traditions are certainly practiced and sustained by people who also inhabit and belong to communities on a smaller scale: their practice is a feature of local life. Even so, in their socialism, their science, or their worship, participants in these cultures look beyond their neighborhoods to a world in which they know millions of others are looking in a similar way to them.[51]

Other parts of the tissue of global culture exist intersocietally rather than interstitially. I have already mentioned the practice of diplomacy, which, though it may take its root from the outward-looking needs of particular societies and may originally have involved nothing more than the formation of alliances, the exchange of spouses and other hostages, and the communication of terms for ending fighting, has in our world developed gradually into a sphere of its own, with its own principles, practices, and traditions.[52] More broadly we may also consider various aspects of what is sometimes called "the state system"—that is, the modern network of nation-states, recognizing one another,[53] maintaining regular channels of contact and consultation on issues of common concern, respecting one another's passports, maintaining treaties of legal comity (on everything from extradition to child custody), applying one another's laws where appropriate (in problems that lawyers call "conflicts of law"), facilitating and sustaining international treaties that make things like safe air travel possible, displaying military force to one another in order to avoid misapprehension and miscalculation, and generally maintaining a common sense of basic order throughout the world (and a common set of categories—war, alliance, neutrality, armistice, etc.—for dealing with disturbances to this order when they arise).[54]

Then there are various arrangements which might be viewed either interstitially or as intersocietal arrangements, or indeed as simply the outward-looking aspect of domestic arrangements. Mercantile law, for example, or the law of international trade, may be understood as the commercial law of municipal legal systems projected out to cover transactions involving parties beyond one's borders, or it can be understood, like the old *lex mercatoria*, as a body of customs which have evolved along the trade routes between societies, and only partly incorporated by them into their municipal law.[55] Law itself may fall into this category:[56] certainly the history of law has been a history not only of transmission, imitation, even boilerplating from society to society, but also the history of the work, study, and influence of at least a civilization-wide community of jurists.[57]

I could go on. But my aim in this chapter is to provide examples only, not a systematic accounting of existing cosmopolitan structures. And the examples are intended to illustrate something. When Martha Nussbaum's opponents want to sneer at her cosmopolitanism, they pretend she is talking about the United Nations, and they poke fun at the fatuous superficiality of UN-style internationalism.[58] I do not wish for a moment to denigrate the UN; but it is worth noticing that the structures we have mentioned in this section have little or nothing to do with that organization. They are much older than the UN, and more substantial; if anything, their existence helps to make the UN work (to the extent that it does); but whether we want the UN to work or not, modern life in any society is unimaginable apart from these interstitial, intersocietal, and outward-looking arrangements. Their existence, in various forms, over millennia gives the lie to those who grudgingly concede that maybe we are in a period of transition from a world of sovereign independent societies to a world of interdependence and cooperation.[59] That seems to me to be predicated on the same old myth—that the default position has been independent societies following their own course on their own respective territories. I hope I have been able to show that historically the default position has been more or less exactly the contrary: intense interaction, and the existence of traditions, cultures, and institutions of interaction, among all societies whenever interaction is a possibility. Societies that can interact do; this is how they form themselves as well as their in between. The myth of pure independence applies at most only to those few societies where, for more or less physical reasons, cultural interchange with others was (for a period) never on the cards. Compared with this dense background of actually existing cosmopolitanism, the very brief flourishing and happy demise of the myth of political sovereignty in the last couple of hundred years, is an insignificant distraction.[60]

C

It was a constant refrain among Nussbaum's respondents that one cannot become a world citizen unless there is a world polity to be a citizen *of*.[61] "Citizenship," says Gertrude Himmelfarb, has "little meaning except in the context of a state."[62] Michael McConnell echoes the sentiment: "Since 'the world' has never been the locus of citizenship, a child who is taught to be a 'citizen of the world' is taught to be a citizen of an abstraction."[63] This argument is not only wrong; it is thoughtless.

To begin with, the position taken by Himmelfarb and others insists confusedly on too tight a connection between citizenship and civic responsibility, on the one hand, and state and government, on the other. They proceed on the basis that, since a *polites* is a member of a *polis* and *polis* means state, any view that a child should be taught to regard himself as a *kosmou polites* must involve advocacy of world government.[64] But I think we should beware of begging the question here. Whether the common connection between citizenship and exclusivity is a *conceptual* connection or not is precisely what discussions like the one in the present chapter are intended to test. But "*polis*" need not mean state in the narrow—and quite modern—sense of a powerful governing organization, any more than the English term "civic" (as in "civic responsibility") implies a connection with "government" (as opposed, say, to "governance"). *Polis* referred originally to the organization of a collectivity: a city, for example, which might have structures and procedures for making various collective decisions, and customs and traditions governing various common activities, but not necessarily any tightly run organization exercising political authority. A citizen was a resident of such a city—a resident conceived as both a right bearer and a duty bearer: his rights included the right to participate in the city's decisions, and his duties included an obligation to respect its traditions and to take some responsibility for its common life. The citizen need not be conceived as a *subject*—that is, he need not be conceived as someone who lives under the power of some overarching organization. In many traditions of civic theory, "subject" and "citizen" are opposites. So it is odd that Gutmann, Himmelfarb, and others cite the absence of a world *power* (to which we might be subject) as conclusive against the notion of world citizenship.

But perhaps it is unfair to say that these critics are simply identifying citizenship with subjection. Maybe the reason for their mistake is more subtle: they associate citizenship primarily with participation in collective decision making, and they infer the impossibility of world citizenship from the absence (or inaccessibility to ordinary people) of institutions of political decision making at a global level. In *every* context, however, citizenship means more than formal participation: at the level of responsibilities, it refers to one's willingness to play a role, even if an informal role, in whatever arrangements there are for the organization of life and activity at a particular level, and to one's willingness to work with others in that regard; and of course at the level of rights, it refers to one's acceptance and enjoyment of the benefits of such organization, in a spirit connected to the shouldering of that responsibility.

Think also of how we invoke the language of citizenship in more informal contexts.[65] When we use the phrase "good citizen" in the context of academic (departmental) life, we use it in relation to institutional responsibility, again without any sense that its use is inappropriate in the absence of an overarching mechanism of government. A good citizen is one who shoulders his share of the burdens of departmental administration, who is willing to advise and supervise students, and who is available to help in crises, etc. He is someone committed to making the department, as an institution, *work* in relation to the goals of education, research, and collegiality. To push the point a little further: one imagines that there was a distinction between good citizens and bad citizens even among the members of "underground universities" and their departments (in, say, Czechoslovakia in the 1980s); and not only did that distinction *make sense* despite the absence of formal ruling structures for the departments in question, it became important precisely because of their absence. Analogously, the phrase "citizen of the world" should not be regarded as meaningless in the absence of a constituted world government. If anything, the absence of such a coercive institution to secure and sustain necessary structures of life and practice at a global level places a greater burden on individual men and women, and makes it all the more important for us to use "citizen of the world" as an idea regulating our actions. The absence of any coercive organization that can do this work for us certainly provides an even greater reason for us as theorists not to peremptorily dismiss (or counsel the peremptory dismissal of) Nussbaum's proposal that people be educated to this cosmopolitan dimension of their civic responsibilities.

Let me now pursue my point about the concrete reality of civic responsibility at this level, using a number of examples.

In Section B, I observed that some of the existing structures of cosmopolitan life exist as aspects or outgrowths of the structures of national or local life. This suggests that some aspects of our responsibility as citizens of the world might be subsumed also under the heading of our ordinary responsibilities as citizens of particular states.[66] For example, in almost every state there are laws that protect foreign embassies against attack by ordinary persons, even embassies of countries hostile to the state in question. Those who attack such embassies—stoning them, storming them, trying to set fire to them—violate local laws. But they are also acting as bad global citizens, since the justification of the laws they violate (the justification that a good citizen would pay attention to, and respect)[67] make essential reference to the importance in the world of the institutions and practices of international diplomacy.[68] So the fact that it is my duty as an American resident not to set fire to the Serbian embassy is not all there is to say about the matter: one of the reasons that that is my duty is that I share a responsibility, with everyone else around here, not to act in a way that makes diplomatic interaction between enemies more dangerous than it already is.

As a second example, consider antiterrorist laws and laws against piracy, which help sustain safe global networks of transportation. The fact that hijacking is an offence against municipal law in most countries (and that there is usually some body of municipal law that applies to any given aircraft, even in international airspace), does not mean that the prohibition on hijacking and the precautions associated with it are not also significant on a cosmopolitan scale.[69] One's responsibility to obey such laws has many dimensions and it is arguably overdetermined: it is a matter both of natural duty and special political obligation,[70] and in my view also a matter of cosmopolitan responsibility—part of the responsibility of a citizen of the world to play his part in securing necessary global structures.[71] As things stand it is also a matter of cosmopolitan responsibility to refrain from voting at a national level in a way that makes it impossible to sustain these international structures. One has a duty to think responsibly—at a global level—before agitating or voting in national politics in regard to the ratification of things like extradition treaties, piracy conventions, and so on. An Irish-American politician, for example, who opposes the extradition of IRA operatives to Great Britain has a responsibility to think the matter through not only in regard to his interests as an American citizen, and not only in regard to his interest in Irish nationalism, but also in regard to his interest in and his honest estimation of the *general* importance of various cooperative antiterrorist endeavors.[72]

This point, about the cosmopolitan dimension of local political activity, is worth amplifying. In a federal context—like Canada, for example—it is not hard to grasp the idea that the citizens of a province may have an obligation not to exercise their provincial voting rights in a way that undermines or damages the confederation.

People have different visions of Canada, of course; so part of that civic responsibility is a duty to participate responsibly in the debate about the shape that federal structures ought to have. One's responsibility to the confederation is not necessarily a responsibility to any particular vision of the confederation. Nevertheless, the citizens of British Columbia, say, or Quebec have a responsibility to think about these competing visions, not just on account of their provincial affiliations but also simply because they are citizens of Canada.

Now I think much the same is true of the exercise of national citizenship vis-à-vis global structures: Canadian citizens have a responsibility to exercise their national voting rights in a way that takes seriously the needs of global structures and the importance of the debates that surround them. For example: we need not assume that *qua* citizen of the world, a Canadian must be in favor of "globalization" as that term is usually understood, that is, in favor of free trade, unrestricted movement of capital without regard to human costs, etc. All that is connoted by the idea of "world citizenship" is that each individual take these issues seriously, and consider justice, efficiency, and economy on a world scale, not just by reference to (say) Canadian interests. One can be a citizen of the world, therefore, and yet act on the ground of serious justice-based opposition to economic globalization: only, that opposition must be articulated with reference to *global* justice, not merely justice for one's fellow citizens in a national (or provincial) sense.

So far I have talked about world citizenship in relation to "official" structures of various sorts: though I have played down things like the UN and its agencies, and various international bodies (such as the World Court or the International Criminal Tribunal or various human rights agencies), I have provided examples of legal and quasi-legal structures at the interface of national and global life that deserve both our consideration and our support. My final point, in this regard, is to remind us that even at the municipal level citizenship is not just a matter of formal participation and civic obligation. It also has to do with various modes of informal participation in civil society—by which I mean the dense network of voluntary and non-governmental groups that gives flesh to civic life. This also is a matter of responsibility, as well as a choice and individual enthusiasm: as a citizen, one has a responsibility to participate in civil society in a way that does not undermine the (sometimes surprisingly fragile) practices and presuppositions on which it rests. Tolerance, openness to debate and interaction, respect for the elementary traditions and procedures that make group life possible, and a willingness to restrain and mitigate sectarian enmities (so that the brightest of lines is drawn between civil society and civil war): all this is important, if civil society is to flourish, and all this must be an accounted part of the informal morality of citizenship. None of this stops at the borders of the nation. As we saw in Section B, there is a dense network of informal global interactions—ranging from participation in the great world religions, to the communities of scholars, athletes, scientists, and socialists, to say nothing of NGO's like Amnesty International and even the international movement for the protection of cultural minorities.[73] Interaction and cooperation at this level do not happen by magic: they are sustained both by the hard work and the forbearance of innumerable men and women around the world, who do not pretend they have no responsibility for the world simply because there is no world state to enforce that as a matter of obligation.

D

In this chapter, I have been able to provide only a very few examples to illustrate the concrete particularity of the world community for which Nussbaum urges us to take responsibility (in our attitudes toward education as well as in the practice of our own civic lives). The aim has been to refute the view of those who condemn cosmopolitanism as an abstraction. I said we should think about cosmopolitan aspects of our legal systems, arts, churches, and economies, on the one hand, and the importance to us all of global structures such as currency markets, the state system, international law, airline conventions, the community of scientists, and the practice of tourism, on the other. When we do that, I think we will be able to see that, between them, these world particularities add up to a set of institutions that makes it perfectly intelligible for Martha Nussbaum, and for us, to use the language of citizenship (the language that clusters together participation, obligation, responsibility, and rights) to describe each person's place in the cosmopolis. My chapter has not addressed the question of what education in this responsibility would consist of: others have talked about that, or have provided—even in their accounts of civic education in a single multicultural nation—some hint of what teaching cosmopolitan right might involve.[74] All I have sought to do here is to specify the concrete topic of this concern, and to vindicate Martha Nussbaum's conception of the urgency of this task against those of her critics who claim it is fatuous.

"No one actually lives in the world of which the cosmopolitan wishes us to be good citizens," says Benjamin Barber.[75] He is quite wrong. We all live in this world; we rely on it in innumerable ways; and the particular characteristics it has *as* such a world are among the most prominent features in our respective cultural landscapes. There is nothing objectionably abstract about insisting that we take responsibility for that world rather than just what we imagine is our own little corner of it—for there are perfectly concrete traditions and practices in the world under whose auspices our children can be taught to discharge that responsibility.

NOTES

This chapter contains material that will appear in a chapter of my book *Cosmopolitan Right* (forthcoming, Oxford University Press). It also includes material from my paper "Multiculturalism and Melange", published in *Public Education in a Multicultural Society*, Robert K. Fullinwider (ed.) (Cambridge: Cambridge University Press, 1996), 90–118. I am most grateful to Carol Sanger for observations and suggestions on this draft.

1. See Martha Nussbaum, "Patriotism and Cosmopolitanism", *Boston Review*, 19 (Oct./Nov. 1994); and Martha Nussbaum and others, *For Love of Country: Debating the Limits of Patriotism*, Joshua Cohen (ed.) (Beacon Press, 1996). See also Chapter 2 of Martha C. Nussbaum, *Cultivating Humanity: A Classical Defense of Reform in Liberal Education* (Cambridge: Harvard University Press, 1997).
2. Nussbaum, "Patriotism and Cosmopolitanism", 7 (quoting Seneca, *De Otio*).
3. Ibid., 11.
4. Ibid., 133 and 144.
5. Benjamin Barber, "Constitutional Faith", ibid., 36.
6. Gertrude Himmelfarb, "The Illusions of Cosmopolitanism," in *For Love of Country*, 77.
7. Michael McConnell, "Don't Neglect the Little Platoons", ibid., 81.
8. Sissela Bok, "From Part to Whole," ibid., 39; but see also the interesting critique of this in Amartya Sen, "Humanity and Citizenship," ibid., 114.
9. Other terms of abuse used by Nussbaum's respondents were "arid", "arrogant", "bleak", "bloodless", "feeble", "halfhearted", "rootless", and "sterile"; even the old slander of "Esperanto" was introduced. (Actually all these epithets can be found in just one of the responses: Robert Pinsky, "Eros against Esperanto," in *For Love of Country*, 85 ff.) The familiarity of this vituperation makes one wonder whether Nussbaum did not flatter her critics when she wrote, "We have so many devious ways of refusing the claim of the humanity" (*For Love of Country*, 132 and 139). The ways of refusal may be many and devious, but they are never new: it is as though the critics always know exactly what to say, and what ancient terms of abuse to dust off and wheel out, whenever claims in behalf of humanity are put forward in opposition to traditional allegiances to blood, kin, and nation.
10. Bok, "From Part to Whole," in *For Love of Country*, 43.

11. This is Nussbaum's reconstruction of her respondents' position, at the end of *For Love of Country*, 142. She sets out an alternative (and more plauisble) account at ibid., 142–4.
12. This is accepted, of course, by those who regard "universalism" as a relic of imperialism. But there is also a history of opposing universalism to imperialism, and of seeing what can be made of it apart from imperialist complacency.
13. So I reject the opposition implicit in Richard Rorty's article "Justice as a Larger Loyalty," in Pheng Cheah and Bruce Robbins (eds), *Cosmopolitics: Thinking and Feeling Beyond the Nation* (Minneapolis: University of Minnesota Press, 1998), 45, at example 56–7: "If we Westerners could get rid of the notion of universal moral obligations created by membership in the species, and substitute the ideal of building a community of trust between ourselves and others, we might be in a better position to persuade non-Westerners of the advantages of joining in that community."
14. For a protracted discussion of this in relation to the Biblical parable of the Good Samaritan (Luke 10: 27–37)—the story of a stranger's immediate and straightforward response to the plight of someone from an alien community— see Jeremy Waldron, "On the Road: Good Samaritans and Compelling Duties," *Santa Clara Law Review*, 40(2000), 1053–1103.

    The Good Samaritan was not a 'telescopic philanthropist', like Dickens' Mrs. Jellaby. Also, unlike his modern namesakes—I mean the Samaritans Organization (an entirely worthy group who maintain a counseling service available by telephone to those who are depressed, lonely, or suicidal)—there is no reason to think that the Samaritan in Jesus' parable was on the look-out for an opportunity to rescue people who fell among thieves or other victims of disaster. He was simply *on the road*, and he came upon the scene of the robbery 'as he journeyed.' When he came near the man who had fallen among thieves, he apprehended roughly what had happened, and straight away gave aid to him as a neighbor. He would have surmised quickly enough that the injured man was probably a Jew rather than a fellow Samaritan. But apparently that did not present itself as an obstacle, for he responded immediately to the injured man's presence and his plight. Awareness of the historic antipathy between Jews and Samaritans does give the story an attractive anti-communitarian edge. But mainly what this cosmopolitan aspect highlights is just the arbitrary immediate 'thrownness' of our being in the presence of another. There is no telling who you will run into—who you will find yourself in the immediate neighborhood of—when you are on the road. That you find yourself side-by-side with an X rather than a Y may be discomfiting—even a source of anxiety and tension—but *there it is*: this is who you are near, and this is who you in particular you have to deal with and respond to.

15. For Nussbaum's apparent indifference to this aspect, see Bruce Robbins, *Feeling Global: Internationalism in Distress* (New York: New York University Press, 1999), 150: her thesis, says Robbins, "has nothing either multi- or cultural about it. No multiculturalist could have written, as she does, that 'the accident of where one was born is just that, an accident' (Nussbaum, *For Love of Country*, 7)." However, she makes much more of it in *Cultivating Humanity*.
16. Of course the average soccer hooligan knows little or nothing of this. But our discussion is normative, and its topic is *good* citizenship for the English, not the caricature of English citizenship that actually disfigures its popular traditions.
17. Immanuel Kant, *The Metaphysics of Morals*, sect. 62: "Cosmopolitan Right," translated by Mary Gregor (Cambridge: Cambridge University Press, 1991), 158 (Vol. 6, p. 352 of the Prussian Academy Edition of Kant's *Works*).

18. Hence the idealized self-description I used in "Minority Cultures and the Cosmopolitan Alternative." There I characterized the cosmopolitan approach to lifestyle, in terms of a person who lives in New York, but came there from California, via Edinburgh, and came in turn to Britain from the other side of the planet, the southwestern corner of the Pacific Ocean, whither his Irish ancestors emigrated in the mid-nineteenth century. I spoke of someone who did not associate his identity with any secure sense of place, or any predetermined subset of the cultural resources available in the world. He did not take his identity to be muddied or compromised when he studied Greek, ate Chinese, wore clothes made in Korea, worshiped with the Book of Common Prayer, listened to arias by Verdi sung by a Maori diva on Japanese equipment, gave lectures in Buenos Aires, followed Israeli politics, and practiced Buddhist meditation techniques. And I said that as long as a person can live like that, it is evident that people in general do not need—what the proponents of cultural identity politics claim they need, claim in fact that they are entitled to as a matter of right—namely, immersion in the secure framework of a single particular culture to which, in some deep sense, they belong.

In the wake of imperialism, global communication, world war, mass migration, and frequent flying—people are not in a position to swallow their cultures whole and pure. We find ourselves listening to a deafening babel of cultural materials, in a bazaar in which no prices have been fixed and no commensurabilities established for the bewildering variety of goods on offer. And in that milieu, each of us makes a discovery about him or herself. We are not so lost or timid that we cannot build an identity for ourselves without the guiding hand of a pre-established framework. Indeed we find ourselves with an identity—a coat of many colors—long before we have the chance to reflect on our ontic relation with community. The Maori *haka* and the Book of Common Prayer were already present in their different language in my consciousness before I had a chance to wonder whether they could really fit comfortably on a single cultural frame.

19. Ibid., sections 42–4, 121–4 (6: 307–12).
20. In "Multiculturalism and Melange", 93 and 96, I proposed the following as "walking-around" definitions of "culture." I said the term seems "to refer to a number of ways of living, acting, and relating, affecting many or most of what are taken to be the more important as well as the more mundane aspects of life, and integrated more or less tightly into a single shared set of meanings, that is, a single way of life... The culture of a community is a way of doing things, particularly the things that are done *together*, throughout the whole course of human life: language, governance, religious rituals, rites of passage, family structures, material production and decoration, economy, science, warfare, and the sharing of a sense of history. It is a way that its members have, as they think their ancestors had and as they hope their descendants will have, of enjoying and enduring the joys and vicissitudes of human life together."
21. The list of seven items that follows is not intended to be complete: it provides one side of the story. My account of the *other* side of the story—more benign bases of interaction—begins later.
22. There is a fine account of the Fijian example in Joseph H. Carens, *Culture, Citizenship, and Community: A Contextual Exploration of Justice as Evenhandedness* (Oxford: Oxford University Press, 2000), ch. 9. (Let me add, though, that my answer to the two questions that Carens poses for me, at ibid., 264, is *affirmative*, in both cases.)

23. For a discussion of the tension between demands for justice now and demands for reparation, see Jeremy Waldron, "Superseding Historic Injustice," *Ethics*, 103 (Oct. 1992), 4.

24. See Jeremy Waldron, "Multiculturalism and Melange" and also "Minority Cultures and the Cosmopolitan Alternative", *University of Michigan Journal of Law Reform*, 25 (1992), 751–92 (reprinted in Will Kymlicka (ed.), *The Rights of Minority Cultures* (Oxford: Oxford University Press, 1995), See also note 18 above.

25. From the website of Oxford's Pitt Rivers Museum (http://units.ox.ac.uk/departments/prm/): "Lieutenant-General Augustus Henry Lane Fox Pitt Rivers...was born in 1827 in Yorkshire. In 1841 he entered the Royal Military Academy at Sandhurst and was commissioned into the Grenadier Guards in 1845...Pitt Rivers was one of the few people who accrued a sizeable collection of ethnographic objects of all varieties during the nineteenth century. His intellectual interest in collecting archaeological and ethnographic objects arose out of his early professional interest in the development of firearms."

26. This does not discredit the relation of the people concerned to their land; it just discredits some of the academic models that are wheeled out to explain it.

27. In "What is Cosmopolitan?" *Journal of Political Philosophy* 8 (2000), 227, I have characterized this disposition as follows: "Humans seem disposed to wander, travel, explore, and settle new regions. Or, if this is not an *innate* disposition, it is at the very least a disposition to respond to certain other vicissitudes of life—such as famine, climate change, overpopulation or attack by other groups—by wandering, traveling, exploring, and settling. At the same time, there are familiar temptations accompanying this movement, exploration, and settlement: the temptation to plunder and conquer, and exploit, enslave, or even exterminate others when one finds that the lands to which one travels are already inhabited."

28. Jared Diamond, *Guns, Germs, and Steel: The Fates of Human Societies* (New York: W.W. Norton, 1997), 215–38.

29. Ibid., 215–18, and 236–8.

30. Ibid., 218: "The two indisputably independent inventions of writing were achieved by the Sumerians of Mesopotamia somewhat before 3000 B.C. and by Mexican Indians before 600 B.C...; Egyptian writing of 3000 B.C. and Chinese writing (by 1300 B.C.) may also have arisen independently. Probably all other peoples who have developed writing since then have borrowed, adapted, or at least been inspired by existing systems." Most of these early systems of writing involved either logograms or syllabaries. Alphabetic writing—with written signs for each basic sound of a given language—was singular in its origin (ibid., 226):

    Alphabets apparently arose only once in human history: among speakers of Semitic languages, in the area from modern Syria to the Sinai, during the second millennium B.C. All of the hundreds of historical and now existing alphabets were ultimately derived from that ancestral Semitic alphabet, in a few cases (such as the Irish ogham alphabet) by idea diffusion, but in most by actual copying and modification of letter forms.

31. See ibid., 248 and (for the characteristics, distribution, and rarity of domesticable animals) 157 ff.

32. Again Diamond provides a good example (ibid., 255): "A simple example is the spread of muskets among New Zealand's Maori tribes. One tribe, the Ngapuhi, adopted muskets from European traders around 1818. Over the course of the next

15 years, New Zealand was convulsed by the so-called Musket Wars, as musketless tribes either acquired muskets or were subjugated by tribes already armed with them. The outcome was that musket technology had spread throughout the whole of New Zealand by 1833: all surviving Maori tribes now had muskets."

33. I make no apology for the use of religious examples, here and elsewhere in the paper (see, e.g. note 14, on the Good Samaritan story, and the discussion of Roman Catholicism as an intercultural presence, below, in the text accompanying note 51). I know that many who talk of cultural rights try to sideline the connection between culture and religion, insisting instead that the particular *language* of a people is much more important in their cultural life than anything associated with religious beliefs and experience: see Will Kymlicka, *Liberalism, Community, and Culture* (Oxford: Clarendon Press, 1989), 165 and 175, and *Multicultural Citizenship* (Oxford: Clarendon Press, 1995), 89. But this position strikes me as question-begging, precisely because the religious component of culture is usually *not* particularist. I suspect that in recent Canadian political theory, this order of priorities—language more important for culture than religion—is a product of the anticlericalism (or, at best, the embarrassment about French Roman Catholicism) associated with the revival of *Québécois* separatism in the second half of the twentieth century: see Jeremy Webber, *Reimagining Canada: Language, Culture, Community, and the Canadian Constitution* (Montreal: McGill University Press, 1994), 44–7, quoted by Jean-Francois Gaudreault-Desbiens, "The Quebec Secession Reference and the Judicial Arbitration of Conflicting Narratives about Law, Democracy, and Identity," *Vermont Law Review*, 23 (1999), 793, at 813–4. For a more balanced view of the relation between language and religion in the constitution of a culture, see Carens, *Culture, Citizenship and Community*, 70–1.

34. Acts 11: 19–21.

35. Acts 15: 1–21. (The compromise that was eventually reached required only minimal observance of Mosaic law: see the letter sent to the church in Antioch, in Acts 15: 22–9.)

36. Acts 17: 16–34 (Revised Standard Version).

37. Acts 17: 26.

38. Acts 17: 26.

39. I believe there is no justification whatever for David Miller's claim, in *On Nationality* (Oxford: Clarendon Press, 1995), 186, that "as cultures become more accessible to outsiders they lose their depth." They may, as he also says, lose "their distinctive character"—but only in the most superficial sense of "distinctive": that is, it will be harder to give a fifteen-word description of the difference between culture A and culture B once they start interacting, or harder to illustrate the difference between A and B in a grade-school coloring book. (See also the discussion in notes 50 and 60.)

40. I knew them as "Chinese gooseberries" when I was growing up.

41. Benedict Anderson, *Imagined Communities: Reflections on the Origin and Spread of Nationalism* (London: Verso, 1983).

42. See E. J. Hobsbawm, *Nations and Nationalism since 1780: Programme, Myth, Reality Edition*, 2nd edn (Cambridge: Cambridge University Press, 1992); and also Ernest Gellner, *Nations and Nationalism* (Ithaca: Cornell University Press, 1983).

43. Ibid., 165–6.

44. In "Minority Cultures and the Cosmopolitan Alternative" I spoke of the importance of pressing communitarians and defenders of minority cultures on the meaning of the term "community."

Many of us have been puzzled and frustrated by the absence of a clear under-standing of the concept in some of the assertions made by communitarians like Michael Sandel, Alasdair Macintyre, Charles Taylor and Michael Walzer. I do not mean the absence of a precise definition. I mean the absence of any settled sense about the *scope* and *scale* of the social entity they have in mind. When they say that the modern individual is a creation of community, or that each of us owes his identity to the community in which he is brought up . . . or that communities have got to have boundaries, or that justice is fidelity to shared understandings within a community—when such claims are made, what *scale* of entity are we talking about? Is 'community' supposed to denote things as small as villages and neighborhoods, social relations that can sustain *gemeinschaft*-type solidarity and face-to-face friendship? What is the relation between community and political system? Is 'community' supposed to do work comparable to 'civil society', picking out the social infrastructure of whatever state or political entity we are talking about? If . . . the concept of *the state* no longer picks out a natural kind, denoting as it does political entities as small as Fiji and as large as the United States, as tight as Singapore and as loose as the [EU], is there any sense in supposing that for every state there is just one community or society to which individuals owe their being and allegiance?

Should we even suppose that communities are no bigger than states? If each of us is a product of community, is that heritage limited to national boundaries, or is it as wide (as *world*-wide) as the language, literature and civilization that sustains us? Are we talking about particular communities, at the level of self-contained ethnic groups, or are we talking about the common culture and civilization that makes it possible for a New Zealander trained at Oxford to write for a symposium in the *Michigan Journal of Law Reform*?

45. Samuel P. Huntington, *The Clash of Civilizations and the Remaking of World Order* (New York: Simon and Schuster, 1996).

46. Indeed, as I say in Chapter 1 of *Cosmopolitan Right*, Immanuel Kant's own dis-cussion of these issues is often quite disconcertingly concrete:

Nature, Kant says, has given us as a world, a *sphere* to live on, not an infinite plain so that those whose actions, beliefs, customs and attitudes offend each other could disperse beyond each others' apprehensions. We live on the surface of a sphere and this means that if I go far enough from you in one direction, I will sooner or later find myself approaching you from the other direction . . . The world of course is very large, and different regions are separated from one anoth-er by uninhabitable stretches of desert or ocean. But even then, Kant says, 'the *ship* or the *camel* (the ship of the desert) make it possible for [men] to approach their fellows over these ownerless tracts, and to utilize as a means of social inter-course that *right to the earth's surface* which the human race shares in common.' Indeed, Kant thinks of the existence of camels, along with marine mammals and driftwood, as evidence of nature's purpose that we should spread out over the whole globe, not just the forested regions.

[E]vidence of design in nature emerges even more clearly [*i.e. even more clearly than in the case of the camel*] when we realize that the shores of the Arctic Ocean are inhabited not only by fur-bearing animals, but also by seals, walruses and whales, whose flesh provides food and whose fat provides warmth for the native inhabitants. Nature's care arouses most admiration, however, by carrying drift-wood to these treeless regions, without anyone knowing exactly where it comes from. For if they did not have this material, the natives would not be able to construct either boats, or weapons, or dwellings in which to live.

I do not know whether Kant took driftwood as a prototype for "the crooked timber of humanity," but at any rate the spherical shape of the earth, together with seals, camels and driftwood are for Kant what David Hume would call the "outward circumstances" of cosmopolitan right.

47. Scott Malcolmson, "The Varieties of Cosmopolitan Experience," in *Cosmopolitics*, 233, at 238: "The cosmopolitanism debate has tended to neglect actually existing cosmopolitanisms, an understandable failing in academic discussions." But Malcolmson's interests are slightly different from mine: he is interested in existent cosmopolitanism as ways of life; in this chapter I am interested in the existing structures that make such ways of life possible.

48. See Christian Meier, *The Greek Discovery of Politics* (Cambridge: Harvard University Press, 1990).

49. This is the term for the arrangement whereby different communities were confined, with their own rules, to their own part of a city, under Ottoman administration.

50. Thus the idea that what is most important about each culture is what *distinguishes* it from others may be seriously mistaken both as a description of the consciousness of the communities in question and as a prescription about what respect for a given culture ought to involve. I argued in "Multiculturalism and Melange," at 99–100, as follows:

> Consider the example... [of] the Breton and Irish cultures. These cultures are markedly different in a number of respects, but there are also marked commonalities. In both... the Catholic Church plays a crucial—and a remarkably similar—role in people's lives. That prompts the following question: to the extent that a Breton or an Irish person actually thinks self-consciously about her culture... is it the *distinctiveness* of the culture that will be important to her—that is, the respects in which her culture differs from others (in the region) as opposed to the respects in which it is similar? I doubt that we can assume this. It seems... probable that an inhabitant of Brittany would regard the teachings and sacraments of the Church as the most important aspect of her culture. If so, it is likely to be both implicit in and essential to that thought that her Church be regarded as *catholic [in the small 'c' sense of universal]*, in precisely the sense of being something shared by other communities. That feature of her life—that *as a Breton* she shares a faith and a church with Irish, Italians, Poles, Brazilians and Filipinas—may be much more important to her identity than anything which (say) a Tourist Board would use to highlight her cultural distinctiveness...
>
> One culture does not need to be clearly and importantly *different* from another, either in its appearance to an outsider or in the consciousness of its practitioners, in order to be the culture that it is. A taxonomist may be interested in qualitative differentiation, and we may want there to be lots of colorful differences in costume, language and ritual so that we can, in a sense, *display* our commitment to multiculturalism to even the most superficial glance. But all this is beside the point so far as the culture itself is concerned. A culture just is what it is, and its practices and rituals are constitutive of it in virtue of their place in a shared way of life, not in virtue of their peculiarity.

51. I pursued this point about the importance of these larger communities in our lives in "Minority Cultures and the Cosmopolitan Alternative":

> Think honestly... of the real communities to which many of us owe our allegiance and in which we pursue our values and live large parts of our lives: the international community of scholars (defined more or less widely in terms of

some shared specialization); the scientific community; the human rights community; the artistic community; the feminist movement; what's left of international
socialism; and so on. These are structures ... which effortlessly transcend national
and ethnic boundaries, and allow men and women the opportunity to pursue
common and important projects under conditions of good-will, co-operation
and exchange throughout the world ... [C]ommunity on this global scale is the
modern realization of Aristotlean friendship: equals orienting themselves in
common to the pursuit of value. It is a form of community that is quite missed
by those who lament the loss of true friendship in modern life. Once we recognize this, the simple Herderian picture of the constitution of an individual by
his belonging to a homogenous group begins to fall apart. Think how much we
owe in history and heritage—in the culture, or the cultures that have formed
us—to the international communities that have existed among merchants,
clerics, lawyers, agitators, scholars, scientists, writers and diplomats. We are
not the self-made atoms of liberal fantasy, fantasy, certainly, but neither are
we exclusively products or artifacts of single national or ethnic communities.
We are made by our languages, our literature, our cultures, our science, our
religions, our civilization—and these are human entities that go far beyond
national boundaries, and exist, if they exist anywhere, simply *in the world*.

52. There is a nice description in Mattingly, *Renaissance Diplomacy* (Dover, 1998).
53. Thus the sovereign independence of separate societies (as something mutually
    recognized) is not the opposite of an international system; it is an artifact of the
    international system. See Martin Wight, *Systems of States* (Leicester: Leicester
    University Press, 1977), 129–36. For such dualism applied more generally to
    law, see Hans Kelsen, *The Pure Theory of Law* (Gloucester, Mass.: Peter Smith,
    1989), 332–3: "If national and international law form a single system,
    then ... [i]nternational law must be conceived either as a legal order delegated
    by, and therefore included in, the national legal order; or as a total legal order
    comprising all national legal orders as partial orders, and superior to all of
    them."
54. There is an excellent account of all this in Martin Wight's book, ibid. See also
    Hedley Bull, *The Anarchical Society: A Study of Order in World Politics*, 2nd
    edn (New York: Columbia University Press, 1995), 3–21.
55. For a good discussion of the development of the law merchant, see Harold J.
    Berman, *Law and Revolution: The Formation of the Western Legal Tradition*
    (Cambridge: Harvard University Press, 1983), 333–56. Berman emphasizes
    (ibid., 342) that in the medieval and early modern period, "[t]ransnational trade
    often predominated over local trade and provided an important model for
    commercial transactions", and that contemporary writers emphasized that it was
    uniform between jurisdictions and "not a law established by the sovereignty of
    any prince" (idem). For the situation in the modern world, see the discussion in
    Keith Highet, "The Enigma of the Lex Mercatoria", *Tulane Law Review*, 63
    (1989), 613.
56. Berman, *Law and Revolution*, 85 ff., connects this (in the West) to the pervas-
    ive influence of modes of administration of the Catholic Church.
57. Compare Frederick Pollock, "The Lawyer as a Citizen of the World", *Law
    Quarterly Review*, 48 (1932), 37, at 38: "[N]o man who aims at being an
    accomplished lawyer can do without making himself a citizen in the common-
    wealth of cosmopolitan jurisprudence." (For this snippet, I am indebted to
    Caroline Bradley, "Transatlantic Misunderstandings: Corporate Law and
    Societies", *University of Miami Law Review*, 53 (1999), 269, at 274.)

58. Thus Robert Pinsky talks, in "Eros Against Esperanto" in *For Love of Country*, 87–8, of a global village "where the folk arts are United Nations institute reports and curriculum reform committees..."
59. Thus Nathan Glazer, "Limits of Loyalty," in *For Love of Country*, 64, writes: "[W]e see fragments of cosmopolitanism emerging as various international treaties and commitments begin to limit the behavior of states for the good of the entire world, as in agreements on the environment, on the treatment of refugees, on the rights of women..."
60. Debunking the old myth is important also for one further reason. Critics of cosmopolitanism sometimes argue that the more we allow cosmopolitan amalgamation of cultures, the more we deprive ourselves of the raw material—the pure cultural resources—upon which any viable cosmopolitanism is parasitic. (Steven Lukes has urged this point to me in several conversations.) But if the argument of this section is basically correct, then it is quite wrong to think of cosmopolitan cultures as forming themselves out of purer, narrower, more particular cultures. Sometimes it is the other way round; or sometimes cosmopolitan cultures have a life of their own; mostly—as I have tried to emphasize—there is nothing but mixture and mingling, all the way down, historically as well as geographically, and even at the most local or parochial level.
61. See, for example, Gutmann, "Democratic Citizenship" in *For Love of Country*, 68: "We can truly be citizens of the world only if there is a world polity. Given what we now know a world polity could only exist in tyrannical form."
62. Himmelfarb, "The Illusions of Cosmopolitanism", ibid., 74.
63. McConnell, "Don't Neglect the Little Platoons", ibid., 81.
64. A slightly different point is made by those who insist that "citizenship" connotes limitation and exclusion. See, for example, Peter J. Spiro, "The Citizenship Dilemma," *Stanford Law Review*, 51 (1999), 597, at 617: "Nor are we ever likely to define ourselves in any meaningful way as 'citizens of the world,' as the very concepts of citizenship and membership inherently implicate something less universal." See also Jean Cohen, "Changing Paradigms of Citizenship and the Exclusiveness of the Demos", *International Sociology*, 14 (1999), 245, at 250–1.
65. I am conscious here of my colleague Gerald Neuman's "plea against the overuse of the rhetoric of citizenship" in his essay "Rhetorical Slavery, Rhetorical Citizenship", *Michigan Law Review*, 90 (1992), 1276, at 1283. But Neuman's plea is mostly aimed at those who talk about the rights of the citizens of a state when they have not thought through the implication that this might be read as withholding the right from non-citizen inhabitants of that state. That is not the issue here.
66. See also the discussion in Nussbaum, *Cultivating Humanity*, 59.
67. Ibid., 59: "The idea of the world citizen...is less a political idea than a moral idea that constrains and regulates political life."
68. The same is true, too, of officials or other national leaders who incite attacks on embassies, even in outrage against injustice—like those who sponsored the attack on the US embassy in Tehran in 1979. In a case like this, where there may be no effective municipal law prohibiting the attack, the political obligation is purely cosmopolitan in character—and not less important for that!
69. Thus a US Justice Department official was heard to observe that Americans are not the only ones who suffer from terrorist attacks directed against American citizens: "In a greater sense, all of the citizens of the world are also victims whenever and wherever the cruel and cowardly acts of international terrorism strikes...And it is up to the authorities of the world [such as the United States]

to respond vigorously and unrelentingly to such terrorist attacks." (See Larry Neumeister, "U.S. Indicts bin Laden in Bombings", *Dallas Morning News* (Nov. 5, 1998), at 1A, quoted by Jami Melissa Jackson, "The Legality of Assassination of Independent Terrorist Leaders: An Examination of National and International Implications", *North Carolina Journal of International Law and Commercial Regulation*, 24 (1999), 669, at 671.

70. See John Rawls, *A Theory of Justice*, Revised edn (Oxford: Oxford University Press, 1999), 98–101 and 293 ff., and Jeremy Waldron, "Special Ties and Natural Duties", *Philosophy and Public Affairs*, 22 (1993), 3–30.

71. To make it probable that such global structures will break down, there are things that a certain number of individuals must do, ranging from say N individual acts of hijacking to, say, N^3 acts of interfering with the responsibilities of airport security personnel. Even if the number N is quite large—maybe there would have to be hundreds of hijackings in a year to break the back of the international air travel system, or maybe many fewer would be necessary—each citizen of the world has a responsibility not to be one of that number. For the general shape of this analysis of civic obligation, see Richard Kraut, *Socrates and the State*. (Kraut is attempting to make sense of the law's reproach to Socrates, as imagined in the *Crito*: "Are you not intending by this thing you are trying to do, to destroy us, the laws, and the entire state, *so far as in you lies?*" in circumstances where one man's disobedience will not destroy the laws but that of N persons will.)

72. I am not making an argument here *in favor of* extradition in such a case, only an argument in favor of there being a cosmopolitan dimension to any responsible thought on the matter.

73. That last point is worth reemphasizing. In an earlier article, "Minority Cultures and the Cosmopolitan Alternative," 779–80, I put it as follows:

[T]hough we may drape ourselves in the distinctive costumes of our ethnic heritage and immure ourselves in an environment designed to minimize our sense of relation to the outside world—no honest account of our being will be complete without an account of our dependence on larger social and political structures that go far beyond the particular community with which we pretend to identify ourselves.

If this is true of the relation of indigenous minorities to the larger state, it applies also to the relation of particular cultures and nations to the world order as a whole. The point is evident enough from the ironies of Article 27 of the International Covenant of Civil and Political Rights, quoted earlier, the article claiming the integrity of indigenous cultures as a matter of human rights. One can hardly maintain that immersion in a particular community is all that people need in the way of connection with others, when the very form in which that claim is couched—the twenty-seventh article of one of a succession of human rights charters administered and scrutinized by international agencies from Ottawa to Geneva—indicates an organized social context that already takes us far beyond specific nation, community or ethnicity. The point is not that we should all therefore abandon our tribal allegiances and re-align ourselves under the flag of the United Nations. The theoretical point is simply that it ill behooves the partisans of a particular community to sneer at and disparage those whose cosmopolitan commitments make possible the lives they are seeking to lead. The activity of these international organizations does not happen by magic: it presupposes large numbers of men and women who are prepared to devote themselves to issues of human and communal value *in general* and who are prepared to pursue that commitment in abstraction from the details of their own particular heritage.

74. I have in mind, for example, a chapter prepared for this volume by Melissa Williams, who emphasizes the importance for citizenship of what Seyla Benhabib and others (following Hannah Arendt) have called "enlarged mentality" or "enlarged thought"—"a capacity to 'mak[e] present to oneself what the perspectives of others involved are or could be, and [to ask] whether I could 'woo their consent' in acting the way I do . . . To 'think from the perspective of everyone else' is to know 'how to listen' to what the other is saying, or when the voices of others are absent, to imagine to oneself a conversation with the other as my dialogue partner.' " See Melissa S. Williams's chapter in this volume. See also Nussbaum, *Cultivating Humanity*, ch. 2.
75. Barber, "Constitutional Faith", ibid., 34.

CHAPTER 2

Liberal Education: The United States Example

K. Anthony Appiah

Liberalism starts with views that are both modern and radical. We are all equal and we all have the dignity that was once the privilege of an elite. When John Locke speaks of "dignity" (in e.g. his draft of the constitution of Carolina) he means the title and privileges of hereditary land owners; it is something associated with a particular station in life. For him, dignity is as much something that the ordinary person does not have as something that belongs to "persons of standing": for modern liberalism, in striking contrast, dignity is something that is to be respected in every human being. Dignity is still, then, as it was for Locke, an entitlement to respect. But now everyone shares that entitlement. Dignity is now human dignity: you get it just by showing up. That is what makes liberalism radical.

But liberals also believe that recognizing individual human dignity entails—in language we owe to Kant—respecting every person's autonomy. The distinctive thought of liberal political philosophy is that individual autonomy is at the heart of political morality. That is what makes it modern.

Kant first articulated autonomy as a philosophical principle, and romanticism lived a peculiarly intense version of this vision.[1] But the central notion is the special province neither of philosophers nor of poets: the claim, put simply, is that what the good is for each of us is shaped by choices we ourselves have made.

This general moral conviction has profound consequences for thinking about the state. Simply put, liberalism values political liberty—freedom from government intervention in our lives—because it holds that each person has the right to construct a life of her own. That right is not unlimited; it must be pursued within moral boundaries shaped, among other things, by the rights of others. But it is fundamental; and every limitation of it is, for liberalism, to be conceded only in the face of a powerful argument.

This picture grew up with Protestantism; which is what accounts for the sense that it is a creature of the West (and, more particularly, of Germany—Kant—and England—Locke). For Protestantism taught, as Locke put it in his "Essay Concerning Toleration," that worship was a "thing wholly between God and me and of an eternal concernment."[2] This notion that the most consequential questions were to be decided individually by each person, searching in his own heart (so that conformity to outer forms was less crucial than inner conviction) placed what mattered most in human life decisively beyond the reach of the government. Locke's major argument in the essay is that state regulation of religious belief is wrong because it is impossible, "[T]he way to salvation not being any forced exterior performance, but the voluntary and secret choice of the mind...."[3] Locke wants religious toleration because the only things the government can regulate—the outward and visible signs—are simply not what matters; like Kant he thought that virtue lies in why you do things not (or not so much) in what you do. This makes him an ancestor of modern liberalism; but our concerns are, I think, somewhat different.

For the modern liberal objection to regulation of religion argues that the choices I make and the understandings I come to in my own search for religious truth are important in part because I chose them in the course of my own search. The modern point is not Locke's—which is that goodness (piety, in this case) is a matter of motive and intention more than behavior; it is that what is good for me to do depends, in part, on my reflective appropriation of the beliefs and values by which I guide my life. Merely adopting views "in gross", as Locke put it, assuming religious "opinions...all at once in a bundle,"[4] is not enough.

It is a crucial point that this moral conviction is not only modern but also, on a world scale, decidedly controversial. It is not the view of the Ayatollahs in Teheran or the Party leaders in Beijing; it is not even the view, to come somewhat closer to home, of His Holiness and the various eminences of the Vatican. For all of these people hold that what is morally required of people is given in advance—by an eternal order for the Ayatollahs and the Curia, by the truths of Marx for the heirs of Mao Tse Tung. All of these positions recognize that one can have obligations that arise out of choice: they recognize promises as binding and duties particular to vocation; and they recognize that roles bring obligations. But none of them agrees with the liberal that sometimes the right thing for me to do is right because I have decided that doing it fits with my chosen sense of the meaning of my own life: none of them therefore accepts the political consequence that in forcing me to do what is best for me according to someone else's conception, you may do me not good but harm.

Notice that far from being relativist or indifferent to moral truth, the claim of autonomy, as made by the liberal, is a universal moral claim: it is something we believe the Pope and the others are wrong about. There is no general answer to the question how one should live one's life: not everyone should be a priest or a poet or a pipe fitter; there are lives worth living that focus on family, and others that center on work. Liberals are pluralists about human flourishing, holding that there are many ways for human beings to live good lives and many projects worth pursuing.[5]

But sensible antiliberals are pluralists too. What is distinctive in the liberal vision is that it holds that there may be an internal connection between what is good for you and the choices you have made: in particular, that your good may depend on the identities you have reflectively appropriated and the values embedded within them. Liberals do not deny that there are some values that are essential components of any good life: honesty, loyalty, and kindness are virtues; and cruelty, thoughtlessness, and unwarranted hatred are vices, no matter what choices you have made. But this essential moral core does not fix everything that matters; nor does it determine how these virtues and vices should weigh against each other in every situation.

Liberalism is a political morality which flows, like all substantial political ideals, from an underlying vision of human life. But, as a political creed, it does not claim to answer every ethical question, every shallow puzzle or deep mystery about how one should live. It stakes out a position about the ethics of relations between the state and the individual, a position that flows from a vision of human life; and that vision proposes that living up to the many values is best when it flows, in two respects, from the "voluntary and secret choices" of your own mind. First, it is best if people do what is right because they recognize that it is right (but this is a point on which the Curia concurs); second, what is best for people depends, in part (but only in part) on what they have chosen. That is why the liberal state has its most distinctive feature: a regime of individual rights, limiting what the state may require of us, even for our own good.

Liberals are not relativists, then. Nor need we be skeptics. We need not argue that each should be allowed by the state to make her own choices because there is no knowing who is right. I may, as a liberal, regard it as proper for the state to allow you to do what is, in my judgment, plainly wrong, provided that, in doing so, you interfere with no one's rights and have freely chosen to do it in pursuit of your aims and in the light of your own knowledge, your best understanding.

This is a separate point from the one about the dependence of the good for you on your choices. Sometimes what is good for me— committing myself to the nationalist struggle against imperial domination—is good because I have reflectively appropriated a nationalist identity; and that identity now gives meaning to much of my life. (Perhaps if I had not developed that identification, a life in the struggle would be worthless, a sham.) But the point I am making now is that sometimes the government should let me do what I have decided to do in the light of my own best understanding, even though what I have decided is wrong. Letting people do something does not, for the liberal, reflect agreement with them. Even when someone is wrong, the state has to have a compelling reason to intervene. And if someone asks why, I would say because it is her life.

It is sometimes said that liberalism is not perfectionist, in the sense that it does not aim to shape the citizen to a vision of human good. I think this is somewhat misleading. Autonomy is a vision of human good; and the liberal state will aim to help the citizen exercise her autonomy, by, for example, providing information and encouraging rational public deliberation. What a liberal will not do is use the coercive power of the state against anyone, except to protect the rights of others.[6] The liberal surgeon-general tells you that cigarettes kill and requires tobacco companies not to sell their products to those, like minors, who are not fully capable of autonomous decision. But if an adult person chooses cigarettes, knowing the harm they do, the most the liberal state may do is limit her access to health care for those harms, if the state does not have the resources to provide it.[7]

Modern American liberalism, as an approach to the realities of politics, goes back to the New Deal, when to the classical liberalism of rights was added a new set of economic commitments: the federal government accepted clearly, for the first time, a national responsibility to guarantee a basic minimum level of welfare to every citizen. This undertaking occurred, of course, in response to the Depression: a massive failure on the part of the private economy to deliver the jobs and the income that were now recognized as a precondition for enjoying the fundamental civil rights—democratic representation, liberty of religion, expression, and association, security of property, equality before the law.

This pious simplification of history ignores a great deal. The New Deal welfare state, for example, did not spring full-fashioned from the brow of the Roosevelt administration. There were already provisions for the poor and the destitute in colonial Massachusetts; there were federal Civil War pensions for veterans and war widows; there were hundreds of charitable institutions, supported by churches and by secular philanthropy, often with tax-exemption from the government, aiming to help people in a thousand kinds of trouble. Still, it was clear to everybody that the New Deal took government provision for the worst off to a new level.

It is natural to see this concern with basic welfare as simply a new addition to the liberal register, not as something growing out of the basic liberal vision. But I think that is wrong. Basic welfare provision flows from the same fundamental concern with dignity. In a world where land has all been parceled out (so that no one can simply acquire land to work by moving into uncharted territory); a world where money is essential for adequate nutrition and proper shelter; where a job (or so much money you do not need one) is increasingly a condition for minimal social respect; guaranteeing that everybody has access to a place to live, food to eat, and a form of work, is simply making sure that everyone has access to the possibility of a dignified existence. It is increasingly clear, I think, that a guarantee of access to health care should be underwritten by the state as well. And, because everybody is equally entitled to dignity, whatever minimum conditions the state must guarantee, it must guarantee to everyone.

More than this, autonomy requires, as we have seen, that people be able to shape a life for themselves, to make choices among options. And this requires, naturally, that there be such options—real choices to make; and that the person has some sense of the way the world actually is.

Each of these conditions is hugely important. The existence of real options is something that argues for multiculturalism within states and cosmopolitanism across them.[8] And the importance of the truth entails that the government has a role in propagating knowledge. To do my will, to act freely, I need not only to have goals but a sense of how I can achieve them. You can undermine my autonomy not only by resisting what I will, but also by depriving me of information—truths—that might allow me to achieve what you desire. Respect for autonomy goes with truth telling, therefore; respect for autonomy entails a concern with knowledge.

There are hard questions here, questions that, as we shall see, matter enormously for the politics of education. Respect for your autonomy means that, where your aims are morally permissible, it is best if you are able to do what you choose. But you choose to do things for reasons, and those reasons are dependent not only on your aims but also on how you believe they can be achieved. Characteristically, in reasoning out what I want to do, I consider what my aims are and what means are available to achieve them. Suppose, then, you know what my aims are, and you know that in pursuing them I am relying on an erroneous belief. Suppose, for example, that I am seeking to abate my fever, and I take the herbs the traditional doctor in my village concocts; and suppose you know that the herbs are mortally toxic in the long run and that I can be cured with the erythromycin in your pocket. If you secretly substitute your authentic medicine for my (as you think) bogus "medicine," are you respecting my autonomy—helping me to the health you know I am after—or failing to do so—by ignoring my clear (but, as you think, fatally misguided) desire to take this stuff that the medicine man provided?

The answer, I believe, is that what respect for your autonomy requires is neither of these things; what it requires is that you tell me what you believe is true (thus putting me in a position to realize my fundamental aim by engaging my goals with the way the world really is). You can urge on me the medicine that will cure me, offering me reasons to believe that it will cure me; but if, in the end, I reject your reasons, if I do not trust you, respect for my autonomy requires that you let me take the worthless portion I believe in. Just as respect for autonomy requires me to recognize your reasons for your choices in matters that affect you, so it requires me to address your beliefs with evidence and reasons; I may not manipulate you into believing what is in fact the truth by offering you phony "proofs" and faked "evidence."

Now I hasten to add that respecting my autonomy is not the only thing that is at stake when I am sick and considering what treatments to undertake. There is also the matter of my physical well-being, which is something that I require for most of my projects and which makes more likely the satisfactory achievement of almost all of them. In dealing with me in these circumstances, you may rank my survival over my autonomy, hoping, perhaps, that once the crisis is over you can persuade me that you have done the right thing. This may be an especially plausible choice if you have a special responsibility for my health—the responsibility, say, of my doctor—or a special concern for my well-being—the concern, say, of my friend or my parent. But even if you make this choice, it should be clear that you have done so against the weight of an important consideration: respect for me, treating me with dignity, surely entails respect for the reflective choices I make, even when they are mistaken.

I have considered this case as if it were one in which your choice was an essential private (i.e. non-state) matter. But if your relationship to me were that of an official to a citizen, then, I think, autonomy would have to loom larger. Governments may not force citizens to do what is good for them, once they have explained why it is good for them and offered them the choice. Provided I am capable of exercising autonomy—provided, that is, I am not mentally incapable at the time that I must think the issue through—my government should let me die, if I choose.

Liberals are not libertarians—our aim is to maximize autonomy not to minimize government involvement. Liberals will normally allow you to take whatever chances you like, once you know the risks; but not if the risk is to your autonomy. Thus, they may regulate access to drugs that threaten—through addiction—the autonomy of every user. In becoming an addict you would give up your autonomy; if you did so willingly, you would be making a mistake from which the liberal state might attempt to save you. This would not be a perfectionist policy: it is not a matter of the state choosing to make you a better person than you would make yourself. Rather, it is the state guaranteeing that you can continue to make the choices that are the substance of your freedom.

I have tried to exemplify what respect for the dignity and autonomy of each person means for a liberal politics. But when we turn to education, we are faced with an immediate problem. We are not born as autonomous adults. We are born, in the Bard of Avon's happy phrase, "mewling and puking", incapable of an even moderately independent existence. Liberalism speaks of respecting the self-chosen projects of others, and of allowing them to pursue them in the light of their own knowledge and their values. But we are born neither with projects nor with knowledge. The fundamental idea of a liberal philosophy of education must be that we need to guide each child from hopeless dependency into an autonomous maturity. Preparing someone to be autonomous requires that we give them access both to values (and the capacity to form projects) and to knowledge (and the ability to learn more). But now there are so many hard questions: who is the "we" here? And which projects should "we" help the child to grow into? And who is to decide, in cases of controversy, what is knowledge and what false opinion?

Many people will say that the "we" that has primary responsibility for our development into autonomy is our parents. It certainly seems right to see this as one of the duties (and pleasures) of parents. There is every reason to think that a loving family is the best place to grow into an autonomous adult. No government has found a way to do better that parents generally do: prudence suggests that states interfere only when they must.

But, as hardly needs saying, my parents can be an obstacle to the development of my autonomy. And when they are, so it seems to me, the state has a duty to intervene.

Just as the New Deal recognized an extensive system of welfare provision as a condition for a dignified adult life in the modern world, so the development of public education reflects the need for a wide range of skills, knowledge, and values, as a condition for an autonomous modern life. These essential prerequisites of autonomy—the elements of a basic education—require time and expertise to teach properly; and in a world where most adults must work for a living, parents cannot be expected to provide them on their own. Further, the elements of a basic education are necessary for all who are not severely mentally disabled: every person, every child, therefore is entitled to a guarantee of at least this minimum. This is why, despite the liberal's general hostility to state intervention in what we ordinarily call private life, the very widespread development of state-funded, state-controlled education, with its intrusion into the relations between children and families, is something liberals are bound to welcome.

Public schools do many things that not every parent agrees with. This seems to me just right: for these liberal reasons. If parents had the right to determine what their children should learn, it would be indefensible that we require parents to chose between public education and publicly licensed private education. That we do require it is a reflection of the fact that we believe children have a right to an education that prepares them for autonomy as adults; and we recognize that this is something many parents cannot, and some parents will not, provide. To the extent that states in the United States license private schools that explicitly aim to limit the child's preparation for an autonomous adulthood, this is a breach of the liberal understanding of the state's obligations to the young.

I do not know whether the framework I am suggesting is likely to seem too radical or too conservative. I suspect that it will seem to many too conservative, in this abstract formulation. I should like to end with a consideration of what it might mean in practice; and here, I suspect, many will find it too radical. But I should like to say that it seems to me that in working out how to proceed in educating our children for adulthood, the notion that we should prepare them for a dignified and autonomous maturity is one that ought to gather support from a very wide range of Americans. This basic idea is, as I have suggested, philosophically liberal: but it is not a liberal idea in the sense in which liberal and conservative are now contrasted in our politics. If contemporary conservatives are skeptical because I have spoken so much of rights, I should remind them that respect for autonomy also entails holding people responsible for their acts and that the existence of rights entails forms of constraint as well as kinds of freedom.

The basic liberal picture lies at the root of democratic thinking: we are each allowed an equal share in shaping the destiny of our nation, subject to the constraint that we acknowledge what flows from the dignity and autonomy of others. This means that the liberal democracy constrains what majorities can do, by the familiar mechanism of a system of legal rights, enforced by a judiciary that is relatively independent of the contemporary majority will. But it also means that the liberal democracy's values are not mere majoritarianism, but public deliberation in which each of us is addressed as a reasoning creature and invited to think through, in the light of his or her own projects and understandings, the choices facing our politics. The exercise of autonomy, as Kant formulated it, was the exercise of reason: I have been developing a picture of autonomy that is not Kant's; but I want it to share this feature of Kant's theory (albeit with a more indulgent understanding of reason).

It follows (unsurprisingly) that liberal democracy is one of the notions that belongs to the core of the liberal conception of political morality, and that teaching it is, therefore, a matter of giving to each child a proper understanding of politics. But we need to give each child not only a grasp of these general notions but an understanding of the particular form through which our political institutions instantiates, in a rough and ready way, these general abstractions; and we need to give her, too, the tools with which to explore the ways in which the current political institutions of our society fail to meet the basic constraints, so that she can, if she chooses, contribute to the citizen's work of improving them.

The key to a liberal education is the development of an autonomous self. But there is a regular misunderstanding of what this means, one to which liberals themselves have contributed: a concern for autonomy is often wrongly seen as inconsistent with valuing sociality and relationship. This is a mistake that should be immediately rejected. An autonomous self is a human self, and we are, as Aristotle long ago insisted, creatures of the *polis*, social beings.

We are social in many ways and for many reasons. We are social, first, because we are incapable of developing on our own, because we need human nurture, moral and intellectual education, practice with language, if we are to develop into full persons. This is a sociality of mutual dependence. We are social, second, because we humans naturally[9] desire relationship with others: friends, lovers, parents, children, the wider family, colleagues, and neighbors. This is sociality as an end. And we are social, third, because many other things we value—literature, the arts, and the whole world of culture; education; money; and, in the modern world, food and housing—depend essentially on society for their production. This is instrumental sociality.

To have dignity and autonomy as values is not, therefore, to refuse to acknowledge the dependence of the good for each of us on relationships with others. Indeed our selves are, in Charles Taylor's fine phrase, "dialogically" constituted: beginning in infancy, it is in dialogue with other people's understandings of who I am that I develop a conception of my own identity. Furthermore, my identity is crucially constituted through concepts (and practices) made available to me by religion, society, school, and state, and mediated to varying degrees by the family. Dialogue shapes the identity I develop as I grow up: but the very material out of which I form it is provided, in part, by my society, by what Taylor has called its language in "a broad sense."[10] It follows that the self whose autonomous desires liberalism celebrates is not a presocial thing—not some inner essence independent of the human world into which we have grown—but rather the product of our interaction from our earliest years with others.[11]

As a result, educating children for autonomy requires preparing them for relationship, not just preparing them to respect, as liberalism requires, the autonomy of others.

Let me exemplify what an education guided by these ideas might be like in the most practical terms, by describing two classroom practices with elementary school children that would, I think, embody the ideals I have been discussing.[12]

The first practice is this: we establish a rule that no discussion is complete until everyone has spoken. The idea, of course, is that everyone is of equal worth, and is, therefore, equally entitled to express her opinion and receive respectful attention. This does not mean that what everyone says is of equal merit: and it is perfectly consistent to ask everyone to play her role in the discussion and, at the same time, to recognize that some contributions move the discussion forward better than others. In practice, living by such a standard requires small discussion groups or long discussions. No doubt in the over-sized classrooms of many schools this will not be possible. But learning that such practical limitations shape real political life is important, too. So saying that a discussion cannot be completed properly because there has not been enough time to let everyone speak or insisting that a discussion be continued later for the same reason might be the best we can practically do.

In the second practice, the teacher makes a habit of asking children to explain what other children have said. This, too, teaches that a dialogue of equals requires listening as well as speaking.

These practices are ways of communicating equality of respect and the place of discourse and reason in the relations of people who respect one another. I am sure that many teachers do both of these things (and many more just like them) already. And they are important because they introduce children to practices of respect, rather than simply announcing to them principles of respect. A child who has learned spontaneously to attend to what other children say and who expects a discussion of a question to be one that requires everyone's voice is learning about dignity and respect and learning to live with them. Such a child is in a better position to understand what the principles I have been talking about mean, when it becomes appropriate, as she grows older, for us to articulate explicitly what she has already implicitly learned through such classroom practices and at home.

What I have just said is, I suspect, likely to seem uncontroversial to many. But it already raises problems in our multicultural society. Not every social group in this country believes that children should be encouraged to speak up: some Chinese–American families teach children that the proper behavior for them is attentive silence in the presence of adults—and the teacher is an adult. Children know nothing, after all; or, at least, nothing of importance. They are in class to learn. From the perspective of certain ways of socializing children, the practices I have just described look guaranteed to produce children who chatter and expect to be listened to; children, in short, who are ill-mannered.[13]

Our liberal principles help us here, too. The raising of children is something in which parents plainly have the central role. I have insisted that the state rightly intervenes to protect the child's growth to autonomy; if the sorts of practices I have described are necessary for that purpose, they may be warranted by that fact. But the parents do not lose their role because the state's experts have a good-faith disagreement with them about what is best for their children. And because they are entitled to the treatment owed to persons with equal dignity, the proper approach, if such procedures are necessary, is to discuss with the parents the ideas they represent and the theories that guide them.

We should go carefully in such encounters. I have already pointed out that the centrality to liberalism of the idea of choices among options (and its correlative, the reflective appropriation of identities) means that we have a strong reason for encouraging the development of many richly socially embedded forms of identity both within nations—multiculturalism—and across them—cosmopolitanism. If a social group takes the attentive silence of its children as the proper and necessary preparation for them to have well-mannered adult lives, then, if they are right, that kind of childhood may be a condition for developing the adult identity embodied in that social group. Because we value the maintenance of a variety of such reflectively appropriated identities, we have a special reason to be careful that we are right in thinking that practices in schools that appear to threaten those identities are either not genuinely threatening, on the one hand, or, on the other, important enough that they warrant the reshaping of the identities they will bring. We need, in particular, to be careful that we are not simply being ethnocentric when we suppose, in our talkative modern Euro-American way, that children's talk really develops autonomy and respect for autonomy, because it is how we have come to want to treat our children.

I do not think that my attraction to the practices I have described is mere ethnocentrism: facility with language and its use in social life requires a lot of practice; children who are talked to and reasoned with do better, on average, at cognitive tasks that are broadly useful in modern life. But Chinese–Americans have not been having a hard time preparing their children to perform well at the cognitive tasks by which our schools measure their success and failure; and it is not an unreasonable hypothesis that the capacity for careful attention and for sustained intellectual work are connected with being able to sit quietly in the presence of adults. I think it is important, therefore, that the practices I have described place value on listening as well as on speaking: and that both of them are consistent with, for example, insisting that children also learn to work quietly together and alone.

At the other extreme from these very practice-based ideas, which have to do with the *form* of our pedagogical practices, are concerns about the *content* of the curriculum. How should a liberal state decide curricular controversy?

There are two major kinds of problems here. First, there are topics in which the controversy is about what the truth is. Religious education is the obvious case here; as is moral teaching on questions, like abortion and homosexuality, about which there is substantial (often religiously based) controversy. To these issues I shall return.

But there are also questions about what weight to place in education on different topics or different approaches. How much American history should children in America know? Within that history, should the focus be on individuals or on social processes; on America's failures or her successes.

Such questions are extremely concrete. We can agree that Frederick Douglass was a slave who brilliantly articulated an ideal of freedom: but we must also accept that that ideal was expressed in terms that made masculinity—and the freedom of men—more central than the freedom of women. Frederick Douglass was by the standards of his day progressive on "the woman question." But by our standards there is something unacceptably masculinist in the central opposition of his narrative between slavery and manhood—with its emblematic moment in Douglass's physical resistance to the slave-breaker Covey: "You have seen how a man was made a slave," Douglass writes; "you shall see how a slave was made a man." The question is, at what stage (if ever) do we teach the problem with Douglass. The issue is not what the facts are, but which ones to focus on, which ones to play up.

My example here focuses on a figure who is much taught these days within the framework of multicultural education; but this sort of question has often been raised recently in resistance to multicultural education. Lynn Cheney objects to a history curriculum that has too much of Harriet Tubman and not enough of Thomas Jefferson. But she also objects to a curriculum whose discussion of Thomas Jefferson focusses more on his betrayal of liberty—in his persistent failure to emancipate his slaves—than on his place, as the author of the Declaration of Independence, as liberty's champion. No doubt a focus too lop-sided shades off into simple untruth: but the real debates here are not about what happened but about what narratives we will embed them in; they are about which of the many true stories we will tell.

From the point of view of liberal political principle, these questions are relatively easy. We need to prepare children with the truth and the capacity to acquire more of it. Because they cannot absorb the whole truth, in all its complexity, all at once, we must begin with simplified stories; sometimes, even, with what is literally untrue. The obvious model where untruth prepares the way for truth is physics: the easiest way, we think, to prepare children for Einstein and Schrödinger is to teach them Newton and Maxwell first. But

Newton and Maxwell did not know about relativity or about the indeterminacy of the fundamental physical laws: and so their physics, which assumes absolute space and the infinite divisibility of matter, is just not true. The teaching of history is full of cases in which we can delve deeper as we grow older into stories we first heard, in simplified versions, in first grade. It is because it is on the way to the truth, or because it is the closest thing to the truth that, at a certain age, they can understand, that these forms of what is, after all, strictly speaking, misinformation, can be seen as aimed at helping children develop toward an autonomy rooted in the best available understanding of the world. To say that these questions of principle are easy to lay out is not to say that the decisions about what to teach (let alone how and when to teach it) are easy to resolve in practice: it is just to say that the disputes about which truths to teach are to be settled by appeal to the notion of a preparation for an autonomous adulthood.

The hard cases for liberal principle, I think—with which I want to deal in closing—are the ones in which the controversy is about what the truth is.

The greatest contemporary controversies about what truths should be taught arise about claims that are, in one way or another, connected with powerful collective identities. At the moment, for example, there is controversy about what shall be taught about evolution, abortion, contraception, and homosexuality; and, if the first amendment did not prohibit the teaching of particular religions in public schools, there would certainly be controversy about that too. It is clear enough that the controversy about evolution flows from the fact that neo-Darwinian accounts of the development of species in general—and of the human species in particular—are at least prima facie inconsistent with the account of human origins proposed in the Old Testament. Some people do not want their children taught that "we are descended from apes" at least in part because they want their children to be, for example, good Baptists; and being a good Baptist requires, in their view, assent to the biblical account. But it seems to me that the controversies about sex and sexuality also have the intensity they do in part because American religious traditions have well-developed moral ideas about the proper use of sex and the proper form of sexuality; and conformity to these prescriptions is also seen as essential to being, say, a good Catholic. And those, on the other side, who are themselves homosexual and have come to celebrate a gay identity, are particularly outraged if it is proposed that children should be taught that their sexuality makes them morally depraved.

So far as the teaching of morality is concerned, all of us plainly have a reason to want children to be taught what we take to be morally true, whether or not we associate conformity to those norms and assent to those moral claims as central to an identity we share. Kant's stress on universalizability as the key mark of the moral reflects the way that treating an assertion as a moral claim entails believing that everyone should conform to it.[14] We want our fellow citizens to know what is morally required and what is morally forbidden because we want them to do what they should and abstain from doing what they should not. But it is noticeable that the greatest controversies surrounding what moral ideas should be taught occur when people feel that their own children are being taught things that are inconsistent with claims that are crucial marks of their own collective identities; or when other people's children are taught things that challenge their own identities. I shall call a claim—whether moral or not—that is, in this sort of way, implicated with a certain collective identity, an identity-related claim.

The currency of controversy about the teaching of identity-related claims is not particularly surprising in this age of what Charles Taylor has dubbed the "politics of recognition." The development, which I have already insisted on, of the liberal idea of an identity, has meant that a great deal of politics—especially nationalist and ethnic politics, but also, for example, a lesbian and gay politics that is somewhat modeled on ethno-national politics—turns on the state's acknowledging a person's identity and protecting each person's ability to flourish while publicly expressing that identity. Each of these state acts recognizes an identity, conferring upon it a certain social respect. Martin Luther King day expresses the state's recognition of African-American identity; antidiscrimination law allows people to express their religion, their ethnicity, and their sexuality in public without the threat of loss of employment or access to housing or assault. As Taylor insists, there is a widespread conviction (which comes, as he also says) from the ethics of authenticity, that, other things being equal, we have the right to be acknowledged publicly as what we already really are. Much debate about what shall be taught in the schools on the teaching of identity-related claims is thus centrally concerned with insisting on the state's recognition of some identities (Christian, say) or its non-recognition of others (lesbian and gay).

Now it will be immediately clear why the notion of raising children to autonomy—with its corollary that we should equip them with the truths they need—does not help much in deciding what should be taught about these particular questions. It does not help because there is substantial social disagreement as to what the truth is; and such disagreements, we can predict, will not be settled by the appointment of commissions of experts to resolve them, in the cases where the claims in dispute are identity related. In the case of moral claims, this is because most modern people do not recognize the existence of experts—perhaps because moral autonomy requires that each of us makes up her own mind about these questions. In the case of the dispute about evolution, it is claimed by some that they are simply operating by different epistemic standards: the authority of the Bible is not, for them, something that could be overridden by other (scientific) sources of evidence.

The constraints of truth do some work, however. Some of the theses of "creation science" (those, in particular, that are not themselves directly biblically derived) might be shown to be false by standards everyone agrees on; and some of the claims made about homosexuality by its enemies—claims about the "recruitment" of children to homosexuality—are completely without serious evidential foundation.

Nevertheless, this does not get us very far. And the question arises: how we can develop, on the sorts of liberal principles I have been articulating, a policy for public education in the cases where the dispute about the facts remains unresolved?

You might think the answer should be to stress the democracy in liberal democracy. Let us have public debate among equals and then vote for what should be taught. This seems to me how we must decide these questions, in one sense. But among the options in that public debate will be one that says that on some topics we may require the state to step back and leave the matter to the parents. It is not the case that the only option is to teach what the majority believes to be true. I should like to defend that option in cases where identity-related beliefs are in dispute.

We must begin by recognizing that the role parents play in the raising of children gives them rights in respect of the shaping of their children's identities that are a necessary corollary of parental obligations. We do not believe that social reproduction should be carried out as it is in *Brave New World*. We believe that children should be raised primarily in families and that those families should be able to shape their children into the culture, identity, and traditions that the adult members of the family take as their own. One liberal reason for believing this is that this is one way to guarantee the rich plurality of identities whose availability is, as I have said, one of the resources for self-construction.

There are imaginable other ways. If the state took over the raising of children and did not aim to raise them all to a singular identity, it would have to assign children, effectively arbitrarily, to one of a range of identities. Once the state had taken over this role, respect for autonomy would require it to teach only such truths as it could decide on; teaching children falsehoods in order to give them "interesting" identities would be a paradigm of treating them as means (to the maintenance of a rich range of identities) rather than as ends. The resources for self-construction available would depend solely on the imagination and the will of the state and its servants, along with whatever "spontaneous" inventions would occur among the adults in such a society. Skepticism about this alternative, however, is surely in order. The intimacy of family life; the love of children for parents (and other relatives) and parents (and other relatives) for children; the sense of a family identity, family traditions: all these would be lost. More than this, the state would be invested with quite an enormous power in the shaping of the citizenry; a power whose potential for abuse is obvious enough.

But once we have left the raising of children to families, we are bound to acknowledge that parental love includes the desire to shape children into identities one cares about, and to teach them identity-related values, in particular, along with the other ethical truths that the child will need to live her life well. A state that actively undermined parental choices in this regard in the name of the child's future autonomy would be a state constantly at odds with the parents: and that would be unlikely to be good for the children. A compromise is therefore necessary: where identity-related propositions are at stake, parents are permitted to insist that their children not be taught what is contrary to their beliefs; and, in return, the state will be able to insist that the children be told what other citizens believe, in the name of a desire for the sort of mutual knowledge across identities that is a condition for living productively together.

Thus, it seems reasonable to teach children about the range of religious traditions in the communities within which they live (indeed, in the world), without requiring them to assent to any of them, so that, to begin with, at least, they will assent only to the religion they have learned at home. This allows the children the knowledge to make identity choices as they themselves grow to autonomy; but it gives parents a special, primary place in shaping those choices. Only when a parent's choice seems to compromise the possibility of an autonomous adulthood—as would be the case with a refusal, on religious grounds, to allow one's children to learn to read—must the liberal state step in.

I have tried to suggest how one might begin to think about some questions in the philosophy of education, guided by the liberal thought that education is a preparation for autonomy. My aim has been to show that this tradition is both powerful enough to help us with this difficult question and rich enough to allow us answers of some complexity. But these are only beginning ideas: and a liberal, who respects his fellow citizens, will offer them into the public debate expecting to learn from others where he is wrong.

NOTES

I owe a great debt of gratitude to the members of a reading group at Harvard named (after its one-time meeting place) the "Pentimento" group. My thinking on *these* questions owes particular debts to four members of that group: Lawrence Blum, Martha Minow, David Wilkins, and David Wong. But, as usual, no one but the author should be held responsible for the views I express.

1. For better or worse, however, Kant's understanding of autonomy was more universalizing and rationalist than the understanding most people now have of it; it will not be a Kantian view that I sketch here.
2. David Wootton (ed.), *Essay Concerning Toleration* in *Political Writings of John Locke* (New York: NAL/Dutton, 1993), 188.
3. Ibid., 189.
4. Ibid., 197.
5. One reason for this is that what makes sense for me depends, very often, on the choices of others: if everyone ceased to care about film, the movie-making career I have set my heart on is going to cease to make sense.
6. I mean here to include, of course, the right to basic welfare and the child's right to an education to autonomy, which I discuss below.
7. There are issues here that are quite complex. My thought is that, if a state cannot afford to provide the most extensive health care provision that is currently technologically possible, then, in rationing access to health care (or in charging for health care beyond what is available free to all), it may take into account whether the sufferers knowingly accepted the risk of the disease.
8. See my "Cosmopolitan Patriotism," *Critical Inquiry* 23 (Spring 1997) pp. 617–39.
9. I mean it is natural to us only in the sense that a normal human upbringing produces creatures with such desires.
10. The broad sense "cover[s] not only the words we speak, but also other modes of expression whereby we define ourselves, including the 'languages' of art, of gesture, of love, and the like." in *Multiculturalism: Examining "The Politics of Recognition."* An essay by Charles Taylor, with commentary by Amy Gutmann (ed.), K. Anthony Appiah, Jürgen Habermas, Steven C. Rockefeller, Michael Walzer, Susan Wolf (Princeton, NJ: Princeton University Press, 1994), 32.
11. See my "Identity, Authenticity, Survival: Multicultural Societies and Social Reproduction" in *Multiculturalism*: Ibid., 149–64.
12. I am conscious of having come to these ideas in conversation with school and college teachers over the last few years, and in reading about education, without being clear as to where exactly they came from. So, either I made them up (which strikes me as unlikely) or I got them from someone, though I have forgotten when and from whom. If the latter is the right hypothesis, I apologize to my source: come forward and I will be happy to acknowledge you.

13. I am especially conscious of the dependence of what I say here on a discussion with the "Pentimento" group.

14. In recent years, Bernard Williams has argued that there are ethical norms, central to the ways in which we construct our lives that do not belong to the universalizing institution of morality; see Bernard Williams, *Ethics and the Limits of Philosophy* (Cambridge: Harvard University Press, 1985). So, if he is right, not every important ethical conviction will share this universalizing logic of moral belief.

CHAPTER 3

Pluralism, Personal Identity, and Freedom of Conscience

KENNETH A. STRIKE

Pluralism, as I shall discuss it here, is the idea that society legitimately contains diverse groups. Obviously much of what this means depends on how we understand the nature of group differences and the values and ends that their toleration or encouragement is thought to serve. Different theorists conceptualize the way in which groups are relevantly different in different ways. Some have emphasized a pluralism of conviction. Rawls,[1] for example, treats pluralism largely in terms of differences in reasonable comprehensive doctrines. This includes religious pluralism, but he expands it to encompass other secular doctrines that play "orienting roles" in people's lives. Rawls's view is primarily a cognitive pluralism. Groups are different because their members subscribe to different beliefs.

Others have viewed pluralism as being about diverse ways of life. Differences of this sort need not, and usually are not, rooted in purely creedal differences. Often the point of an emphasis on diverse ways of life is to assert the equal worth of individuals by providing equal recognition to their cultures.[2] The idea that cultural pluralism is a servant to equal recognition assumes an intimate connection between culture and identity. It tends to see one's identity as one's culture writ small. Otherwise we could not recognize people by recognizing their culture. These different emphases on what pluralism is are neither equivalent nor mutually translatable. While conviction is one thing that may differentiate culture, it is also true that people who share common convictions may come from quite different cultures. Similarly, people who share common cultures may not share common convictions. The phrase "Irish Catholic" is not a redundancy.

Different conceptions of pluralism may be associated with different visions of the values and ends that pluralism should serve. Some who defend pluralism may emphasize freedom of conscience and worship, a marketplace of ideas, or freedom of association. Others may emphasize resistance to domination and oppression, or equal recognition. The way in which pluralism is conceived may serve some ends and values well and others poorly. Here my lead example is freedom of conscience. I argue below that it is difficult to conceptualize what is at stake about freedom of conscience if one is working with a view of pluralism that emphasizes diversity of culture and identity. Similarly, however, an emphasis on diversity of comprehensive doctrines may not well serve the goal of resistance to oppression and domination or the demand for equal recognition.

In this chapter I emphasize some of the potential liabilities of conceptualizing pluralism largely in terms of diverse identities. I do not claim that we should abandon this way of thinking about pluralism. It has rational uses. However, I believe that this emphasis poorly serves some values, such as freedom of conscience or a marketplace of ideas, and it ill serves those who do not view their identities in terms of their relationship with a discrete and well-bounded culture. I am concerned that we are coming to employ the language of identity uncritically and without attention to its costs. We need to be more conscious of these costs and limitations. We need a pluralism of pluralisms.

3.1. Introduction

One repository of discourses about pluralism is the law. I do not claim here that there is a legal view of pluralism that is to be contrasted with a non-legal view. Nevertheless, the law is a source of views about how pluralism has been conceived that carries some weight. Hence, I begin with a few US Supreme Court cases. In 1925, the Supreme Court handed down *Pierce* v. *Society of Sisters* (1925).[3] The Court said:

The fundamental theory of liberty upon which all governments in this Union repose excludes any general power of the State to standardize its citizens by forcing them to accept instruction from public teachers only. The child is not the mere creature of the state; those who nurture him and direct his destiny have the right, coupled with the high duty to prepare him for additional obligations. (p. 9)

There is much debate about the basis of this case. The fundamental theory of liberty appealed to is not well described. The argument may be represented so as to appeal to parents' rights, the free exercise of religion, or freedom of expression.[4]

Wisconsin v. *Yoder*,[5] a case that granted an exemption to the Amish from Wisconsin's compulsory education laws for reasons rooted in the free exercise clause of the First Amendment, contains this comment:

A way of life, however virtuous and admirable, may not be interposed as a barrier to reasonable state regulation of education if it is based on purely secular considerations; to have the protection of the Religion Clauses, the claims must be rooted in religious belief. (p. 205)

Here the Court suggests that freedom of conscience provides a stronger warrant for protection than does "mere" cultural diversity. Conscience matters more than difference.

United States v. *Seeger*[6] concerns conscientious objection to military service. In *Seeger* the Court quotes former Chief Justice Harlan Stone as follows:

Both morals and sound policy require that the state should not violate the conscience of the individual. All our society gives conformation to the view that liberty of conscience has a moral and social value which makes it worthy of preservation at the hands of the state. So deep in its significance and vital, indeed, is it to the preservation of man's moral and spiritual nature that nothing short of the self-preservation of the state should warrant its violation. (p. 163)

Finally, in *Bakke* v. *CA Davis*,[7] the Supreme Court took up the question of using race as an admissions criterion. In United States law, race is a suspect classification. In order to justify the use of a suspect class there must be a compelling state interest. The compelling state interest the Supreme Court discovered to justify the use of race as a criterion in university admissions was diversity, which the Court held to be in the penumbra of the First Amendment. Here the Court links the First Amendment to the view that universities are to be a marketplace of ideas, and, if they are to be such, the bearers of diverse views must be represented there.

It appears from this modest sample of cases that the legal apparatus the US Supreme Court has used to discuss pluralism has emphasized three values. One is freedom of conscience. The second is the marketplace of ideas. Implicit in these two is freedom of association.

Why see these cases as about pluralism? The word does not occur. Moreover, they might be viewed primarily as concerned with the rights of individuals. But *Pierce* and *Yoder* concern the rights of the members of *groups* to associate together to preserve distinctive, religiously based ways of life, and to transmit their convictions to their children. The primary beneficiaries of legal provisions protecting conscientious objectors were pacifist groups such as Quakers. Nor would *Bakke* make sense were it not believed that underrepresented minorities had interests and held ideas associated with their membership in groups. While the rights defended in these cases may belong to individuals, the meaning of these rights often depends on group membership. Freedom of conscience, freedom of expression, and freedom of association are the fundamental legal building blocks of pluralism so far as the US Constitution is concerned.

Little is said in these cases about a pluralism of identities. (An exception may be *Roberts* v. *Jaycees*.[8]) Nor is the conception obviously implicit in them. As I argue below, to protect conscience is one thing; to protect identity another. One commenter on this chapter has suggested that identity is implicit in affirmative action cases claiming that minorities have different ideas *because* they have different identities. But this seems wrong. It is more likely, or at least more typically, the case that minorities have different ideas because they have different experiences, different cultures, or different interests. They may, for these reasons, also have different identities, but, in *Bakke*, it is not differences in identity the court seeks to protect or promote. It is the dialogue among groups with different views.

While the law is not the only source of views about pluralism, it surely provides useful clues as to the central traditions and values of our society as they apply to pluralism. Moreover, with the exception of *Seeger*, these are education cases. Given this, it is noteworthy that many who write about pluralism in education seem to take it for granted that the fundamental form of pluralism is a pluralism of identities. For example, Walter Feinberg entitles his fine book on diversity *Common Schools and Uncommon Identities: National Unity and Cultural Difference*.[9] The assumptions of the title seem to be that culture shapes identity and that the pluralism at issue in education is a pluralism of identities. The issue to be debated in the book is described as follows:

Historically, schools were justified as critical in bringing different peoples together to participate in a common and shared identity, one in which every person was recognizable to every other person as a citizen of the same nation. Today the emphasis appears to have shifted, and what was once taken as an important role of the schools—advancing a common identity—is sometimes viewed as advancing the interests of the dominant group over those who are different and powerless. Yet if the historical mission of the common school is now of uncertain value, the question remains, How should children from different cultural backgrounds be treated by the public schools, and what, if any, identity work is appropriate for public education? (p. 4)

Feinberg's way of discussing pluralism and multiculturalism, linking these notions strongly to different identities, seems notably different from the way pluralism is discussed in the law. Yet this way of thinking about pluralism also has a long and honorable pedigree. I am not suggesting that Feinberg is wrong. Instead, I am suggesting that the nature and significance of these different conceptualizations needs to be explored. Are these ways of conceiving pluralism at odds in any important ways? If so, should we care? We should care to the extent that different ways of conceptualizing pluralism serve different ends and different values.

3.2. The Insufficiency of Identity Talk: Two Examples

Consider the case of religious pluralism. Suppose that religious diversity came to be discussed more in the language of religious identity and less in the language of religious conviction, how might this change what we take religious diversity to be about? Consider how the emphasis on a pluralism of identities differs from freedom of conscience. What a pluralism of identities often seeks is equal recognition of individuals through equal recognition of their cultures.[10] The harm involved in the lack of equal recognition is to one's sense of self-worth or self-esteem. If my identity is bound up with my culture, then to denigrate it is to denigrate me. If one assumes that the basis of equal rights is equal recognition, then equal recognition of identities is also connected with equal citizenship.

What is the harm involved in freedom of conscience? It is this: Conscience commands. Commands may originate from God or from reason, but what matters is that I have internalized these authoritative "voices" of conscience.[11] To violate my conscience is to compel me to do that which I must not do or to prevent me from doing that which I must do.

Compare the US Supreme Court cases *Barnette* v. *West Virginia*[12] with some recent discussions in England about disestablishing the Church of England. *Barnette* concerns the exemption of Jehovah's Witnesses from the obligation to salute the US flag, an activity they view as idolatry. This seems a straightforward case of freedom of conscience. There is no demand for recognition. Jehovah's Witnesses do not demand that schools recognize the value of their religion or assert that it is of equal worth to the faith of others. There is only the demand that Jehovah's Witnesses not be compelled to do what they believe God commands them not to do.

In contrast, there is a discussion now emerging in England concerning whether the Church of England should be disestablished. This issue is sometimes linked with the coronation of the next king. Will the Church of England be privileged in the coronation ceremony? No great issue of conscience is raised here. What is of concern is the equal recognition of all faiths in the civic life of the nation. Establishment of the Church of England no longer threatens the conscience of dissenters, but it does give special recognition to the Church of England in civic affairs and, thereby, suggests that non-members are second class citizens.

The demand for freedom of conscience is linked to the objectivity and authoritativeness of commands. The voice of conscience may be the voice of God or of reason, but commands are not commands if they are mere matters of opinion. No one's conscience would be greatly troubled by violating one of the Ten Suggestions. The reasoning that leads to obedience says, "I must do this, because the voice that commands me is true and authoritative." Identity language also provides a way of reasoning about the grounds for action. It often has this form: "I am a member of group G. I do this because this is what we members of G do." Such an argument may conceal an appeal to group solidarity or to a form of authenticity where one sees doing what Gs do as an expression of one's group based identity.

Such identity based claims do not do adequate justice to what is involved in conscience. Imagine Martin Luther standing before the Diet of Worms and declaring "Here I stand. I can do no other. Why? Because I am a Lutheran, and this is what we Lutherans do." This makes no sense not just because at the time there was no religion called Lutheranism, but also because what obligated Luther was, in his view, God and God's truth. Most religions assert truth claims. These claims are essential to the authoritativeness of religious commands. Solidarity and authenticity do not bind the conscience in the same way. Talking about religious pluralism in the language of religious identities at best misses what conscience is about. At worst, it may intimate a religious epistemology that is inconsistent with the self-understanding of many religious people.

These comments apply, to a degree, even when the religious justification for some practice does seem to express solidarity with a group. Suppose that someone who is a Jew is asked why he wears a *yarmulke* and answers, "Because I am a Jew." What does this say? It may well be that many Jews wear a *yarmulke* as an expression of solidarity with other Jews or as an expression of a Jewish identity. However, the wearing of a *yarmulke* may not be adequately understood if this is all that is said. One internet source[13] claims "The Talmud says 'cover [the child's] head so that he will have the fear of heaven.'" The Talmud also associates a covered head with humility. I do not know whether this is good Judaism. What is important, however, is that here the practice of wearing a *yarmulke* is seen as having a point that is not conveyed by talk about identity. "I wear a *yarmulke* because I am a Jew" is not like saying "I eat pasta because I am Italian." The *yarmulke* honors a command or symbolizes a religious conception. Much of its point is lost if it is viewed merely as an expression of solidarity or of an identity.

Consider a second issue. Viewing pluralism as concerned with diverse identities tends to frame the issue of political stability or national unity in a way that might be viewed as broadly communitarian. Political stability is seen as a matter of solidarity developed through a shared national identity. (This is the view that seems captured in the quotation from Feinberg above.) Presumably to share a national identity is to see ourselves as members of a national community where others whose identities may be in some ways different from ours are nevertheless seen as part of some larger *We* with a shared identity. Consider some comments of Daniel Bell who argues for a communitarian view of justice:[14]

Any effective scheme of distributive justice ... presupposes a bounded world of people deeply committed to each other's fate—most of us will not agree to enshrine actions in law, and to live by those laws, if we can't identify in some way with the recipients of those generous actions—and it just so happens that the nation state has emerged ... as the unit within which our sense of solidarity is strongest. (p. 138)

The very act of framing the question of the basis of political stability as one of identity tends to erect a preference in favor of thinking of stability as a matter of shared bonds and a shared culture, and against views such as those of Rawls which emphasize a commitment to a conception of justice which is distinguished from a morality of association.[15]

Identity language involves a view of what is at stake in pluralism and a conception of how pluralism is connected with political stability. If it becomes the dominant language of pluralism, issues of freedom of conscience recede and issues of recognition advance to the forefront. If it is, the language used to discuss political stability views that emphasize a shared culture are emphasized over those that emphasize shared principles.

3.3. *Identity: Does Everyone Have One?*

Having an identity is not like having hands or feet. It is far from clear
what it is to have an identity. Indeed, I suspect that on some views of
what it means to have an identity many of us do not have one.
Consider three different views as to what people's identity is. First,
their identity might be their core; that is those values and commitments that are important to people's way of orienting in the world.
Second, their identity might be their essence, those characteristics
that are durable and defining. Third, their identity might be the
internalized values of, and attachments to, their culture and its members. We are our primary groups writ small. It is the last of these
views that often seems central in discussions of identity, pluralism,
and recognition. All are problematic. Many of us lack the kind of
relationship to some primary group that would allow us to view ourselves as our culture writ small. Identities are too contextual for the
notion that my identity is my essence to work well. And one may
have a core without thinking of this as one's identity.

Suppose I am asked these two questions:

1. Tell me about yourself?
2. Describe your identity?

In my own case, I have a great deal to say in answer to the first,
but I am puzzled as to how I would answer the second. I believe that
my difficulty is informative about the weakness of identity talk. The
reason I have this difficulty is not, I believe, that I am anomic, suffering from an identity crisis, or that I lack stable convictions or preferences. Instead, the reason is that none of these views of what it is
to have an identity work well for me.

In *Sources of the Self,* Taylor claims that for many people their identity is specified by their relationship to some spiritual or moral tradition.[16] He claims "it is this that provides the frame within which they
can determine where they stand on questions of what is good, or worthwhile, or admirable, or of value" (p. 27). I have convictions and preferences that play such a role in my life, but it is less clear that they root me
in a single tradition or that they cohere into a single frame. My sources
are eclectic. Plato, Aristotle, Mill, and Kant are there, as are Moses and
Jesus. None of these account for my love of Mozart or my enjoyment of
canoeing. I am Athens and Jerusalem and a good deal more. One can
have a core without having a primary source or a primary group.

This makes it difficult for me to use the language of identity
to describe my core. I can say "Here are my durable tastes and

convictions. This is my core." But I cannot easily name my core by naming a tradition. I cannot say "I am a member of this group" in a way that tells you what my core is. Moreover, much of what I think of as my core commitments are not salient in the way in which identity should be salient. I think of myself as honest. Indeed, honesty is a core commitment for me. I can say "I am an honest man." Hopefully this is a true description. It is puzzling as to what it would mean to view "I am an honest man" as a claim about my identity.

Perhaps I should look for my identity, not in some relationship to a core that is connected with a tradition, but in some set of characteristics that are durable and defining. They need not connect me with any particular tradition. They merely need to be what I am. Perhaps I am like an angel. I have my own essence and that is my identity. But not every sentence of the form "I am an X" asserts something about my identity. I currently live in Ithaca, New York. But am I an Ithacan? That depends on more than the mere fact of my residence. It depends on how central being an Ithacan is to my sense of self. I am about to move to Maryland. Will my essence change? Can I live in Maryland and still be an Ithacan? I have a beard. Is my beard part of my identity? Presumably, this too depends on the connection between my beard and my sense of self. Would a clean shaven me still be me?

These examples suggest the "matter of degreeness" of identity. Things are not sharply me or mine, essence or accident. And these examples also suggest that the me/mine distinction is not firmly linked to the notion of my tradition, my culture, or my way of life. Nor is it necessarily strongly linked to my group or my city, state, or nation.

Those things that are salient to me are relational and contextual. Who I am may depend on where I am or whom I am with. When I travel abroad the fact that I am an American becomes more salient. When I am in Montreal the fact that I am an anglophone becomes important. Hence if I try to cash out identity talk by looking for my essence rather than for my constitutive community, I still find it hard to apply it to my own case.

Suppose that one's identity is a relationship between one's self and a distinctive culture or way of life. Perhaps it is an idea such as this that is expressed if one claims to have a Jewish identity or an American identity, or an African-American identity. Such claims are often made in order to support a demand for equal recognition. If one's identity is strongly linked to the culture of one's group, then the failure to provide equal recognition can be an attack on the integrity of the self. Taylor links the demand for recognition to the notion that the self is socially and dialogically constituted such that one's culture is part of one's identity, and the image of one's culture reflected in the discourse of others inevitably effects one's self-appraisal.[17] Hence, we cannot claim to grant equal respect to individuals while refusing to extend equal recognition to their cultures.

Consider how Michael Sandel sees the relationship between individuals and the communities that constitute their identities.[18] He writes:

And in so far as our constitutive self-understandings comprehend a wider subjectivity than the individual alone ... to this extent they define a community in the constitutive sense. And what marks such a community is not merely a spirit of benevolence, or the prevalence of communitarian values, or even certain shared final ends alone, but a common vocabulary of discourse and a background of implicit practices and understandings within which the opacity of the participants is reduced if never finally dissolved. (pp. 172–3)

A community, then, is a group of people linked by a shared consciousness born of a common life. It is not merely a group connected by common purpose, trust, or by bonds of mutual regard or attachment. In communities people are transparent to one another because they understand and see the world in the same way. Common identities are rooted in these shared understandings. Sandel's community is a *Gemeinshaft* community,[19] a Folk, a people.

Here a community seems more like a tribe than a congregation. By a tribe, I mean a group of individuals that share a variety of common understandings because they share a way of life that spans many domains of life. They are together in religion and love, in work and in play. In this sense, the Amish are a tribe. If the kind of common understanding that Sandel claims is associated with membership in a community through possession of a shared vocabulary and shared practices is to go very deep, then it seems that communities must be like tribes. When we think of a culture as a way of life, we suggest that it is tribe-like. In contrast, by a congregation I mean a group of people who associate because they share certain convictions, interests, or purposes. In my sense, Presbyterians are a congregation, but so are stamp clubs and volunteer fire companies. Presbyterians share some things, perhaps some important things, in common. But they are plumbers and professors, Asians and Africans, speakers of many languages, Republicans and Democrats, and holders of many diverse views on many topics. What is common to members of congregations does not generate a shared life, deep and pervasive shared understandings, or create a shared identity.

Members of liberal democratic societies are often associated with many congregations, but few are associated with a tribe. Our various religions, races, and ethnicities may shape us, but they do not constitute distinct and discrete ways of life. Members of a given race do not inevitably share the same religion or speak the same language. They will be members of different professions, and they may be shaped more by religion or profession than by race.

Hence, while we may be shaped by our various communities, it does not follow that we have constitutive communities if this requires that we belong to some primary community characterized by a distinctive way of life. In my own case, this partly explains why I have difficulty in answering questions about my identity. If I take people to be asking me for my primary community, my constitutive community, my tribe, I can only respond by giving them a list of congregations. I am a Presbyterian, a canoeist, a philosopher. All of these shape me and suggest things about me. Some go deeper than others. None is a constitutive community and none enables me to assert any clear statement about my identity.

It might be argued that for most of us the best candidate for our constitutive community is our national community. "I am an American," says something about who I am that is different from "I am a canoeist." National communities, however, also seem poor candidates for constitutive communities. If Americans share a constitutive community that generates common understandings and a shared identity, it is hard to say in what it consists and how it distinguishes Americans from Canadians or Russians. In most liberal democratic societies the internal cultural diversity is enormous.

Sometimes I do understand Americans better. When I watch a baseball game, for example, it makes sense in a way that cricket does not. I know how the phones work, what side of the road to drive on, and what is thought to be ill-mannered. It is far from obvious to me, however, that this sense of cultural familiarity is a significant feature of my identity. Moreover, many Americans will feel more cultural affinity with, and achieve understanding of, members of some other nation than they do with many other Americans. Presbyterians from the Northeast United States may feel more at home with and understand Scots more than Baptist Texans.

Perhaps constitutive communities have to do with those whom we perceive as ours. To say that I have a constitutive community is to say both that before there was an I there was a We, and that this We consists of a group of people with whom I have a distinctive relationship.

I have strong attachments to my family, but my family is not, in the required sense, a community. Here are a few other people and groups I occasionally identify with: the New York Knicks, the

Philadelphia Phillies, the New Zealand All Blacks, YoYo Ma, Ritchie Ashburn. This list is not altogether frivolous. It has some connection to my history: where I was raised (near Philadelphia), where I (as of this writing) live (New York State), where I have spent a sabbatical leave (New Zealand), to whom I see myself as in some way similar, and some of my preferences (certain sports and music). But these identifications provide few clues as to my identity. I do not care greatly about any of the teams or individuals. I am certainly not bonded with them if bonding requires reciprocity or deeply shared common understanding. None of these groups and individuals know anything about me. I do not share a significant common culture with them. Are they a part of my identity? They are only in a sense that trivializes the very idea of an identity by making everything that is true of me a part of my identity.

Perhaps the idea of my identity as having to do with those with whom I identify works better when we think of a national identity. I do normally identify more strongly with Americans than members of other nations. I am apt to root for American athletes in international competitions. But I also identify in varying degrees with members of other nations, with Scots more than Lithuanians, for example. Indeed, I find many Scots more transparent and comprehensible than I do members of many American subcultures.

Are there other groups or people with whom I identify? I enjoy small boats, but I cannot think of an individual canoeist with whom I identify. I am a Presbyterian. I was once a Methodist. I could easily be an Anglican. I am a philosopher by training. Here, indeed, is a group affiliation that has shaped how I think. I find that I have much by way of shared understanding with other philosophers (at least of my genre) even if they hail from around the globe. Nevertheless, these identifications tell me about my congregations, not my tribe. All of these associations say something about me. They say that I have eclectic tastes in sports and music. They say that I have no strong sense of place. They say that I belong to various congregations, some of which span the globe; that I have formed tastes, acquired convictions, and developed associations and attachments from a wide and diverse set of sources. They say that I am a citizen of the world because I have a wide range of tastes, convictions, and congregations to choose from, as do most citizens of liberal democratic societies. If my identity is supposed to be formed by a single constitutive community, by those who I see as mine, by a shared culture that sharply distinguishes me and mine from others, I have no identity. I lack a tribe. Were I to have one, I would feel constrained. Nothing about my core leads me to a tribe.

What follows? If having an identity is to have a core, then I have an identity because I have an orienting set of values and convictions. Yet I find it difficult to think of my core as an identity rather than a set of durable convictions because it does not readily connect me to a single group or a tradition. If having an identity is to have a strong relationship to a primary culture or a constitutive community, I have no identity. I have many congregations, but no tribe. If having an identity is to have an essence, I do not have an identity. My sense of self is too varied and contextual. The metaphysics of identity does not work for me. I suspect it does not work for many others for similar reasons. This is, I think, a fact of some significance concerning how we think about pluralism.

3.4. Identity and Recognition

That I am a WASP male is an important fact about me. Among other things, it gives me an easier claim on things—recognition, access, cultural capital, power, resources—that are less available to others on the basis of characteristics such as race, ethnicity, or gender. I have no doubt that this is true and unjust. It is not, however, clear that this is significant factor about my identity. I do not think of myself as a WASP. Being a WASP is not to be a member of a constitutive community. WASPs are neither a congregation nor a tribe. WASPishness is not my essence. It is not salient. That I am bearded or tall is more salient to me even if being a WASP is more important about me. One of the privileges of being a member of the majority culture or the dominant group is that one's race or gender need not be salient. I have only experienced being white as salient when I spent a month in South Africa. Usually it is as water to the fish.

These last observations, however, help us to be mindful of one point of talking about equal recognition of identities. Characteristically, claims for recognition are made by members of minority cultures who find their ways of life invisible, marginalized, or threatened, and themselves oppressed. Since they are oppressed because they have certain visible characteristics, these characteristics are inevitably salient to them. Recognition may be a matter of their achieving genuine equality in their societies or of the survival of their way of life. I have had several Native American graduate students. These individuals talk a good deal about cultural recovery and the need for protection of their cultures from the overwhelming competition of the dominant culture. The link between their identities and their culture is far clearer than is the link between my culture and me. Very likely their connection with their culture is such that one cannot disparage their culture without disparaging them. They may experience the loss of their culture as a loss of self. It is cases like this where the language of identity does clear work. These students seem to have communitarian souls whereas I do not. Literally, they have a tribe.

In such cases the demand for recognition can be turned to the goal of cultural survival. It is a tool to resist domination and repression. Minority status is one of the factors that may contribute to forging strong connections between identities and a culture or community with distinctive boundaries. For my Indian students the broad out-line of what is involved in the demand for equal recognition of their identities is clear enough. What is wanted is legitimization, support, autonomy, recognition of the value of their cultural practices, pro-tection from cultural imperialism, and an end to oppression and domination. To link these demands to claims about identity is to point out that the absence of these things does violence to the self.

This is, I believe, the key and indispensable role that the notion of identity performs in discussions of pluralism. It is a role that seems to require the concept. People can object to discrimination and injus-tice without introducing the notion of identity. It is not, for example, required to explain why exclusion based on race, gender, ethnicity, or culture is wrong. Statutes prohibiting such exclusion need not refer to identity. But the concept is required to explain why dis-paragement does violence to the self of those whose identity is strongly shaped by their differences.

In many other cases, however, it is not clear that claims about dif-ferent identities can do such work. Were I to demand equal recogni-tion for my identity, it is far from clear what I would be asking for. One reason may be that I do not need recognition for my culture because I already have it. The argument I have made above suggests, however, that the difficulties lie elsewhere. They lie in the fact that my identity is not strongly shaped by membership in some primary group that has been the object of discrimination. I have many congrega-tions, but no tribe. I am someone who has a beard and likes Vivaldi. Do I want someone to say that having a beard is every bit as good as not? Do I want them to say that Vivaldi is every bit as good as Mozart or jazz? Do I want equal time for Vivaldi on public radio? Do I want people to say that my religion is equally true to that of others?

The difficulty is that much of my culture stands to me, not as something that defines me, but as a rich repertoire of things I may choose. Even when I have fallen into something rather than having chosen it, I can often change my mind if there are reasons to do so. Those parts of the cultural repertoire that I have appropriated may forge some sense of connection with members of a wide and diverse range of different congregations. I may have some bonds with other Vivaldi lovers or other Presbyterians or other bearded men or other middle-aged male academics. Some of these associations may be more important to me than others, but none forge strong links between my identity and anything that can be called my culture. I am not easily able to transform such identity claims into demands for recognition. I can, of course, suffer disparagement, but not for the fact that I belong to a tribe.

Thus it seems that identity talk does not work equally well or in the same way for everyone. Identity talk is likely to be a vehicle to protect the self from disparagement and to secure recognition primarily in those cases where there is a clearly delineable link between one's identity and a particular culture or group. Such links are often forged or maintained by difference and by oppression. Hence the language of identity has a point. However, it may have significant weaknesses if it is employed in more sweeping ways than it is, I suspect, if we attempt to use it to develop a general theory of pluralism or to assert a theory of equal rights. Then the fact that the language of identity does not serve us all equally seems to become a liability.

3.5. The Costs of Identity Talk

Thinking about pluralism through the language of identity can have costs. Some of them are likely to be visited on members of oppressed minorities.

Suppose that there is a tight link between one's identity and a group culture, perhaps one that is forged substantially because of what or whom one looks like, and in virtue of the reactions of others to these characteristics. There may be two consequences. First, one's choices and options may be shaped and constrained by the expectations of others. Second, adopting the practices and products of one's group may become more than a matter of individual taste and appraisal. It may become a matter of affiliation and solidarity.

To affirm the practices and products of a group is to affiliate. To abandon the practices and products of one's group weakens solidarity. It may be viewed as betrayal. To be sure, groups can maintain solidarity and accept considerable diversity.[20] At the same time if there is to be a group there must be limits to the flexibility of identity.

Moreover, because the solidarity of a group identity may be necessary to pursue justice, and because others may view minorities as members of a minority group regardless of their own sense of affiliation, individuals may have a greater need to affiliate.

If this is right, then oppressed minorities and members of majority or dominant groups stand in different relation to the range of cultural products in their societies. Members of the majority are more able to view the cultural products of others as options for choice and adoption than are members of oppressed minorities because they have less need for group solidarity. It may also be that the cultural options of members of oppressed minorities are constrained by the expectations of others. In either case, the consequence is a narrowing of the cultural repertoire available to members of oppressed minorities as well as a narrowing of the range of associations. No one suggests that I am breaching solidarity with my race because I like jazz (in truth more than I like Vivaldi). Nor do I view this as involving a significant alteration of my identity. African-Americans may be less free to love Vivaldi. Developing such tastes may be viewed as both a breach of solidarity and as the adoption of an inappropriate identity. The point of such terms as "oreo", "apple", and "banana" seems to be to accuse people of such transgressions against their group based identity. I am told that there are comparable terms for white people who adopt practices or products from other cultures. That I have not found anyone (after a brief survey down the hall) who knows what these terms are is telling about their coercive force.

A tight link between identity and group based culture makes identities subject to cultural criticism. Many African-Americans are psychologically invested in the thesis of Black Athena. Many Indians find the claim that the Iroquois Confederation influenced the US Constitution to be a confirmation of their identity. To deny these theses is to do harm.

Here is a criticism of Vivaldi. It says that it is not true that Vivaldi wrote over seven hundred concertos. Instead he wrote one concerto seven hundred times. We Vivaldi lovers as a rule find this humorous. To be a member of a majority and to lack a tight link to a distinct culture enables one to have less at stake in cultural criticism. I may love Vivaldi, but I am not a Vivaldi lover.

To accept the thesis that there is a strong link between identity and a group culture is to have an incentive to accept some version of cultural relativism. If we are relativists, some imagine, we can know in advance that all cultures, hence all identities, are equal because there can be no rational grounds on the basis of which members of one culture can criticize another. Taylor has pointed out that the recognition provided by relativism is of doubtful worth.[21] It is rather like saying to one's beloved, "My darling there are no objective standards of beauty, therefore you are as beautiful as anyone, but no more so." Where we cannot appraise, neither can we praise. Nor can we condemn baseness or evil when they are the baseness or evil of cultural others. The cost of relativism is high.

Taylor claims that cultures and cultural products can be appraised and then proceeds to root equal recognition in the claim that all cultures are presumed to have something of worth.[22] However, that cultures and cultural products can be appraised warrants comparative judgments among cultures and, hence, on Taylor's thesis, comparative judgments among identities. The development of a fusion of horizons of the sort Taylor recommends does not obviously eliminate this potential. If criticism of cultural products is possible, it is not clear that the discovery that every culture has something of value affords grounds for equal recognition.

If it does not, then a tight link between identity and a group culture leaves us with a dilemma. We must either find a way to view the criticism of the cultural products of one group by another as inappropriate, or we must deal with the difficulty that cultural criticism can undermine equal recognition. We are given a choice between a marketplace of ideas and equal recognition. One way out is the Kantian and Judeo-Christian thesis that people are of inherent worth apart from any individuating facts about them. We may also claim that a prima facie duty to respect other cultures flows from the duty to respect the members of other cultures. To make this move would be to make the basis of multiculturalism akin to the traditional basis of religious liberty, in that the obligation to respect the faith of one's neighbor is rooted in the need to respect the neighbor's conscience and is consistent with believing the neighbor's religion to be false.

A strong link between identity and equal recognition can truncate the marketplace of ideas. There are two reasons. First, if there is a strong link between identity and culture then cultural criticism becomes personal assault. If the thesis that the Iroquois have had a significant impact on the framing of the US Constitution is a part of the identity of some Indians, then a free and open debate about the historicity of this claim puts the selves of these individuals at risk. Second, if we are relativists, then cultural products may only be appraised within the culture. Outsiders not only cannot understand, but will employ the wrong standards. Cultural criticism is thus both harmful and wrongheaded. If so, a marketplace of ideas can only be a display of different, presumptively equal, cultural products the purpose of which is to provide a vehicle for providing recognition and developing tolerance. It cannot involve appraisal or become a debate. The Millsian view that truth is discovered via criticism and debate has little place where a demand for equal recognition dominates.

A strong link between identity and a group culture raises certain problems for democratic citizenship. Suppose that Bell is correct that "Any effective scheme of distributive justice ... presupposes a bounded world of people deeply committed to each other's fate ..." Let me interpret this comment to mean that the basis of citizenship is solidarity rooted in a shared identity. This view assumes that the people to whom individuals are primarily bonded are one's fellow citizens—members of a common nation-state. This, however, is exactly what is in doubt for members of minority groups whose primary attachments may be to members of their group. A view that roots justice or citizenship in bonds born of a shared identity has reason to insist that the primary bonds of citizens must be to the national community and that these bonds must trump more particularistic connections when they conflict. Those for whom this is untrue are unlikely to be viewed as good citizens.

Such a view is likely to strain both freedom of conscience and multiculturalism. It will strain the first because those who say "I must obey God rather than man" or who feel a stronger bond to members of their faith than to members of their polity can be accused of a defect of citizenship. Similarly, people who feel a stronger bond to their racial or ethnic subgroup may be viewed as less than good citizens and multiculturalism may be viewed as a threat to citizenship.[23] This may be true despite the fact that members of minority groups may be perfectly willing to deal justly with all their fellow citizens.

This difficulty arises from reliance on national identity as the basis of citizenship apart from a commitment to a set of principles. Suppose that the essence of citizenship is viewed as a sense of justice involving a commitment to something like Rawls's overlapping consensus.[24] Such an account has two advantages. First, it allows us to view those who feel a stronger connection to some group other than their nation to be viewed as good citizens so long as they are willing to treat their fellow citizens with justice. Nor is there any contradiction in the idea that people may be committed to justice while feeling stronger ties to a subgroup than to the nation. Second, such a view permits a principled account of when we may prefer our own or act on the convictions of our local group, and when we must not. We can know that Jehovah's Witnesses who will not salute the flag can still be good citizens. And we can know that African-Americans who work primarily for the betterment of their race are still good citizens. In neither case, however, should these primary attachments be carried into the performance of public roles. There is no deficiency of citizenship if Jehovah's Witnesses work for the promotion of their church, if African-Americans attend AME Zion churches or celebrate Kwanzaa, just as there is no deficiency of citizenship if I identify more strongly with Scots than Texans. If the same persons are judges, impartial justice is required in their court.

3.6. Conclusions

I would draw three conclusions from these discussions. The first is that pluralism serves a variety of values. These are generally praiseworthy. They may also be in tension. We need to keep them all in view and to balance them when required. An exclusive reliance on identity talk as the way to approach pluralism is likely to bias the discussion so as to prefer some values over others. It may, for example, promote the importance of self esteem, but diminish the protection granted to conscience. Moreover, while identity talk provides potential benefits for oppressed groups, it also imposes costs on them. It can render their group identities impermeable and isolate oppressed minorities from the cultural products of the larger culture. It can lead to viewing uncommon identities as a deficiency of citizenship. Identity talk is theory embedded talk. We ought to mean it when we use it.

Second, this discussion provides some support for a Rawlsian picture of identity. In *Political Liberalism* Rawls develops what he terms a political conception of a person.[25] Here we have a roughly Kantian view of the basis of rights that views people as of equal value apart from their cultural identities. Since this political conception is not viewed as rooted in empirical facts about individual personal identities, it is consistent with the recognition that there are people whose real identities are firmly rooted in a subgroup. Because, in a Rawlsian view, one of the primary goods to secure for everyone is the basis of self-respect, we have grounds to promote recognition of diverse cultures. We thus avoid some of the difficulties of a view that connects equal justice to equal recognition of different identities. However, we may still recognize the need to accommodate multiple identities.

Finally, I have claimed both that the language of identity tends to invoke the tribe more than the congregation and that that is its import and its liability. The Constitutional/liberal values with which I began this chapter are most easily associated with "congregationalism." They support the right of people to freely associate for purposes that are their own while also viewing others as members of a larger polity. They do not, however, usually view these associations as expressions of a thick common culture and a broadly shared and distinctive life. The US Constitution assumes that Americans will go to church in free associations of the like minded and work, shop, play, and study in other, differently constituted associations. In many ways, it seeks to welcome free association and thwart sectarianism. Identity pluralism inclines to a more tribal picture of community. The questions of pluralism and nationalism tend to become questions about the relations between local tribes and the national tribe. If we think this way, we may begin to see liberal societies as political associations of tribes. It is more accurate and more desirable to see them as associations of congregations.

Yet modern liberal democratic states do have tribes. Sometimes they create them or perpetuate them through oppression. Hence a vision of pluralism that failed to protect tribes or recognize and respect their members would be deficient. However, my argument also suggests that most of us are not members of tribes. Identity talk, thus, may not serve us well.

Do we need identity talk? I suspect so. We will need it so long as we have tribes and so long as we have group based oppression. We should not, however, view it as the sole or primary language of pluralism. To do so is to erode our commitment to values such as freedom of conscience, autonomy, and the marketplace of ideas. We need a pluralism of pluralisms.

NOTES

The research reported in this article was made possible, in part, by a grant from the Spencer Foundation. The data presented, the statements made, and the views expressed are solely the responsibility of the author.

1. J. Rawls, *Political Liberalism* (New York: Columbia University Press, 1993).
2. C. Taylor, "The Politics of Recognition" in A. Gutman (ed.), *Multiculturalism: Examining the Politics of Recognition* (Princeton: Princeton University Press, 1994).
3. *Pierce v. Society of Sisters of the Holy Name of Jesus and Mary*, 268 U.S. 510 (1925).
4. M. Yudof, D. Kirp, and B. Levin, *Educational Policy and the Law* (St. Paul: West Publishing Company, 1992).

5. *Wisconsin* v. *Yoder*, 406 U.S. 163 (1972).
6. *United States* v. *Seeger*, 380 U.S. 163 (1965).
7. *Board of Regents* v. *Bakke*, 98 S. Ct. 2733 (1978).
8. See N. L. Rosenblum, *Membership and Morals: The Personal Uses of Pluralism in America* (Princeton: Princeton University Press, 1998).
9. W. Feinberg, *Common Schools: Uncommon Identities* (New Haven: Yale University Press, 1998).
10. Taylor, *Multiculturalism* (1994).
11. T. Green, *The Formation of Conscience in an Age of Technology*.
12. West Virginia State—*Board of Education* v. *Barnette*, 319 U.S. 624 (1943).
13. Ask a Rabbi (2000) http://www.ohr.org.il/ask/ask221.htm#Q3.
14. D. Bell, *Communitarianism and Its Critics* (Oxford: Clarendon Press, 1993).
15. J. Rawls, *A Theory of Justice* (Cambridge: Harvard University Press, 1971).
16. C. Taylor, *Sources of the Self: The Making of the Modern Identity* (Cambridge: Harvard University Press, 1989).
17. Taylor, *Multiculturalism* (1994).
18. M. Sandel, *Liberalism and the Limits of Justice* (Cambridge: Cambridge University Press, 1982).
19. F. Tonnies, *Community and Society* (New Brunswick: Transaction Books, 1988).
20. I. M. Young, *Justice and the Politics of Difference* (Princeton: Princeton University Press, 1990).
21. Taylor, *Multiculturalism* (1994).
22. K. A. Strike (1997) "Taylor, Equality, and the Metaphysics of Persons" in F. Margonis (ed.), *Philosophy of Education* (Urbana: Philosophy of Education Society, 1996).
23. See A. M. J. Schlesinger, *The Disuniting of America* (New York: W.W. Norton & Company, 1992).
24. Rawls, *Political Liberalism* (1993).
25. Ibid.

CHAPTER 4

Between State and Civil Society: European Contexts for Education

Joseph Dunne

I take it to be true of political liberalism generally that over the past decade or two it has ceded greater importance to, and reflected more fully on, the role of culture in the formation of identity. There seems to be a greater readiness among liberals now to acknowledge the reality and significance of group affiliation or collective heritage in defining who one is, and a corresponding readiness either to valorize individual autonomy less strongly or to redefine it so that it is less suggestive of a sovereign self, independent of any particular identity or culture. At a more reflexive level, too, there is a keener appreciation both of the extent to which the ideal of individual autonomy is itself the achievement of an historically specific culture (broadly that of Western modernity) *and* of the fact that this achievement can be viewed as problematical from the point of view of other cultures—in ways, moreover, that make the universality of this ideal much more difficult to defend.

All of this I take to be philosophical gain. A question I shall raise in this chapter, however, is whether the inflection of "self" by "culture" has been matched by a comparable and perhaps no less necessary inflection of culture by "institution"—or whether the notion of culture in the prevailing discussion of multiculturalism does not float too free of the institutional apparatus to which culture, in any really efficacious sense of the term, remains anchored. I raise this question in the context of an analysis of nation-states and of the function that schooling has to come to serve for them. Although education for democratic citizenship is an intelligible role for schooling to play, my analysis will tend toward the unwelcome conclusion that this is largely eclipsed by another role: that of reproducing the socio-economic structure, with a hugely homogenizing effect. Whether this homogenization is reinforced or threatened by globalization is, I suggest, an open question. I shall find some basis for optimism in the recent evolution of the European Union and especially in the reconfiguration of the nation-state and the greater prospects for civil society that it seems to portend. This will lead me to sketch a possible realignment between the state and civil society that would allow greater scope to cultural pluralism. But, in my own corner of it, the European Union has also been a site of deep cultural antagonism and communal strife. I shall conclude, then, with some reflections on the kind of ethico-political response that this situation demands. In doing so I shall outline three models of imaginative exchange suggested by the French philosopher, Paul Ricoeur, and ask what their entailments for education may be.

4.1. Schooling and the Nation-State

The dominant institutions in a modern society are those of the market and the state. People who work at the same kind of computer terminals, or watch the same kind of television programmes, or drive the same kind of cars on the same kind of highways, or shop in the same kind of malls under the influence of the same kind of advertisements, share a substantially *common* culture. Large and important areas of their lives are subject to the same imperatives. Such differences as exist between their "cultures" are ones that have already made their peace with these imperatives. The imperatives just adverted to are those of the market. But the homogenizing pressures of the modern state system are hardly less formidable.

The primary institution of the state in this regard is the school. Not only has schooling developed, in its universal and compulsory aspect, through state support, funding, and regulation but, conversely, it has itself played a crucial role in expanding and stabilizing state formation and concomitant processes of nation-building throughout the modern period. Historically, the second of these lines of causation is the more striking. For the pace setters in establishing national systems of education in Europe were not the countries already most successful in terms of economic prosperity or political cohesion. As distinct from the indisputably major powers of France and England, it was countries "that had yet to attain economic and political success in competition with other states, or that had yet to integrate their own populations around national symbols of a common identity, that took the lead in instituting compulsory state-directed schooling for the masses."[1] A perceived deficit in economic and political efficacy or a crisis of national morale have provided the strongest impetus for state involvement in education. For example, it was to offset the centrifugal effect of stubborn localism on the part of German princes that Frederick the Great attempted to create a schooling system that would instil Prussian patriotism in all the children of the state; or, half a century later, it was in the aftermath of Napoleon's humiliating victory at Jena that Fichte's *Addresses to the German Nation* called for a reconstructed, state-governed education to inspire children to be good Germans and to equip them with the attitudes and competencies to reassert Prussian power—a call answered in a spate of educational reforms over the next few decades that would help to create Bismark's unified and powerful Germany. Or Europe's first effective system of national schooling was established in Denmark in the early nineteenth century within a few years of Denmark's losing Norway to Sweden, and not without the considerable influence of a "Danish Fichte," N. F. S. Grundtvig, who saw education as the key instrument for regenerating the spirit of the nation.

A classic statement of this political function of education is by Napoleon: "There cannot be a firmly established political state unless there is a teaching body with definitely recognized principles. If the child is not taught from infancy that he ought to be a republican or a monarchist, a Catholic or a free thinker, the state will not constitute a nation; it will rest on uncertain and shifting foundations; and it will be constantly exposed to disorder and change."[2] Still, Napoleon himself did not get to establish a mass system of primary education and the first serious attempts to do so in France (beginning in 1833 under Louis Philippe) were strongly influenced by the Prussian precedent. Foiled by subsequent political instability and regime changes, these attempts were not to be effectively realized until defeat in the Franco–Prussian War, and a widespread perception in France that the war had "been won by the Prussian schoolmaster" motivated the major school reform programme that the newly established Third Republic saw as the essential tool of national regeneration. Meanwhile in England a less volatile political situation was accompanied by much greater tardiness on the state's part in replacing or regulating voluntary, ecclesiastically sponsored provisions for education. When the spur to compulsory schooling came, the threat to England's mercantile supremacy posed by Germany and the burgeoning economy of the United States (dramatically highlighted by the perceived inferiority of the British display at the Paris Exhibition of 1867) did much to supply it.

This brief historical advertence seems to point up a few significant features in the emergence of nationalized systems of schooling. The latter can be seen as responding to indigenous needs and crises. And in their commitment to nationalizing projects, with emphasis on vernacular languages and cultures, they represented a turn away from the more cosmopolitan emphasis of Latin and Greek in earlier forms of education or indeed the more universalist thrust of a shared religion in earlier Christendom. Still, their plural particularities notwithstanding, the European countries were responding to a common imperative which had to do with their standing in a newly emerging world order of sovereign nation-states. For each of these entities, increased capital accumulation and, to this end, greater levels of state management of the economy were to define the requirements for national well-being and prestige. To these shared structural features—equally imposing for all nations, whatever the differences in their respective histories and self-understandings—there would gradually be added a different kind of universality: a broadly liberal-democratic conception of the kind of compact that the state should establish with individual members in conducting its affairs. In working out this compact, the school as institution would come to play a crucial role. On the one hand, it would be the state's instrument for equipping the young with ranges of knowledge and skill to contribute to national economic development and for socializing them into the norms necessary to preserve a stable social and political framework for the pursuit of this development. On the other hand, the liberal-democratic determination of this transaction would ensure that the process of socialization was at the same time a process of individuation: the knowledge and skills acquired would *also* enable students to enhance their own individual life chances and to develop a form of autonomy that could enable them to steer their own life courses. Egalitarianism in state provision of education reflects both sides of this compact: it releases the potential of all to contribute to national prosperity and at the same time it affords them the opportunity to profit from education on the basis of their own individual merit.[3]

4.2. *State, Nation, and Citizenship*

The complex—and potentially conflict-laden—role of schooling cannot be adequately understood apart from the conflictual emergence of nation-states with which it has been so intimately linked. As political entities, nation-states—by contrast with, say, kingdoms, city-states (singly or in loose federations), and empires—are specifically modern formations. "State" connotes, in crude terms, a more or less concentrated system of power over a defined territory, the borders of which it can secure and the inhabitants of which it can rule. As distinct from this irreducibly political concept, "nation" can be seen as a primarily cultural—and therefore prepolitical—concept, connoting a social grouping held together by an amalgam of factors such as shared descent, historical experience and memory, language, custom, and belief. If capitalism was the engine of modernization through the unleashing of great new productive resources and the expansion and unfettering of trade, the early modern state was the political instrument which facilitated the development of capitalism by providing an infrastructure of rational administration and a legal framework for free individual and group action. Within this perspective, nations might be seen as somewhat amorphous precipitates of earlier historical processes, whose givenness in the modern era provided the prime matter, as it were, for the formation of states.

This assertion of givenness, however, must not make the process of formation seem too natural; for in fact it involved a complex dialectic. Nations after all were not just facts of geography or history; they were also constructs of the specifically modern ideology of nationalism. As a new form of cultural integration, nationalism emerged in response to the dislocation, mobility, and isolation of individuals under conditions of early capitalism; and at the same time it gave a reflexive character to national consciousness by mediating the latter through a newly self-conscious historiography which itself bore the impress of Romantic ideas. This artificial aspect of nations—the fact that building them was a task—meant that they did not supply already defined masses, of land and people, on which state apparatuses could supervene. For their very definition had to be negotiated: a process in which state apparatuses themselves played a substantial role—not least through their newly developing national systems of education. To every nation, then, a state—for self-expression and self-assertion; but conversely, too, to every state a nation—for internal coherence and legitimacy. And of course this whole process, in which coveted natural resources as well as cultural privileges were at stake, involved a great deal of forceful homogenization, as nation-states often succeeded only by suppressing ethnic, linguistic, or religious minorities (and surviving internal agitation and insurrection) or by appropriating neighboring rivals (through diplomacy or war). Thus the volatility and apparently endemic violence which has characterized the modern history of Europe—from which, as we in Ireland know only too well, not even those blessed by geography with island status have been exempt.

Another strand in the evolution of modern politics, closely interwoven with capitalism and nationalism but distinct from and potentially in tension with them, has been an ever more inclusive democratic ideal; if the nation-state was a vehicle for capitalist consolidation and expansion, it was also the ground in which modern democracy grew up. Some aspects of the democratic ideal were clearly serviceable to nationalist aspiration—the idea, for example, of self-determination through popular sovereignty, classically propounded by Rousseau. In other respects, however, democracy, as a political form, can be seen to make normative claims which do not depend on—and may indeed conflict with—the prior existence of a "people" whose collective identity has already been secured ethnically, culturally, or linguistically. For a people must now *constitute* itself—and not by appeal to blood and soil but, rather, by engaging in procedures and fulfilling requirements that have an irreducibly ethical basis. Liberty, equality, and mutual recognition must now be embodied as principles in the political practices which mediate relations between "the people" (as state) and individual persons; through these practices, then, the former acquires legitimacy at the same time that the latter become *citizens*.

Citizenship enshrines basic rights in law but also looks beyond these rights to modes of active civic engagement. Through the latter citizens participate in the deliberative conduct of affairs in the polity. Since this is a *praxis* that cannot be legally enforced, it is less an assigned status than an always precarious achievement. It requires the cultivation of civic virtues, not least the virtue of patriotism. And these virtues can take root only in a political culture that defines freedom not only in terms of individual liberties but also as a joint practice of self-rule. Self-rule entails an ability and willingness to adopt a "we" perspective that relativizes—and sometimes even displaces—the "I" perspective of each virtuous citizen. The difficult question of course is how this "we" is to be constituted and whether it can be constituted at all without a shared allegiance to a set of goods that is more than—though it must indeed include—the good of self-rule itself. We touch here on the fundamental issue of solidarity and the motivational resources that it must muster. It is here that democracy is tempted—if it does not simply succumb to administering a system for efficient production and fair competition between disaffiliated, self-interested individuals—to fall back on already charged ethnic or national idenities, with the passions and allegiances that they can so easily harness.

Is this temptation resistible? Has the undeniable conjunction in the modern period of nationalism and democracy been necessary or only contingent—necessary, because the formal nature of the latter always leaves a void which can be filled with substance only by the former; or contingent, because this formality can be seen not as empty but rather as bearing universalist seeds which contain the promise of a post-nationalist version of citizenship? But perhaps this is not quite the right way to pose the question. In construing a symbiotic relation with the nation as a "temptation", it presupposes that the latter must have a corrupting effect that a properly pure democracy ought to resist. But might we not envisage the possibility of a genuine complimentarity between nationality and democracy, such that the nation provides sources of solidarity which anchor the democratic process, while the latter provides a universalist thrust which protects these sources from closure on internal difference and dissent, or on external cooperation and exchange?

The tensions that these questions reveal between nationality and democracy are not the only ones we face here. The meaning of democratic citizenship is itself open to rival interpretations. The robust conception I have already hinted at looks askance at any reduction of citizenship to a legal status guaranteeing entitlements and immunities, or any substantial devolution of civic responsibility to a cadre of professional politicians, mandarins, or bureaucrats. Putting a premium on political participation and care for the common weal, it assigns an unabashedly educative role to politics, seeing it as a proper function of the state not just to deter from vice but to cultivate those dispositions of mind and character that make good citizens.[4] But from the perspective of a newly cherished privacy this classical conception of citizenship can seem too arduous (in Oscar Wilde's characterization of socialism, it takes too many evenings) and too charged with authoritarian potential; not only may one not want to participate in endless political debate but, more seriously, one may not want to have to submit to its outcome, especially when it has designs not only on one's behavior but on one's character. If exclusion from public life was the characteristic oppression of the ancient world, over-immersion in it appears as the characteristically modern nightmare—something the "good citizen" has been subjected to from Robespierre to the Red Guards and Pol Pot. The objective of a more chastened politics, then, is to deliver more opportunity to people to shape their own lives according to their own choices. In this their economic agency (so loftily disregarded in the ancient notion of citizenship) becomes paramount. Access to and competence on the market is a primary requirement; and the state's main function, in addition to efficient management of the economy, is ensuring equitable access and developed competence for all its citizens. It is in the discharge of this function that schooling has come to play such a cardinal role.

4.3. Homogenization and the Ambiguities of "Postmodernity"

This excursus on the evolution of the modern nation-state indicates a number of tasks for the system of schooling which has been so closely bound up with it: transmitting a national culture, training for democratic citizenship (whether strongly or weakly defined), developing individual autonomy, and preparing young people for the disciplines and opportunities of the market. However, I should not deny a bias in the analysis toward the view that the last of these greatly outweighs the others. Despite its uncongeniality, a functionalist view of schooling seems to me compelling. This suggests that whatever particular substance or *content* may be inserted into schooling through the discretion of particular groups, or even by the state itself, will always in the end be trumped by the *function* schools play in the reproduction of the overall socioeconomic system. There is no lack of philosophical argument for such a view,[5] and there is also more empirical, local evidence to support it. As is generally the case in Europe (with France as the conspicuous exception), in Ireland there is no constitutional principle to disbar the state from supporting different religious groups in running their own schools; and in fact most schools are Catholic. But the overwhelming dynamic of education in Catholic schools is no different from that which imposes itself on students in other schools: to achieve the maximum points in the competitive Leaving Certificate examination at the end of second-level schooling, on which access to third level places and variously desirable career pathways crucially depends. The explicit content of the curriculum as Catholic is overridden by the implicit function of the school as institution.

Where does this thesis about the nation-state and the school as classic institutions of modernity—crudely deterministic and undifferentiated as it may seem—leave us? (The question it may seem to suggest is not so much whether the liberal-democratic state ought to allow different subgroups their own schools as how much difference it would make anyhow if they did.) Well, in stressing a double process of homogenization—where nation-states first assimilated or suppressed regional and ethnic differences within themselves and then accommodated to a transnational, increasingly global institutional order—I do not mean to suggest that this process is immune from critique. I have intended rather to suggest that with respect to the central issue of how to reconcile the claims of unity and cohesion with those of particularity and difference a great deal is already entrenched that weighs heavily towards the first—even in efforts to foster the second. This is the case of course in countries that have successfully modernized (and I do not want to underestimate the merits of this success in terms of technological and economic development as well as in greater levels of equality and individual freedom). There seems to be greater readiness now to acknowledge a lopsidedness in the modernizing project carried by the nation-state, the fact that, in Bhiku Parekh's trenchant formulation, it "recognized only the individuals as the bearers of rights, nationalized its citizens, insisted on equality (which it equated with uniformity), and represented a homogeneous legal space made up of identical political units regulated by identical institutions."[6]

If the substance of Parekh's critique is now on our agenda, perhaps what puts it there is not just a philosophical conscience of modernity but the onset of postmodernity as a sociological condition. This is indeed a highly ambiguous condition. On the one hand it seems to accentuate rather than reverse central modernizing tendencies, not least toward homogenization. Thus the global market links the economic activities and fates of human beings across the whole inhabited world, creating a universal borderless space for the movement of capital and (more selectively) of labor, giving ubiquitous visibility to the same commodities, spawning not only multinational corporations but supranational agencies (IMF, OECD, World Bank, etc.), and generating a logic of "performativity," of relentlessly uniform quantification, through which all things—goods, activities, services, and even people—are made commensurable and interchangeable. This is the postmodern as hypermodern, and one might suppose that it can accommodate difference only as a variant of what Stanley Fish has called "boutique multiculturalism."[7] Still, in its very intensity the globalizing phenomenon is also—through instant communication of images and information and greatly increased travel and migration of people—also a process of dislocation and hybridization. What was stable and central has been more promiscuously exposed to the peripheral and marginal. The very boundlessness of the new environment can facilitate the small and flexible at the expense of the large and unwieldy. By reaction, too, individuals and groups seek to salvage some meaningful sense of belonging, leading to the recrudescence of older ethnic and religious identities but also to attempts to redefine them through exposure to novel influences.

If the nation-state, with its centralizing organs, could be seen (as I intimated earlier) as a functional element in the rise of capitalism, it seems to have become markedly dysfunctional in the new era of "late capitalism." "The development of the world market saps the foundation of nations. From the point of view of the market, any act of national government is a restrictive practice, an unwelcome act of protectionism, and national central government itself, the raiser of taxes, the spender of other people's money, the originator of regulations, the fixer of bank rates and would-be fixer of exchange rates, is just another vested interest, another unjustified obstacle to the free flow of capital."[8] Here, too, however, the situation is ambiguous, containing both opportunities and threats—as I shall now try to show in relation to the project of European Union. On the one hand, the very impotence of the nation-state in the context of economic globalization indicates a logic in the move toward European federalism. On the other hand, the *anomie* brought about by the global market can generate a more acute need than ever for just that kind of rootedness and belonging—however factitious and "imagined"[9]— that nations have provided.

4.4. The European Union and the Texture of Civil Society

At its best, the European Union is an attempt to reconcile the contrary pulls here by reconfiguring the relation between state and nation. By divesting important functions previously vested in states to European institutions, nations can play a more benign part in offering some of the resources for finding/forging identities—not least by becoming more relaxed about those regional and local differences that they felt compelled to suppress in their heyday as nation-states. With "Europe" anchored politically in shared institutions the challenge for "culture" in Europe is to become what it most needs to become in face of the global market—plural, polyglot, and diverse. Federal institutions have played a cultural role by supporting regions and provinces (and cities and towns) in developing what is distinctive to each and by facilitating encounter, exchange, and cooperation between them.[10] Only if there is real difference—of customs, language (including accent, dialect, and gesture), dress, cuisine, music, dance, even philosophy—is there anything significant to encounter; and there may be only a modest amount that any central administration can do genuinely to encourage a particular culture—if it is not simply to embalm it or invest it with ersatz charm as a commodity on the tourist market. But the more widely based institutions do sponsor modest initiatives to facilitate exchange across diverse cultures (through e.g. student exchanges, networking of women's groups or trainee workers, or town twinnings).

Within the separate countries of this reconfigured Europe, the search is on for a new kind of citizenship vitiated neither by the sense of "blood and belonging" that, at the limit, can lead to drives for "ethnic cleansing" *nor* by an insouciant cosmopolitanism which may fail to meet people's needs for identity (and by this failure help to open the door to the very xenophobic nationalism that it wishes to repudiate). Such a citizenship calls for a renewed, more pluralized "civil society", related more pluralistically to the state. This will provide a space for older minority groups and new migrant ones to develop their own cultures and to do so in dialogue with each other and with the majority culture. In a healthy civil society the latter is itself plural and diverse and thus more open to influence from and modification by the others. Civil society is a domain of interaction that is neither political in the sense of being coterminous with state action nor private in the sense of being confined to the individual or familial spheres. It creates space for free association in which people come together for all kinds of purposes—including the purpose of simply coming together. It is realized in networks of common action and supported by civic spaces. As its name suggests, civility is the essential quality that it creates and sustains. This quality gives buoyancy to social life through a kind of trust and civic friendship which cannot be secured by legal entitlement, purchased on the market, or enforced by the state.

Civil society is a bulwark of freedom, affording scope to gather people together to exercise initiative in the pursuit of common interests and goals. It is only because the commitment of many people—over decades or across generations—has sustained different practices, traditions, and communities that other individuals can exercise the thinner freedom of joining in or exiting from them. Moreover, through the openings for participation in diverse enterprises and agencies which it creates, civil society provides the essential complement to representative democracy, the danger of which is that citizens will become "spectators who vote"—or, as is increasingly the case with young adults, who do *not* vote. These openings bring people out of a privacy that would leave them isolated—and therefore all the more vulnerable—before state-bureaucracy and market-automatism. In a modern society, however prized "autonomy" may be, the forces that affect people's lives are so complex that it is only in concert with others—through channels of communication, organization, and action—that people can hope to get any effective purchase on them. By providing such channels, then, more or less directly, civil society is a kind of training ground for citizenship and the wider freedom it embraces.

Civil society is also a focus for solidarity. Given its essential plurality and diversity, however, this solidarity cannot be one of uniformity or monopoly. This fact implies that civil society can be neither theocratic nor ultranationalist. But it excludes, no less, the "liberal" form of orthodoxy that would wash out differences in a reductively secular or putatively universalist bleach. And so it is hospitable to the presence and contributions of different religious, ethnic, and linguistic groups, with, for example, their own senses of identity and historical memory, practices, customs, norms, and patterns of family life. If civil society is receptive to such substantive or "thick" contributions, however, its own essential identity is as an overall ensemble that incorporates many other contributions too, so that all are exposed to and modifiable by each other. If no voice can hope in a civil society to be the only voice, differences may be marked and conflicts unavoidable. Still the very multiplicity of the sites of possible engagement can bring some hope of mediation. Conflicts are more tolerable when enough overlapping of different groupings ensures that people who are apart or opposed on one front may find common interest or cause on another. A healthy civil society is composed of very many densely interwoven strands of association and action; its strength is more like that of a rope than an iron bar.

4.5. *The State, Civil Society, and Cultural Pluralism*

Here, inevitably, the question arises about the relation of civil society to the state. As an entity that stands apart from the concerted activities of an engaged citizenry, our notion of the "state" is foreign to ancient republicanism (it does not at all correspond to the Greek *polis*). And because of this very externality, it was natural that in its eighteenth century origins civil society should see itself as a check on the state—especially through the emerging "fourth estate," with a proliferation of newspapers and pamphlets giving new meaning to "public opinion" as an informed and critical tribunal to which the state would now be made answerable. The canonical maxim in this regard was coined by an Irishman, John Curran: "the condition on which God hath given liberty to man is eternal vigilance." Now, as in the eighteenth century, however, this "vigilance" has ambiguous potential. When it is expressed as principled withdrawal from, and even hostility to, the state, it represents the antipolitics of both early and late economic liberalism.[11] But it can also take the opposite path of engaging with the state and ensuring that the latter actively furthers its own best impulses. The relation between state and civil society then becomes more reciprocal and complex. To be sure, the effectiveness of the state will be seen to depend on the extent to which it latches into and builds on existing competencies and solidarities (so that e.g. the Welfare State will function best as complement to a caring society and not only as attempted compensation for an uncaring one). But it is also the case that, for all its vernacular energy and cohesiveness, civil society remains, even in the best case, the scene of divisions and conflicts and that the state commands enormous power and resources, in the disposal of which it cannot remain neutral with regard to these conflicts.

As a necessary focus of unity and the agency of collective decision making, the state must have an interest in fostering solidarity in civil society; and it cannot do so without laws and policies that protect basic liberties and embody some—inevitably contested—notion of equality. Here the classic liberal separation of public and private will not serve well. For solidarity is inhibited when some minority groups have a precarious status, there is little sympathy or support for their practices and values, and state organs maintain a principled aloofness or—as this will inevitably amount to in practice—reinforce some more or less unreflective version of the dominant majority culture. If a state is really to cherish its minority cultures then it will have to offer them moral and material support; without this, their advancement in educational and economic life, for example, will be at the cost of an assimilationist loss of identity. But it is not only through one-way sponsorship of their legitimate cultural aspirations that the state needs to relate to its constituent cultures. It also has to ensure that they are in fact *constituent*, by not only ensuring sensitivity to them in its laws and policies, but also by finding ways of reflecting their presence in its own myths, rituals, and emblems. Responsiveness to difference is the only way to worthwhile political unity; without it, the polity invites disaffection and fragmentation. By making different groups less embattled, it may also be the way to facilitate *within* each group a greater measure of critical reflection, tolerance of dissent, and openness to outside influence.[12]

The kind of pluralism I am urging here with respect to different cultural communities will be greatly enhanced, I believe, by a pluralist conception of civil society as itself constituted by irreducibly different spheres, each with its own relative autonomy. There is of course the economic sphere regulated mainly by the market but there are also, for example, the spheres of education, health, communications media, organized sport, and religion. I speak of the "relative autonomy" of these spheres because each has its own specific goods, as well as its own specific ways of relating to need, aptitude, competence, interest, or faith. It is when these specificities are not respected and advantage in one is translated into and magnified in another that inequalities become intolerable and the civic fabric is threatened—as when those with large business interests come also to control important organs of communication, or when businessmen are favored by politicians, or politicians become beholden to businessmen (or deferential to bishops). Democracy is endangered when the same people come to wield influence in all spheres—as happens when the rich may use their wealth to purchase political patronage (irrespective of persuasion), and better health care (irrespective of need), and a better education for their children (irrespective of need, interest, or talent). But it is damaging too that the goods of other spheres are reduced to economic goods (i.e. commodities) and their internal logics are reduced to an economic logic (i.e. the "bottom line"). Here I return to a theme of the opening section of this chapter: the homogenizing effect of the economic imperatives that now bear so heavily on education. To be sure, the state must have a policy on the goods to be achieved through education—indeed on the good that *is* education. But a genuinely pluralist state—one that is more or less post-nationalist and that sponsors the type of civil society sketched here—will have to ensure both the proper differentiation of education from other spheres and also a good deal of differentiation within education itself. To this end, there is much scope for partnerships between the state and various elements within civil society. In most European countries (unlike the United States) this has long been the case with the churches and—with due safeguards—can, I believe, be extended to other groupings.

4.6. A Divided Society: The Case of Northern Ireland

Having earlier given some profile to Europe, and having just depicted civil society in a positive light, I want to conclude this chapter by adverting to one place in the European Union where civil society has been very much in abeyance, Northern Ireland. The case of Northern Ireland does not of course present us with the normal issue of "multiculturalism:" how to accommodate different ethnic, linguistic, or religious identities within a polity whose basic integrity and legitimacy—however much internal reconstruction or reform it may be deemed to be in need of—none of them seriously challenges. This case has its roots in settlement and conquest in the late seventeenth century and in the inability then or since of the settler community, and the metropolitan state (Britain) to which it pledges loyalty, to subdue or assimilate the native population. The history of this conflict has precipitated two communities deeply and bitterly divided by ethnic origin *and* national allegiance *and* religious adherence.[13] The political entity that was to contain these two communities was created by partition of the island as part of an attempt to solve the wider "Irish problem" in 1922. But disabilities which the native people had suffered over the three previous centuries were continued in the new state. There was systematic gerrymandering of electoral constituencies to unionist advantage (indeed the very boundaries of the new state could be seen as the result of a master act of gerrymander), widespread discrimination in employment and housing policies, failure to establish through organs of the state (especially policing and the civil service) an impartial system of administration, delegitimation of basic political aspirations of the nationalist community, and refusal of recognition to its cherished cultural tokens (e.g. the Irish language).

Disaffection in the oppressed group was matched by a threatened and embattled posture on the part of the dominant group—a not unreasonable posture given that what they confronted was a very substantial internal minority (never less than 40 per cent and augmented by higher Catholic birth rates), a larger state to the south which had irredentist claims on their territory and to which this minority professed loyalty, and a state across the water whose support—notwithstanding their own loyalty to it—was prone to depletion by liberal and democratic scruples. All of these were a recipe for deep instability; and while the antagonism between the two communities could be covered by some layers of civility at a local level, the potential for violent outbreaks was endemic. At various stages these could be contained by influential elites or moderating influences on both sides; but when a concerted civil rights campaign was aborted in the late 1960s, and the British government felt constrained to despatch a large garrison of British troops to the province, the scene was set for a campaign of paramilitary violence on the republican side that was to last for thirty years.

Violence created its own force field whose power to attract and distort all the normal recourses of politics and civil life remained unchecked by any established sovereignty with authority unambiguously to criminalize it. Through spirals of reactive tit-for-tat killings, violence became representative: a person was killed not for individual qualities or acts but just because she or he was Protestant or Catholic. Already polarized by history, people on both sides were driven more tightly than ever into identification with their own "tribes," into communities of fear and distrust exposed not only to the danger of random reprisal from the other side but also to extremists on their own side who had power not only to provoke these reprisals but also to offer perhaps the only available defense against them.

As yet one can write about this situation in the past tense only very provisionally. But the ceasefires on both sides over the past few years and the vigorous pursuit of political initiatives that has filled the vacuum they created give grounds for hope. It seems clear that the momentum both for the ceasefires and for the subsequent political developments has come mainly from the British government's gradual abandonment of the fiction that the "troubles" were an internal problem of the United Kingdom and from its willingness to share responsibility for the problem with the Irish government. What has made the difference over the past decade or so has been the determination of the two governments to work constructively together—indeed to bring forward joint proposals at every step. This has been made possible by the abatement of animosity between the Irish and British peoples and the readiness by both states to move beyond their ancient quarrel to a "special relationship" buttressed by their partnership within the wider framework of the European Union. This readiness has been manifested in Britain's declaration that it has "no selfish or strategic interest" in retaining Northern Ireland as part of the United Kingdom and in the Republic's abandonment, through constitutional amendment, of its irredentist claim to the North and its formal acceptance of the principle of consent (no United Ireland without the consent of a majority in Northern Ireland). These larger constitutional undertakings have been accompanied by a raft of measures enshrined in the Good Friday Agreement that guarantee rights, equity, and "parity of esteem" to both communities economically and culturally, establish a power-sharing legislature and executive at political level, and complement these internal arrangements with a delicate balancing of North–South (Northern Ireland-Republic) and East–West (Ireland and Britain) institutions.

Can all this work, so that "hope and history rhyme?"[14] Support for the Agreement in the Unionist community is on a knife edge, and hugely contentious matters still remain to be resolved (not least the disposal of paramilitary weaponry, policing, and the ever-thorny issue of symbols and flags). Most of all there is the legacy of suffering, grievance, distrust, and enmity on which neither side can claim a monopoly. When every resource of political intelligence and imagination has been exhausted in crafting constitutional and legal frameworks and institutions, what other work remains to be done if there is to be a healthy civil society and if the two traditions are to learn what is required of them to live together in justice and peace? Whatever work this may be, it surely lies at the heart of what education must become in a society such as Northern Ireland.

In a closely analogous European context—reflecting on the problem of political power sharing by countries whose histories have embroiled them in bitter wars with each other (especially France and Germany)—Paul Ricoeur writes: "it would be a mistake to believe that transfers of sovereignty in support of a political entity . . . can be successful at the formal level of political and juridical institutions without the will to implement these transfers deriving its initiative from changes of attitude in the ethos of individuals, groups, and peoples."[15] Ricoeur goes on to respond to this ethico-political problem by outlining three models of imaginative exchange that have no less salience, I believe, for the situation in Northern Ireland.

4.6. Three Kinds of Imaginative Interaction: Translation, Exchange of Memories, and Forgiveness

The first model is that of *translation*. The fact that there is not just one language means that translation is necessary; the fact that all the many languages are not self-enclosed or other-excluding makes it possible. There may indeed be an ultimate incommensurability between any one language and another; but short of this limit there is the perpetual challenge of rendering in the one what is said in the other. In carrying through this process, there is no "master" Language—supplying a kind of neutral template on which correspondences between the two languages might be registered—to which the translator can have recourse. Rather, as bilingual, the latter must live into the distinctiveness (at many levels—phonological, lexical, syntactical, stylistic, etc.) of the other language and try to bring this over, without semantic loss, into her own language. Any attempt to subdue the otherness of what is to be translated or to impose on it the frame of the home language as "dominant" is foreign to the spirit of translation. This spirit is essentially one of hospitality, of readiness on the part of the receiving language to put itself out so that the content in the other is made at home in it. It is on this account—that rigor here is a form of courtesy—that translation offers such a significant model (and that the learning of another language can be such an educative experience). But in fact its full significance is realized only when the encounter extends beyond language to the other culture in all its density of meaning, custom, and belief—when, in Ricoeur's words, it takes on an "*ethos* whose goal would be to repeat at the cultural and spiritual level the gesture of linguistic hospitality"[16] implicit in the act of translation.

This extension brings us to the second model, that of *the exchange of memories*. For Ricoeur, memory is not just the psychological faculty through which we recall the past; rather, by structuring our whole way of being in time, it constitutes our very identity. The primary work of memory—the genre through which this structuring happens and identity is created—is narrative. A story gathers actions and events that are otherwise dispersed by the ineluctable passage of time; but in telling her story a person also configures *herself* and achieves a more or less stable identity. The "more or less" here is important; for, as construed narratively, identity is neither fixed nor self-enclosed. It is not self-enclosed because my story is always entangled with the stories of significant others (such as my parents, neighbors, friends, and enemies)—which are themselves, of course, similarly entangled with mine as well as with each other. And it is not fixed because the formative actions and events that are configured in a story can always be *re*configured: through account being taken of other hitherto excluded events or through a shift in "point of view" an established narrative can be displaced by one of perhaps several alternative "readings."[17]

It is most particularly through confrontation with the stories of others that a space is opened for such a recounting of my own story. And it is the spirit in which these confrontations occur that Ricoeur is concerned with when he introduces his model of "the exchange of memories." In the present context, of course, this whole theme must be transposed from the level of individual persons to that of peoples and cultures—on the assumption that one can speak meaningfully of "collective memory" and that "the identity of a group, culture, people, or nation, is not that of an immutable substance, nor that of a fixed structure, but that, rather, of a recounted story."[18] In the case of a nation, the story will profile "founding events" which, because they are primordial and have been much commemorated and celebrated, tend to hold the story in a fixed mould, to the point even of generating an "identity which is not only immutable but also deliberately and systematically incommunicable."[19] In relation to founding events or generative moments in the life of a nation, Ricoeur calls neither for abandonment nor amnesia but rather for "an effort of plural reading." This effort, then, is not to be conducted against tradition (but only against the kind of fixation required by tradition*ism*): "Tradition represents the aspect of debt which concerns the past and reminds us that nothing comes from nothing. A tradition remains living, however, only if it continues to be held in an unbroken process of reinterpretation."[20] This reinterpretation can bring liberation not from the past but *of* the past, or rather of the frustrated potential of the past. For "the past is not only what is bygone—that which has taken place and can no longer be changed—it also lives in the memory thanks to arrows of futurity which have not been fired or whose trajectory has been interrupted. The unfulfilled future of the past forms perhaps the richest part of a tradition."[21]

The project of "reinterpretation", with the debates between "plural readings" that it gives rise to, can of course be undertaken within one community—as it has been, for example, by French historians responding to the bicentenary of the French Revolution, or by German historians in relation to the Nazi period, or by Irish historians in relation to the physical force movement and the constitutional nationalism which it eclipsed in the events leading up to the foundation of the Irish Free State. When Ricoeur speaks of "exchange of memories", however, he has in mind an attempt by people of one community to enter imaginatively and sympathetically into the story or stories of *another* people—while at the same time allowing *their own* story or stories to be reconfigured through the impact of this recognition of the other. This attempt would have to reproduce at the level of memory and identity the ethics of empathy and hospitality already operative at the linguistic level in the art of translation. But so fraught are the materials that arise at this level—so marked are they by past conflicts still charged with lethal possibilities of further conflict—that they may require an even more demanding ethical response: what Ricoeur invokes with his third "model", that of *forgiveness*.

The kind of "revision" that can bring about a release from the irreversibility of the past (and thus a real shift in identity) runs up against a limit in the ungainsayable reality of past suffering: what has been endured by one side and inflicted by the other. Not only at the level of *realpolitik* but also even at the level of a political morality incorporating principles of reciprocity and justice, past suffering calls for retribution—all the more so indeed when a faithful memory has kept it alive and no mere narrative strategy has been able to efface it or to remove the burden of guilt which it imposes on those who have inflicted it. The drive for retribution, and the justification to which it can lay claim, can be overcome only at a level where the logic of reciprocity gives way to the "surplus" logic of *gift*. Short of the latter, both perpetrator and victim remain bound to a cycle of reaction— even if, in cases where the oppressing force is overwhelming, retaliation must be deferred and take the form of an as yet unreleased potential. It is an act of for*giving* that most conspicuously brings release from the "relentless automatism" of this cycle. Some important clarifications remain to be made, however, if forgiveness is not to be thrust as an undue burden of expectation on the victim and if, in particular, it is to lead to *reconciliation*.

First, there must be no attempt on either side to "forget" the terribleness of what has been done. Second, while forgiveness exceeds justice it cannot be turned into a substitute for it. And this means that, beyond remembrance, the perpetrator must both acknowledge responsibility and show contrition for his deed—which will entail an intention not to reoffend and, where still practicable, an attempt to make restitution. It is only when these conditions are fulfilled that the perpetrator can *receive* forgiveness (as distinct from *taking* it, which in fact he can never do) and that, in forgiving, the victim can be released from emotions not only of resentment and revenge but also of righteous anger. Even with these requirements, forgiveness remains a gratuitous act—and one, moreover, for which the perpetrator remains dependent on the victim. For, of its nature, forgiveness is something that an individual can never give to himself; in that respect it subverts the very idea of sovereignty and reflects the character of identity as always already entangled.[22] Moreover, in this entanglement the role of perpetrator or victim can seldom be assigned exclusively to either side; even if one side was innocent when first attacked, in its reaction thereafter it is unlikely to have remained entirely guiltless. And all this carries over to the political sphere where, in the relations between peoples and nations, forgiveness is as relevant and even as necessary as it is between persons. Nor, fortunately, do we lack recent examples of it in this sphere— Nelson Mandela's donning of the Springbok jersey being perhaps the most vividly memorable.

There is, I think, a kind of universality in these "models" of dialogue: one that does not suppress but rather embraces particularity, while at the same time remaining capable of transcending it.[23] It remains important of course to distinguish the civic bond from cultural or ethnic attachments. This bond must be founded on principles of equality, liberty, and reciprocal recognition, principles that are properly translated into codifications of rights in constitutional/legal documents such at the Good Friday Agreement. I do not believe, however, that such rights can in the end be vindicated unless the primary cultural and ethnic attachments are in some way worked through—rather than bypassed or wished away. It is in bringing out what is involved in this "working through"[24] that Ricoeur's insights may be helpful. As translation challenges the limits of a language through the friendly contest it opens up with other languages—without thereby hankering for a single Language—so the exchange of memories goes beyond uses of history that reinforce chauvinist sentiment and nourish old grievances or enmities—without thereby succumbing to the illusion of a sterilized vantage for the construction, free of all prejudice, of the one definitive "objective" account.[25] This refusal of an apparently attractive—but ultimately repressive—universalism, and the corresponding acceptance of plurality ("difference", "otherness")[26] is not a refusal of the idea of transcultural accord; it is, rather, a necessary condition for any real movement toward it. This movement can take place only as the different communities open to each other—and to the refocusing of their own identities brought about through this opening; and of course it requires more than symbolic gestures by political leaders, however edifying these may be.[27]

I have profiled these insights of Ricoeur's hermeneutical ethics because I believe them to be heavy with implication for the educative task. While it is beyond the scope of this chapter to spell out their entailments for curriculum, pedagogy, and schooling policy, it may be worthwhile in conclusion to forestall possible misunderstanding by indicating one implication that they do *not* carry. Education, it may be claimed, should create some kind of distance from the urgencies and abridgements of students' present situations and release them into the wider spaces of great literature and science, thereby involving them in a "self-forgetting that is experienced not as a loss of self, but as the free buoyancy of an elevation above oneself."[28] And even if self-understanding is a valid aim of education, is it not to be achieved *in education*—as distinct from psychotherapy—by indirection, by attention to a world beyond the self and its own immediate tribe? Moreover, in a society with a history such as that of Northern Ireland (and perhaps *all* societies have histories that are not too dissimilar) should young people not be helped to break free from the past and from any limiting polarity of "self" and "other"— as if there were not many selves and many others that education might properly enable them to discover? There is real force in these questions. Far from pulling against Ricoeur's analysis, however, this force is actually acknowledged within it. For the latter does not protect inherited identities from multiple claims that may break open their particularistic limitations; its aim, rather, is to show how "particular" and "universal" must be mediated together. But an education instructed by this mediation will *also* realize that we cannot escape the past by evading the task of understanding it. It is the merit of Ricoeur's hermeneutical insights that they neither deny the past nor imprison us in it. They contain the promise of an education through which young people may realize "the unfulfilled future of the past" by coming to understand both themselves and the estranged other in ways that open them to a deeper understanding of a shared humanity.

NOTES

1. Francisco O. Ramirez and John Boli, "On the Union of States and Schools" in G. M. Thomas, J. W. Meyer, F. O. Ramirez, and J. Boli (eds), *Institutional Structure: Constituting State, Society, and the Individual* (Newbury Park: Sage, 1987), 187. My historical account here is much indebted to this paper.
2. Ibid., 188.
3. I refer here to egalitarianism as an official aspiration of state policy on education in developed Western democracies. In practice, of course, as a great deal of sociological literature makes plain, elusive factors still militate against the scholastic attainment of poorer children and thus remain as formidable barriers to real "equality of educational opportunity."
4. "Any *polis* which is truly so called, and is not merely one in name, must devote itself to the end of encouraging virtue. Otherwise, a political association sinks into a mere alliance...[and] law becomes a 'mere guarantor of men's rights against one another'—instead of being, as it should be, a rule of life such as will make the members of a *polis* good and just." Aristotle, *Politics*, 3,9, 1280b6-11.
5. For example, in Horkheimer and Adorno's analysis of the "dialectic of enlightenment," in Habermas's thesis on the "colonisation of the life world" by the "steering media" of money and power, or in Foucault's account of the construction of the modern subject and the role played in it by disciplinary institutions (the prison and asylum as well as the school).
6. Parekh, "A Commitment to Cultural Pluralism", http://kvc.minbuza.nl/parekh.html.

7. See Fish, "Boutique Multiculturalism" in M. Meltzer, J. Weinberger, and M. Zinman (eds), *Multiculturalism and American Democracy* (Lawrence, KA: Kansas University Press, 1998).

8. Nicholas Boyle, *Who are We Now: Christian Humanism from Hegel to Heaney* (Notre Dame: Notre Dame University Press, 1998)

9. In Benedict Anderson's sense: see his *Imagined Communities: Reflections on the Origin and Spread of Nationalism* (London: Verso, 1983).

10. There has for example been a considerable resurgence in the past decade or two of Irish traditional music and dance, of the Irish language as a spoken and written medium, and of what might, perhaps nebulously, be called national morale. But this has been due not to the pursuit of the kind of introverted and often authoritarian policies that were understandable, if almost entirely counterproductive, reflexes when we lived within an exclusively Anglo-American axis but, in fair measure, to a new sense of being one of many minority cultures and languages, each of which is strengthened by the kind of solidarity with others, that has been fostered through inter-regional structures within the European Union.

11. The idea of civil society first crystallized in reaction to eighteenth century absolutism (though it had some antecedents in mediaeval social formations). It arose with the claim (e.g. contra Hobbes) that sovereignty vested in an absolute ruler was not the only source of political authority or of social cohesion. This antiabsolutist impulse, however, would itself prove only too capable of assuming absolutist forms. For the "people" whose sovereignty was counter-asserted (most classically in Rousseau's doctrine of the "general will") would foreshorten to the "nation" or the "proletariat" and inspire all the terror and even attempted extermination that has defaced the past century. Painfully learned resistance to all-inclusive designs by *any* kind of state apparatus, then, is internal to the idea of civil society. But this idea *also* entails resistance to another legacy from the eighteenth century, whose absolutist potential we have perhaps been even slower to recognize beneath its original antiabsolutist appearance. When the whole nexus of production and exchange not only expanded to create new opportunities for wealth, loosened from the old privileges of birth, but came to be seen (in the writings of the Physiocrats and Adam Smith) as having its own laws—that is, as forming an autonomous sphere of *economy*—it could be welcomed as a curb on the ambitions of monarchs and emperors. But when this sphere itself becomes sovereign—so that no other hand can moderate the invisible hand of the market, and freedom is equated with "free enterprise"—then it too (notwithstanding earlier historical connections between the two) becomes inimical to civil society. And so our lesson now is to recognize civil society as the reality that was not only suppressed in the collapsed totalitarian regimes of the eastern bloc but is also threatened by neoliberal policies. (See Charles Taylor, "Invoking Civil Society", *Philosophical Arguments* (Cambridge, MA: Harvard University Press, 1995), 204–24.)

12. I follow here Bhiku Parekh's argument in "Integrating Minorities", in T. Blackstone, F. Parekh, and P. Sanders (eds), *Race Relations in Britain* (London: Routledge, 1996), 1–21.

13. Although language did not become the strong badge of identity in Northern Ireland that it did in the case, for example, of Czech and Polish nationalisms, even single words in the common English language can still carry huge historical freighting. To say "Derry," for example, rather than "Londonderry" is to betray a whole political orientation. And the core-word "Ulster" is deeply contested: for Unionists it names their territory, the six county state, whereas for nationalists this is a misappropriation of the name for the historic province of

nine counties artificially truncated by the partitionist settlement in 1922 to ensure an inbuilt Unionist majority.

14. The phrase is Seamus Heaney's, in oblique reference to Northern Ireland, in his *The Cure at Troy* (London: Faber).
15. Paul Ricoeur, "Reflections on a New Ethos for Europe", *Philosophy and Social Criticism*, 21(5/6) (1995), 3. (This essay is a translation by Eileen Brennan of "Quel ethos nouveau pour l'Europe?" in *Imaginer l'Europe*, sous la direction de Peter Koslowski (Paris: Editions du Cerf, 1992), 107–19.)
16. Ibid., 5.
17. For further development of points here, see my "Beyond Sovereignty and Deconstruction: The Storied Self", *Philosophy and Social Criticism*, 21(5/6) (1995), 137–57.
18. Ricoeur, ibid., 7.
19. Ibid.
20. Ibid., 8.
21. Ibid.
22. I go beyond Ricoeur here, drawing on a thinker whom he does not mention, Hannah Arendt. Arendt conceives of action in a way that highlights the web of relations within which it transpires, the incapacity of the agent to contain the chain of consequences which it unleashes (the phrase, "relentless automatism" in the text is hers), and the unavailability of anything which can bring relief from this chain other than the free act of forgiveness. See H. Arendt, *The Human Condition* (Chicago: University of Chicago Press, 1958), part V, esp., 236–43.
23. A similar kind of ethical universalism is implicit in Simone Weil's understanding of a culture as a "vital medium" and in her corresponding characterization of patriotism. "There is one's own particular vital medium; but there are others besides. It has been produced by a network of causes in which good and evil, justice, and injustice have been mixed up together, and so it cannot be the best possible one." To avoid "the contradictions and lies that corrode the idea of patriotism", Weil suggests as the essential sentiment of the latter, not pride in, but compassion for, one's culture as for some "precious, fragile, and perishable object." "Whereas pride . . . is by its nature exclusive, non-transferable . . . compassion is by its nature universal; it is only more potential where distant and unfamiliar things are concerned, more real, more . . . charged with effective energy where things close at hand are concerned" (Weil, *The Need for Roots* (London: Routledge, 1978), 155–56). Compassion is a virtue that surely deserves an important place in moral and civic education; if this education is to be truly cosmopolitan it will strive to make more real the "potential" toward what is "distant and unfamiliar."
24. "Working through" is an important concept in Freud's elaboration of psychoanalysis as a healing art; see "Remembering, Repeating and Working-Through" in J. Strachey (ed.), *Standard Edition of Complete Psychological Works* (London: Hogarth Press, 1968), XII, 147–56.
25. That prejudice is legitimate, and in any case inevitable, in all historical interpretation, as in all encounters between different viewpoints, cultures, or traditions—and that it is to be overcome not by the construction of a neutral, "scientific" horizon but by a "fusion of horizons" (between the historian and his intended subject matter or between the two cultures)—is a cardinal point in the work of Ricoeur's fellow-hermeneuticist, Hans–Georg Gadamer; see Gadamer, *Truth and Method* (London: Sheed and Ward, 1975), 238ff., 273ff.

26. On "plurality" as a necessary condition of the public space of democratic politics, and on its abolition as the constant mark of tyranny, see Arendt, op cit., 220ff.
27. An act with very powerful symbolic resonance in the recent history of Northern Ireland was David Trimble's (leader of the main Unionist party) attendance at the funeral in Co. Donegal of three young victims of the Omagh bomb in 1998.
28. Hans–Georg Gadamer, "On the Problem of Self-Understanding" in D. E. Linge (trans. and ed.), *Philosophical Hermeneutics* (Berkeley and Los Angeles: University of California Press, 1997).

CHAPTER 5

The Burdens and Dilemmas of Common Schooling

Terence H. McLaughlin

Schools of every kind, place, and time shoulder burdens and face dilemmas. Many of these burdens and dilemmas are universal in that they are inherent in the very activity of schooling and teaching. Every school faces the burden of arousing the interest of students in what it is in their interests to learn, and of ensuring that the learning in question is satisfactorily brought about. Every school also faces dilemmas arising from the relative weight and priority to be given to contrasting and competing demands such as those captured in tensions between reassurance and challenge in the handling of individuals, breadth and depth in determining what is to be learnt, and equality and excellence in the overall aims and ethos of the classroom and school.[1]

Common schools in pluralist, multicultural, liberal democratic societies, however, shoulder burdens and face dilemmas of very specific and demanding kinds. These burdens and dilemmas relate to the particular educational role and mandate which common schools are given in such societies which is in turn related to, and derived from, the complex principles, values, and practices which articulate and underpin societies of this kind. Bhikhu Parekh expresses in a clear way the centrality to these principles, values, and practices of the achievement of a certain kind of balance between unifying and diversifying imperatives and forces: "Multicultural societies throw up problems that have no parallel in history. They need to find ways of reconciling the legitimate demands of unity and diversity, achieving political unity without cultural uniformity, being inclusive without being assimilationist, cultivating among their citizens a common

sense of belonging while respecting their legitimate cultural differences, and cherishing plural cultural identities without weakening
the shared and precious identity of shared citizenship."[2] Common
schools are typically seen as having an important educational role
and mandate in relation to these challenges. It is widely argued that
a common school, underpinned by an appropriate conception of
common education, is the most favored context in which these challenges can be met and liberal democratic educational aims, values,
and processes realized.

In this chapter, I shall explore some of the neglected resultant burdens and dilemmas faced by common schools in pluralist, multicultural, and liberal democratic societies. The potential weight and
complexity of these burdens and dilemmas is reflected in Stephen
Macedo's observation that common schools give rise to questions
relating to some of the "deepest divisions" and "most intractable
conflicts" characterizing the public lives of modern states.[3] The
chapter has five sections. Section 5.1 outlines some general considerations relating to common schooling and a conception of common
education, and Section 5.2 offers a sketch of some general features
of such conceptions. In Sections 5.3 and 5.4 respectively, some of
the burdens and dilemmas of common schooling are explored.
Although these burdens and dilemmas are brought into focus by the
sort of philosophical reflection and analysis attempted in this
chapter, they have a pre-eminently practical character. Neglected
questions relating to this important truth will be addressed in
Section 5.5.

5.1. Common Schooling and a Conception of Common Education

At the most basic level, a "common school" can be regarded as a
school which is open to, and intended for, all students within a given
society regardless of their specific differentiating characteristics. Ideals
of "common schooling," however, normally specify not merely a particular institutional arrangement for schooling but also a "conception
of common education" which the school should embody and enact.
The notion of a "conception of common education" prescribes a range
of educational outcomes of wide ranging kinds as appropriate and
desirable for all members of the society in question.[4] Conceptions of
common education, and therefore the role and mandate which is given
to the common school, vary across differing societies. In theocratic

societies, common schools typically embody the form of religiously based education and formation judged appropriate for all citizens and for the maintenance of favored forms of moral and cultural monism and homogeneity.[5] In the former Soviet Union common schools sought to transmit, and shape students in the light of, a particular view of the good expressed in part in the sort of unified, detailed, moral formation contained in the notion of *vospitanie*. A range of differing philosophical resources can be appealed to in articulating a conception of common education.[6] In the context of the sorts of pluralist, multicultural, and liberal democratic societies which are the focus of the present discussion, however, "common schools" are seen as a favored context in which to realize a "conception of common education" based on liberal democratic philosophical and educational ideals and embodying an appropriate balance between the kinds of complex unifying and diversifying imperatives and forces mentioned earlier. This "conception of common education" is seen as an entitlement for all students and as therefore in tension with the claims of diversity, parental rights, and the mechanisms of the educational marketplace. It generates a series of educational aims and processes which involve not merely the development of relevant forms of knowledge and understanding, but also of forms of sensitivity, disposition, virtue, and commitment.[7]

It is useful to make a number of preliminary general points about the "common school" and a "conception of common education" in pluralist, multicultural, and liberal democratic societies. First, "common schools" are not, and cannot be, "common" in every respect. Walter Feinberg acknowledges that common schools differ in their material and intellectual resources, in their curriculum and pedagogy, and in their racial, gender, and social class composition and effects.[8] Common schooling, understood as requiring similarity of educational provision, experience, and outcome does not, and cannot, exist. In the United States and in England and Wales, there are marked and widely recognized differences in publicly funded schools related to such factors as location, and in both contexts greater diversification in publicly funded schooling is being urged. What is fundamentally "common" in common schools is the "conception of common education" which they seek to embody and certain *de jure* provisions relating to such matters as open admission criteria and a learning environment which is hospitable in different ways to diversity. In addition, the de facto realization of such provisions, albeit imperfectly, is also significant. However, whilst conceptions of common education are compatible with certain kinds of variety in common schooling, both *de jure* and de facto, the unifying and egalitarian elements inherent in such conceptions imply that some differences among common schools are troubling, for example, those which have implications for equality of educational opportunity in its various aspects. Parameters within which variety in common schooling should be contained can therefore be derived from most conceptions of common education[9], as can criteria for the limits of accommodation between conceptions of common education and such aspects of diversity as religious belief.[10]

Second, and relatedly, it is a "common conception of education" and not common schooling per se which is seen as of fundamental value. The "common school" is regarded as valuable not as an end in itself but to the extent that it is an appropriate context for the realization of the underlying conception of common education. Common schools are widely considered to be particularly favored contexts for this purpose, however, since in bringing together students from many diverse backgrounds in a common institution, common schools constitute an educational environment which is both intimately related to the requirements of conceptions of common education and unobtainable elsewhere.[11] Be this as it may, however, the practical shortcomings of common schools in particular contexts, the impossibility of deriving conclusions for schooling arrangements from philosophical and political premises alone, and complexities inherent in conceptions of common education themselves, mean that the relationship between common schools and a common conception of education is at best a presumptive one.[12] I have argued elsewhere that certain forms of "non-common" educational provision, such as certain kinds of religious schools, can be compatible with conceptions of common education.[13]

Third, the extent to which a conception of the "common school" and a "conception of common education" is explicitly articulated and implemented at the level of policy and practice in any particular pluralist, multicultural, liberal democratic society varies. In the United States the political, legal, and historical context of the "public school" has given a sharpness of focus to central matters of educational principle and their relationship to practice, even though these matters have been subject to development and require careful interpretation.[14] In England and Wales, there is less sharpness of focus given to matters of educational principle by the political and legal context, in part because of the lack of separation between church and state and a different history of the relationship of publically funded schooling to religion.[15] Religious education and an act of worship are compulsory in all publically funded schools, and around one third of schools in the publicly funded sector are religious schools to which the sponsoring religious body makes a financial contribution in exchange for control over certain aspects of the life and work of the school, including admissions of students, religious teaching, certain staff appointments, and school ethos.[16] Until relatively recently, educational aims and values have been not been explicitly and systematically addressed and articulated at the policy level in England and Wales[17] and insufficient attention has been given at this level to specific concerns, such as education for citizenship and the appropriate handling of controversial issues, which are inherent in "conceptions of common education."[18] The theoretical articulation of ideals of the "common school" and a "conception of common education" at an abstract level is one thing, and the articulation and realization of those ideals at the level of educational policy and practice is another. Meira Levinson is correct in drawing attention to the limitations of purely theoretical reflection about educational ideals and the need to pay attention to contextually sensitive matters of policy and practice if a full understanding of the matters at stake is to be achieved.[19] Before proceeding, it is worth noting that the term "common school" is not widely or unproblematically used in either the United States or in England and Wales, although it has a long history in the United States. The "common school" is exemplified in broad terms in the United States by the "public school" and in England and Wales by the "non-voluntary" school in the "maintained" or publicly funded schooling sector (*viz*: a school which does not have a religious sponsor). The use of the term "common school" in the present discussion is intended to focus attention upon certain matters of broad principle relating to schooling rather than the details of particular institutional arrangements.

Fourth, the notion of a "conception of common education," and therefore of the precise role and mandate of the "common school" within pluralist, multicultural, liberal democratic societies, is the subject of continuing debate and dispute at the theoretical and practical level. Some of these debates and disputes will emerge in the discussion of the burdens and dilemmas of common schools which emerge in this chapter.

5.2. Common Conceptions of Education: Some General Principles

In approaching the specific burdens and dilemmas faced by common schools in pluralist, multicultural, liberal democratic societies, it is helpful to begin with an outline of the basic framework of principle and value typically employed in the articulation of conceptions of common education for such societies. This basic framework can then be elaborated and sophisticated to enable the burdens and dilemmas to emerge.

A good starting point in the articulation of this framework is the report of the Swann Committee of Inquiry into the Education of Children from Ethnic Minority Groups.[20] The report captures well a number of the central features of such frameworks, including the centrality of a judicious balance of unifying and diversifying imperatives and forces. In the report, a pluralist democratic society is characterized as one which "... values the diversity within it, whilst united by the cohesive force of the common aims, attributes and values which we all share"[21] and which therefore seeks to achieve a balance between "... on the one hand, the maintenance and active support of the essential elements of the cultures and lifestyles of all the ethnic groups within it, and, on the other, the acceptance by all groups of a set of shared values distinctive of the society as a whole."[22] The vision of the report is therefore one of a society stressing "diversity within unity",[23] in which a stark dichotomy between assimilation and separatism with respect to minority groups is avoided.[24]

With regard to unifying elements, the report insists that, in a genuinely pluralist society, there must be a "... framework of commonly accepted values, practices and procedures..."[25] which embodies a common political and legal system and fundamental democratic commitments, such as those relating to freedom and to justice and equality.[26] The framework also acts as a limitation upon the scope of diversity within society. Thus all members of society have an obligation "... to abide by the current laws of the country and to seek to change them only through peaceful and democratic means",[27] and whilst the majority community within a pluralist society cannot be untouched by the presence of minority groups, those minority groups "... cannot in practice preserve all elements of their cultures and lifestyles unchanged and in their entirety ... if they were to wish to do so it would in many cases be impossible for them then to take on the shared values of the wider pluralist society."[28]

With regard to diversifying elements, the report urges that ethnic minority groups should be allowed and encouraged to maintain their distinct identities within this common framework. They must be free "... within the democratic framework to maintain those elements which they themselves consider to be the most essential to their sense of ethnic identity—whether these take the form of adherence to a particular religious faith or the maintenance of their own language for use within the home and their ethnic community—without fear of prejudice or persecution by other groups."[29] Although the Swann Report is concerned with ethnic diversity, many of its basic principles are relevant also to a number of other aspects of significant diversity.

The educational conclusions which the Swann Report draws capture several of the central elements of the framework of thought relevant to common conceptions of education. The report argues that all children must be educated to "...an understanding of the shared values of our society as a whole as well as to an appreciation of the diversity of lifestyles and cultural, religious, and linguistic backgrounds which make up this society and the wider world."[30] The insistence of the report that all pupils must be given the "knowledge and skills" needed not only to contribute to British society but also "...to determine their own individual identities, free from preconceived or imposed stereotypes of their 'place' in that society"[31] reflects the centrality to common conceptions of education of the autonomy of the child. Thus the report regards as "entirely wrong" any attempt to "...impose a predetermined and rigid 'cultural identity' on any youngster, thus restricting his or her freedom to decide as far as possible for themselves their own future way of life."[32]

As I have remarked elsewhere,[33] such a general conception of education involves the exertion of a complex twofold educational influence. On the one hand, education seeks to bring about the commitment of pupils to the shared, or common, values of the society. In the Swann Report, the autonomy of the child is seen as in an important sense non-negotiable, as are the sorts of qualities and dispositions to be developed in all pupils, including flexibility of mind, an ability to engage in "rational critical" analysis, a global perspective, a willingness to find "...the normality and justice of a variety of points of view" non-threatening and stimulating, and the skills to resolve conflicts positively and constructively.[34] Similarly non-negotiable is the "genuinely pluralist perspective" that should characterize the content and teaching materials of the curriculum and be brought to bear on "the hidden curriculum"[35] and the need for an appropriate form of political education.[36] Racism is presented as wrong and all schools are invited to combat it.[37] Such elements of non-negotiability underlie the insistence of the report that all pupils should "...share a common educational experience which prepares them for life in a truly pluralist society."[38] This leads to a strong emphasis on the value of the common school, and the majority view of the report expresses an opposition to the establishment of separate schools of a religious, or other, kind by ethnic minority groups within the publicly supported school system.[39]

On the other hand, with regard to values which are not shared or common (e.g. those relating to a particular religious faith) the report insists that the common school has no role in bringing about substantive commitments in pupils, as distinct from the development of understanding and critical reflection. With regard to religion, for example, the report holds that it is not the role of the school to encourage in pupils belief in a particular religion: "It is . . . the function of the home and of the religious community to nurture and instruct a child in a particular faith (or not), and the function of the school to assist pupils to understand the nature of religion and to know something of the diversity of belief systems, their significance for individuals and how these bear on the community."[40] Pupils must therefore be enabled, through an approach to religious education which seeks to illuminate the character of the religious domain rather than to engage in religious nurture, to ". . . determine (and justify) their own religious position."[41] This leads the report to call into question the legal requirement that all schools in England and Wales (including common schools) provide an act of collective worship which is broadly Christian in character,[42] and (with the exception of the minority report) to express the attitude to separate religious schools within the publicly supported system which was reported earlier.[43] This general framework of principle and value relating to a pluralist, multicultural, liberal democratic society and the form of common conception of education which is typically related to it is a familiar one in broad outline, as is the range of philosophical assumptions on which such frameworks typically rest. Frameworks such as these are far from being unproblematic, and are open to a number of significant and searching lines of enquiry and criticism. For example, the Swann Report does not address tensions between the unifying and diversifying elements of the framework arising from fundamental or deep-seated conflicts. Further, central features of the report, such as its commitment to the autonomy of the child, clearly invite more extended interpretation and defence. Whilst it is unreasonable to expect a report such as this to engage in such reflection and argumentation, the need for such an engagement in a fuller account of the matters at stake is manifest. Some of lines of enquiry and criticism addressed to general frameworks of the sort articulated in the Swann Report touch upon the fundamental justification of the framework itself. For example, Alasdair MacIntyre claims that, since there exists in liberal societies a number of rival and incompatible accounts of the virtues none of which can establish its superiority by criteria of rational argument which are generally shared and agreed, there can be no shared programme for moral education which is rationally defensible, but only a range of rival and conflicting programmes based on specific standpoints.[44] The present discussion does not pursue these more fundamental challenges to general frameworks such as those developed in the Swann Report and concentrates attention upon the burdens and dilemmas of common schooling which arise within their parameters. These burdens and dilemmas come into clearer focus in exploring in more detail how central elements of such a framework can be variously interpreted.[45]

5.3. Conceptions of Common Education and the Common School: Light and Heavy Burdens

The burdens of a conception of common education on the common school can be located on a continuum of "lightness" to "heaviness" according to the precise interpretation which is offered of, and emphasis placed upon, central elements in the conception, relating to both its unifying, common, or public aspects and its diversifying, non-common, or non-public aspects. Questions relating to the unifying, common, or public aspects involve issues concerning the nature, status, and grounding of the public values, such as the form and scope of the sort of personal autonomy which is proposed for development and the kind of democratic citizenship which is being aimed at. Questions relating to the diversifying, non-common, or non-public aspects involve issues relating to the nature and extent of the diversity which should be valued, the sense(s) in which it should be valued, and the general question of the role which the common school is invited to play in the "non-public" domain. The respects in which all these questions are related to underlying philosophical positions such as "ethical" or "comprehensive" liberalism on the one hand and "political" liberalism on the other can be readily discerned.[46]

To put matters roughly, "light" burdens arise for the common school from conceptions of common education which embody *inter alia* an uncomplicated view of public values and the public domain generally (e.g. one which invokes uncontroversial de facto consensus as a basis for common moral influence), a restricted view of the form and scope of personal autonomy and of democratic citizenship, an uncomplicated view of the nature of diversity and its implications, and a reluctance to extend its educative ambitions into the non-public domain. "Heavy" burdens arise for the common school from conceptions of common education which embody *inter alia* an account of public values and the public domain which is articulated in terms of (often complex) matters of principle which need to be understood by students, an expansive view of the form and scope of personal autonomy and of democratic citizenship, a view of diversity and its implications which is sensitive to complexity and subtlety, and an ambition to engage educationally in a significant way with the "non-public" domain.

At the "light" end of this continuum, therefore, are conceptions of common education of the sort which Eamonn Callan describes as "minimalist" because the character of the education is determined merely by a contingent "lowest common denominator" consensus in society about what all children should learn (e.g. basic literacy, respect for law and order, and the educational prerequisites of economic productivity and competitiveness).[47] Such conceptions generate "light" burdens for the common school because the disagreements characteristic of pluralist, multicultural, and liberal democratic societies are simply evaded: any personal autonomy aimed at is restrictively conceived, any education for citizenship attempted is seen in minimal terms as little more than low-level civic socialization;[48] and the "non-public" domain is seen as off-limits.[49] Also at the "light" end of this continuum is William Galston's well known view of civic education.[50] Galston sees civic education as primarily concerned with supporting and strengthening a particular political community and not with truth seeking and rational enquiry, which are, in Galston's view, in tension with the development of citizens who will embrace the core commitments of a liberal society. Civic education requires a pedagogy which is "rhetorical" and "moralizing" rather than rational.[51] Further, Galston insists that civic educational requirements do not extend to an interest in how children think about different ways of life.[52] In Galston's view public education may not "...foster in children skeptical reflection on ways of life inherited from parents or local communities"[53] because promoting a Socratic ideal of self-examination in the public education system of a liberal state both goes beyond what is functionally necessary for its sociopolitical institutions and conflicts with the liberal freedom to lead an unexamined life.[54] Galston's view imposes "light" burdens on the common school because the school has little work to do in achieving a critical and principled understanding of the public domain on the part of students or an engagement by students in a fair and balanced way with issues in the non-public domain.

Also at the end of the continuum which involves "light" burdens for the common school are conceptions of common education which seek to promote in an unequivocal way *via* education a form of "ethical" or "comprehensive" liberalism as a view of the moral life as a whole. In such views, there is no recognition of the significance and demands of normative diversity and the non-public domain;[55] Macedo, in accusing Dewey of a kind of "civic totalism", sees him as advancing a kind of view of education of this kind.[56] Such conceptions impose relatively "light" burdens upon common schools because of the straightforward value influence they propose. There is little work for the school to do in, for example, the area of the interface between the "public" and the "non-public" and in relation to complexities relating to the latter.

Conceptions of common education which impose "heavier" burdens on common schools specify the achievement by students of independent critical reflection and judgment (if not a full blown notion of personal autonomy) which is sensitive to, and engaged with, matters of diversity and difference. Conceptions of this general kind vary somewhat in their detailed formulation. To sketch matters roughly, Gutmann and Callan see the demands of civic virtue as requiring a form of autonomous deliberation about matters relating to the common good which include the capacity to evaluate values, commitments, and ways of life. Once developed, however, this capacity cannot be confined to the political realm and its development leads to a form of autonomy which is exercised across wider aspects of the life of the person, including those which fall into the "non-public" domain.[57] Callan's view, for example, embodies a substantial account of the nature and demands of the attitudes, habits, and abilities required by public virtue.[58] In particular, Callan sees "public virtue" as requiring the development by students of Rawlsian "reasonableness" involving acceptance of the Rawlsian "burdens of judgment" (the sources of ineliminable rational disagreement)[59] thereby leading to the development of a grasp of the scope of reasonable diversity and the grounds of freedom of conscience and reasonable toleration. Callan therefore concludes that "...the development of the virtue of justice under pluralism implies the growth of autonomy to a notably sophisticated level."[60] Callan resists Galston's claim that civic tolerance of deep differences and civic deliberation are compatible with unswerving and unshakable beliefs and commitments relating to one's own way of life[61] and insists that a proper understanding of the Rawlsian "burdens of judgment" requires them to be actively rather than passively embraced by students and brought to bear by them on matters which extend beyond the political realm to wider conceptions of the good.

In this way, Rawls's attempt to restrict the intentional scope of education to political matters in the light of a "political" and not an "ethical" conception of liberalism comes to grief.[62] For Callan, a proper embrace of the "burdens of judgment", together with the development of other aspects of "civic virtue", brings a form of ethical liberalism and wide ranging Rawlsian "reasonableness" in "through the back door", together with educational influence that, contra Rawls, cannot be confined to the political domain and leave "non-public" commitments undisturbed.[63] Thus Callan sees education as requiring a sympathetic, critical, and serious engagement with beliefs, ways of life, and conceptions of the good which are different from, and at odds with, those which the child has inherited from his or her parents and background culture.[64] For Callan, therefore, "... the education we should want for our children would transform the character of the self in ways that have large consequences for how they will live beyond the realm of civic responsibility ..."[65] It is important to note, however, that Callan is careful not to characterize his position as advocating a full blown form of autonomy or "Socratic self-examination", but merely the kind of autonomy necessary to avoid a state he describes as "ethical servility."[66]

Kymlicka holds that autonomy in the sense of a capacity to engage in rational reflection upon, and possible revision of, our conceptions of the good life is not in itself one of the basic virtues of liberal citizenship, although it is closely related conceptually and developmentally to various civic virtues. However, although autonomy in this sense is not a direct aim of education for citizenship, it will nevertheless be indirectly promoted by it.[67]

Macedo, although making clear that his account of civic education is based on a form of "political liberalism",[68] places great emphasis upon its wide-ranging transformative implications. For Macedo, an excessive deference towards diversity and the "non-public" domain is unwarranted by liberalism properly understood[69] and by the need to shape diversity in support of the demands of liberal citizenship and a shared public life.[70] According to Macedo, this process requires "... a certain ordering of the soul"[71] and a shaping of our deepest moral commitments so that they are supportive of liberalism.[72] However, this is governed by a restraint which respects the non-public domain and a commitment to a form of autonomy.[73] Similarly, Feinberg insists that the common school is "... an instrument of individual and cultural change ... [which] ... alters the way people think, changes basic moral understandings, and alters commitments and loyalties"[74] yet within a framework of restraint similar to that invoked by

Macedo. The complexities of the burdens on the common school arising from positions such as these are illustrated by Macedo's observation that "Public schools intervene in the most private of
relationships, for the most sensitive of purposes"[75] and Feinberg's
recognition that the common school is seeking to bring about a standpoint which is "...neither natural nor easy to learn."[76]

Further along the continuum of burdens for the common school in
the direction of "heaviness" are various views which assign to the
common school a significant role in relation to the non-public
domain. Jeff Spinner-Halev claims that common schools should
become involved in various forms of cooperation with religious
schools and homeschoolers and should include, in a fair way in its
curriculum and life, religious students and religious perspectives, trying to accommodate where possible the special needs of religious students.[77] Spinner-Halev accepts that, in general, good citizens should
be autonomous in a robust fashion[78] and that common schools
should, in general, encourage the virtues of autonomy and liberal
autonomy and facilitate appropriate engagement with diversity of
ideas.[79] However, Spinner-Halev provides a defence of the legitimacy
of, and the need to secure the conditions for choosing, a conservative religious life in a "community of obedience" within the
principles of liberal citizenship and the context of a diverse autonomy-
supporting mainstream society. Two claims are central to Spinner-
Halev's argument here. The first is that: "Liberalism aims to enable
the life of individuality, but it does not insist that people choose this
life. The religious conservative may lead a life of minimal autonomy,
a life guided by one main choice. But this life is safely within the
confines of liberalism, as long as this life is chosen, people are given
a decent education, and are not coerced. Liberalism demands that
people choose the sort of life they want to lead, not that they live
lives couched in constant choices."[80] The second claim is that each
condition for autonomy (appropriate mental abilities, an adequate
range of options, and independence)[81] should not necessarily apply
to every community within a liberal society.[82] Spinner-Halev draws
attention to the fact that, despite appearances to the contrary, the
religious conservative in a liberal society is more likely to be
autonomous in significant ways than many people in the mainstream
of the society who lead unreflective lives, and that restrictive communities can aid autonomy.[83] Spinner-Halev's proposals relating to
the common school are designed to entice religiously conservative
parents to send their children to such schools as part of a pragmatic
and flexible attitude of inclusion and the maximization of goods.

The forms of cooperation which are envisaged, including allowing students from religious affiliated schools in common schools for some part of their curriculum and life,[84] encouraging the teaching of religion in the curriculum of the common school,[85] and providing for the accommodation in different ways of religious views and perspectives within the common school[86], give rise to a range of potentially complex questions and resultant burdens.

Heavy burdens arise for the common school from Kenneth Strike's argument that the demands of the "non-public" require greater recognition and salience in the common school than they receive in much contemporary discussion.[87] Strike points to several neglected aspects of "non-public" educational interests, including the significance of reasonable and coherent comprehensive (or partially comprehensive) theories of the good in the Rawlsian sense as resources for the practical reasoning of students in relation to good lives, together with difficulties in seeing such comprehensive theories as apt for presentation merely as objects of choice for students. To enable students to understand such theories and to achieve "competence" in them, claims Strike, it is necessary for the common school to acknowledge the significance of initiation and of "conversational fora" insulated to some extent (and, no doubt, pro tem) from criticism from other, rival, comprehensive doctrines.[88]

The sorts of concerns addressed by Strike are taken up in an extended way by John Tomasi, whose conception of the role of the common school specifies particularly heavy burdens for it.[89] Tomasi claims that civic education should be as much about the "ethical situatedness" of students as about their political liberation[90] and should attend to the *fit* between the public and the non-public views which students affirm. This includes not merely discerning how the students own non-public views support public views, but also how the public norms support their non-public views.[91] For Tomasi, civic education for political liberals "... must address issues that lie deep in the moral worlds of individual citizens."[92] This view stands in stark contrast to a view such as that of Feinberg, who argues that, if as a result of their education children develop a more questioning attitude, then "... the school has done its job regardless of the accommodations the student makes to her familiar environment."[93]

Lying behind Tomasi's educational claims is his view that political liberalism should pay more attention to the non-public virtues and personality traits which should characterize citizens in a liberal society and which are not related solely to questions of justice and legitimacy. For Tomasi, "... the normative domain of liberal theory construction is importantly wider than the domain of public, deliberative value"[94] in the context of a liberal polity based on political liberalism which is as welcoming as possible to "...the aims and self-understandings of all politically reasonable citizens."[95] Tomasi argues that attention needs to be paid to the ways in which citizens construct their lives as a whole in such a society as part of placing issues of human flourishing and well-being at the heart of citizenship.[96]

For Tomasi, citizenship requires the skilful exercise of non-public reason by diverse good souls[97] as part of making a success of a life "...lived on the interface of public and personal identity components"[98], and he therefore sees ethical development in a liberal society as requiring the finding by persons of personal meaning in life across this interface.[99] This is turn requires citizens to deploy "compass" concepts which are "thick" and "identity dependent" and which provide a set of bearings in the background culture of a society enabling citizens to discover what their political autonomy means for them in the light of their fuller conception of their good, and which guide them in the way in which they should exercise their rights.[100]

Tomasi therefore specifies a range of virtues of the liberal citizen which relate to the interface between the public and the non-public domains, and which concern such matters as the ability to achieve an appropriate equipoise between one's political standing and the fuller commitments characteristic of one's fuller non-public life. What this requires of citizens of different kinds varies. Citizens who are religious believers, for example, require dispositions to enable them to resist the commercial and secular nature of modern society.[101] In giving a role for common schools in the development of non-public virtues of this kind, a range of significant consequent burdens come readily into focus.

A range of other burdens arise for common schools from other sources, most notably concerns about the conditions required for the provision of equality of opportunity in its different aspects.[102] Space precludes a consideration of these further burdens at this point. It is time now to turn to a consideration of a range of the dilemmas arising from the burdens which have been identified.

5.4. Conceptions of Common Education and the Common School: Burdens and Dilemmas

The range of burdens which have been identified in relation to the common school generate a range of corresponding dilemmas.

"Dilemmas" rather than (say) "problems" best captures the intractability of what is at stake here and the lack of availability of clear unambiguous solutions. The need for common schools to achieve the trust and support of diverse citizens sharpens the force of the dilemmas which such schools face and the need to discover at least "best possible" resolutions of them.

The dilemmas are felt at a number of levels. At the theoretical level, they pose the sort of quandaries which philosophers of education (and educational theorists more generally) puzzle over and try to clarify and resolve. Educational policy makers are also confronted by some of the dilemmas in that they have implications for such matters as the structure of the educational system and the determination of policy on many relevant matters. However, many of the dilemmas are constituted by fine-grained subtleties which require a practical response at the level of the school and classroom by educational leaders and teachers *via* the exercise of a form of pedagogic *phronesis*.

For example, issues relating to the achievement by students of a proper understanding of the nature and scope of such notions as "respect" and "toleration," and to the fair and balanced conduct of controversial issues, can only be dealt with in detail at this level. The practical aspect to these dilemmas will be considered in due course.

In what follows I identify a range of dilemmas arising for common schools from the kinds of burdens identified in Section 5.3. For convenience, the discussion is divided into matters relating to the public domain, the non-public domain, and the interface between the two, although clearly this categorization is somewhat artificial.

Before proceeding, it should be noted that these burdens and dilemmas arise not only in relation to *what* is taught, but also to the *way* in which it is taught, to *whom* it is being taught, and the general *context* in which it is being taught. This general point reinforces the significance of the sort of pedagogic *phronesis* to which attention has been drawn.

Burdens and Dilemmas Relating to the Public Domain

Common schools based on a rationale which goes beyond the minimalistic yet which does not stipulate unequivocal value influence based on a form of ethical or comprehensive liberalism, bear the burden of ensuring that their students are not merely socialized into the public values but achieve a critical understanding of their nature and scope. As I have argued elsewhere[103], students in such schools must achieve a grasp of the salience and importance of public values for political purposes, but also come to appreciate the limitations of these values with respect to overall moral evaluation and to life considered more broadly. Such an awareness is implicit in the achievement of the sort of "moral bilingualism"[104] on the part of students which is often seen as a major aim of the common school, and which involves an appreciation by students that the language of public evaluation is a kind of "moral pidgin."[105] One of the major implications of this point is that, whilst accepting that public values have potentially transformative implications of the sort which Gutmann, Callan, Macedo, and Feinberg identify, and which cannot therefore leave values in the "non-public" domain just as they are, the common school must not underplay the role which reasonable moral views in the non-public domain play in overall moral evaluation and in human life more generally. Moral debate in the common school should not therefore be confined to public values and to the exclusive adoption of what Thompson and Gutmann call "moral economizing."[106] The common school should not promote a liberal view of life as a whole, nor a secular one.[107] David Archard's privileging of a liberal choice and consent based sexual morality as a basis for sex education in the common school seems to be problematic on precisely these grounds.[108] Nor should deep seated moral disagreement be smoothed away by (say) presenting homosexual practice as morally acceptable by invoking only public values as criteria for judgment and excluding, or failing to bring to bear adequately, reasonable non-public perspectives on the matters at stake.[109] Tomasi's insistence that political liberals must be concerned "... about ways of gently *protecting* diversity from the pursuit of legitimate public ends"[110] seems justified here, as does his concern that "... by teaching children the detached, rights-based forms of thinking central to public reason, liberal civic education unintentionally encourages those forms of thinking in all domains of reason, including ones where such ways of thinking are transformative beyond what the bare attainment of political autonomy requires."[111] Whilst common schools cannot aspire to influence which is wholly neutral across all aspects of diversity, or which is completely fair to every viewpoint,[112] Tomasi may have a point in arguing that because of unavoidable "unintended spillovers" within the classroom, lessons about public value must include an "internal corrective."[113]

A number of burdens arise in relation to achieving for students a proper understanding of notions in the public domain, such as "respect." The common school must encourage "civic respect" for

reasonable differences of view which goes beyond a grudging attitude of "live and let live." Callan captures something of the deeper,
more principled basis underlying civic respect in his invocation of
the Rawlsian "burdens of judgment" as part of his account of the
nature of public virtue.[114] However, the common school needs to
achieve a fine-grained understanding of "respect" on the part of its
students. "Civic" respect does not constitute the only form of respect
and students should be made aware that what is worthy of "civic"
respect is not necessarily worthy of respect considered from all
points of view. Further, care must be taken by the common school
not to convey the impression that giving "respect" requires the necessary approval of the choices which people make within the limits of
their rights. Macedo points out that such a requirement would be
self-defeating from a liberal point of view, since an important aspect
of liberal freedom is allowing people to disagree about important
matters.[115] It may, however, be difficult to avoid a relativistic implication being drawn from encouragement to give "respect." Spinner-
Halev identifies a central problem here when he asks: "How do we
teach mutual respect and appreciation for others while avoiding
teaching that each way of life is equally acceptable to the others?"[116]
What is required of common schools in these matters is the achievement by students of an understanding of significant aspects of moral
texture and complexity.[117]

One dilemma which arises from an attempt to encourage a fine-
grained understanding of "respect" on the part of students is that an
attempt to achieve "civic" respect for (say) a particular lifestyle may
be undermined by too much emphasis on critical evaluations of the
lifestyle to be found at the non-public level. For example, an attempt
to overcome blatant forms of ignorant prejudice against, and hatred
of, homosexual people may be undermined by the successful illumination of reasonable non-public perspectives which make a distinction
between homosexual orientation and practice and hold that the latter
is morally unacceptable.[118] From such perspectives, "civic respect" for
homosexual persons, important though it is, is importantly distinguishable from moral acceptance of homosexual practice. However,
some students, especially if they are ignorant and prejudiced in relation to homosexual persons, may not find such distinctions easy to
grasp and may see them as lending support to their ignorant and prejudiced civic attitudes. For example, the notion of "homophobia" is
often invoked in the process of establishing civic respect for homosexual persons. However, an illumination of moral texture and complexity is likely to problematize "homophobia", especially uses of the

term which imply that all moral criticism of homosexual practice is *ipso facto* homophobic. Gary Colwell, for example, argues that the term "homophobia" is part of a "...rhetorical tactic that has been used with increasing success to prevent the moral discussion of the rightness or wrongness of homosexual practice from ever taking place."[119] It is, in his view, a "fending-off mechanism"[120] which serves to preempt necessary moral debate in a democracy. Such points, legitimate as they may be within the framework of political liberalism, may provide some comfort to those resisting its civic demands. The dilemma of the relative prioritization of "public" and "non-public" perspectives also arises in this particular example in judging the appropriate educational response to students who are themselves homosexual. A similar kind of dilemma arises in other aspects of sex education, where the need to protect health and safety may be in conflict with illumination of the fact that, from some non-public perspectives, many "safe-sex" practices are immoral.

However, the achievement of "moral bilingualism", and the fine grained (and potentially conflicting) forms of respect and evaluation which it embodies, is an important consequence of taking seriously the claim that we are confronted by serious value conflicts, as distinct from mere differences of view, in a pluralist multicultural liberal democratic society. The sorts of dilemmas to which attention has been drawn are intensified by a realization of the important point that there is no escaping forms of "moral distress" in serious dialogue about value diversity.[121] Callan sees such distress as involving "...a cluster of emotions that may attend our response to words or actions of others or our own that we see as morally repellent,"[122] a "discriminating susceptibility" to which he sees as a fundamental aspect of virtue and of moral education in a pluralist multicultural liberal democratic society. In such a society we encounter strangers as well as friends.[123]

Another aspect of the "public" dimension of conceptions of common education involves the concept of autonomy. Macedo indicates the centrality of the notion of personal autonomy to such conceptions in his observation that the common school and its associated educational ideals is based in part on "distrust" of particular groups regarding the extent to which they can and will promote autonomy.[124] A crucial issue, however, is how autonomy is to be properly interpreted.[125] Parekh is right to insist that autonomy "...is difficult to define and impossible to measure or demonstrate"[126] and to draw attention to the role of culture in structuring in a particular way a person's understanding of, and capacity for, autonomy.[127] Dilemmas arise for the common school in the determination of the nature and extent of the kind of autonomy which should be promoted, and the matters in relation to which autonomy is seen as appropriately exercised.

The complexities inherent in such dilemmas are captured in distinctions such as those between "autonomy" and "autarchy,"[128] and between "autonomy promoting" and "autonomy facilitating" education.[129] One ingredient in judgments here is the extent to which autonomy can be confidently expected to be developed outside the school.[130] The position which the common school takes with respect to these matters can be quite significant for the perceived fairness of the overall value influence which it exerts, and to whether, for example, it is promoting a form of ethical or comprehensive liberalism. It seems important for the common school to encourage reflection about the limits of an examined life.[131]

It is also important for the school to confront dilemmas inherent in the complex unifying and diversifying influence which it seeks to exert. In relation to public matters, the school seeks to achieve a strong substantial influence on the beliefs of students and their wider development as persons, whilst in relation to matters in the "non-public" domain, the school exerts a principled forbearance from influence. The school therefore faces dilemmas inherent in simultaneously trying to bring about, on the one hand, affirmation, and on the other, hesitation and problematization, in the experience of students.[132]

Further dilemmas arise from the fact that abstract philosophical principles alone cannot provide us with a precise uncontroversial answer to the question of which matters should be regarded as public and which as non-public in a particular liberal democratic society.[133] These matters require complex judgment and perhaps negotiation, with attention to the significance of "default" norms. There is room for considerable debate about matters of cultural salience in the common school, not least because the common school cannot be culturally neutral and must have a cultural content which selectively favors some beliefs, practices, and values in ways that go beyond what could be justified from a strictly neutral point of view.[134]

Another source of dilemmas arise in relation to the requirements of ensuring that common schools are communities in a significant sense.[135] The role of ethos and community is manifested in many of the educational tasks of the common school. With regard to ethos and community, one of the central difficulties concerns the extent to which, given its commitment to a principled forebearance from influence in significant matters, the common school can satisfy the demands of substantiveness and determinacy which are constitutive of the notions of ethos and community.

Burdens and Dilemmas Relating to the Non-public Domain

Conceptions of common education vary in the extent to which they require the common school to enter into the non-public domain. "Liberal silence"[136] with respect to this domain is highly problematic for a range of reasons, as is any attempt to exclude non-public perspectives from a discussion of moral issues.[137]

Acceptance of the burden of fairly illuminating aspects of the non-public domain for the purposes of understanding gives rise to a range of dilemmas. Many of these concern religion.[138] As noted earlier, both Spinner-Halev and Tomasi call for a form of teaching religion in common schools in the United States.[139] Such teaching has been adopted in common schools in England and Wales for many years. The form of education at stake here can be described as "education in religion and spirituality from the outside."[140] In this form of education, no one religious or spiritual tradition is given normative status. Issues of meaning, truth, and value relating to the religious and spiritual domains are seen primarily as matters for exploration, discussion, and critical assessment. Religious and spiritual belief, commitment, and practice on the part of individuals are neither presuppositions nor aims of the enterprise. What is being sought on the part of students are appropriate forms of understanding and autonomous judgment and response. For these reasons, education of this kind can be described as "from the outside" of particular religious and spiritual traditions.[141] Dilemmas relating to the fair illumination of diversity here include concerns about the appropriate kind of critical enquiry considered appropriate for the domain of religion[142] and the extent to which religious and spiritual understanding can be achieved independently of religious and spiritual practice and forms of life.[143] The danger of superficiality involved in any attempt to exhibit, however sympathetically and imaginatively, a range of religious and spiritual traditions "from the outside" for consideration has significant philosophical support. There is a danger, as Callan notes, of religious practices being "...celebrated as so many charming ornaments of ethnicity."[144] Further dangers include the possibility that students may be given the impression that relativism in its various forms is an appropriate (or inevitable) perspective to take toward the possibility and nature of "truth" in and across the religious and spiritual domains, that differing religions should be seen as apt for choice by individuals simply on criteria relating to individual appeal, that spirituality should be seen under a merely therapeutic aspect, that religion should be seen in reductionist or functionalist terms, and so forth.[145]

The need for the common school to take care in the view of these matters which it transmits to students is reflected in Macedo's observation that whilst political liberalism does not assert a "particular view of the whole truth", this does not mean that "there is no truth about these larger matters."[146] The pedagogic challenges involved in conveying the relevant distinctions are, however, extensive.

A number of similar difficulties arise in relation to the widely voiced perception that the school should, in relation to a contested moral issue, illuminate a range of alternative perspectives for consideration. To what extent can such an illumination really bring to life the different views at stake (given e.g. their housing in fuller moral traditions) and avoid giving the impression that the alternatives in question are "exhibits" to be viewed spectatorially or as *mere* alternatives under (say) a relativistic aspect which does not invite the need for, and possibility of, serious moral evaluation? On what grounds can the range of views at issue be selected? Although it is tempting to think it appropriate that an attempt be made to "represent" each of a range of views along a spectrum, this approach has its difficulties. Apart from the impossibility of representing *all* views, there is a need to ensure that the differing views are in dialogue with, and not merely juxtaposed against, each other in the interests of promoting a coherent debate and bringing about appropriate forms of understanding. Another problem which arises in relation to a strategy of "representation" is the phenomenon of diversity *within* (say) religious traditions. Which "representation" is to be seen as the correct or most balanced one? Dilemmas such as these are part of a larger range of concerns about what is involved in making a "deliberative arena" genuinely inclusive.[147]

In addition to dilemmas arising in relation to the fair illumination of diversity, the dilemmas arising from the phenomenon of moral distress which was alluded to in the last section should also be borne in mind.

A particularly interesting question relating to pluralism and multiculturalism concerns the degree of acceptance and tolerance that common schools can consistently extend to features of "minority" belief and culture which appear to infringe, or to be in significant tension with, a number of the values typically insisted upon as "common" or "public" (and therefore importantly non-negotiable).[148]

A useful resource in conceptualizing the range and nature of diversity in a liberal democratic society and the limits of toleration is Tomasi's categorization of four main types of adult citizens as types A–D, according to the extent to which the values of autonomy and individuality govern their lives.[149]

Burdens and Dilemmas Relating to the Interface of the Public and the Non-public Domains

Particularly significant burdens and dilemmas arise for the common school in relation to conceptions of common education which require the common school to engage significantly in the area of the interface of the public and non-public domains. Here there is space only to consider the views of Tomasi, which exemplify this kind of conception in a particularly striking way.

As we saw earlier, Tomasi rejects the view that the liberal virtues can be identified by "...making a list only of those virtues whose need happens to be common to all citizens."[150] For Tomasi, the good liberal citizen must possess additional virtues enabling her to construct her fuller life within the confines of justice by negotiating the interface of public and non-public normative structures. Tomasi holds that liberal civic education cannot be confined to fitting students for the role they will play as public persons in the light of public reason, but must extend to equipping them to lead their non-public lives in a rewarding way in the light of a relevant form of non-public reason.[151] Thus students must come to have an understanding of the *fit* between public reason and "...the more local, internal understandings of value particular to the various politically reasonable narrative traditions each citizen will inhabit",[152] thereby enabling them to consider the meaning of their rights within the context of their lives considered more fully. The interface of public and non-public norms are therefore at the heart of Tomasi's conception of civic education as concerned not merely with the political liberation of citizens, but also with their eventual "ethical situatedness."[153]

What are the implications of this view for the common school? At the outset it is important to note that Tomasi supplies a number of conditions to his educational proposals which reflect the location of his view within the framework of political liberalism. Thus, all students are to be prepared for "full political autonomy" and all school environments should include a mandatory and non-optional provision designed to ensure that its requirements are met. Further, the consideration by students of their non-public values and commitments is

situated within an awareness of this political autonomy and its constituent values and principles. Therefore "controlling" as distinct from
"compass" concepts are ruled out, as are beliefs (such as those held by
Tomasi's "D" citizens) which are incompatible with public reason and
civic virtue. Further, no one view in the non-public domain is to be
favored, or given normative status, in the common school.[154]

Within this framework, however, Tomasi calls not only for the
teaching of religion in common schools[155] but also for careful attention to the nuances and subtleties inherent in the discussion of controversial matters, an approach which he considers in relation to the
case of *Mozert v. Hawkins*.[156] Tomasi is sensitive to the existence of
"informal assimilative pressures" in large common schools[157] and
for the need to attempt to "level the playing field" within the domain
of the politically reasonable, however possible. For Tomasi, this
means "... allowing *all* reasonable reintegrative ideals a more equitable share of influence in classrooms and hallways and on athletic
fields"[158] thereby creating an educational environment which is
"ethically charged" in a more "open" and "even handed" way. The
activities which Tomasi mentions as arising from this perspective
include inviting parents into schools to speak of matters of work,
family, and religion, and allowing students to express their own non-
public views and perspectives[159] in significant contexts, including
school ceremonies, where this has not previously been seen as appropriate in the US public school. A central feature of Tomasi's
approach is that students should not be disrupted from the ethical
worldviews formed within their families beyond "... what an appreciation of their own nascent political autonomy requires..."[160]
Therefore, Tomasi holds that common schools must be "ethically
subservient" to children's (politically reasonable) parents in relation
to "reintegrative questions."[161]

Tomasi argues that the schools he has in mind are "... vibrant
places, full of the color, warmth, and variety found in the society
they are to serve."[162] Tomasi's position stands in need of further
interrogation and defence. Does the position assume, for example,
that students come to school with non-public "identities" which are
more fully and coherently formed than is in fact typically the case?
In the absence of a full consideration of Tomasi's position, however,
it is clear that the burdens arising from it for the common school are
extensive and highly complex,[163] and they give rise to many dilemmas.
The dilemmas which have been identified in the discussion so far are
intensified by the more wide ranging and less predicable salience of
non-public considerations in Tomasi's account of the role of

the common school. Whilst Tomasi invokes principles which restrict the expression of non-public views that are politically unreasonable, within the domain of politically reasonable non-public belief and commitment, dilemmas arise relating to the achievement of appropriate forms of coordination and control with respect to the presentation of views and the conditions needed for balanced overall value influence.[164] Dilemmas arise also from the role given to parents on Tomasi's view. How should this role be balanced against the need for respect to be given for the developing autonomy of the child? The logic of Tomasi's own position would seem to require that the school take an active part in the achievement by students of an understanding of the "fit" between their non-public commitments and public norms. However, this would seem to involve the school in a form of "diagnosis" of the beliefs and perspectives of individual students.[165] The dilemmas which arise here are extensive and include questions relating to the objectivity and fairness with which such "diagnoses" could be undertaken, the nature of the mandate which the school can be said to possess with respect to these matters, and the need to achieve forms of trust on the part of parents and society generally.

5.5. *Policy, Pedagogy, and Practical Judgment*

The role of the common school in addressing the sorts of complex dilemmas which have been indicated in the previous sections invite attention at the level of, and pose specific challenges to, educational policy, pedagogy, and practical judgment. Tomasi rightly insists that there is an important gap between abstract philosophical and political principles and their realization in particular practical contexts.[166] Central questions which arise here concern the way in which the subtleties and complexities inherent in the dilemmas which have been identified can best be addressed and eased, if not resolved.

At the level of general educational policy making it is important to note the limitations of the extent to which the sort of complex subtleties which have been identified can be embodied clearly and extensively in policy guidelines and documents capable of guiding schools and teachers in relation to the dilemmas in a detailed way. The best that can be hoped for here are statements of general principle.[167] An underlying question here is the extent to which a complex philosophical characterization of an educational principle can be made to "bite" upon educational practice.[168]

It is important to note that central to the resolution of many of the dilemmas which have been identified is a form of practical judgment on the part of educational leaders and teachers at school level. Callan accepts that reasonable disagreement about matters of timing and sensitivity in pedagogy in controversial matters is likely to be expected under pluralism[169] and this is a major area in relation to which practical judgment needs to be exercised, as are areas potentially inviting appropriate forms of accommodation and compromise.[170] Many of the dilemmas which have emerged in this discussion require resolution at the classroom level via a form of pedagogic *phronesis*. This kind of judgment is required by, and exercised in relation to, a myriad of questions about *inter alia* what fairness, balance, and objectivity require in the articulation of a particular controversial matter, when weight should be placed in a particular situation upon a civic norm at the expense of non-public considerations which might tend to undermine it, and when to pursue or not to pursue a particular line of argument, perspective, or objection at a particular time in the interests of (say) sensitivity to moral distress. As indicated earlier, the influence exerted by the common school extends far beyond teaching in the classroom to embrace teacher example and the ethos and community of the school. The burdens of the common school demand from teachers considerable qualities of attentiveness, skill, commitment, and understanding which are not sufficiently summed up in the notion of the "reflective teacher."[171]

What seems clear is that the teacher who can realize the educational mandate of the common school must be a *certain sort of person*, who possesses not merely an abstract understanding of the features of the conception of common education in play (though this is important), but can also exhibit the kind of pedagogic *phronesis* of the sort which has been referred to. The implications of this for teacher formation are extensive.

The ideal of the common school is a complex one which gives rise to a range of significant burdens and dilemmas. These burdens and dilemmas do not in themselves undermine the coherence and importance of the ideal or constitute insuperable obstacles to its realisation in practice. However it is important to note that a realization of the complex ideal of the common school requires considerable understanding, contextualized judgment, and professional skill on the part of teachers, amounting to a form of "pedagogic *phronesis*." The conditions required for the development of this capacity repay attention. After all, the task of clarifying and justifying the ideal of the common school is idle in the absence of clear reflection on some of the central conditions required for its realization.

NOTES

1. The extent to which such dilemmas are experienced at school level is, of course, dependent in part on the extent to which the dilemmas are resolved by convention or circumstance, or at a higher level within the educational system of which the school is a part.
2. B. Parekh, *Rethinking Multiculturalism: Cultural Diversity and Political Theory* (London: Macmillan, 2000), 343.
3. S. Macedo, *Diversity and Distrust: Civic Education in a Multicultural Democracy* (Cambridge: Harvard University Press, 2000), 39.
4. Callan, Eamonn, *Creating Citizens: Political Education and Liberal Democracy* (Oxford: Oxford University Press, 1997), 163–6.
5. Parekh defines "moral monism" as the view that "...only one way of life is fully human, true, or the best, and that all others are defective to the extent that they fall short of it", B. Parekh, *Rethinking Multiculturalism: Cultural Diversity and Political Theory*, 16.
6. For an Aristotelian perspective on public education, see R. R. Curren, *Aristotle on the Necessity of Public Education* (Lanham: Rowman and Littlefield Publishers, 2000).
7. See, for example, Callan, *Creating Citizens*; A. Gutmann, *Democratic Education* (Princeton: Princeton University Press,1987); W. Feinberg, *Common Schools/ Uncommon Identities: National Unity and Cultural Difference* (New Haven and London: Yale University Press, 1998); M. Levinson, *The Demands of Liberal Education* (Oxford: Oxford University Press, 1999); T. H. McLaughlin, "Liberalism, Education and the Common School", *Journal of Philosophy of Education*, 29(2) (1995), 239–55. Macedo, *Diversity and Distrust*; K. A. Strike, "On the Construction of Public Speech: Pluralism and Public Reason", *Educational Theory*, 44(1) (1994), 1–26. K. A. Strike, "Liberalism, Citizenship and the Private Interest in Schooling", *Studies in Philosophy and Education*, 17(4) (1998), 221–9; P. White, *Civic Virtues and Public Schooling: Educating Citizens for a Democratic Society* (New York: Teachers College Press, 1996).
8. Feinberg, *Common Schools/Uncommon Identities*, 2–3.
9. See, for example, the discussion of the compatibility of certain recent proposals for school reform in the United States with civic educational ideals in Macedo, *Diversity and Distrust*, ch. 11. On the limits of tolerance with respect to kinds of schooling within a liberal democratic perspective see also, for example, H. Brighouse, *School Choice and Social Justice* (Oxford: University Press, 2000); Callan, *Creating Citizens*, ch. 7; Levinson, *The Demands of Liberal Education*, ch. 5, section 2; R. C. Salomone, *Visions of Schooling: Conscience, Community and Common Education*, (New Haven: Yale University Press, 2000) ch. 8.
10. For an expansive account of such limits emphazing flexibility and inclusion see, for example, J. Spinner-Halev, *Surviving Diversity. Religion and Democratic Citizenship* (Baltimore: The Johns Hopkins University Press, 2000) 135–41. For arguments in support of pluralism in schooling in liberal democratic societies in which common schools are not given pride of place, see F. Schrag, "Diversity, Schooling and the Liberal State", *Studies in Philosophy and*

Education, 17(1) (1998), 29–46; E. J. Thiessen, *In Defence of Religious Schools and Colleges* (Montreal: McGill-Queen's University Press, 2001). See esp. ch. 13.

11. Of common schools, Macedo writes: "That the schools bring children from many backgrounds together in a common institution is the whole point" (*Diversity and Distrust*, 232). On the significance of this feature of common schools, see also Spinner-Halev, *Surviving Diversity*, 112–14. On general considerations supporting common schooling, see Callan, *Creating Citizens*, 174–8.

12. On the relationship between philosophical considerations and educational policy see T. H. McLaughlin, "Philosophy and Educational Policy: Possibilities, Tensions and Tasks", *Journal of Educational Policy*, 15(4) (2000), 441–57. On complexities concerning the relationship between conceptions of education and schooling arrangements, see Callan, *Creating Citizens*, ch. 7.

13. T. H. McLaughlin, "The Ethics of Separate Schools" in M. Leicester and M. J. Taylor (eds), *Ethics, Ethnicity and Education* (London: Kogan Page, 1992). On these matters, see also Callan, *Creating Citizens*, ch. 7; E. Callan, "Discrimination and Religious Schooling" in W. Kymlicka and W. Norman (eds), *Citizenship in Diverse Societies* (Oxford: University Press, 2000); Spinner-Halev, *Surviving Diversity*, 115–23; E. J. Thiessen, *Teaching for Commitment: Liberal Education, Indoctrination and Christian Nurture* (Montreal: McGill-Queen's University Press, 1993); Thiessen (2001). For a discussion of relevant considerations, see Macedo, *Diversity and Distrust*, 234–6, 260–8. For arguments against religious schools see, for example, J. G. Dwyer, *Religious Schools v Children's Rights* (Ithaca: Cornell University Press, 1998).

14. On the history of the "public school" in the United States see, for example, Macedo, *Diversity and Distrust*. chs 2–4. On these matters, see also Salomone, *Visions of Schooling*, chs 1–6. For an argument against the claim that state funding to religiously affiliated schools violates US constitutional principles, see Spinner-Halev, *Surviving Diversity*, 120–3.

15. On this history see, for example, P. Chadwick, *Shifting Alliances: Church and State in English Education* (London: Cassell, 1997).

16. On proposals to extend the number of faith based schools in the publicly funded schooling sector in England and Wales see, for example, Archbishops Council, *The Way Ahead: Church of England Schools in the New Millennium* (London: Church House Publishing, 2001).

17. A significant recent initiative in this respect was the consultation process on educational values launched by the former Schools Curriculum and Assessment Authority, which involved the establishment of the National Forum for Values in Education and the Community and culminated in the statement of values included in the new National Curriculum (see School Curriculum and Assessment Authority, *National Forum for Values in Education and the Community: Consultation on Values in Education and the Community* (London: SCAA, 1996), and QCA Department for Education and Employment and Qualifications and Curriculum Authority, *The National Curriculum Handbook for Secondary Teachers in England: Key Stages 3 and 4* (London: DfEE, 1999), 195–7; M. Talbot and N. Tate "Shared Values in a Pluralist Society?" in R. Smith and P. Standish (eds), *Teaching Right and Wrong: Moral Education in the Balance* (Stoke on Trent: Trentham Books, 1997). For criticisms of this initiative see, for example, J. Beck, *Morality and Citizenship in Education* (London: Cassell, 1998), esp. 85–95; G. Haydon, *Values, Virtues and Violence: Education and the Public Understanding of Morality* (Oxford: Blackwell, 1999), esp. chs 3, 13 and 14; R. Smith, "Judgement Day" in

R. Smith and P. Standish (eds), *Teaching Right and Wrong: Moral Education in the Balance* (Stoke on Trent: Trentham Books, 1997); P. Standish, "Fabulously Absolute" in R. Smith and P. Standish (eds), *Teaching Right and Wrong: Moral Education in the Balance* (Stoke on Trent: Trentham Books, 1997); J. White, "Three Proposals and a Rejection" in R. Smith and P. Standish (eds), *Teaching Right and Wrong: Moral Education in the Balance* (Stoke on Trent: Trentham Books, 1997). Most recently, an exercise has been conducted by the Qualifications and Curriculum Authority to determine the overall aims of the school curriculum for the new millennium. This exercise, which has involved the participation of philosophers (see R. Aldrich and J. White, *The National Curriculum Beyond 2000: The QCA and the aims of education* (London, Institute of Education: University of London, 1998)) has yielded for the first time a set of published aims for the National Curriculum (Department for Education and Employment and Qualifications and Curriculum Authority, (1999), 195–7). For concerns about the adequacy of the statement of aims and the extent to which the aims are being brought to bear on the curriculum itself see S. Bramall and J. White, *Will the New National Curriculum Live up to its Aims?* (Impact No. 6, Philosophy of Education Society of Great Britain, 2000).

18. For recent developments in relation to these matters, see Qualifications and Curriculum Authority, *Education for Citizenship and the Teaching of Democracy in Schools: Final Report of the Advisory Group on Citizenship* (London: QCA, 1998), sect. 10; and Qualifications and Curriculum Authority, *Citizenship at Key Stages 3 and 4: Initial Guidance for Schools* (London: QCA, 2000), Appendix 2. For a philosophical appraisal of recent policy developments relating to citizenship education in England, see T. H. McLaughlin, "Citizenship Education in England: The Crick Report and Beyond", *Journal of Philosophy of Education*, 34(4) (2000), 541–70.

19. Levinson, *The Demands of Liberal Education*, 109, see also ch. 4; and Brighouse, *School Choice and Social Justice*, ch. 8.

20. "Swann Report", Great Britain Parliament House Of Commons. *Education for All*, The Report of the Committee of Inquiry into the Education of Children from Ethnic Minority Groups, cmnd 9453 (London: Her Majesty's Stationery Office, 1985).

21. Ibid., ch. 1, para 6.

22. Ibid., ch. 1, para 4.

23. Ibid., ch. 1, para 6.

24. Ibid., ch. 1, para 3.

25. Ibid., ch. 1, para 4.

26. Ibid., ch. 1, para 2. Thus the framework is seen as generating an obligation for government to ensure "... equal treatment and protection by the law for members of all groups, together with equality of access to education and employment, equal freedom and opportunity to participate fully in social and political life... equal freedom of cultural expression and equal freedom of conscience for all" (Ibid., ch. 1, para 4).

27. Ibid.

28. Ibid.

29. Ibid.

30. Ibid. The report therefore insists that a good education "... must reflect the diversity of British society and ... the contemporary world" (Ibid., ch. 6, para 2.1); and the curriculum for all pupils must be "... permeated by a genuinely pluralist perspective which should inform and influence both the selection of content and the teaching materials used" (Ibid. ch. 6, para 3.1).

150   Terence H. McLaughlin

31. Ibid., ch. 6, para 1.4.
32. Ibid., ch. 6, para 2.5.
33. T. H. McLaughlin, "Liberalism, Education and the Common School."
34. Swann, ch. 6, para 2.7.
35. Ibid., ch. 6, para 3; chs 7 and 8.
36. Ibid., ch. 6 paras 3.7–3.12.
37. Ibid., ch. 2; ch. 6, para 2.3.
38. Ibid., ch. 8, II, para 2.11.
39. Ibid., ch. 8, II. It should be noted that the report allows for separate schools on grounds of gender. On this, see Ibid., chs 8, 11, para 2.15. For the minority report on separate schools, see Ibid., 515.
40. Ibid., ch. 8, I, para 2.8.
41. Ibid., ch. 8, I, para 2.11.
42. Ibid., ch. 8, I, para 5.3.
43. Ibid., ch. 8, II.
44. A. Macintyre, "How to Seem Virtuous Without Actually Being So" in J. M. Halstead and T. H. McLaughlin (eds), *Education in Morality* (London: Routledge, 1999).
45. The conclusions of the Swann Report did not have a decisive impact on educational policy and practice in England and Wales. For a recent report, see Commission On The Future Of Multi-Ethnic Britain, *The Future of Multi-Ethnic Britain* (The Parekh Report, London: Profile Books, 2000).
46. On such matters see, for example, Callan (1997), ch. 2; A. Gutmann, "Civic Education and Social Diversity", *Ethics*, 105 (1995), 557–79.
47. Callan, *Creating Citizens*, 169–71.
48. T. H. McLaughlin, "Citizenship, Diversity and Education: A Philosophical Perspective", *Journal of Moral Education*, 21(3) (1992), 235–50.
49. For criticisms of such conceptions, see Callan, *Creating Citizens*, 171–4.
50. W. A. Galston, *Liberal Purposes: Goods, Virtues, and Diversity in the Liberal State* (Cambridge: University Press, 1991), ch. 11.
51. Ibid., 242–4.
52. Ibid., 251–5.
53. Ibid., 253. For criticism of Galston's claim that children will become autonomous through other influences see Callan, *Creating Citizens*, 133.
54. For criticisms of Galston see, for example, Callan, *Creating Citizens*, ch. 5; Spinner-Halev, *Surviving Diversity*, 103–4; Brighouse, *School Choice and Social Justice*, ch. 5; Gutmann, "Civic Education and Social Diversity." For a defense of Galston's version of democratic liberalism, but a claim that he seriously underestimates the incompatibility of "deep" diversity with public schooling, see Schrag, "Diversity and Schooling..."
55. Callan describes an education derived from any form of comprehensive liberalism as "...wide in scope, transforming the selves of future citizens in ways that push beyond the sphere of political obligation as they learn to live according to the prescribed comprehensive values...(and requiring)...a pedagogy pitted against all sources of diversity at odds with those values" (*Creating Citizens*, 16).
56. Macedo, *Diversity and Distrust*, 139–45.
57. Gutmann, *Democratic Education*; Callan, *Creating Citizens*.
58. Of these attitudes, habits, and abilities, Callan writes: "These include a lively interest in the question of what life is truly and not just seemingly good, as well as a willingness both to share one's own answer with others and to heed the many opposing answers they might give; an active commitment to the good of the polity, as well as confidence and competence in judgment regarding how

that good should be advanced; a respect for fellow citizens and a sense of common fate with them that goes beyond the tribalisms of ethnicity and religion and is yet alive to the significance these will have in many people's lives" (*Creating Citizens*, 3).
59. J. Rawls, *Political Liberalism* (New York: Columbia University Press, 1993), 54–8.
60. Callan, *Creating Citizens*, 68. For a discussion of the scope of the justification of autonomy required by Callan's overall thesis, see chs. 3 and 6.
61. Galston, *Liberal Purposes*, 253. See especially Callan, *Creating Citizens*, ch. 5.
62. Gutmann calls into question whether political liberalism is more hospitable to social diversity via civic education than comprehensive liberalism. See Gutmann, "Civic Education and Social Diversity."
63. Callan, *Creating Citizens*, ch. 2.
64. Callan, *Creating Citizens*, 133. Callan writes, "...the relevant engagement must be such that the beliefs and values by which others live are entertained not merely as sources of meaning in *their lives*; they are instead addressed as potential elements within the conceptions of the good and the right one will create for oneself as an adult...to understand ethical diversity in the educationally relevant sense presupposes some experience of entering imaginatively into ways of life that are strange, even repugnant, and some developed ability to respond to them with interpretive charity, even though the sympathy this involves must complement the tough-mindedness of responsible criticism" (Callan, *Creating Citizens*, 133). For criticism of Callan's "moral psychology", see Spinner-Halev, *Surviving Diversity*, 99–102, 132–3.
65. Callan, *Creating Citizens*, 51.
66. Ibid., ch. 6.
67. W. Kymlicka, "Education for Citizenship", in J. M. Halstead and T. H. McLaughlin (eds), *Education in Morality* (London: Routledge, 1999), 90–3. Here Kymlicka holds that the promotion of autonomy may be justifiable as part of a person's broader well-being and education.
68. Macedo, *Diversity and Distrust*. chs 7 and 9. On forms of political liberalism see, for example, Ibid., chs 7–9; J. Tomasi, *Liberalism Beyond Justice: Citizens, Society and the Boundaries of Political Theory* (Princeton and Oxford: Princeton University Press, 2001), ch. 1; Callan, *Creating Citizens*, ch. 2. On the notion of "reasonable disagreement", see, for example, A. Gutmann and D. Thompson, *Democracy and Disagreement* (Cambridge: Harvard University Press, 1996). ch. 1.
69. Macedo rejects a conception of liberalism as "...a kind of anemic non-judgmentalism, a position that is morally uninspired and uninspiring, incapable of pressing even its own core values in the face of disagreement" (*Diversity and Distrust*, 8).
70. Ibid., e.g. chs 1 and 9.
71. Ibid., 30.
72. Ibid., 164.
73. Ibid., 236–40. On the relationship between the positions of Macedo and Callan on matters such as the Rawlsian "burdens of judgment", see S. Macedo, "Liberal Civic Education and its Limits: A Comment on Eamonn Callan", *Canadian Journal of Education*, 20(3) (1995).
74. Feinberg, *Common Schools/Uncommon Identities*, 56–7.
75. Macedo, *Diversity and Distrust*, 145.
76. Feinberg, *Common Schools/Uncommon Identities*, 239.
77. Spinner-Halev, *Surviving Diversity*, 110.

78. On Spinner-Halev's discussion of citizenship in relation to his overall theory, see Spinner-Halev, *Surviving Diversity*, ch. 4.

79. Ibid., 112–14. Despite his defense of religiously affiliated schools, Spinner-Halev argues that the liberal state should try to "entice" parents to send their children to common schools by encouraging cooperation between public and private schools (p. 125).

80. Ibid., 54.

81. On these conditions, see Ibid., 32.

82. For Spinner-Halev's arguments relating to the inadequacy of liberal theory with respect to the recognition of points such as these, see Ibid., esp chs 2 and 3.

83. On the elements of autonomy involved in living a conservative religious life in liberal societies and the respects in which restrictive communities can aid autonomy, see Ibid., chs 2 and 3, respectively.

84. Ibid., 125–8.

85. Ibid., 128–35.

86. Ibid., 135–41.

87. Strike, "Liberalism, Citizenship and the Private Interest in Schooling."

88. For a discussion of Strike's arguments relating to these matters, see T. H. McLaughlin, "Kenneth Strike on 'Liberalism, Citizenship and the Private Interest in Schooling'," *Studies in Philosophy and Education*, 17(4) (1998), 231–41.

89. Tomasi, *Liberalism Beyond Justice*.

90. Ibid., 95.

91. Ibid., 86.

92. Ibid., 88.

93. Feinberg, *Common Schools/Uncommon Identities*, 241.

94. Ibid., xvi.

95. Ibid., 74.

96. Tomasi refers to the nature of the person postulated by political liberalism as "hybridized" in virtue of the presence of differentiated public and non-public normative components (*Liberalism Beyond Justice*, 36).

97. Ibid., 71.

98. Ibid., 75.

99. Ibid., 84.

100. Ibid., ch. 3.

101. Ibid., 77.

102. On the notion of equality in relation to education see, for example, Brighouse, *School Choice and Social Justice*, ch. 61.

103. McLaughlin, "Liberalism, Education and the Common School", 248–50.

104. K. A. Strike, "Ethical Discourse and Pluralism" in K. A. Strike and P. Lance Ternasky (eds), *Ethics for Professionals in Education: Perspectives for Preparation and Practice* (New York: Teachers College Press, 1993).

105. Strike, "On the Construction of Public Speech", 19.

106. Spinner-Halev, *Surviving Diversity*, 155.

107. For concerns about common schools along these lines see, for example, Thiessen, *Teaching for Commitment*, ch. 13.

108. D. Archard, "How Should We Teach Sex?" *Journal of Philosophy of Education*, 32(3) (1998), 437–49. D. Archard, *Sex Education. Impact No 7* (Philosophy of Education Society of Great Britain, 2000); cf. T. H. McLaughlin, "The Moral Basis of Sex Education: Principles and Controversies." *Sex Education* (forthcoming).

109. On this matter see, for example, P. White, "Parents' Rights, Homosexuality and Education", *British Journal of Educational Studies*, 39(4) (1991),

398–408. McLaughlin, "Liberalism, Education and the Common School." 248–50; Callan, "Discrimination and Religious Schooling." 58–63; J. M. Halstead and K. Lewicka "Should Homosexuality be Taught as an Acceptable Alternative Lifestyle? A Muslim Perspective", *Cambridge Journal of Education*, 28(1) (1998), 49–64. J. Beck, "Should Homosexuality be Taught as an Acceptable Alternative Lifestyle? A Muslim Perspective: A Reply to Halstead and Lewicka", *Cambridge Journal of Education*, 29(1) (1999), 121–30. J. M. Halstead, "Teaching about Homosexuality: A Response to John Beck", *Cambridge Journal of Education*, 29(1) (1999), 131–6.

110. Tomasi, *Liberalism Beyond Justice*, 107.
111. Ibid., 90.
112. Macedo, *Diversity and Distrust*, ch. 8. Parekh observes that, in a liberal environment "... the very awareness of other traditions alerts each to its own contingency and specificity, and subtly alters the manner in which its members define and relate to it" (Parekh, *Rethinking Multiculturalism*, 220). For an argument against the value and possibility of "world view neutrality" in the common school, see S. Sandsmark, *Is World View Neutral Education Possible and Desirable? A Christian Response to Liberal Arguments* (Carlisle: Paternoster Press, 2000).
113. Ibid., 126.
114. Callan insists that: "To give the respect due to ethical viewpoints in deep conflict with our own, we must learn to enter them imaginatively and to understand that much of the pluralism that permeates our social world is a consequence not of evil or folly but of the inherent limits of human reason" (*Creating Citizens*, 43).
115. Macedo, *Diversity and Distrust*, 223. Feinberg argues that students must learn to respect members of other groups without necessarily understanding them or agreeing with what they say (*Common Schools/Uncommon Identities*, 212). See also chs 5–7.
116. Spinner-Halev, *Surviving Diversity*, 133.
117. On the difficulty that acceptance of liberal political values such as mutual respect might come at the price of an enfeebled acceptance of the fuller ethical values held by citizens, see E. Callan, "Liberal Virtue and Moral Enfeeblement" in D. Carr and J. Steutel (eds), *Virtue Ethics and Moral Education* (London: Routledge, 1999).
118. For example, in a recent statement of the late Cardinal Hume on the teaching of the Catholic Church on homosexual people, it is insisted that all persons, including those of homosexual orientation, should be treated with dignity, respect, and fairness, that the oppression and contempt which homosexual people have suffered should be combated by the church, and that homophobia and violence against homosexuals in speech and action should be condemned (B. Hume, "A Note on the Teaching of the Catholic Church Concerning Homosexual People", *Briefing*, 16 (Mar. 1995), 3–5. paras 12, 14, 15). Further, the statement acknowledges that civil legislation relating to the elimination of injustice against homosexual people requires practical judgment and the assessment of social consequences in relation to which Catholics may reach diverse conclusions (Ibid., para 13). These remarks indicate a form of valuing and respect for homosexuality. However, the value and respect which is accorded to homosexuality is restricted in an important way. Drawing a distinction between homosexual orientation and homosexual acts (Ibid., paras 6, 7), the statement reiterates church teaching on the immorality of the latter. Thus, whilst it is suggested that it might be appropriate to acknowledge legal rights of some kind to engage in homosexual acts, it is insisted that " ... there can be

no moral right to homosexual acts, even though they are no longer held to be criminal in many secular legal systems" (Ibid., para 5 cf. para 12).

119. G. Colwell, "Turning the Tables with 'Homophobia' ", *Journal of Applied Philosophy*, 16(3) (1999), 207–22.

120. Ibid.

121. Callan, *Creating Citizens*, ch. 8.

122. Ibid., 200.

123. On the complexity of the ethical difficulties, attitudes, and virtues demanded by liberalism, including the role that certain forms of hypocrisy play in sustaining liberal democratic society, see J. Shklar, *Ordinary Vices* (Cambridge: Belknap Press of Harvard University Press, 1984).

124. Macedo, *Diversity and Distrust*, 240.

125. An indication of Macedo's conception of autonomy is given in his reaction to the case of the Amish with respect to exemption from public education: "All children should have an education that provides them with the ability to make *informed* and *independent* decisions about how they want to lead their lives in our modern world. Liberal freedom to choose is the birthright of every child" (Ibid., 207).

126. Parekh, *Rethinking Multiculturalism*, 253.

127. In criticizing the notion of a "transcultural" and "culturally untainted" "power of autonomy", Parekh notes how culture shapes people in many ways. As a result, he argues, a person's capacity for autonomy " ... is structured in a particular way, functions within flexible but determinate limits, and defines and assesses options in certain ways" (Ibid., 110). Parekh charges contemporary liberal responses to diversity with absolutizing liberalism by equating "non-liberal" with "illiberal" and by failing to distinguish between a universal and a liberal moral minimum in relation to human values (ch. 3). Whilst supporting diversity, Parekh argues that autonomy needs to be given a more nuanced role in the values of a pluralist society (see esp chs 7 and 10).

128. McLaughlin, "The Ethics of Separate Schools", 126–7.

129. Brighouse, *School Choice and Social Justice*, chs 4 and 5.

130. On this matter see, for example, Schrag, "Diversity and Schooling in the Liberal State"; Spinner-Halev, *Surviving Diversity*.

131. Macedo, *Diversity and Distrust*, 245–53.

132. Galston notes that one danger which needs to be guarded against is not that children will believe in something too deeply, but that they will believe in nothing very deeply at all (Galston, *Liberal Purposes*, 255). For critical comment on this claim, see Callan, *Creating Citizens*, 133. On the complex kinds of education in character and virtue required in the common school, see T. H. McLaughlin and J. M. Halstead "Education in Character and Virtue" in J. M. Halstead and T. H. McLaughlin (eds), *Education in Morality* (London: Routledge, 1999).

133. McLaughlin, "Liberalism, Education and the Common School." 245–8.

134. On these matters, see also Parekh, *Rethinking Multiculturalism*, 257–63. Tomasi notes that school classrooms and the wider school community are "ethically charged" in ways that " ... extend far beyond what is politically relevant or required" (*Liberalism Beyond Justice*, 98) and Spinner-Halev draws attention to the limits of the extent to which the common school can avoid transmitting the dominant culture as a default norm (*Surviving Diversity*, 116–7).

135. K. A. Strike, "Schools as Communities: Four Metaphors, Three Models and a Dilemma or Two", *Journal of Philosophy of Education*, 34(4) (2000), 617–42.

136. Strike, "Ethical Discourse and Pluralism", 178.

137. McLaughlin, "Liberalism, Education and the Common School", 250–1. On the difficulty in separating out religious from other considerations in relation to many issues see, for example, Spinner-Halev, *Surviving Diversity*, ch. 6.

138. On the role of religion in liberal societies see, for example, Ibid., esp ch. 8; see also N. L. Rosenblum (ed.), *Obligations of Citizenship and Demands of Faith: Religious Accommodation in Pluralist Democracies* (Princeton: University Press, 2000).

139. Spinner-Halev, *Surviving Diversity*, 128–30; Tomasi, *Liberalism Beyond Justice*, 89–90.

140. H. Alexander and T. H. McLaughlin, "Education in Religion and Spirituality" in N. Blake, P. Smeyers, R. Smith and P. Standish (eds), *The Blackwell Guide to the Philosophy of Education* (Oxford: Blackwell, 2003).

141. It is important to insist, however, that education of this form cannot remain "on the outside" in the sense that no attempt is made to understand the religious and spiritual domains from the insider's point of view. Such attempts are necessary if religious and spiritual traditions and ideas are to be properly illuminated for the purposes of understanding and assessment.

142. On the relationship between religious and secular forms of reasoning, see R. Audi, *Religious Commitment and Secular Reason* (Cambridge: University Press, 2000).

143. On this matter see, for example, T. H. McLaughlin, "Wittgenstein, Education and Religion" in P. Smeyers, and J. Marshall (eds), *Philosophy and Education: Accepting Wittgenstein's Challenge* (Dordrecht: Kluwer Academic Publishers, 1995).

144. Callan, "Discrimination and Religious Schooling." 57.

145. Spinner-Halev insists that while the common school may teach about different beliefs relating to salvation they should not teach that each answer is equally true (*Surviving Diversity*, 128–35).

146. Macedo, *Diversity and Distrust*, 197.

147. On this matter see, for example, Callan, "Discrimination and Religious Schooling."

148. On the attitude which liberal societies should take towards ways of life which are culturally self-contained in different ways, see, for example, Parekh, *Rethinking Multiculturalism*, 170–2.

149. Tomasi, *Liberalism Beyond Justice*, ch. 2. According to Tomasi, A-people give the values of autonomy and individuality a governing role in their lives, affirming ethical or comprehensive liberalism as a world view in their public and non-public lives, and rejecting the authoritativeness of any ethical doctrine based on authority. B-people (which Tomasi takes to be the vast majority of citizens) affirm liberal principles such as freedom and equality in their public lives, but do not affirm general or comprehensive doctrines in their non-public lives, which are characterized by a degree of muddle and variability. C-people affirm liberal principles in their public lives, but some general ethical doctrine based on religious authority in their non-public lives. D-citizens affirm a comprehensive doctrine in both their public and non-public lives and reject liberal principles and public reason, seeking (e.g.) to impose their distinctive beliefs on others politically.

150. Ibid., 78.

151. Ibid., 86–7.

152. Ibid., 87.

153. Ibid., 95. For Tomasi, the central challenge for political liberals in relation to education is " ... to devise reintegrative forms of schooling that prepare students to live lives of integrity affirming their own (diverse and incompatible)

doctrines as true, even once recognizing a common moral foundation for the political standing of diverse others." (Ibid., 96)

154. On all these matters, see Ibid., ch. 5.
155. Ibid., 89–90.
156. Ibid., 91–5. For discussion of *Mozert* v. *Hawkins* see, for example, S. Burtt, "Religious Parents, Secular Schools: A Liberal Defense of an Illiberal Institution." *Review of Politics*, 56 (1994) 51–70; Callan, (1997), ch. 6; Macedo, *Diversity and Distrust*. chs 6–8; Spinner-Halev, *Surviving Diversity*, ch. 5.
157. Ibid., 98.
158. Tomasi, *Liberalism Beyond Justice*, 99.
159. Ibid., 27–8.
160. Ibid., 98.
161. Ibid., 97. On these matters, see also S. Burtt, "In Defense of *Yoder*: Parental Authority and the Public Schools" in I. Shapiro and R. Hardin (eds), *Political Order: Nomos XXXVIII* (New York: New York University Press, 1996); Burtt, "Religious Parents, Secular Schools."
162. Tomasi, *Liberalism Beyond Justice*, 126.
163. Tomasi sums up the task which each student should take up as part of the liberal social world in the following way: "Become just, but do so in a way that makes sense of the importance that your own particular history up to now has to you. The great good of social justice is not the only good recognizable from a political liberal perspective. For you, citizenship involves not only the performance of public duties but the way you build your life. We encourage you to build that life, not *in spite of* the ethical background culture of your society, but *through your use of* that background culture and the distinctive forms of communication made available there. We must prepare each of you to excel within the particular kind of social world you are now entering—a world where human lives must be built across the interface of public and non-public normative structures. It is as political liberals, therefore, that we respectfully play our part in preparing you all to be good people. For it is in your capacity to live well that the liberal settlement finds its mortal point" (Ibid., 99–100).
164. Macedo acknowledges the historical reality of "... the pretenses and hypocrisy of claims to public school neutrality with respect to religion, and... morality" (*Diversity and Distrust*, 42).
165. For a similar perspective, see B. Ackerman, *Social Justice in the Liberal State* (New Haven: Yale University Press, 1980), ch. 5.
166. Tomasi, *Liberalism Beyond Justice*, 105–7.
167. On guidance given to teachers in England and Wales in relation to the teaching of controversial issues in citizenship education, see Qualifications and Curriculum Authority, (1998), sec. 10; also Qualifications and Curriculum Authority, (2000), Appendix 2.
168. On these matters see, for example, McLaughlin, "Philosophy and Educational Policy."
169. Callan, *Creating Citizens*, 158–9.
170. Spinner-Halev, *Surviving Diversity*, 135–41.
171. T. H. McLaughlin, "Beyond the Reflective Teacher." *Educational Philosophy and Theory*, 31(1) (1999), 9–25.

CHAPTER 6

Should We Teach Patriotic History?

HARRY BRIGHOUSE

Cosmopolitan liberals often deny the propriety of public education reinforcing in children the particularistic ties they learn in their families and communities. The role of public education should be to expand children's horizons, to teach them that they are part of a larger moral community than that in which they were raised, and that their life options should not be limited to those endorsed by their parents and communities. Thus the cosmopolitan aims both to liberate children from their roots, and to induce proper moral concern with the rest of humanity.

But cosmopolitans also often assume, or in some cases argue, that this project justifies encouraging patriotic identification with the liberal democratic state. This state, after all, embodies universalistic values, and identification with it is liable to distance people appropriately from their more parochial concerns. Arthur Schlesinger Jr's much discussed *The Disuniting of America*, for example, has two central themes. First he criticises multiculturalists who want to use "history as a weapon" to sustain or even create separate ethnic identities in America. Consciously echoing Edward Said, he says that "History as a weapon is an abuse of history. The high purpose of history is not the presentation of self nor the vindication of identity, but the recognition of complexity and the search for knowledge"[1] and later that "history as therapy means the corruption of history as history . . . honest history calls for the unexpurgated record."[2] On the other hand he criticises the same multiculturalists for promoting a history and pedagogy which may lead to the "decomposition of America": the breaking of the bonds of identity which unite an ethnically and culturally diverse population in loyalty to a single nation state: "Above all, history can give a sense of national identity. We do not have to believe that our values are absolutely better than the next fellow's or the next country's, but we have no doubt they are better for us, reared as we are—and are worth living by and dying for. For our values are not matters of whim or happenstance. History has given them to us."[3]

In this chapter I cast doubt on the desirability of using schooling to encourage loyalty to, or identification with, the nation state, and criticize the arguments for it. I want to address the particular question of whether it is permissible for patriotism to be taught to children in schools; and whether, if it should, the teaching of history is the right vehicle for teaching patriotism. I argue that there are good reasons for being deeply suspicious of teaching patriotism in schools: there are additional reasons for thinking that even if it should be taught, history is a particularly inappropriate discipline with which to convey it.

This goes against the grain of the thought of just about everyone concerned with teaching history in the United States today. Open any US high school American History text book, and you will find it imbued with a sense of identification with the country whose history it relates. Uses of "we", "our", and cognates abound, identifying the reader and author with their, in many cases long dead, compatriots. So, in many books, do identifications of "America" or "the nation" as an intentional agent. So, finally, do moralizing commentaries on the motives and characters of individual agents in history. Here are some examples from a bestselling textbook, Daniel Boorstin and Brooks Mather Kelley's *A History of the United States since 1861* (all emphases are mine):

Explaining the entry of the US into the First World War: 'Most Americans, including the President, were drawn by powerful unseen forces toward the British cause. *We* spoke the English language . . . *our* laws and customs were built on English foundations *We* had fought the American revolution to preserve *our* rights as Englishmen.'[4]

Concerning the Red Scare: 'The mania of these times would last even after the war. The *virus* of witch-hunting and super-patriotism was not so easy to cure.'[5] General Douglas MacArthur was '*a true American hero*' but, in his dispute with Truman over Korea 'more and more Americans came to see that Truman was talking sense.'[6]

Rosa Parks was a 'tired black seamstress;' Martin Luther King: 'a natural leader, *American to the core*'; in response to segregation he was 'indignant and saddened but not angry. He was a *thoughtful* man and a Christian.'[7]

A section called "Why we were in Vietnam" contains the following:

'A third reason for going into Vietnam was to protect *our* reputation. *We* wanted other free countries to believe that *we* would stand by them if they were attacked by Communists. This was called *our* 'credibility.' If *we* did not protect South Vietnam, *we* feared other nations would not believe *we* would help them. Then *our whole worldwide system* of defense and deterrence against the Communists might collapse.'[8]

Different textbooks moralize in different ways, emphasize different virtues and faults; and disagree about both the significance and moral content of events. But the consensus favoring such commentary on, and identification with, the past is striking.[9] This may seem surprising given the apparent place of history in America's so-called culture wars, and the charges that the authors of history standards are unpatriotic and unconcerned with their student's identification with the nation. In fact, there is no disagreement. Gary Nash, himself a prolific author of high school texts, comments: "the argument is in fact between two visions of patriotic history. On one side are those who believe that young people will love and defend the United States if they see it as superior to other nations and regard its occasional falls from grace as short pauses or detours in the continuous flowering of freedom, capitalism, and opportunity. . . . On the other side are historians who believe that *amor patriae* is nurtured by looking squarely at the past, warts and all. Only this clear-sightedness will obviate the cynicism that sugar-coated history produces when youngsters get older and recognize 'the lies my teacher told me.' "[10]

The chapter proceeds as follows. In Section 6.1, I discuss briefly the justifications of patriotism and the further arguments that patriotism is something that should be taught to children in school, and in particular that history is an appropriate vehicle for teaching it. Section 2 casts doubt on the arguments for patriotism and even more doubt on the idea that it should be taught. In Section 6.3, I argue that history is a discipline particularly inappropriate for conveying patriotic feeling.

6.1. Why Patriotism?

What is patriotism? For the most part I shall mean a special sense of identification with one's state and one's compatriots, which inclines one sometimes to give them prior consideration to non-compatriots. One's compatriots are normally the citizens of the state of which one is a citizen, though there may be exceptions (e.g. people who have been unjustly stripped of citizenship, and others who actively want but are unjustly denied citizenship).[11] On some accounts patriotism involves distinctive obligations to compatriots. But on others it just involves a special sense of attachment or fellow feeling: John White writes of the sentiment involved when he contemplates "the relative flatness of the landscape and the rainy weather after returning from a week in Maderia; hearing about the knife attack on George Harrison by a fellow Liverpudlian, two women waiting for the 184 bus and wondering why it was late; the New Years Honours list."[12] I understand patriotism narrowly, as including just the sense of fellow feeling, though it will be vital to discuss the stronger sense of patriotism since the idea that we have distinctive patriotic obligations is a major motivation for thinking that we should encourage fellow feeling for them. I shall restrict my attention to views which are, broadly, compatible with a liberal democratic outlook. Historically patriotism and its justifications have stood apart from the liberal democratic tradition, but since no set of social arrangements could be just or legitimate unless it was liberal and democratic, justifications of patriotism which are incompatible with this outlook are non-starters. Liberal democratic justifications of patriotism are simply the best available, so it is on them that I want to cast doubt.

There are four broadly liberal justifications of patriotism.

First is the claim that we have particularistic obligations to our compatriots which we do not have toward non-citizens, by virtue of sharing their nationality. These are not the only obligations we have, and they are sometimes overridden by universalistic obligations. The model is usually that of the family: it is an accepted part of common sense morality that we have duties to our family members that we do not have toward non-family members, and it is hard to reconcile these special duties with an exclusively universalistic approach to morality.[13]

Second is the claim that the character of political institutions, and the relationships that hold within them, mean that the universal obligation of respect for persons yields a duty of partial concern toward compatriots. Richard Miller argues that the mere fact of sharing a state with someone else gives us a reason to prioritize their interests over those of foreigners because our political choices will result in laws which they are bound to obey. "Equal respect for all is incompatible with supporting the coercive enforcement of terms of self-advancement under which some are seriously burdened, regardless of their choices, in ways that could be alleviated at relatively little cost to the advantaged."[14]

A third argument avoids describing patriotism as a duty, but still asserts that it is, or at least can be, a very good thing. This is the argument that patriotism facilitates the stability of the (just) liberal state. Trust is a practical necessity for stability: since citizens will make conflicting demands on the polity and will do so based on different judgments about what is the right or best thing for the state to do, it is vital for the stability of the liberal state that citizens be able to interpret their disagreements as due to the burdens of judgment rather than the self-seeking behavior or unreasonableness of their opponents. Since the burdens of judgment are heavy, and the amount of disagreement they permit is great, citizens need to be able to trust those with whom they conflict in order confidently to attribute their error to the burdens of judgment rather than unreasonableness. Patriotism facilitates this trust, and according to Eamonn Callan it is "only through initiation into a just polity, and coming to care about the people and the particular institutions it encompasses" that we "come to draw on that reservoir of trust" that is achieved over time by the work of other citizens.[15]

Finally, it is often argued that patriotism is instrumental for distributive justice. The idea is that the fellow feeling engendered by patriotism helps citizens with correct views about distributive justice to act justly, since their motivation from duty is buttressed by their motive of association. Patriotic ties can direct our attention toward our duties to fellow citizens, and provide a sort of backup motivation for action in accordance with justice when the motive of principle, for whatever reason, fails, thus helping to secure justice. Principle and association are distinct, but in a liberal state complementary, sources of motivation.

It never follows immediately from the fact that some trait or kind of behavior is good that it should be taught to children. There are many goods, and some can be instilled in people only at the expense of others. Many goods are consciously neglected by schools, on the assumption that they, or non-compatible alternative goods, will be taught to children elsewhere.

The first two cases for patriotism mentioned above are those that most naturally lend themselves to supporting a policy of universal teaching of patriotism. Both justifications claim that we have direct duties to our compatriots that we do not have to others, and if it is true that we have these duties it is incumbent on us to carry them out, in so far as doing so does not conflict with other, more stringent, duties. If a correct theory of justice must observe a standard of publicity—that is, if its principles must not only be fulfilled but must also be transparently known, and known to be fulfilled, by citizens, as if as a matter of common agreement, then it is important that the duties be known by citizens.[16] Teaching them in school is not the only way of carrying this out, but it is a convenient and natural way of doing so.

The case from instrumentality for some other good to teaching patriotism is more complex. Three further conditions are needed to justify promoting patriotism. It must be claimed: first, that no alternative good is instrumental for stability or justice which can be as readily taught with as few opportunity costs; second, that the good for which patriotism is claimed to be instrumental is important enough to justify whatever opportunity costs are involved in teaching patriotism; and third, that teaching patriotism *universally* is needed in order to ensure the threshold level of uptake required in order to secure the good for which patriotism is supposed to be instrumental; or that, if it is not, there is some independent reason for teaching it universally given that one is teaching it at all. These are instances of general conditions on justifying state action to provide or secure something which is either merely a public good or is merely instrumental (but not necessary) for some other good which is necessary as a matter of justice.

With respect to the second necessary claim, I must admit that justice and stability are extremely important goods, and it is hard to see what opportunity costs could be claimed that would justify not contributing to their security, if their security were in doubt absent the presence of a high level of patriotism. But I shall cast doubt on the first and third claims as well as on the instrumentality claim itself.

6.2. *Problems with Teaching Patriotism*

The first problem is that the instrumental justifications all assume an extremely benign version of patriotism. David Miller, in an early article on the subject, cites the peculiarly English insularity of the Water Rat in *Wind in the Willows*:

Beyond the Wild Wood comes the Wild World. And that's something that doesn't matter, either to you or me. I've never been there, and I'm never going, nor you either if you've got any sense at all. Don't ever refer to it again, please.[17]

Nationalism is not, he says, necessarily illiberal, as evidenced by the Rat's non-imperialistic parochialism. While "it is descriptively true in many historical cases" that "national identities are . . . biased in favor of the dominant cultural group, the group that has historically dominated the politics of the state", it is not integral to national identities that they should be loaded in this way.[18] Eamonn Callan similarly assumes that patriotism need not be illiberal and would not endorse teaching an illiberal patriotism. Patriotism need not have the spillover effect of turning children into jingoists.

In this Miller and Callan are examples of a recent trend of emphasizing nationalism's kinder and gentler face.[19] But the mere compatibility of patriotism with liberalism is not greatly reassuring. Callan remarks of induction into the role of citizen that individuals do not become attached to schemes of cooperation in general, but to "this scheme of just cooperation...*these* fellow citizens."[20] Similarly, one does not learn patriotism in general, but *this* particular version of patriotism—the patriotism of this country. Even the most benign actual patriotisms of existing countries are tainted by xenophobia and jingoism: certainly, the Water Rat's patriotism is by no means representative of the British (or English) patriotism we should expect to be taught in schools, whether through the hidden or the open curriculum. The mere possibility that nationality or patriotism can be inoffensive tells us nothing about the likelihood that the versions of patriotism promoted by real states will be inoffensive in the appropriate way.

National identities vary from nation to nation. Within many national identities *is* a sense of superiority that justifies overriding the legitimate interests of non-nationals (as well as some just claims of co-nationals). Callan may be right that patriotism can lend a supporting hand to justice, or to stability, in a long-lived liberal polity whose national identity has already been tamed. But in many actual liberal countries, even those with relatively inoffensive national identities, patriotism all too often cuts against justice: the attachments and precepts it involves pull citizens in the opposite direction, and help to obscure the actual working of social and political processes. This is never truer than in times of national crisis. Given the *actual* content of British national identity, I believe that the handful who protested against the British war against Argentina in 1982 were indeed (as accused by the press) traitors, not to the state, but to the prevailing ideal of Englishness or Britishness.

National identities also, of course, vary from person to person. And here lies a second problem. Friends of patriotism, or national identification, like to claim that there are coercive and non-coercive ways in which the state can promote a sense of attachment. Andrew Mason, for example, draws this distinction with regard to assimilationist policies:

"*Coercive* measures might include laws which prohibit members of a cultural community from engaging in their customs and practices.... *Non-coercive* measures, in contrast, might include giving the customs and symbols of the dominant culture public status and respect (giving public holidays for festivals recognized by the dominant culture but not others); employing the language of the dominant culture in public affairs; requiring that state schools teach in that language and educate children in the history, geography, and literature of the dominant culture; subsidizing the dominant culture in various ways or giving tax cuts to those who participate in it."[21]

David Miller also draws the distinction, giving the example of protecting national culture through "inducements rather than by coercion: farmers can be given incentives to preserve their hedgerows; the domestic film industry can be subsidized out of cinema revenues; important works of art can be purchased for national collections; and so forth."[22] But each of Mason's and Miller's mechanisms *is* coercive. Miller's examples coerce the cinema goer and the taxpayer, who are forced to pay for something they would not choose to pay for voluntarily, and in the name of a culture which the coerced person has shown no interest in when making cultural choices. The inducements they are forced to provide must be inducements to do *something*, and the content of that something depends on some fixed idea about the proper content of the national culture. In the case of cinema it is that the culture is more truly British (or French, or German, or whatever) if the movies people watch are made in the native country by (largely) native production companies. In the case of the farmer the view is that hedgerows are more important to British culture than less expensive and more efficiently produced foods. Similarly with Mason's purported examples of non-coercion. National holidays restrict the options of those workers and employers who would rather not observe them; state schools are funded through coercively acquired taxation and (usually) are the only realistic option for most children to get an education.

Of course, dissenters are likely to prefer the purportedly "non-coercive" strategies which merely force them to subsidize other peoples cultural practices over the more determinedly coercive strategies which prevent them from engaging in their own. But the strategies are, nonetheless, coercive. Miller says of his preferred strategies that they can "provide an environment in which the culture can develop spontaneously."[23] But if subsidies are to be provided to maintain and develop a "national" culture, those subsidies have to be provided by a granting authority. That authority, if it is responsible, does not distribute the subsidies randomly—instead it has in mind some set of criteria which projects have to meet in order to qualify. Those criteria must be explicit, and they will guide the development of the culture. The development of the culture will not be spontaneously based on the diverse and fluid cultural interests of the population, but will be guided by the non-spontaneous criteria of a cultural elite (since members of this, rather than some randomly selected group of citizens, will most likely comprise the granting authority).

These problems with state promotion of national attachments are especially telling against teaching them to children. Children are uniquely vulnerable and capable of developing full-fledged views of their own about the good life. If their own views of the good life and of the place of their loyalty to country within it are to be truly their own, and not merely explainable by the inculcating activity of the state, it is important that they be encouraged to reflect critically on the character of their national identity. This could be done while they are taught to be patriotic, but it could just as easily not be done. Furthermore if the national culture, and hence the content of the nation's "patriotism," is to be a function of the spontaneous activity and critical reflection of engaged citizens, it is at least dangerous to give the state the authority to determine the content of the patriotism that will be instilled in children, even when that state is democratic. Just as with the trajectory of a national culture, if the state directs teachers and schools to imbue a sense of identification with and loyalty to the state and nation in schools, it must have some guidelines both on how to do it and on what the character is of the state and nation toward which the children's attachment is to be directed. That will guide the future direction of people's senses of what it is to be "British" or "American" or "Italian." The development over time of the national identity is not spontaneous and based on the fluid and diverse interests of individuals, but is shaped in part by the state's sense of the proper content of the patriotic idea.

It is familiar now that, with respect to the circumstances in which they develop their conceptions of the good life and stance toward the state, children must be subject to *some* coercive authority, and that, as long as the family is taken for granted, that authority must be either that of the parents or some agent of the state. Children cannot develop their views authentically without any paternalistic influence. Elsewhere I argue that with respect to some aspects of the child's moral development it is important for the state to have coercive authority. Does not this mitigate the objection that teaching patriotism coerces children?

No. The objection here is not that the state does a wrong to children by *coercing* them. It does two wrongs. It wrongs the child by conditioning his or her consent to the state, thus jeopardizing his or her ability to give the freely offered consent that is the marker of liberal legitimacy. And it wrongs the whole of society by distorting the process of cultural formation and reformation, and in particular by distorting the development of the national idea. There is a strong case for depriving the state of authority with respect to the stance the child develops toward the state: not because this allows the child to develop its views without the influence of any authority, but because granting parents authority will more reliably reproduce a diversity of stances toward the state which constitute the patriotism of conationals who are free and equal.

A further problem with teaching patriotism is that patriotic attachments may interfere with other loyalties and attachments which are instrumental for justice (if not necessarily for stability). Consider the case of Britain. The gradual move toward a more distributively just state over the course of the hundred years beginning around 1870 was driven mainly by two motors: the universalistic idealism of the liberal and latterly the socialist traditions, and the class loyalties and self-interested activity of the labor movement. Patriotism has interfered with these developments—it has been a weapon of the conservative class, wielded with too much success, though less than they would have liked. Some historians see the successful promulgation of the American national loyalty as a key explanation of the failure of the United States, unique among advanced industrial countries, to develop an effective and politically powerful working-class movement. In other countries which have approached egalitarian ideals of distributive justice, class loyalties have played a far greater role than national loyalties, and again, patriotic loyalties have served more to disrupt than to propel the movements toward justice.

It is instructive here to turn to consider Richard Rorty's discussion of the reformist left in *Achieving Our Country*.[24] His main thesis in the book is that the contemporary academic, or "cultural", left in the United States has been misled by theorists like Lasch that America is irredeemably corrupt, and by theorists like Lacan and Foucault that human agency is ineffectual. The reformist left of the first half of the last century, by contrast, loved America, and this love enhanced their effectiveness: "Few of the people who wrote for leftist periodicals, either those aimed at workers or those aimed at bourgeois intellectuals like my parents, had any doubt that America was a great, noble, progressive country, in which justice would eventually triumph."[25]

His characterization of this left as one which never doubted that there was greatness in America is correct (broadly speaking), as is his description of the optimism about the reformability of social institutions. But it is not at all clear that this left was patriotic in his sense, or that, if it was, its patriotism contributed to its effectiveness. The reformist left, unlike Rorty, and unlike the culturalist left that he criticizes, believed in universal values, such as equality, liberty, and democracy. It believed, at least officially, that working class Americans had more in common, both in their experience and their interests, with working class Europeans and Asians than with ruling class Americans, and it believed that the commonalities of class either were, or should be made, more motivationally efficacious than the ties of nationality. Even after its "Americanization" the Communist Party remained slavishly devoted to the leadership in Moscow. Class (albeit, in the Communist Party's case, a grotesque notion of it) was the fundamental loyalty, not nation. Socialists, even more than liberals, have distrusted patriotism and national loyalties. In addition to the reason they share with liberals, the fear that national loyalties lead to unacceptable disregard for the universal obligations owed to all persons, socialists have feared, reasonably, that national loyalties and ties disrupt class loyalties which socialists have seen (not without reason) as the primary motor of moves toward justice. Nor is the fear that workers will fail to unite across the world, but that ties to the members of their own domestic bourgeoisie will inhibit their ability to unite with other members of their domestic working class.

Need Eamonn Callan be troubled by all this? Maybe not. Once a fully just liberal society has been established, and that society's sense of what it is is conditioned by justice, patriotism may play a role much more like the one that Callan assigns to it. This may be true, and the objection I have presented above does not imply that it is impermissible to teach it in such circumstances. But I do want to emphasize that we cannot read off from the propriety of teaching patriotism within a well-ordered Rawlsian just society whether it would be appropriate in the societies we actually inhabit.

But there is another problem which Callan cannot shrug off so easily. His argument for the instrumentality of patriotism for stability and justice assumes (*à la* Rawls) that the purpose of morality of association is to shore up whatever tendency individuals have to treat justly others within their scheme of social cooperation. This is all very well if the boundaries of the state coincide with those of a scheme of social cooperation. But it is almost never the case that the boundaries of a state coincide with those of a scheme of social cooperation. Although it is now a cliché to talk about the globalization of the economy, it has been the case ever since the discovery of the New World that many of us interact in morally important ways with distant strangers even in peacetime. My car was made in Japan; my employer licenses sportswear that is made in Indonesia and sold all over the world; I drink tea grown in India, blended in England, and sold in Wisconsin; I pay taxes to a government which uses them to sue the European Union for favoring Caribbean over South American banana growers.

Neither Rawls nor Callan says much about the identity conditions of schemes of social cooperation (I say this not to fault them). But once a certain level of economic interaction has been established, it must be the case that the boundaries between schemes of cooperation have been breached, and that then the polity includes only a small part of the scheme of social cooperation. Patriotism will not help us to carry out our duties to those with whom we share a scheme of social cooperation. Richard Miller's invocation of the special character of political interactions does not help to counter this objection, at least in the real world.[26] For our interactions with foreigners are governed by collective coercive institutions: there are tax treaties, trade agreements, military alliances and enmities, immigration and emigration laws. Organizations such as the WTO, the IMF, the World Bank, and the various agencies of the UN, all rely for their functioning on coercively raised funds, and operate through the authorization of participating governments. They formalize the coercive character of international interactions, and demonstrate the international character of schemes of social cooperation.

6.3. Why History is an Especially Inappropriate Vehicle for Teaching Patriotism

In Section 6.2, I have cast a good deal of doubt on the propriety of teaching patriotism to children, at least in schools. In this section I want to set those doubts aside (though they may creep back in), and assume for the sake of argument that there could be some place for teaching patriotism in the school curriculum. Here, instead, I want to argue that that place should not be within the history curriculum. There are particular problems with teaching patriotism through history.

First consider an argument that *fails* to establish that patriotism should not be taught through history. This is that the *telos*, or the distinctive aim, of history is to access the truth about the past. There are two problems with this view. First, history has a number of legitimate aims—truth is not the only one. Second, we may properly have different aims in teaching history than we do in practising it. This is true of many activities: the practitioner of a sport may aim at excellence in the sport; but someone teaching the sport may properly aim merely to ensure that his students enjoy themselves playing sport, whether or not they achieve excellence. The practitioner of Spanish aims to communicate with other Spanish speakers; but the teacher of Spanish may aim to give the student a full appreciation of the ways in which different natural languages can have different grammars and structures. The responsible teacher of philosophy does not seek to instill true beliefs in her students, though approaching the truth is a major motivation in her practice of the subject.

I want to show that teaching patriotism would conflict with other purposes which clearly are legitimate, and in my view are central. If a positive argument could be given for the legitimacy of teaching patriotism as a purpose of teaching history, and that doing so is more important than the other purportedly legitimate purposes with which it conflicts, I would be proven wrong. The previous section, I hope, shows that such an argument will be very difficult to make. But my aim here is to shift the burden of proof—to show that a positive argument is needed and cannot be assumed.

Here are three legitimate purposes for teaching history:

1. Truth: it is legitimate to try to convey the truth about history to children; to teach them what actually happened, insofar as we know. It is legitimate to teach children that Europeans came to the Americas in the fifteenth century; that the British colonies rebelled late in the eighteenth century and established an independent federation of States; that Prince Metternich's diplomacy was motivated by the desire to delay the collapse of the old order in Europe for as long as possible; that Henry Kissinger was a biographer of Metternich; that there were revolutions throughout Europe in 1848; that Henry VIII established a church of England; and so on.
2. A second purpose is to teach them how to discern causal connections in social processes and, perhaps, more importantly, to teach them what difficulties are involved in discerning such connections. It is legitimate to teach them that there are disagreements about the causal processes which led to the invasion of England in 1066; to the First and Second World Wars, and the Civil War in the United States; about the fall of the Roman

Empire and the rise of the English industrial working class. It is legitimate to teach them what kinds of evidence scholars consider to count in favor of and against such causal claims.

3. It is legitimate to teach them the history of the particular institutions they can be expected to inhabit, so that they can more effectively and knowledgeably negotiate those institutions. In the American context this would involve teaching about the development of the two-party system; the evolution of the constitution and changes in constitutional interpretation, and the kind of reasoning which is accepted as legitimate in public debate and judicial review; the development of the New Deal and Great Society programs and the paths not taken; the ways that political power has been sought by different movements and interest groups. It is legitimate both to teach this so that children can come to understand the institutions they will operate within, and to think critically about those institutions themselves, so that their endorsement or rejection of the institutions is reasoned and informed.

There is no deductive argument that encouraging patriotism through the teaching of history will conflict with these other legitimate purposes. Some examples will help illustrate the difficulties.

Take the first aim. A good deal of what actually happened makes any country distinctly unlovable to someone possessed of an effective sense of justice. I suspect the conservative patriots are right to want anti-Communism, Hiroshima, Watergate, the secret war on Cambodia, and slavery to be glossed over rather quickly. The persistence of poverty in the midst of the American Dream and the lengths to which the state has gone at various times to inhibit the success of movements for social justice is quite impressive, and cannot reflect well on the nation itself. Britain's history is similarly flawed. While the empire may have been relatively benign, British imperialism is distinctly unlovable—and the manifest willingness of less advantaged Britons to partake in the benefits of imperialism makes it hard to think of imperialism as incidental to the history of the "true" nation.

Of course, in the history of both countries, from the perspective of justice, there is a great deal to admire: Roman rule; the Peasants revolt; the Diggers and Levellers; the War of Independence; the First Amendment; the Chartists; the antislavery campaign; the underground railroad; the early Labour Party; the suffragettes; the rise of the CIO; the Labour Landslide of 1945 and some of what that government did; the civil rights movement. But even within these episodes there is much of which to be critical: the Pankhurst's autocratic and elitist practice; Labour's support for World War One; Martin Luther King's personal failings; John L. Lewis's manipulation of the Communist Party; and the Communist Party's support for Stalin. Teaching the truth about these episodes not only involves one in teaching children that the agents of social justice have usually been deeply and widely hated by many of their compatriots, but also in teaching them of the flaws and problems with even those whose actions pushed history in the direction of justice. Will the warts and all approach to history (which must surely include a warts and all approach to the beauty spots) enhance love of country, as Nash and the new textbook writers think it will? There are good reasons for doubting so, at least for many children.

Take the second aim. An educator aiming to instill love of country will have difficulties teaching about the causal processes which led up to the Civil War in the United States, especially given the preconceptions her children are likely to have. Take three radically different interpretations. The war was about protecting states' rights from the encroachments of an increasingly powerful federal government; it was about preserving the union and abolishing slavery; it was about creating flexible labor markets and liberalizing trade. Only one of these explanations reflects well on the moral character of the war; while it is not the least plausible, it is not the most plausible, and the others all have some plausibility. Given the second purpose, the pedagogue's aim must be to encourage reflection in the light of the best evidence she can present, and discourage that any of that reflection be distorted either by her desire or that of any of her students to present the events in a favorable light. Patriotic concerns when teaching the Civil War are also likely to inhibit the third aim. It continues to have a central place in the moral story Americans tell themselves about their country. One cannot understand contemporary American political institutions without an accurate picture of the Civil War; yet teaching the complexity of motives on both sides (many of which were morally obnoxious) is unlikely to contribute to love of country.

Consider again how the presentation of Rosa Parks in the Boorstin textbook distorts learning about social processes. What he says about her is true: she was a tired black seamstress. But what is conveyed is that she just finally snapped, and thought something to the effect of "I am not going to take this any more"; and that her spontaneous refusal prompted a spontaneous protest movement. Read Gary Nash's own textbook covering the issue and we find a different, more revealing story: "Protests like Parks's were not new, but hers was the kind of case community leaders had been waiting for. Parks was dignified, soft-spoken, well-liked. She was a former secretary of the local NAACP chapter and was active in her church. The previous summer she had attended an interracial workshop at the Highlander Folk School in Tennessee. Now, local civil rights leaders asked if she would be willing to fight her case for as long as it took to win."[27] The impression left by the Boorstin textbook risks obscuring the role of non-spontaneous organization in promoting social change in this case.

0It might seem from my approving quote from Nash's textbook that my position is just his position in disguise, but I do not think that is true. Nash claims that the truth—warts and all—will serve the development of patriotic attachment and that this aim is a proper aim of teaching history. My position is that patriotic purposes have no legitimate role in the teaching of history: so I would endorse the "warts and all" pedagogy, but entirely without regard to whether it serves the development of patriotic attachments. If it did not, that would not in any way count against the pedagogy, as, for Nash, it presumably would (though maybe not decisively—since he does not investigate the possibility of conflict there is no way of discerning whether truth or patriotism is more important to him).

There is, I think, a third position which lies between Nash's and mine: that while patriotic purposes may be permissible in the teaching of history, their pursuit is strictly constrained by truthfulness and other legitimate purposes I have identified. However, at the level of textbook composition, the three positions may be very similar, because in practice it is so hard to pursue the patriotic purposes while respecting the truth. Certainly, when searching for turns of phrase or modes of presentation that are inimical to my own view, I was unable to find any offenders in Nash's own textbooks. At the level of classroom teaching, there may be a difference: the non-patriotic educator would disregard the effects of her questions and the direction of classroom discussion on the attachments of her students, and may be more willing than the patriotic educator to delve into the moral significance of the private failings of historically important figures whose public lives are liable to inspire attachment to country. For example, let us assume that Martin Luther King's multiple infidelities and plagiarism are not historically significant. Then the warts and all patriot and the non-patriot will concur on omitting mention of them from textbook treatments. They will also concur (I presume) that they should not be denied if a child raises questions about them in class. Nevertheless the warts and all patriot may, believing that dwelling on them could have the misleading effect of diminishing the greatness of King's leadership in the minds of her students, wish to move on promptly from the question. The non-patriot, unconcerned with that possible effect, although she believes the private behavior was not historically significant, may be more willing to entertain *discussion* of their historical significance (with children of an appropriate age), and may even raise the issues herself for the purpose of having that discussion.

6.4. Concluding Comments

How, then, should history textbooks be written? Any book, after all, has to be written from *some* point of view. If they may not be written from a patriotic point of view, is it permissible for them to promote class loyalty (and if so, which class), or identification with one's cultural group (or the cultural group of another)?

I shall answer this question very briefly, but first I want to clarify the conclusion of my argument. Although I have focused on textbook writing, my real concern is with the way history is *taught*. The Boorstin book could quite well be used in conjunction with other materials by a sensitive teacher to perform the legitimate functions of teaching history and to avoid the illegitimate. The teacher could introduce source materials concerning the Selma bus boycott and the Red Scare showing what actually happened and how, and could point out and encourage discussion about the many attempts by Boorstin to get his audience to identify with "America." Or the teacher could counter the Boorstin text with something like Howard Zinn's *A People's History of the United States*, a book which, although patriotic in something like Rorty's sense, clearly aims to expose the warts of America's history in order to stimulate criticism of America's leaders and to encourage a deeply critical identification with the nation. From the conclusion that history should not be used to teach patriotism we cannot conclude that history books, even history textbooks, may not be written from a patriotic perspective.

While I cannot vindicate this claim here, my belief is that using history to promote the other kinds of loyalties mentioned would encounter many difficulties similar to those I have raised with promoting patriotism. One view is that African-American children should be taught history in a way that affirms and encourages their identities as African-Americans; in the 1930s a series of textbooks were written presenting history for working-class children to encourage their identification as working class. I suspect that whatever the identity being promoted, its promotion jeopardizes the required functions of teaching history, and risks indoctrinating children so that their affirmations of the identity will lack authenticity. But presenting children with a variety of texts, all constrained by the truth, while presenting a variety of viewpoints might be an adequate way of stimulating them to reflect on the loyalties the authors hold and are trying to promote. It seems reasonable to use textbooks that are written from an angle as it were, so long as children read a variety of such books and their teachers can help the students negotiate the complexity of the views. However, the primary attention of liberal authors of textbooks should not be on directly encouraging identities in, or teaching values to, readers, but on teaching them what happened and teaching them the skills essential to figuring out why.

NOTES

1. Arthur Schlesinger, *The Disuniting of America* (New York: Norton, 1992), 72.
2. Ibid., 93.
3. Ibid., 137. Schlesinger never explicitly advocates using history teaching to promote national identity, but it does seem to be a subtext of his book; albeit that any teaching of history must, in his view, be constrained by the truth and the "unexpurgated record" (I discuss this possible position in Section 4). An excellent discussion of Schlesinger can be found in Robert Fullinwider, "Patriotic History" in Robert Fullinwider (ed.), *Multiculturalism and Public Education* (Cambridge: Cambridge University Press, 1996). Fullinwider's essay was a major stimulus to my own thinking on this issue, and the present essay is an attempt to circumvent Fullinwider's defence of patriotic history.
4. Daniel Boorstin and Brooks Mather Kelley, *A History of the United States since 1861* (Needham, Mass: Prentice Hall, 1990), 208.
5. Ibid., 221.
6. Ibid., 366.
7. Ibid., 379.
8. Ibid., 441.
9. There are exceptions: some Africanist educators, for example, writing primarily for Black students, emphasize identification not with America but with the experience of African-Americans in the past. However, they share the idea that students should be offered a "usable past", one which encourages their identification with some appropriate group.
10. Gary Nash, Charlotte Crabtree, and Ross E. Dunn, *History on Trial* (New York: Knopf, 1999), 15.
11. In the first case I think of Americans who have been stripped of citizenship because of their engagement with communist regimes; in the second I think of Turkish adults who have been born and raised in Germany.
12. John White, "Patriotism without Obligation" (Unpublished), 4.
13. David Miller, *On Nationality* (Oxford: Oxford University Press, 1995), 50.

14. Richard Miller, "Cosmopolitan Respect and Patriotic Concern", *Philosophy and Public Affairs*, 27 (1998), 202–24 at 215.
15. Eamonn Callan, *Creating Citizens* (Oxford: Oxford University Press, 1997), 88.
16. See John Rawls, *A Theory of Justice* (Cambridge: Harvard University Press, 1971), esp pp. 55–6 and Andrew Williams, "Incentives, Inequality, and Publicity", *Philosophy and Public Affairs*, 27 (1998), 225–47 for useful discussions.
17. "In Defence of Nationality", *Journal of Applied Philosophy*, 10 (1993), 3–16 at 3.
18. D. Miller, "In Defence of Nationality", 11.
19. See, for example, Yael Tamir, *Liberal Nationalism* (Princeton: Princeton University Press, 1995), several contributions to Robert McKim and Jefferson McMahan, *The Morality of Nationalism* (Oxford: Oxford University Press, 1998), several contributions to Kai Nielsen, Jocelyn Couture, and Michel Seymour (eds), *Rethinking Nationalism* (*Canadian Journal of Philosophy* Supplementary Volume 22, 1996), and the other works referred to in this article.
20. Callan, *Creating Citizens*, 93.
21. Andrew Mason, "Political Community, Liberal-Nationalism, and the Ethics of Assimilation", *Ethics*, 109 (1999), 261–86 at 268 (emphasis in original).
22. David Miller, *On Nationality*, 87–8.
23. Ibid., 88.
24. Richard Rorty, *Achieving our Country* (Princeton: Princeton University Press, 1998).
25. Ibid., 59.
26. "Cosmopolitan Respect and Patriotic Concern." See also Thomas Hurka's contribution to *The Morality of Nationalism*.
27. Gary Nash, *American Odyssey: The United States in the Twentieth Century* (New York: McGraw Hill, 1999), 674–5.

Part II

LIBERALISM AND TRADITIONALIST EDUCATION

CHAPTER 7

Comprehensive Educations and the Liberal Understanding of Autonomy

SHELLEY BURTT

7.1. Introduction

The starting point for this chapter is a juxtaposition of two texts, one from the Bible, and the other from the bible of the Enlightenment, Locke's *Essay on Human Understanding*. Consider first this quotation from Proverbs: "Train up a child in the way he should go and when he is old he will not depart from it."[1] I take this to be a succinct statement of the aim of a certain sort of religious education, generally viewed with suspicion by secular liberals. The idea is to provide a child with an identity, sense of purpose, and orientation to life strong enough to tie him to that life and identity throughout adulthood. Education is seen as fitting the child with the worldview, personal commitments, and moral understandings that his parents and the faith community that he inhabits believe to be necessary to live a good life. While the analogy is not perfect, at least some sorts of education into a particular cultural identity can also be thought of as guided by a similar principle. In this chapter, I refer to upbringings characterized by these goals as "comprehensive educations", in the sense that those responsible for a child's education (parent or teacher) seek to inculcate in her a comprehensive vision of the good in the manner and toward the end just described.

Compare this ideal to the one articulated by Locke early on in the *Essay on Human Understanding*. Here, in a paragraph heading at the end of Book I, Locke formulates a central credo of the Enlightenment and in so doing crafts a classic definition of liberal autonomy: "Men must think and know for themselves."[2] His particular point is that we are not to accept political or philosophical doctrines as true simply because others say so. Thus, we are not to "give up our assent only to reverend names" but must "employ our own reason to understand those truths which gave them reputation." We are not to "[take] up another's principles without examining them" but must "use of [our] own reason and judgement" in deciding what propositions about human nature, politics, morality, and religion are true or not.[3] To think and know for ourselves in this way is to be autonomous and it is what liberals want for liberal citizens.

Critically juxtaposing these texts offers one way of reflecting upon an issue at the heart of the current debate about children's education in a pluralistic society: is it true that to "train up a child in the way he should go" is subtly or not so subtly to reject the idea that "men must think and know for themselves"? Is the sort of comprehensive religious education valorized in the quote from Proverbs (or its cultural counterpart) at odds with the development of individual autonomy as prized by liberals and the liberal democratic state? My answer to these questions is no. The achievement of individual autonomy correctly understood is not threatened by the major sorts of religious and cultural education on offer today. Friends of autonomy are thus in error if they target comprehensive educations as inimical to autonomous thought and action simply because they are comprehensive.

Note, however, that this claim does not mean that all forms of comprehensive education automatically produce autonomous individuals. As I make clear in the next section, the capacity for autonomous thought and action depends on the development of both moral and intellectual virtues which not every education will provide. As Eamonn Callan's most recent work makes clear,[4] this is a charge that can be leveled against versions of mainstream, secular educations as much as against comprehensive ones. It is also important to keep in mind that the capacity for autonomous thought and action does not in itself guarantee a willingness to defend liberal freedoms. While it is plausible to expect many recipients of an autonomy-facilitating education to develop affinities for liberal ways of life, the capacity to "think and know for oneself" does not on its own lead an individual to embrace liberal, egalitarian, or democratic ends. To the extent that such commitments are important to us, we must move beyond considerations of autonomy to the inculcation of civic virtues.

I return now to my assertion that comprehensive educations do not as a class threaten the achievement of individual autonomy. To defend this conclusion, I seek first of all to get a better understanding of the sort of education religious or culturally committed parents seek to give their children. What room would education of this sort, correctly described, leave for autonomy understood in the Lockean sense? At first glance, the Biblical saying appears to place little value on an adult's autonomy. It suggests that proper training during childhood successfully "captures" an individual, binding him to particular habits or ways of life which he will find difficult to break as an adult. The promise that we will reproduce the way of life of our ancestors appears tantamount to the promise that we will lack sufficient independence of thought to judge for ourselves which principles to live by.

One possible response to this concern begins by rereading the quote with the following emphasis: "train up a child in the way he *should* go . . ." The import thus becomes that only a good education, an education to satisfying, humanly fulfilling ends will "capture" a person's heart. The quote then serves as both a promise and a warning to parents. Choose the ends you hold out to your children well. If these ideals are indeed worthy of human commitment, your child will embrace them as she matures and continue to live by them as an adult. The warning to parents contained in this passage, then, is that only good educations win the hearts and minds of your children. If you educate a child in a way that retards or restricts his development, the education may not "take."

The obvious objection to this interpretation is that parents are perfectly capable of profoundly misdirecting a child's ambitions and understanding, whether in the service of a fundamentalist zealotry or equally corrupt secular hatreds and prejudices. The fact that a child affirms the values of his parents, kin, or faith community and goes on to reproduce their way of life is therefore not in itself a sufficient guarantee that the way of life is worthy of the child's commitment. Bad educations create bad habits and perverted understandings of what sorts of lives are good or even possible. While good educations to worthy ends may capture a child's soul, so too may corrupt or abusive ones.

Still, the possibility of a comprehensive education toward unworthy ends does not mean that all comprehensive educations are unworthy. The question at issue here is whether even benign forms of comprehensive education (those in which the values inculcated are neither intolerant of nor antithetical to liberal democratic political ideals and processes) are properly criticized as inimical to human freedom because unfriendly to the development of personal autonomy. I argue that this concern is seriously overstated in the current literature on the subject, although defending this conclusion requires recasting our view of what liberal autonomy demands.

Contemporary liberal theory typically associates the capacity for autonomy with the willingness and ability to distance ourselves critically from the roles or ends we have been raised to value. Political theorists who adopt this view most often prescribe generous amounts of school-based exposure to alternative ways of life as the most effective antidote to excessive parental parochialism.[5] Children given this sort of education for autonomy will generally think of the principles by which they live their lives as being self-consciously selected from a range of worthy options, choosing freely between various attractive prospects on the basis of some personal interrogation of desire. Advocates of this "informed consumer" model of autonomous action admit that teaching children to think in this manner about their ultimate ends makes certain ways of life not reprehensible in themselves either impossible or difficult to embrace. However, this consequence is generally accepted as a reasonable price to pay given the "fundamental right" we have "to govern our own conduct."[6]

Understood in this manner, autonomous thought and action will appear beyond the reach of children raised in the manner envisioned in the quote from Proverbs. Such children are not encouraged to choose their ends, but rather to grow into roles and life goals already affirmed as worthy by their family and faith or cultural community. In fact, a truly successful comprehensive education creates adults with a sufficiently rich sense of a cultural or religious identity such that breaking away from that identity would seem to strike at the heart of who one is as a person. These individuals cannot, and will not, approach moral reflection on issues of identity and ultimate goals with the consumerist mentality generally taken by liberal theorists as evidence of autonomous capacity.

But does the ability to choose freely between alternative understandings of the good life exhaust what it means to "think and know for oneself"? To the extent that such a definition is affirmed, liberal theorists have missed the chance to describe in detail the possibilities for autonomous thought from within a comprehensive education to a particular way of life or understanding of the good. Part One of this chaper takes up this challenge, offering several reasons why the central demand of autonomy—to think and know for oneself—is well within the reach of individuals who receive this sort of "grounded" education. In Part Two, I look more closely at liberal theories of autonomy, particularly aspects of those accounts which encourage the idea that comprehensive educations are at odds with the development of autonomy. I argue that such characterizations overstate the difficulties that exist and conclude by reaffirming the possibility of combining an education for autonomy with education toward a comprehensive vision of the good life.

7.2. Part One

As part of considering the resources for autonomy available to individuals receiving comprehensive educations, I turn now to two sketches of persons brought up in a way that, for liberals, make them autonomously challenged: the "encumbered self" familiar from the work of Michael Sandel and the person of "simple integrity" described in Eamonn Callan's recent book, *Creating Citizens*.[7] These individuals, by definition, lack the ability (or desire) to frame their fundamental religious or cultural commitments as matters of personal choice. Contemporary liberal theory considers such incapacity as evidence that an individual lacks autonomy. But if we think about what autonomy really demands, such a conclusion seems too hasty.

Encumbered selves "conceive their identity... as defined to some extent by the community [religious or ethnic] of which they are a part. For them, community describes not just what they *have* as fellow citizens, but also what they *are*, not a relationship they choose (as in a voluntary association) but an attachment they discover."[8] As Richard Dagger usefully elaborates, "the self-identity of the encumbered self... [teaches] the individual that he or she is entangled in a network of unchosen attachments and commitments."[9] Sandel describes these unchosen attachments as "loyalties and convictions whose moral force consists partly in the fact that living by them is inseparable from understanding ourselves as the particular persons we are—as members of this family or community or nation or people, as bearers of that history, as citizens of this republic."[10] One way we can think of the religious and cultural education that worries liberals, then, is as an attempt to create "encumbered" selves, selves that understand themselves in some important way as lacking a choice about what they do or who they are.

Callan uses the idea of "simple integrity" to raise similar concerns about educations which compromise the achievement of adult autonomy. Persons whose lives are characterized by what he calls the value of simple integrity typically embrace a comprehensive understanding of the good life, located within the "shared practices" of a circumscribed community. In addition, the individual "identifies wholeheartedly with the role or configuration of roles that structures her life, and she lives in close fidelity to its requirements." Finally, "the responsibilities [her] roles entail are harmonized, so that there is ordinarily no or at most modest friction between them."[11] Callan believes that "membership of a particular religion is a role that commonly entails acceptance of the ideal of simple integrity."[12] I think we can also imagine individuals embracing certain ethnic or cultural identities with "simple integrity" as well.

Callan worries that "the value of simple integrity might be used to argue against an education that would conduce to autonomy."[13] As he explains it, parents who wish to encourage in their child a close identification with a comprehensive idea of the good will not want their child's faith to "have to pull against the appeal of rival values. To subject her faith to that crisis would be to endanger the whole-hearted commitment upon which simple integrity depends."[14] The implicit assumption is that developing the capacity for autonomous thought and action requires widespread and sympathetic exposure to alternative understandings of the good life (preferably ones in direct confrontation with parental ideals), such that young adults will be required self-consciously to choose rather than accept their core identities or the moral principles by which they wish to live their lives.[15] Parents who oppose such exposure are said to be hostile to an education in autonomy.

As these citations indicate, contemporary liberals generally assume that the autonomous individual is one who has distanced himself sufficiently from his parents' and community's values to see them not as heritage or birthright but as one of many possible ends awaiting his selection (or rejection) as a thoughtful adult. Autonomous individuals are those who self-consciously *select* rather than *accept* the principles which govern their lives. But such characterizations represent a very narrow conception of what autonomy requires. Once we place independent thought and action rather than free choice at the center of our understanding of autonomy, comprehensive forms of religious and cultural education do not seem quite so restrictive of individual freedom as liberal theorists would have us believe.

Consider Callan's not atypical description of the autonomous person: "I am autonomous to the degree that I have developed powers of practical reason, a disposition to value those powers and use them in giving shape and direction to my own life, and a corresponding resistance to impulses or social pressures that might subvert wise self-direction."[16] What is being recommended here are the virtues of practical reason and moral courage. An education designed to elicit *these* capacities does not seem immediately incompatible with wholehearted commitment to a particular vision of the good life or with an understanding of oneself as constituted by certain unchosen loyalties. In fact, comprehensive educations can typically be expected to encourage these dispositions as part of their effort to bring children to embrace a particular vision of the good life. Every belief system will encounter "hard cases" in which the right thing to do is not immediately evident no matter how unquestioning a commitment one has developed toward acting within it. Even the demand to use Scripture or God's will as a guide to the resolution of conflicts requires a capacity for critical reflection, without which the nature of Scriptural commands or God's intentions for His children will remain frustratingly obscure. Part of doing a good job of raising children to embrace a comprehensive vision of the good life thus involves equipping them with the "powers of practical reason" with which to confront crises of faith and identity. The ability to resist "impulses or social pressures" will also figure prominently in many comprehensive educations as parents seek to give their children the courage to live by ideals outside of the cultural mainstream. The capacities for autonomous thought as set out in Callan's definition are thus compatible with educations designed to raise children who understand themselves as irrevocably constituted by certain cultural or religious commitments.

Admittedly, not every single form of comprehensive education will encourage the sort of independent thought described here. Some versions of religious orthodoxy, for example, prescribe an unquestioning obedience to the dictates of a religious leader. To the extent that this view is strongly in evidence and adherents of a particular religion appear to live faithfully by it, there is no difficulty in concluding that that particular form of comprehensive education does not promote a critical element of autonomous thought. But my point here is that there is nothing in the fundamental structure or aim of comprehensive educations per se which is incompatible with developing the powers of practical reason and moral courage and that, in many instances, such educations will encourage such development.

I want now to consider what it is about contemporary liberal theory which generally blinds it to the possibilities for autonomous thought available to individuals from within comprehensive visions of the good life. What leads so much of contemporary liberal thought to contest this compatibility? At least part of the reason is the insistence found in so much of the literature on remaking autonomous individuals over in the image of the free chooser. Consider Eamonn Callan's otherwise illuminating discussion of how moral agents choose the principles by which they live. Drawing on the work of Meir Dan-Cohen, Callan distinguishes two sorts of choice—the choice we make when something appears as categorically valuable, as compelling our choice, and the choice we make between an "array of more or less eligible options", when we "select one on the basis of our preferences."[17] Are choosers of the first sort non-autonomous? While Callan does not say so directly, his comments point in that direction.

The possibility that a cultural or religious identity might cease to be conceived as a choice of the first sort and begin to appear more like a choice of the second sort is, Callan says, one thing that worries communitarian critics of autonomy-facilitating education. "The fear of some such transformation is doubtless familiar to many who resist educational practices that would expose their children to alternatives to a prescribed way of life." And he continues:

After all, it is one thing to be taught to identify with a particular religion categorically as the locus of meaning and fulfillment for human beings always and everywhere; it is another to learn to see it as the most attractive item on a menu of spiritual possibilities, to be chosen only so long as it maintains its edge over the competition.[18]

The implication of this comparison is that deeply religious or strongly culturally identified parents want their children to understand their ends in the first (non-autonomous) manner, while an education for autonomy promotes self-understanding of the second sort.

There are two difficulties with an analysis of this sort. First, the capacity for autonomous thought and action is reduced to a requirement that individuals relate to their ends in the manner held out by the metaphor of the menu. I have already pointed out that, even on their own terms, liberal accounts of what autonomy consists in do not necessarily require such a stance. As Callan suggests elsewhere in his book, independent thought depends especially on "the powers of practical reason" and the moral courage to use it, virtues which can be elicited from within educations to comprehensive visions of the good life.

A second problem concerns the characterization of what comprehensive understandings of the good life point toward. While the most intolerant versions of fundamentalist religions might teach children to identify with them "categorically as the locus of meaning and fulfillment for human beings always and everywhere", such an expectation seems alien to the more common sorts of education toward a comprehensive understanding of the good life on offer in Western democracies today. In this sense, the opposition set out in Callan's text is a false one. Between the consumerist menu of spiritual possibilities and the totalizing vision of the crusading fundamentalist is a third alternative of an education into comprehensive ideals which are worthy of commitment because of the particular sort of person one is—born into this family, of this nationality, sharing in this heritage, fated to this physical condition, stuck with these relatives. Hasidic Jews, for example, do not raise their children to understand their faith as "the locus of meaning and fulfillment for human beings always and everywhere." Rather the Jewish faith is presented as the right way for *them* to live *their* spiritual life, because of who they are, how their parents grew up, what their grandparents experienced, etc. Education into a particular ethnic or cultural identity seems equally an example of teaching a child to embrace certain ends conditionally—because of the sort of person *he* is, *his* particular cultural setting, family history, etc. Thus my friend sends her daughter to Chinese school not because "being Chinese" is some universal good to which we should all aspire, but because she believes her child should grow up understanding herself not only as an American with one parent of Chinese ancestry but as part-Chinese herself.

The message not explored by Callan's two-part schema, then, is that parents conforming to an ideal of simple integrity share with their children the moral message: this is the good life for you because of who you are, where you were born, and who your family is. Individuals who cultivate, accept, or adopt this sort of relationship to their ends act autonomously when they reason responsibly and critically about what it means to be the sort of person characterized by the ends they accept as given. "What does it mean to be a person who..." is a core question of this sort of autonomous thought, and raising children capable of asking and answering this question in an intellectually responsible and independent manner is fully compatible with an education towards a comprehensive vision of the good.

The compatibility I affirm here is of two sorts. First, the skills involved in thinking critically about "what does it mean to be the sort of person who..." are compatible with comprehensive educations in the sense that they could be taught in public schools without engendering the sort of hostility which currently arises between liberals wedded to a consumerist vision of autonomous thought and religious parents opposed to it. Liberal education theory now virtually commands public schools to function as cultural counterpoints to parental teachings regarding the good and worthy life: "The essential demand is that schooling properly involves at some stage sympathetic and critical engagement with beliefs and ways of life at odds with the culture of the family or religious or ethnic group into which the child is born."[19] But understanding autonomy as the ability to think independently about what the sort of person one has been raised to be would enable schools to work toward such independence of thought without any direct challenge to parental values and commitments.

A second sort of compatibility is more contingent. If educating a child to a particular religious or cultural identity is conceived simply as a matter of ensuring her slavish conformity to a set of rules or cultural practices, critical reflection on questions of identity will not be encouraged. But such an account caricatures the vast majority of comprehensive educations. Living an identity (even if defined within a life of "simple integrity") is simply too complex a matter to imagine that it can be achieved without any confrontation with the question of what that identity means. At a minimum, it seems that children must be taught to distinguish between true and false understandings of what that identity means so as to live that identity most genuinely and fully. But children given the intellectual tools necessary to separate false doctrines from true are not only being exposed to alternative conceptions of the good life ("false" doctrines), they are also being handed the resources necessary for independent, critical thought. Children being raised to adopt comprehensive forms of religious or cultural identity are constantly being instructed in what it means to be "the sort of person who..." (A Jehovah's Witness is not the sort of person who salutes the flag, accepts blood transfusions, celebrates birthdays, etc.) But because it is impossible to provide any complete answer to the question of what a person with a particular identity or commitment does, they are often and properly given the opportunity to cultivate habits of thought which provide the groundwork for independent reflection on this issue as well.

Not everyone will agree with the characterization I give here of the resources for autonomous thought within "encumbered" educations. Children who are both taught that the best way of life involves unquestioning obedience or submission to the will of another person, whether priest, parent, or politician, and who accept this mandate obediently and live by it, will certainly lack autonomy—as will children who unquestioningly receive their understanding of the good from peer groups, television, or the latest arbiter of "what's cool." To place oneself at the disposal of another's point of view is certainly not to "think and know for [oneself]." In addition, any adult who, out of fear of rejection, overwhelming guilt, or false understandings of filial duty, finds it emotionally unbearable to make choices at odds with his parents' understanding of the good life is not an autonomous actor. He or she lacks the ability to engage critically with the powers of custom and authority which Locke believed crucial to independent thought and action. This is the "ethically servile" individual, sensitively described and properly condemned in Callan's book.[20] But it seems hardly credible that all comprehensive educations run the risk of creating such stunted lives.

I have now suggested a number of reasons why one should not automatically assume that encumbered selves, or lives lived with simple integrity, lack the autonomy valued in liberal theory. Of course, exposure to a comprehensive education does not guarantee the development of autonomy any more than does exposure to any other sort of upbringing. However, if autonomy is understood in the Lockean sense of non-subordination to the will and opinion of others, we can see that comprehensive educations are not only compatible with autonomous thought and action, but contain within them resources which contribute to the development of autonomy (in particular, a built-in interest in developing the powers of practical reason and the virtue of moral courage). I have also suggested that critical engagement with the question, "What does it mean to be the sort of person who..." will be the way in which those who receive comprehensive educations demonstrate their autonomy. But nagging doubts may remain. Will children raised to understand themselves as encumbered by unchosen obligations to other persons and ways of life truly possess the resources for *independent* thought about such identities? Will they be able, given such an education, to think and know for themselves?

Bringing up children to understand themselves as encumbered by certain obligations or loyalties (to kinship groups, ethnic identities, or religious faiths) does make impossible a certain sort of ethical reflection, one that begins with the sense that everything is on the table. Children given educations designed to elicit comprehensive commitments to certain ways of life will not experience the world as presenting a "menu of spiritual possibilities", nor will they be apt to understand themselves as free to select any identity from among the hundreds of thousands on offer in the modern world. But such ungrounded choice is not a prerequisite for autonomous thought and action. What is necessary, however, is a sense that things (and people) might be other than they are—that the life we are given is not the *only* life we might make for ourselves. At this point, liberals generally prescribe exposure to diversity as both a necessary and sufficient guarantor of autonomous thought, recreating the clash between proponents of autonomy and comprehensive educations that I have sought to avoid. Can we look, then, for other enablers of autonomous thought, more compatible with comprehensive educations but still able to provide children and adults with the critical distance on their experience necessary for independent reflection on their commitments and identities?

I want to begin a discussion of this question by proposing three key contributors to autonomous thought, all of which are compatible with a comprehensive education and at least some of which are probably necessary to ensure that a comprehensive education will also enable autonomous thought. This list is not complete and I trust additions and alternatives to my suggestions will be easily made. The idea is to encourage reflection on what sorts of qualities or experiences, other than exposure to diversity, can encourage the independent thought we think of as characteristic of autonomy. The three goods I have in mind are moral courage (already discussed), familiarity with the idea of "character pluralism", and a belief that good lives must feel right "from the inside."[21]

The virtue of moral courage gives one the ability to resist pressures to conform, to act on one's understanding of the good in the face of familial and peer disapproval. I have already suggested why I believe comprehensive educations encourage the virtue of moral courage and why moral courage facilitates autonomy. The moral courage that children learn from parents who set themselves against the dictates of popular culture provides the emotional capacity necessary to act on concerns they may have about the life they are being raised to endorse.

The idea of "character pluralism" teaches one that individuals come with different needs, characters, gifts, and abilities. It implies that the good life for one person may not be a rewarding life for another, even someone within the same family. I understand it to be an important enabler of autonomous thought, for it provides a basis from which children can make constructive sense of any misgivings they may have about the sort of comprehensive education they are receiving. Rather than interpreting their resistance as moral recalcitrance or personal failing on their part, they might come to see it as grounded in the sort of person they are. Their parents' devout practices may not be right for *them*. Nor is the idea of "character pluralism" a subversive secular invention necessarily at odds with the ideals and values of a comprehensive education. To value an encumbered life is not to believe that one life fits all. The Christian teaching that "there are diversities of gifts, but the same Spirit" (I Corinthians 12: 4) or that "in my Father's house, there are many mansions", for example, can be interpreted to reflect this idea that human beings will not all approach even a shared end in the same way.

It is additionally helpful to autonomous thought if children are taught that the way of life they adopt and the ultimate ends they affirm ought to feel right "from the inside." As Harry Brighouse explains, "[Some] ways of life are ... good. But some whose parents try to pass those ways of life down cannot endorse them from the inside: although the ways of life are good, these people cannot live them well. They have opportunities to live well only if they can exit into other good ways of life."[22] This idea, elaborated as well in Kymlicka[23] and Norton,[24] encourages the individual to insist that the fundamental principles to which he conforms be experienced as right for him, the sort of person he is and has, through his experience, circumstances, and education, come to be. Most comprehensive educations already hold out such an ideal in teaching that a certain way of life is right for a child because of who he is, the particular circumstances of his birth, family history, nationhood, etc. or in the idea that God has a particular plan and purpose for each individual. If this ideal is assimilated along with the notion of character pluralism, adolescents and young adults will have the cognitive tools to reflect on whether the way of life their parents urge is right for them.

Together, these qualities make it possible for individuals to "think and know for themselves" without forcing them to recast their ends as matters of personal preference to be selected after a state-encouraged sampling of available alternatives from within and without their native culture. They are thus compatible with a comprehensive education to a particular religious or cultural identity—and necessary to it, if such an education is to produce autonomous citizens.

One question that might arise at this point concerns just how malleable our identities and educations can be. Communitarian critics of liberal autonomy sometimes speak as if liberals have misunderstood questions of identity. From this perspective, we are all inevitably encumbered by certain unchosen attitudes and loyalties, and to pretend otherwise is to misconceive the necessary starting point for moral reflection and autonomous action. If this communitarian critique were true, *all* autonomous thought would take the form, "what does it mean to be the sort of person who ..." To imagine that anyone is a "free chooser," let alone to glorify free choice as the hallmark of autonomy, is simply to be mistaken about important aspects of the human condition. At other times, communitarian criticism adopts a more elegiac tone: since we can come to think of almost identity, commitment, or way of life as freely selected on the basis of personal preference, the important thing is that we not succumb to such temptation. This criticism concedes that certain people are autonomous in the way contemporary liberal theory conceives of that term. Once this point is conceded, the question becomes whether it is the only or best way possible for people to "think and know for themselves."

Perhaps one reason this debate continues unresolved is that both perspectives have something to be said for them. The extraordinarily porous boundaries of First World cultures means that almost no locus of identity *needs* to be understood as an "unchosen" starting point for moral action and reflection. The National Health Service in Britain, for example, underwrites several thousand sex change operations a year. A world in which even our gender identity is open to government-subsidized revision is certainly one in which ethnic, religious, and racial identities can similarly be construed as goods to be chosen or rejected based on conscientious considerations of one's personal preferences. On the other hand, it seems that *some* decisions regarding our identity are not only ours to make. For better or worse, those we come in contact with will use visual and aural cues to make their own decisions about our identity and react to us accordingly. Wherever in the world we live, my adopted son will "be Korean" in some way that he cannot choose to ignore. And were we to revisit Korea, everything about him from his language to the way he dressed and carried himself would mark him as "American" in a way he would have to confront as well. Finally, the radical dependence of the human infant, and the universal human need for relations of intimacy and trust without which normal maturation is impossible, means that each of us will come to questions of our values and identities with a unique and inescapable emotional history.

These considerations suggest that no understanding of autonomy will be complete which insists that individuals relate to their ultimate ends in a purely consumerist fashion. All individuals are entitled to an upbringing in which identities are not simply grafted onto them in ways which are experienced as profoundly unfree or alienating. We do not however owe children an education which guarantees they come to adulthood with the emotional and cognitive capacity to remake themselves in any manner they wish. The starting point from which we begin to build an independent, individual understanding of our own identity is not entirely within our control. We do better to think of an education for autonomy as equipping children with the cognitive and emotional tools with which to sort out what it means to live well, given who they are. And who they are will be, in part, a function of what their parents have made them as well as of their ascriptive characteristics which resist transformation. To manage autonomously within these boundaries requires, as I have already suggested, moral courage, a familiarity with the idea of "character pluralism", and a commitment to the idea that lives need to be good "from the inside." These dispositions are compatible with educations toward comprehensive visions of the good and enable children and adults to ask, "Is this life right for me?", "Am I the sort of person who...?" which are rich and respectable building blocks for independent thought and action.

To summarize: remaking our world into one in which all children are encouraged to cast all of their commitments as selected on the basis of personal preference does not seem to me either necessary for their autonomy or possible given certain fundamental facts about what it means to be human. The question of how far we could and should go in this direction remains open for debate, but it is not necessary to explore this question here. Like Sandel, I believe it is independently a good thing to see ourselves as encumbered by unchosen attachments and loyalties. But the independent worthiness of the encumbered life versus the life of Macedo's Californian is not what is at issue here.[25] The question is whether children given a very non-Californian understanding of the good life can develop the capacities necessary for autonomous thought.

7.3. Part Two

To explain more completely, and from a different perspective, why I think the answer to this question is yes, I turn now to the second text I promised to comment on: Locke's injunction that "men must think and know for themselves." As already indicated, I believe that contemporary liberals are in error when they reduce this classic definition of what it means to be autonomous to the image of the "free chooser." But to explain why distancing ourselves from our ends and educations such that we experience ourselves as self-consciously choosing the principles by which we live is not necessary to being autonomous, we need a better understanding not just of what it means to think independently, but of why liberals believe it is important to do so. What I hope to do in this discussion is to show that the core concerns of liberal theory regarding autonomy can be met by forms of autonomous thought compatible with the comprehensive educations already discussed in Part One.

What is it about the effort to "train up children in the way they should go" such that as adults they enter wholeheartedly into their parents' way of life that so disturbs liberal thinkers? What features of the human good do they fear are missing from a life shaped by such a commitment? Liberal theory tends to value autonomy for two sorts of reasons; one political, the other personal. Politically, the capacity for autonomy is important because it helps to secure the virtue of liberal justice. Personally, it is important because without it human beings cannot be said to live well. The first position on the importance of autonomy corresponds with the concerns of political liberalism; the second with so-called comprehensive or perfectionist liberalism.[26]

In *Creating Citizens*, Eamonn Callan gives a thoughtful account of how the capacity for autonomy serves liberal justice. "Good citizens have the virtue of justice", he writes:

The justice we need under pluralism requires us to think for ourselves in a much more radical way than we must when all can take for granted the same conception of the good and the right. To give the respect due to ethical viewpoints in deep conflict with our own, we must learn to enter them imaginatively and to understand that much of the pluralism that permeates our social world is a consequence not of evil or folly but of the inherent limits of human reason.[27]

Callan's concerns seem entirely valid. If all comprehensive educations left individuals unable "to give the respect due to ethical viewpoints in deep conflict with our own", liberals would indeed have deep cause for concern. Thus, the liberal state properly insists that children whose parents wish to initiate them into comprehensive visions of the good life at a minimum learn the skills necessary for mutually respectful civil cooperation. (This is not a particularly stringent test, but will exclude certain visions of the good: the extreme fringe of the survivalist movement in the United States, for example.)

Yet Callan obviously has in mind more than mutual tolerance when he speaks of the requirements of liberal justice. The capacity for responsible political deliberation in pluralist states requires, he says, imaginative empathy with understandings of the good life very different from our own. And the sort of imaginative empathy required by the virtue of liberal justice is nurtured by the same exposure to alternative ways of life that is said to be necessary to the development of autonomy. If Callan is correct about the importance of imaginative empathy, it would be a significant blow to my thesis regarding the compatibility of comprehensive educations and liberal political virtues. My assumption throughout this essay has been that comprehensive educations legitimately resist children's exposure to alternative ways of life and that this resistance is not incompatible with developing the capacities necessary to think autonomously (or, in this case, to act justly). But while I agree that the virtue of justice requires more of individuals than grudging tolerance of others' views, I think the capacity for autonomous thought and action serves liberal justice in a somewhat different way than Callan suggests (and in a manner more compatible with comprehensive educations).

No political order is perfectly just. Recognizing this truth, the best polities will cultivate citizens who have not only the capacity but the will to examine existing and proposed political practices against their society's best understandings of what justice requires. Even more to the point, good citizens must be able to challenge the community's dominant understandings of justice in the first place. A good civic education thus includes encouragement to reflect independently on the strengths and weaknesses of the existing social and political order. Children whose parents seek to initiate them into certain comprehensive understandings of the good life should not be exempted from the requirement to develop this civic capacity (which is different from the "imaginative empathy" Callan recommends).

In fact, educations to strong religious and cultural identities, because such commitments fall somewhat outside of the cultural mainstream in liberal polities, almost inevitably encourage reflection of this sort. The message children receive from such an education is that the normal way of doing things is not entirely correct or just; that they must stand up for what they think is right regardless of the consequences; that the principles by which a majority lives its life is not for that reason necessarily the best. (The children involved in the Supreme Court flag salute cases and Amish education cases, for example, were all taught these sorts of lessons.) The circumstances of a comprehensive education in a liberal society thus provide the skills and dispositions which will enable individuals to reflect upon the justice of the existing social order—without requiring the sort of imaginative empathy generally discouraged by the goals of a comprehensive education.

One more concern having to do with the relationship of justice and autonomy needs to be addressed. I have argued that children receiving comprehensive religious or cultural educations can generally be expected to develop the ability to reflect critically on the justice of the existing social order. But an education which encouraged children to adopt their parents' understanding of the good life without providing them with any ability to reflect on the justice of *this* vision would be deeply problematic. That is, the child of Muslim fundamentalists may be well equipped to challenge the understanding of justice dominant in secular democracies, but what resources has he been given with which to probe the worthiness of his own ideals? Thus, in assessing the compatibility of comprehensive educations with autonomy, we need to ask whether encumbered selves have been given the emotional and cognitive tools necessary to distance themselves sufficiently from their familial or societal educations to ask, "Are the principles by which I have been raised just? Is this a way of life worthy of human commitment in the first place?"

What it would take to prepare adults to ask that question thoughtfully and consistently is not a topic I can address in any detail now. The briefest reflection on the world around us makes it obvious that far too many citizens of any political stripe lack the interest or capacity for substantive self-critical reflection along these lines, so the problem hardly lies with comprehensive religious or cultural schooling alone. An optimistic resolution of this issue would say that children taught to question the justice of the existing social order from the point of view of their parents' religious commitments possess the capacity, in theory at least, to direct that critical sensibility against the principles by which they were taught to live. Any way of life will in practice fall short of at least some of its expressed ideals. It is perhaps in the space opened up by this disjunction that those raised to embrace comprehensive visions of the good life will find the room to reflect on the justice of their own ideals. But we may need to think more about how such self-critical reflection is elicited, both within and without comprehensive educations. (The ideas of "character pluralism" and a life that feels right "from the inside" do not engage this question of justice as directly as one might like. What might be useful in this context would be the discouragement of hypocrisy. Children raised to condemn the vice of hypocrisy would at least be attuned to circumstances in which the ideals they had been taught fall short in practice, a circumstance which could potentially invite critical reflection on the worth of these ideals.)

One reason liberals value autonomy then is for the work it does in promoting justice. If comprehensive educations toward particular visions of the good stripped individuals of the ability to think critically about the justice of the existing social order or the principles by which they lived, we would have to admit that it discouraged virtues which liberal citizens ought to have. Liberal concerns regarding comprehensive educations would then be at least partially justified. I have argued, however, that educations toward comprehensive visions of the good life, while rarely urging imaginative empathy with "ethical viewpoints in deep conflict" with one's own, nevertheless lay the groundwork for independent thinking about the justice of existing social arrangements. Children who receive this sort of education are taught to stand up for culturally marginalized ways of life and are encouraged to develop the moral courage necessary to resist pressures for conformity. If they are given as well a sensitivity to the vice of hypocrisy, they may develop the skills necessary to reflect critically on the justice of their parents' principles as well. If not, it is only fair to acknowledge that the inability to probe the justice of the ideals with which we have been raised is a problem faced across the educational spectrum, not limited to those promoting strong religious or cultural identities.

I turn now to the case for autonomy made by perfectionist liberals. Here, autonomy is commended as a good in itself, something human beings in general (or, less ambitiously, citizens of a liberal polity) require in order to live well. We need now to consider first, whether perfectionist liberals are correct (that to live a good life, human beings need to be autonomous) and second, if they are correct, whether comprehensive educations definitively thwart the development of this capacity. The best account of why autonomy should be understand as a fundamental human good is still the explanation Locke worked out in the *Second Treatise*: if men cannot "think or know for themselves," they are by default at the mercy of others' opinions and orders. To be subjected to others' wills or whims in this way is to lack the freedom to which men are entitled by virtue of their innate moral equality.[28] If parents' efforts to "train up a child in the way he should go" resulted in individuals whose adult lives were characterized by direct subordination to the personal will of another, the liberal state would be justified in seeking to create the social conditions under which such educations became rare if not impossible. However, and for reasons I have already discussed in Part One, the charge that comprehensive educations seek to secure the subordination of adult wills in this way is unpersuasive.

Admittedly not all children given comprehensive educations will become the sort of independent thinkers Locke hopes will people the liberal polity. But an inability to think for oneself is hardly an affliction suffered by the products of comprehensive education alone. As others have also begun to point out, the capacity for autonomous thought is not an automatic consequence of being raised in a world in which the good life is defined principally in terms set by Hollywood, the Gap, and MTV.

So far, so good. It is at least possible to argue that, using the Lockean definition of autonomy, children receiving comprehensive educations have at least as much a chance of achieving a satisfactory level of personal independence as do their robustly liberal counterparts. But by a process which I cannot unravel here, contemporary liberals have come to interpret the demands of autonomy in a very different way than does this Enlightenment vision. In place of a readiness to submit their beliefs to rational examination and to resist the tyrannical authority of their moral equals, autonomy is now presented as a function of "the extent that [people] choose the principles by which they live."[29] This shift of emphasis has given rise to a sort of hyperliberalism in which the requirements of autonomy are described in ways that are both unconvincing and ontologically problematic. Furthermore, by defining autonomy in this manner, liberals perpetuate the assumption that comprehensive educations are opposed to autonomy, when in fact they are not. I have already made this point in Part One. I want to conclude by saying a little more about the deficiencies of hyperliberalism in its own terms.[30]

The first difficulty is ontological. If self-making is the measure of autonomy, something must be said about the degree to which external factors (such as socialization and parental ideals) can influence us before such influence compromises the "self" of "self-legislation." Since the brute facts of human dependence in childhood are difficult to explain away, liberal theorists who begin by asserting the connection between autonomous thought and self-legislation almost immediately begin to qualify the amount of self-making autonomy requires. Thus Callan:

The truth is surely that whatever reflection autonomy requires does not demand that we can detach ourselves from all our ends. The requirement is only that we be capable of asking about the value of any particular end with which we currently identify and able to give a thoughtful answer to what we ask.[31]

Or Brighouse:

Many of our commitments *must* be formed non-autonomously. Many of our most deeply held beliefs were not selected through careful and rational weighing of the reasons for holding one belief or another, but by internalizing impressions, by trusting the testimony of others, or by trusting our hunches... Commitments generated by non-autonomous processes become autonomous when the agent reflects upon them with an appropriate degree of critical attention.[32]

I take these qualifications to represent an acknowledgement that any unqualified requirement that we "choose the principles by which we live" is too stringent; these principles are best understood as given in the course of our education and maturation. What is required to relate to these ends in an autonomous manner is some disposition to reflect on whether they are good or worthwhile goals—given the sort of person one is, the circumstances one encounters, and the challenges with which one is faced. But this is to bring us back to an image of autonomous reflection fully compatible with understanding one's ends as constitutive of one's identity. Here Callan's conclusion seems absolutely correct: "Liberal theory invites us to conceive the self as revocably encumbered in the sense that we can reject ends currently constitutive of identity should we come to see them as worthless."[33] This option remains available even to products of comprehensive education to the extent that such education includes the various "enablers" of autonomous thought discussed in Part One. Once again, when correctly understood, autonomous thought and action do not seem as much at odds with comprehensive educations as perfectionist liberals initially fear.

Another way in which hyperliberalism undercuts its own initial insistence on completely free choosing is its acceptance of a certain baseline stability in a child's education. While autonomy supposedly requires us to be the sort of people who choose our own ends, even the most robust hyperliberal is willing to concede that not all our self-understandings and commitments can be reserved for a time when we are old enough to choose freely and rationally. Some ideas of the good must be conveyed earlier as a necessary feature of human socialization. This requirement is usually excused away as the need for "cultural coherence." Levinson provides a nice account of this need:

Our conception of autonomy must incorporate a commitment to the development and preservation of cultural coherence. Individuals must be able to feel embedded within a culture or set of cultures, and to mediate their choices via the norms and social forms constitutive of their culture(s). Cultural coherence . . . both aids individuals' senses of identity and hence agency, and helps to limit individuals' range of choices to a manageable level so as to prevent their development of anomie . . .[34]

Once again we must ask whether, given such qualifications, liberal accounts of autonomy are really at such odds with the goals of comprehensive education. The initial objection to such educations is that children receiving them are not left free to choose central aspects of their identity or life goals for themselves. (In hyperliberal speak, they are not autonomous.) But the free choosing held up by liberals as central to autonomy turns out to require a background cultural embeddedness without which the individual cannot possibly choose independently. Comprehensive educations pride themselves on providing just this sort of cultural embeddedness. Why then is the provision of "cultural coherence" an acceptable and even necessary element of the development of autonomy, while inculcating comprehensive understandings of the good life are deemed autonomy-thwarting? Presumably the liberal objection to the latter is that they provide too much coherence to the developing child, but such a distinction seems strained.

It turns out then that the impulse in modern liberalism to link autonomy with the free choice of one's ends is continually being undercut by liberal political theory itself. Any attention at all to the circumstances of human development forces the realization that human beings come to maturity with an understanding of the world and what is good within it that cannot be described as freely chosen. Nor could we remake the experience of childhood and adolescence to provide such freedom without, for a start, doing away with the family as a social institution. Most liberals who recognize this developmental fact back off their initial characterization of the requirements of autonomous thought and action. The necessarily grounded nature of our understanding of the good is grudgingly acknowledged and the possibility of autonomy from within such understandings admitted. The hyperliberal account of autonomy may thus be less wedded to the idea of the completely free chooser than some of its less guarded pronouncements suggest. If so, it will be increasingly difficult to demonize comprehensive educations as antagonistic to independent thought and action. Callan's idea of the "revocably encumbered" self, for example, goes a long way toward making liberal understandings of autonomy available to the products of a comprehensive education.

But an additional problem with contemporary liberal definitions of autonomy remains. Let us go back to Dagger's definition: "People are self-legislating, autonomous rather than heteronomous, to the extent that they choose the principles by which they live."[35] There is nothing too objectionable about this definition once it is qualified in the ways I have just discussed. The choice at issue is less a choice in the void than a capacity to consider and if necessary set aside the principles given to us as part of the process of becoming social, culturally grounded beings. Autonomy understood in this fashion is available to encumbered selves. An encumbered self is autonomous when it reflects on the value of its (unchosen) loyalties, either in universal terms (is this a good way of life from the perspective of justice? is it worthy of human commitment in the first place?) or in strictly personal ones (is this a good way of life for *me*? the child of *these* parents? raised in *this* country? having *these* physical characteristics? etc.) What I now want to discuss is the liberals' view of the sort of education children need in order effectively to evaluate their ends in this manner. What does an education toward autonomy conceived in this manner entail?

Contemporary liberal thought speaks with a unified voice on this question. An education for autonomy requires children to be given a sense of the "very different lives which could be theirs."[36] Choosing freely the principles by which we live requires us critically to compare our parents' favored way of life with other alternatives on offer in the world today. Only once we have subjected our views to such a comparative evaluation can we be said to identify with our ends autonomously. No critical comparison; no autonomy.

This is the feature of contemporary liberal understandings of autonomy that I said earlier was unpersuasive. Even if we agree that "autonomy is the ability to control our lives by reasoned choice",[37] the liberal understanding of how to cultivate this ability seems profoundly off the mark. Eamonn Callan's able work is once again the focus of my comments.[38] He begins his discussion of education for autonomy in a liberal democracy by quoting Ackerman's account with approval. ("The entire educational system will, if you like, resemble a great sphere. Children land upon the sphere at different points, depending on their primary culture; the task is to help them explore the globe..."[39]) He then describes the "normative core" of this idea in the following way: "The essential demand is that schooling properly involves at some stage sympathetic and critical engagement with beliefs and ways of life at odds with the culture of the family or religious or ethnic group into which the child is born."[40] In other words, good polities will ensure that children who attend public schools receive educations which challenge rather than affirm their parents' values and ways of life, and that such education is necessary to ensure their autonomy.

Apart from the astonishing arrogance of this claim and the fact that it is rarely applied with vigor to enthusiasts of the mainstream secular, consumer culture, its persuasiveness as a prescription for autonomy depends in part on why such engagement is deemed essential. Ignorant antipathy toward other ways of life encountered in one's polity is incompatible with the requirements of liberal justice.

Schooling properly attempts to remove such prejudice and some sympathetic exposure to other ways of life in order to prevent their political demonization may be necessary to this end. But perfectionist liberals pursue a different agenda. They seek to assure that no child receive an education which condemns him to a life of "ethical servility" or to a role or identity which he experiences as alienating or profoundly unsuited to his temperament or circumstances. I have already argued that every child needs to be able to consider whether a particular vision of the good life is worthy of her allegiance, from both a political and personal perspective, considered separately from the commitments of her parents. But this sort of autonomous reflection, which the liberal state justifiably seeks to ensure, does not require the thorough comparative knowledge of different ways of life championed by Ackerman and Callan. Rather, children receiving educations toward certain comprehensive visions of the good life could equally well be exposed to the very different ways in which persons committed to similar understandings of the good life or similar cultural identities interpreted these ends. Questions such as "Who am I? What goods ought to compel my allegiance? What weight do I give to the different components which make up my identity?" all encourage reflection on what counts as a good life for me without requiring extensive familiarity with how very different sorts of people from very different circumstances choose to live their lives. In fact, resources for this sort of education exist within the cultural scripts of most comprehensive religious or cultural identities.

It is also important to ascertain what "at some stage" means. Much of the liberal vision regarding an appropriate education for autonomy would be unremarkable if it were presented as a program for secondary education in liberal democracies. Children over the age of sixteen possess the cognitive capacities and self-awareness to begin to make the identities they have evolved as children their own. In this process, the opportunity to evaluate their own commitments in the light of others' values may be helpful. I am still not sure the liberal state possesses the authority to insist on such exposure over parents' or children's objections—this is in part the question raised by the debate over *Wisconsin* v. *Yoder*.[41] But much recent advocacy in liberal educational theory has been directed toward the worth of exposing much younger children to points of view not specifically endorsed by their parents.[42] The children at issue in *Mozert* v. *Hawkins*, for example, were only in the sixth grade. Liberal theory needs to be clearer about the stage at which exposure to alternative understandings of the good life is appropriate, linking this claim to a better understanding of what we now know about children's psychological and cognitive development.

Callan goes on to gloss his "essential demand" in the following manner: "My claim is that to understand ethical diversity in the educationally relevant sense presupposes some experience of entering imaginatively into ways of life that are strange, even repugnant, and some developed ability to respond to them with interpretive charity."[43] Another disturbing prescription, again made more worrisome by uncertainty about the age at which such exposure is recommended (Five? Fifteen? Twenty?). Philosophers from Plato to Rousseau have expressed concern about the impact on individual character of mimetic exercises. A recommendation that children be encouraged to "enter imaginatively" into ways of life they or their parents find repugnant needs to confront such concerns.

Again, the liberal state may demand of its citizens sufficient appreciation of alternative ways of life such that civil cooperation between cultural groups is made possible. This may include some sympathetic engagement with lifestyles certain liberal citizens initially find repugnant. But this education has a different emphasis than one which presumes to ensure that citizens' *own* allegiances are made freely, autonomously. To secure this end it seems to me that exposure to "repugnant" ideals is not only unnecessary but counterproductive. As discussed in Part One, achieving an autonomous relationship to our ends or identity requires reflecting on whether they are "right for me", a practice which will be impossible without certain enablers of autonomous thought such as moral courage, a familiarity with the idea of character pluralism, and the valuing of a life that feels right "from the inside." Familiarity with the different ways in which others who share one's ideals go on to realize them is also helpful. However, familiarity with and appreciation for ways of life completely alien to one's own is unnecessary. My daughters' autonomous relation to the values our family holds about women's equality will not be particularly enhanced by any exhortation seriously to consider the life lived by the veiled Muslim girls they have seen in London. That life is simply unavailable to them given who they are. What they need to make their identities their own is an understanding of the different ways in which Americans committed to the principle of women's equality live this principle in practice. (How does the balance between work and family life struck in our household differ from the balance chosen by their friends' parents, for example? What about the division of household labor?) Sustained, sympathetic exposure to different ways of life creates a cosmopolitan person, not an autonomous one.

Insisting on such exposure to alternative ways of life as the pre-condition of autonomy is also counterproductive. It creates the false impression that a truly autonomous relation to one's ends or identity requires individuals to "shop" for their ideals—or at least agree to take a "taste test" before sticking with the brand their parents "bought." But this image of the autonomous individual as informed consumer misconceives the relationship between choice and autonomy. The effort to be autonomous seems better characterized as a struggle to fit our already internalized ideas of what it means to live well with various challenges we encounter in our effort actually to live a good life. Deciding what to do in these circumstances does not seem to involve first and foremost a rapid polling of all the various ways in which humans understand what it means to live well. Rather we try to sort out, as the occasion arises, what it means for me, this person, to live well given these circumstances. To think independently at these moments (in conscious resistance to the pressures of convention, tradi-tion, and authority) requires us to look inwards not outwards. "Is this the best understanding of what it means to be the sort of person I believe I am?" is the sort of question autonomous individuals ask in dif-ficult circumstances. "What sort of person am I? and why?" are neces-sary subsidiary questions which must be answered as well. (A good example of this sort of deliberation, its causes, and effects, are provided by Edward Norton's character in the recent film, *American History X*. His character also provides a useful warning that the capacity to reflect critically upon one's parents' ideals and way of life does not in itself lead one to embrace either liberal or democratic values.) Instruction in the capacities necessary for this sort of reflection is the type of education for autonomy which could usefully be provided at the primary and secondary level, and to which parents skeptical of mainstream liberal culture would have less reason to make objection.

7.4. Conclusion

"We . . . need to teach children the skills needed to make comparative evaluations between their parents' and others' ways of life in order to give them a real opportunity to live well."[44] Here is the perfec-tionist liberal claim in all its glory. In order to ensure that individuals have the chance to be autonomous, the state needs to give children the tools with which to weigh the comparative worthiness of the way of life their parents think best against an unspecified selection of alternative possibilities. If the view Brighouse espouses here is correct, comprehensive educations cannot but appear inimical to the development of autonomy.

Comprehensive educations call for children to be protected from premature exposure to alternative ways of life, both because children are understood as lacking the necessary emotional and cognitive maturity to judge correctly between them and because too early an invitation to understand one's ends as "selectable" undermines the possibilities for certain non-consumerist but still choiceworthy ways of life. In Part One I provided some reasons why comprehensive educations which reject such exposure ought not on that account to be interpreted as hostile to the development of autonomy. But little headway can be made in this direction as long as liberal theory affirms, with Brighouse, that "autonomy with respect to one's religious and moral commitments requires exposure to alternative views."

Is this connection a necessary one? I have tried in Part Two to give some reasons for interpreting the requirements of autonomy more liberally than contemporary liberalism generally allows. Such a recasting of liberal autonomy would have the triple advantage of bringing contemporary liberal views into closer connection with core commitments of the liberal tradition (i.e. Locke on autonomy); into greater harmony with how individuals actually experience the demand to think and act autonomously (i.e. we do not go shopping for principles in some grand moral IKEA), and into deeper appreciation of the resources for independent thought and living well made available by educations which seek to "train up a child in the way he should go" in the hopes that "when he is old he will not depart from it."

NOTES

For comments on earlier drafts of this article, I am especially grateful to Richard Dagger, John Gould, Meira Levinson, and James Murphy as well as to fellow participants in the June 2000 conference on Collective Identities and Cosmopolitan Values at McGill University.

1. Proverbs 22: 6.
2. John Locke, *Essay on Human Understanding* (Atlantic Highlands, NJ: Humanities Press, 1978), 39.
3. Ibid., 41.
4. Eamonn Callan, "Autonomy, Child-rearing, and Good Lives." in David Archard and Colin M. Mcleod, eds. *The Moral and Political Status of Children* Oxford: Oxford University Press, 2002.
5. Theorists who argue along these lines include Bruce Ackerman, *Social Justice in the Liberal State* (New Haven: Yale University Press, 1980); Stephen Macedo, *Liberal Virtues* (Oxford: Oxford University Press, 1990); Eamonn Callan, *Creating Citizens* (Oxford: Oxford University Press, 1997); Richard Dagger,

Civic Virtues: Rights, Citizenship and Republican Liberalism (Oxford: Oxford University Press, 1997); Meira Levinson, *The Demands of Liberal Education* (Oxford: Oxford University Press, 1999); Harry Brighouse, *School Choice and Social Justice* (Oxford: Oxford University Press, 2000); and Rob Reich, *Liberalism, Multiculturalism, and Education* (Chicago: The University of Chicago Press, 2002). Obviously these authors do not exhaust the contemporary literature on autonomy, but because they have had the most to say about the supposed threat comprehensive educations pose to autonomous capacity, their works are the ones I confront most directly in this essay. For criticism of comprehensive educations from a democratic perspective, see Amy Gutmann, *Democratic Education* (Princeton: Princeton University Press, 1987) and Richard Arneson and Ian Shapiro, "Democratic Autonomy and Religious Freedom: A Critique of *Wisconsin* v. *Yoder*", in Ian Shapiro and Russell Hardin (eds), *NOMOS XXXVIII: Political Order* (New York: New York University Press, 1996). I do not address the concerns raised in these works here.

6. Dagger, *Civic Virtues*, 26.
7. Michael Sandel, "The Procedural Republic and the Unencumbered Self", *Political Theory*, 12 (1984), 81–96; and Callan, *Creating Citizens*.
8. Michael Sandel, *Liberalism and the Limits of Justice* (Cambridge: Cambridge University Press, 1982), 150.
9. Richard Dagger, "The Sandelian Republic and the Encumbered Self", *Review of Politics*, 61 (1999), 181–217.
10. Michael Sandel, "The Procedural Republic and the Unencumbered Self", *Political Theory*, 12 (1984), 23.
11. Callan, *Creating Citizens*, 60.
12. Ibid., 60.
13. Ibid., 60.
14. Ibid., 60–1.
15. Ibid., 133.
16. Ibid., 148.
17. Ibid., 56.
18. Ibid., 57.
19. Ibid., 133.
20. Ibid., 152–7.
21. For a different account of the place of the final two criteria in enabling autonomy to which I am indebted for my discussion, see Brighouse, *School Choice and Social Justice*, 69–75.
22. Ibid., 69–70.
23. Will Kymlicka, *Multicultural Citizenship* (Oxford: Oxford University Press, 1995), 80–4.
24. David Norton, *Democracy and Moral Development: A Politics of Virtue* (Berkeley: University of California Press, 1991).
25. "Liberalism, holds out the promise, or the threat, of making all the world like California." Macedo, *Liberal Virtues*, 278.
26. Brighouse, *School Choice and Social Justice*, and Levinson, *The Demands of Liberal Education* are among recent works to suggest that so-called political liberalism necessarily builds on a perfectionist base. Even if this is true, it is still helpful to separate the political and personal reasons for valuing autonomy under these rubrics.
27. Callan, *Creating Citizens*, 43.
28. John Locke, *Two Treatises of Government* (Cambridge: Cambridge University Press, 1960); Dagger, *Civic Virtues*, ch. 3.

29. For an account in which Rawls plays the central role in this shift, see Dagger, *Civic Virtues*, 38.
30. These are not the only criticisms that can be made of liberal understandings of autonomy, although they are the ones that bear most directly on the problems posed by comprehensive educations. For a more expansive critique, see especially Jennifer Nedelsky, "Reconceiving Autonomy: Sources, Thoughts and Possibilities", *Yale Journal of Law and Feminism*, 1 (1989), 7–36.
31. Callan, *Creating Citizens*, 54.
32. Brighouse, *School Choice and Social Justice*, 67.
33. Callan, *Creating Citizens*, 54.
34. Levinson, *The Demands of Liberal Education*, 31.
35. Dagger, *Civic Virtues*, 38.
36. Ackerman, *Social Justice in the Liberal State*.
37. Dagger, *Civic Virtues*, 38.
38. These views are modified in Callan, "Autonomy, Child-rearing and Good Lives", which offers a more appreciative account of the resources for autonomy available from within traditional religious upbringings. My comments here focus on the claims made in *Creating Citizens*.
39. Ackerman, *Social Justice in the Liberal State*, 159.
40. Callan, 133.
41. Shelley Burtt, "In Defense of *Yoder*: Parental Authority and the Public Schools," in Ian Shapiro and Russell Haredin, eds., *NOMOS XXXIX: Political Order* (New York: New York University Press, 1996).
42. James Dwyer, *Religious Schools* v. *Children's Rights* (Ithaca: Cornell University Press, 1998); Nomi Stolzenberg, " 'He Drew a Circle That Shut Me Out': Assimilation, Indoctrination, and the Paradox of Liberal Education", *Harvard Law Review*, 106 (1993), 581–667.
43. Callan, *Creating Citizens*, 133.
44. Brighouse, School Choice and Social Justice, 73.

CHAPTER 8

Citizenship as Identity, Citizenship as Shared Fate, and the Functions of Multicultural Education

Melissa S. Williams

8.1. Introduction

To what extent must liberal democracies accommodate particularistic identities, and to what extent must they focus, instead, on inculcating a shared identity of democratic citizenship? This is the question that has predominated in current debates over group identity and democratic education in liberal societies. In this chapter, I want to explore the possibility that it is the wrong question; I wish to cast doubt on its implicit premise that meaningful citizenship and stable constitutional order must be grounded in a shared identity among citizens. More specifically, I want to challenge the idea that we should understand citizenship in terms of an allegiance to certain moral commitments, and the function of democratic education as the inculcation of those commitments. Ideas of citizenship as loyalty, allegiance, patriotism, and commitment have their roots, I believe, in much older rites and conceptions of trustworthiness (such as feudal oath-taking). Although I will not be able to explore these historical connections as deeply as I would like, they help to us to envisage the possibility that *any* notion of citizenship as identity—as deeply constitutive of the individual's sense of self—will lead to implicit or explicit standards of loyalty as the precondition for full membership. And wherever loyalty becomes the standard, there is a natural tendency to be suspicious of those whose outward forms and inward habits of mind are different from those of commonly recognized paragons of citizenship.

The concept of citizenship as identity is thickly interwoven with the emergence of the modern nation-state. It is now a commonplace that the modern nation-state, and the conception of national sovereignty that accompanies it, are under growing pressure from the cluster of phenomena we call "globalization." This ongoing transformation in the foundation of political order offers us an opportunity to reconsider the meaning of citizenship, particularly in view of the fact that the sites and targets of political involvement are so rapidly changing (witness the demonstrations by transnational labor, environmental, and human rights groups against the transnational WTO in Seattle and Genoa, and the IMF in Prague). These changes lead us to ask new questions about the various ways in which meaningful citizenship is (or is not) contingent upon boundaries of various sorts, and in the second part of the chapter I will explore this question. The basic line of argument here is that most of our current understandings of citizenship are based on the historic *convergence* of boundaries of citizenship (territorial, cultural/national/linguistic, institutional, and moral) that are now pulling apart. The heightened salience of the concept of "multicultural society" in the last decade or so is, perhaps, largely traceable to these changes.

In Section 8.3 of the chapter, I want to explore the idea that, instead of a model of citizenship-as-identity, we should move toward an idea of citizenship as membership in a community of shared fate. Here, the idea is not that membership entails a shared *identity* with any particular content, but comes by virtue of being entangled with others in such a way that one's future is tied to theirs. For most of us, membership in such a web of relationships has resulted from a multiplicity of causes, and is chosen in some regards and not in others. Certainly, the conditions in which we find ourselves have many historical roots which are obviously not objects of our choice (though, as Burke taught us, we have some choice about how to interpret our history and its implications for our future). When coupled with a rudimentary conception of democratic legitimacy, that we should be able to justify our actions to those who are affected by them, the notion of a community of shared fate can yield a *pragmatic* conception of citizenship that is freed from the pernicious tendencies that (I will have argued) are inherent to notions of citizenship as identity.

In the final part of the chapter, I will discuss the implications of this view of citizenship for democratic education. Although my thinking on these issues is quite preliminary, I am inclined toward the view that preparing children to participate as citizens of shared fate would emphasize teaching them to understand themselves as connected to others through a history that was not of their making, but as having the agency to remake those connections according to their own best judgments.

8.2. *Citizenship as Identity and the Project of Nation-Building*

Much of contemporary democratic theory begins from the supposition that meaningful democratic citizenship requires that citizens share a subjective sense of membership in a single political community. This sense of shared membership, theorists argue, constitutes a distinctive *identity*, that is, it partially constitutes individuals' understandings of who they are.[1] Political membership is internalized as an *affective bond* to the political community and its other members. Joseph Carens calls this the psychological dimension of citizenship: "[One] way to belong to a political community is to *feel* that one belongs, to be connected to it through one's sense of emotional attachment, identification, and loyalty."[2] As Benedict Anderson famously expressed this idea in his study of nationalism, individuals internalize a political identity by seeing themselves as members in an "imagined community", a community comprised of individuals with whom they never have any face-to-face contact.[3] In modern democratic societies, it is this imagined community—not the city within its walls, whose citizens know one another—that constitutes the "self" of political self-rule, and the "people" of popular sovereignty.

But not just any collection of human beings is eligible for the status of a democratic people; there must be some substance that binds them together in order that individuals should have a reason to identify with *this* political community rather than any of the other communities in the world. Recent work on nationalism has yielded two candidates for this binding substance: culture or values. These options correspond to the distinction between ethnic nationalism, in which the political community is defined by a shared language, history, and culture, and civic nationalism, in which the political community is defined by a shared commitment to core principles of democratic legitimacy.

Liberal democrats have joined other theorists of democracy in affirming that democratic citizenship rests on some shared substantive identity among citizens, but have argued that a commitment to certain core liberal principles—equality, freedom, toleration, and constitutionalism—is substance enough to sustain a stable democratic community. So long as the great majority of the population affirms these principles as morally authoritative, at least with regard to *political* relations among individuals, we have met a necessary (though perhaps not sufficient) condition of popular self-government, a coherent "people." Whether one wishes to call this "civic nationalism", "constitutional patriotism", or simply "civic community",[4] the crux of this view is that by grounding political community in a shared commitment to core principles liberal democracy can overcome the dark side of ethnic nationalism, in particular its tendency to exclude people outside the *ethnos* from full political membership, whether or not they live within state boundaries.

Nonetheless, critics of the distinction between ethnic and civic nationalism have argued persuasively that liberal theory relies covertly upon the nationalist strategy in its account of political community and democratic citizenship. It must do so, they argue, because liberalism itself offers no principle by which to define the demos, to establish *which* affirmers of core liberal principles owe the peculiar obligations of liberal democratic citizenship to each other. Yet liberal democracy does distinguish the rights and obligations of citizenship from the thinner class of rights and obligations that attach to humanity as such. Liberal democracy needs the boundaries that define a demos, but cannot provide them from within its own concepts and principles. Voluntary consent would be the obvious liberal principle for inclusion, but consent by itself does not do the necessary work, for even liberal democratic states must be established in a particular territory, with particular borders, with the inevitable consequence that some of their members will arrive in their jurisdictions by birth and not by choice. Liberal democracies that are fully civic, in the sense that they are free of the taint of any ethnic basis of citizenship, nonetheless confer legal citizenship on the basis of birth.[5]

But citizenship by birth is not the only continuity between liberalism and nationalism, as Yael Tamir argues persuasively in her book, *Liberal Nationalism*. It will not suffice, for liberal democracy, that individuals merely affirm the validity of core liberal principles. In addition, it is important that they feel an *affective attachment* to those principles, to the citizens who share them, and to the regime that embodies them. In short, it is important that they have some sense of *loyalty* to the principles, to fellow citizens, and to the constitutional order that connects them. Why does liberalism require more of citizens than that they affirm the valid authority of basic legal and constitutional norms? Why does it require, further, that they *internalize* these norms as part of their subjective sense of self, that is, as part of their identities? And why does it require a sense of attachment to the particular others who share political society with them?

Two broad liberal ends seem to depend upon an affective attachment to the regime and to co-citizens. The first is distributive justice. Tamir argues that the liberal conception of distributive justice "is only meaningful in states that do not see themselves as voluntary associations but as ongoing and relatively closed communities whose members share a common fate. Within such communities, members develop mutual attachments that supply the moral justifications required for assuming mutual obligations... The 'other' with whom we share the fruits and burdens of cooperation must be identifiable and familiar."[6] She continues: "Communal solidarity creates a feeling, or an illusion, of closeness and shared fate, which is a precondition of distributive justice. It endows particularistic relations with moral power, supporting the claim that 'charity begins at home.' Moreover, the morality of community can serve as grounds for justifying the allocation of resources to the well-being of future generations, and to the study and preservation of the communal past. Consequently, the community-like nature of the nation-state is particularly well-suited, and perhaps even necessary, to the notion of the liberal welfare state."[7]

Eamonn Callan similarly views citizens' emotional attachment to each other and to the political community—what he calls "liberal patriotism"—as a necessary condition of liberal justice. "So far as citizens come to think of justice as integral to a particular political community they care about, in which their own fulfilment and that of their fellow citizens are entwined in a common fate, then the sacrifices and compromises that justice requires cannot be sheer loss in the pursuit of one's own good."[8] Walter Feinberg is even more forthright in stating a connection between nationalism and social welfare provision: "The source of national identity is often connected... to the belief that a people share a common origin in terms of historical experience, culture, or language. It is also connected to a web of mutual aid that extends back in time and creates future obligations and expectations."[9]

The second liberal end that appears to depend upon a strong attachment to the regime is political stability. This connection has been made most clearly and consistently by John Rawls in his explication of the idea of an overlapping consensus, particularly in his historical account of how an overlapping consensus on a political conception of justice comes into being. If we take a snapshot view of Rawls's idea of an overlapping consensus, the issue of citizens' emotional stance toward principles of justice and political institutions does not seem to arise. That is, the overlapping consensus consists in individuals' substantive moral agreement on core ideas and principles that provide a sufficient basis for a political conception of justice. This moral agreement, Rawls argues, lends stability to the regime grounded in the political conception of justice, because individuals conscientiously affirm its core principles. In contrast to a "mere *modus vivendi*", in which individuals agree to be governed by certain rules and institutions because it serves their self-interest, a political order that has the support of an overlapping consensus need not fear that individuals will defect from its scheme of social cooperation the moment the balance of power shifts.[10] To put it slightly differently, the stability of a regime based on an overlapping consensus arises from the fact that its basic principles constitute a part of individuals' *moral identity*. To abandon those principles would be an act of self-betrayal, a compromise of personal integrity much more costly than the sacrifice of marginal gains to material self-interest. Stephen Macedo expresses this idea especially forcefully: "[T]he civic health of liberal democracies depends not simply on a clear division of spheres, but on a deeper convergence of public and private values: a convergence of individual consciences and the public good powerful enough to ensure the political supremacy of public values and institutions against competing imperatives."[11]

The relationship between individual moral identity and the basic principles of a political conception of justice provides one source of individuals' affective attachment to a political liberal regime, in Rawls's view. In addition, his *historical* account of the emergence of an overlapping consensus provides a second reason for this attachment. There, he argues that the regime of liberal toleration that arose out of the religious wars of the sixteenth and seventeenth centuries was originally an agreement based on mutual advantage, a *modus vivendi* or peace treaty which was unstable insofar as parties had no reason not to defect as soon as circumstances would allow them to dominate the others. In time, however, this interest-based agreement thickened into what Rawls calls a "constitutional consensus", then finally into an overlapping consensus among individuals on the fundamental intuitive ideas from which a political conception of justice could be built.[12]

For my purposes here, what is most fascinating about this story is the different ways in which individuals come to participate in the overlapping consensus. For some, they affirm it because their comprehensive conceptions of the good (some religious views, all comprehensive liberalisms) include the principles of individual freedom and equality that also define the core of political liberalism. For others, though, there is no immediate substantive connection between their comprehensive views and political liberalism. In their cases, their affirmation of the political conception arises out of prolonged experience with liberal institutions, the sense that those institutions benefit them and create the conditions for a healthy society, and the fact that they have become accustomed to them. In other words, they become attached to these institutions because they have been socialized through them and like the results, and this is sufficient to secure their commitment to the political conception as it has been embodied in a particular constitutional order through time.[13] This, then, may include an unreflective emotional attachment that has been internalized as part of individuals' sense of their own identity, but which does not entail a conscious or self-critical stance toward basic principles themselves. Rawls does not appear to count the stability that comes from this sort of political identification as any less desirable than the stability that comes from a reflective affirmation of the basic principles, so long as the principles and institutions themselves *could* be justified to a more questioning citizenry.[14]

Eamonn Callan and Stephen Macedo—both of whom acknowledge their indebtedness to and sympathy with Rawls's view—state liberal democracies' reliance on their members' strong attachment to the political community much more overtly than does Rawls himself. Callan notes both the distributive and the stability-based reasons for this reliance: "[T]he justice of the society [Rawls] envisages depends partly on people not being strongly disposed to leave whenever they would benefit more from the distributive principles that apply elsewhere ... And the stability of the society depends in part on ethnic or other subgroups being disinclined to pursue secession."[15] Although the liberal project begins from the presupposition of religious and moral pluralism, there is a limit to its capacity to absorb all forms of diversity. When pluralism is partly constituted by religious or other groups that disavow an attachment to the liberal regime and its core principles, it threatens the stability of just liberal institutions. Macedo's recent work makes this point very strongly: "[D]iversity needs to be *kept in its place*. ... Diversity is sometimes invoked as a way of taking liberal democratic principles more seriously, but at other times the invocation of diversity and multicultural ideals undermines the very possibility of a public morality."[16] "Talk of diversity", Macedo argues, "often proceeds without taking adequate account of the degree of moral convergence it takes to sustain a constitutional order that is liberal, democratic, and characterized by widespread bonds of civic friendship and co-operation."[17]

According to this view of democratic stability, the proliferation of some forms of diversity in liberal democratic societies is likely to have grave consequences. "A liberal democratic polity *cannot endure* without citizens willing to support its fundamental institutions and principles."[18] It therefore "behooves us to try to understand what must be done from a political standpoint to keep Sydney from becoming Sarajevo, or Boston from becoming Beirut."[19] These worries about threats of diversity—and of being too generous in accommodating difference within public policy—are twofold. On the one hand, they express a concern that an overindulgent attitude toward non-liberal minorities will threaten liberal values directly, perhaps by violating the interests in freedom or equality of individuals *within* the groups, perhaps by diminishing other citizens' confidence in the legitimacy and sufficiency of liberal principles to ground a just political order. On the other hand, there is a danger in exception making itself, whether or not the group in question is actually opposed to core liberal principles. This latter concern is the worry about "balkanisation" or governability, that once groups develop a sense of entitlement to exceptions or exemptions or special accommodations, they "open a floodgate of complaints and requests for exemptions" that quickly overwhelm the capacity of political officials and agencies.[20]

The difficulty, according to Macedo and Callan, is that liberal democracies do not *necessarily* or *automatically* generate only acceptable forms of social diversity. With somewhat different emphasis, they both criticize Rawls for presupposing that just liberal institutions will tend to produce citizens who feel the requisite attachments to liberal principles and to the political community. "[L]iberal citizens do not come into existence naturally", Macedo tells us.[21] Yet having a critical mass of citizens with appropriate moral commitments and affective attachments is too important to leave to chance. Repeating an enduring theme in the history of political philosophy, theorists such as Macedo, Callan, and Walter Feinberg argue that a just regime must not merely adapt itself to its citizens, but must consciously mould citizens who are capable of living within it. The project of democratic education in pluralist societies must include "the task of creating citizens who share a sufficiently cohesive political identity", Callan argues.[22] As Macedo puts it, "[o]ur constitutional order must shape citizens, and not only establish political institutions."[23]

What sort of identity should a program of civic education inculcate in citizens? Although defenders of citizenship as identity acknowledge that individuals are bearers of multiple and sometimes conflicting identities—through their roles within families, through their work lives and choice of career, through their cultural memberships, through their religious commitments—they tend to argue that *political* identity depends on attachment to a *particular* political community, and to only one such community. Civic education, then, has the task of inculcating individuals' loyalty and attachment to one and only one national political community. As Walter Feinberg puts it, "What children pick up when they take on a national identity is the idea that nationhood involves collective inclusion and exclusion in a past, present, and future stream of activities, sufferings, and anticipations.... Through the nation individuals are brought together as *a people* and as such ... they stand in distinction from others who are brought together as a *different people*."[24]

Moreover, the other attachments that compete for individual loyalty must not be so strong that they conflict with political loyalty. In effect, this means that whatever other sources of identity shape individual action, in cases of conflict it is their political identity that must prevail. Shared citizenship thus requires "a commitment to a common authority that can *override local interests, local decisions, and local ways of knowing*."[25] Macedo argues: "A liberal polity does not rest on diversity, but on *shared political commitments weighty enough to override competing values*."[26] One of the functions of education is to encourage individuals to "assimilate in non-oppressive ways and toward justifiable values."[27] Such education must go far beyond merely teaching children about their rights and obligations as citizens. In a stable liberal polity, "liberal institutions and practices shape *all* of our *deepest moral commitments* in such a way as to make them supportive of liberalism."[28] As I discussed above, the idea of citizenship-as-identity rests on the supposition that political identity shapes and constitutes the individual conscience itself.

We have seen that the stability that liberal regimes enjoy as a result of individuals' moral and emotional identification has the same *form* as political stability in other types of regime. Any regime can find resources for stability in its subjects' identification with its ideological principles and their affective attachment to the regime and its populace. However, the *content* of the moral identity these liberals seek to inculcate is distinctive to liberalism. In particular, they agree that a robust liberal democratic citizenship depends on individuals' affirmation of basic principles of equality, freedom, and toleration. Whether this moral identity is relatively thick, involving a commitment to the ideal of individual autonomy and an acceptance of what Rawls calls the "burdens of judgment", or relatively thin, requiring only a general belief in principles of individual equality and political liberty, is a matter of some disagreement among theorists.[29]

Related to this substantive conception of individual identity is the liberal account of the developed *skills, capacities,* and *virtues* on which a healthy liberal democracy depends.[30] Especially important is the developed capacity for critical reflection on matters of public concern: to fulfil the protective function of democratic self-government, individuals must be able to judge whether or not public officials are acting justly and in the public interest. And to participate in the work of democratic self-rule, they need to be able to engage with other citizens in an ongoing reasoned deliberation about matters that affect them. This capacity must include an ability to formulate and articulate arguments through the use of reasons that other citizens can recognize and accept, as well as a capacity for engaged listening to other citizens. Associated virtues include civility, a respectful demeanor toward other citizens even when one disagrees with them. All of these interrelated capacities and virtues are among the important aims of democratic education in a liberal society.[31]

On this view of liberal citizenship, then, creating the conditions in which citizen identity can flourish is a crucial part of the project of nation-building. At the same time, these theorists recognize that the project of building national identity has historically had a dark side. Not only has there been a strong tendency, in liberal democracies as in other regimes, to read the identity of dominant social groups into the content of citizen identity. Beyond this, the project of nation-building in the United States and elsewhere has been based on the conscious and intentional marginalization of women and ethnic minorities. As Rogers Smith has powerfully demonstrated in the American case, "for over 80 per cent of US history, American laws declared most people in the world legally ineligible to become full US citizens solely because of their race, original nationality, or gender."[32] This exclusion was no oversight or accident; it was directly tied to the project of constructing a stable political order through the promotion of particular understandings of national identity. Similar stories can be told about Canada.[33] Exclusion and marginalization have not been the only costs of constructing national identities; policies of forcible assimilation for indigenous peoples have devastated their communities and are clearly tied to contemporary phenomena of anomie, poverty, ill health, and extremely high suicide rates in many of those communities.

Given these historic costs of projects aimed at constructing citizen identity, liberal theorists who wish to defend an identity-building civic education are at pains to distinguish their agendas from those of the past. Tamir argues that while it is impossible to construct a liberal state that is culturally neutral, it is imperative for the legitimacy of liberal regimes that they respect the rights of self-determination of national or cultural minorities within their boundaries.[34] A program of democratic education within a liberal state should include an education for national–cultural identity (particular to each cultural community), an education for democratic participation, and an education for a respect for cultural diversity.[35] Macedo also argues that civic education is fully compatible with respect for those forms of social, cultural, and religious diversity that are consonant with liberal democracy. Callan and Feinberg pay particular attention to the requirements of a democratic education which is not oppressive to cultural and religious minorities.[36] Despite the differences among them, all of these theorists, then, believe that inculcating citizen identity through democratic education is fully compatible with respect for diversity and a commitment to equality within a multicultural society.

I am less confident than these theorists that an educational project of inculcating citizen identity is easy to reconcile with the egalitarian treatment of citizens from cultural and religious minorities. Nor am I persuaded that this educational project is the most promising route to robust democratic citizenship in diverse societies, particularly in an age of globalization, when the nation-state and the conception of popular sovereignty which it enabled bear a diminishing resemblance to the nexus of political relationships in which individuals find themselves.

Let me begin by explaining why I believe that a conception of citizenship as identity stands in tension with an inclusive and egalitarian approach to minority citizens. We saw above that various theorists have linked the project of inculcating citizen identity to the idea of *loyalty* to the political community, its basic principles of justice, and its other members. A loyal citizenry sustains political stability by being willing to make sacrifices of narrow self-interest in difficult times, even when exit from the community might yield more benefits to the individual than staying within it. The virtue of loyalty does not necessarily entail amoral patriotism, the attitude of "my country, right or wrong." It may, indeed, emphasize the contribution to legitimacy and to long-term stability of "loyal opposition", in which individuals criticize the regime for failing to live up to its own principles or to the highest standard of the public good. These were precisely the terms in which many articulated the goals of abolitionism, the Black Civil Rights movement in the United States, and the women's suffrage movement.

I do not dispute, then, the idea that a loyal citizenry can contribute to political stability in ways that are fully consonant with democratic equality. My concern, rather, is with the valorization of citizen loyalty as a virtue that we should attempt to inculcate through the use of state institutions, and as a measure of the worth or standing of citizens in a democratic society. The dark side of the claim that we have good reason to trust fellow citizens who affirm their commitment to liberal principles and constitutional order is the implication that we have good reason to *distrust* individuals who refuse to affirm this commitment. The confidence we feel in the stability of our political order when most citizens have internalized a sense of political loyalty has its mirror image in the *fear* of disorder that we feel when we observe other citizens who disavow a sense of loyalty or whose beliefs contradict core liberal values.

The articulation of a substantive content of a healthy citizen identity—an identification at the level of individual conscience with core liberal values, an affirmation of the value of tolerance toward those whose ways of life are different from our own, and a commitment to reasonableness as the standard of political deliberation—tends to slide very easily into an argument that individuals who do not display this identity are unhealthy as citizens and are unworthy of political trust. Thus, although the Amish "pose no threat to the health of the wider liberal society" because of their insularity and small size, Protestant fundamentalists do pose such a threat because "[t]hey are far more numerous and powerful, and they are actively engaged in political activity."[37] On this view, individuals or groups whose beliefs earn the label "illiberal" or "unreasonable" should not have equal standing to be heard or respected within liberal democratic politics. "[S]ome groups have been pushed to the margins of society for good reason, and the last thing we want is a politics of indiscriminate inclusion."[38] Further, the substantive standards of good citizenship may lead us to probe into individuals' consciences to ascertain whether "liberal institutions and practices shape *all* of [their] *deepest* moral commitments."[39]

Anxieties about political stability, and related suspicion of groups that do not converge on mainstream values and ways of life, are nothing new in the politics of liberal democracies. It is no surprise that such anxieties might lead us to seek assurances from those who do not conform to the standards of healthy citizenship. As the late Judith Shklar emphasized, Americans have been particularly enamored of extracting loyalty oaths from suspect citizens, irrational though this practice is: the distrust that motivates the requirement of an oath is not likely to be assuaged by its utterance.[40] Although few if any contemporary liberals would endorse loyalty oaths as a permissible way of according standing to citizens whose commitments are suspect, the project of citizenship-as-identity sometimes comes quite close to that. As Stephen Macedo notes approvingly, American Catholics seeking judgeships or elective office, suspected of greater loyalty to their church than to American constitutional principles, "have effectively 'been forced to proclaim the practical meaningless-ness' of their religious convictions as a condition of being allowed to serve." "Such rituals are bound to be educative, and ... express our commitment to ensuring that political power will be exercised on the basis of reasons that we can share, for purposes that we can hold and justify in common, notwithstanding our religious differences."[41] Macedo seems unperturbed by the fact that such assurances of secu-lar purposes are politically necessary for Catholics, but not for Protestants. From where I stand, however, it seems a clear double standard to presume that one citizen's religious identity casts her political loyalty into doubt, whereas another's religious commit-ments are fully supportive of liberal democratic principles. That this is a moral double standard—and so a violation of the principle of equality—seems particularly clear in the American context, where nineteenth century Catholics were stigmatized as incapable of demo-cratic citizenship (a legacy Macedo fully acknowledges).[42]

The liberal tendency to view Catholics with suspicion arises from a logical inference from Catholic doctrine to assumptions about what Catholics will do in practice. The doctrine of papal infallibility, com-bined with the Pope's status as earthly head of the Church and the supremacy of religious over all other obligations, lead logically to the conclusion that Catholic individuals will follow the dictates of their religion *rather than* the dictates of political obligation when the two happen to conflict. A similar process of reasoning characterizes liberal assessments of Islam as a theocratic religion, and feminist assess-ments of all three major monotheistic religions as fundamentally antithetical to gender equality.[43] Similarly, many liberals characterize fundamentalist Protestant sects, some of which reject ideals of critical self-reflection and individual autonomy, as essentially "unreason-able" because their doctrines are incompatible with the exchange of mutually acceptable reasons as the condition of political legitimacy.[44] In each of these cases, religious confessors' capacities for genuine democratic citizenship and for political loyalty are called into ques-tion because the content of their consciences is inconsonant with the content that healthy citizenship requires. Although individual mem-bers of these faiths are seldom questioned directly about their con-scientious religious commitments and the relationship thereof to political membership, such questioning (which is obviously odious from a liberal point of view) is not seen as necessary because we can deduce their commitments from religious doctrine.

Moreover, even if they are not actively hostile to principles of individual equality, individual freedom, and toleration, groups that have experienced a history of marginalization may have good reasons to be reluctant actively to affirm those principles. All the basic principles of constitutional regimes contain an element of indeterminacy, and if that indeterminacy has historically been exploited to give the principles a content that is biased against certain groups, those groups have good reason to be wary of expressing allegiance to the principles themselves. For many groups, though, the reluctance to praise key virtues and principles of democratic citizenship arises from a critical assessment of the consequences they have had for themselves or others. Since the principles of individual equality and individual autonomy have historically been used to deny cultural minorities recognition or accommodation within the law, these minorities may have very reasonable reservations about these principles. If groups identify critical thinking with moral relativism, and moral relativism with a weak capacity to resist pleasures that are damaging to well-being, they might have reason to oppose critical thinking. If groups identify the celebration of individual autonomy with atomism and the rejection of the duties to family and community, they have some reason for refusing to celebrate autonomy. Given that critical thinking and individual autonomy are, in any event, regulative ideals that are at best imperfectly realized in our societies, and imperfectly served by institutions of public education, to deny groups an equal place in political discourse because they fail to affirm these principles strikes me as closefisted.

Once our assessment of a religious or cultural community's expressed commitments (or of their unwillingness to express a commitment to liberal principles) yields the judgment that it is illiberal or unreasonable, we are clearly relieved of any strong obligation to accommodate or even to tolerate them. Although liberal theorists tend to disavow the use of force toward illiberal groups, and prefer gentler means of bringing them around, they argue that we should be prepared to do what is necessary to protect the stability of the regime.[45] As Macedo puts it, "Fastening our bayonets should be a last resort . . . Our politics might well come down to holy war with some people, but we do not know in advance with how many or exactly whom."[46]

So far, most of what I have written in characterizing the liberal view of citizenship as identity would not be taken by these theorists

as critique. Macedo argues that although it is perfectly true that liberalism marginalizes some groups, they are by and large the groups
that *should* be marginalized because their commitments are incompatible with legitimate and democratic political order. But once we
have labeled a particular group's *doctrines, claims,* and *arguments* as
unreasonable or illiberal, there is a common tendency to attach these
labels to the group in general and to all of its members. The danger
here is that we may prejudge a group's claim to recognition or
accommodation and unjustly deny that recognition because we have
wrongly generalized from one argument to another, and from doctrine to practice. Of the *Mozert* case, for example, liberal theorists
have emphasized parents' objections to their children's "mere exposure" to beliefs and ways of life different from their own, and have
argued persuasively that acceding to this argument is incompatible
with a liberal commitment to tolerance. Yet this was not the only
argument the *Mozert* parents made, and some of their arguments are
indeed quite reasonable from a liberal point of view. In particular,
the argument that the school readers were unfairly biased against
Protestant Christianity is widely acknowledged as valid.[47] Moreover,
as Judge Boggs emphasized in his concurring opinion in that case,
the adversarial structure of the courtroom may have worked against
the parents' more reasonable claims, particularly insofar as they
were led by sophisticated cross-examination to make arguments that
would make them appear much more opposed to their children's
education about other visions of moral life than they actually were.[48]
In short, by focusing in on the parents' arguments that *were* unreasonable from a liberal point of view, and generalizing from those
arguments (and from assumptions about their beliefs that were
extrapolated from religious doctrine), liberal commentators on this
case have demonstrated an inclination to close off the possibility of
fruitful political deliberation—prematurely, in my view.

Selective attention to "illiberal" or "unreasonable" doctrines or
arguments is not the only possible source of faulty generalizations
about religious or cultural groups and a consequent inclination to
view them as justly marginalized in political discourse. In addition,
the structure of inference from doctrine to identity to probable practice is itself flawed. First, it is highly unlikely that individual identity
is ever constituted completely by religious commitments, especially
in a pluralistic society. Even in relatively closed communities, individuals occupy different roles in different moments, and so learn to
use different structures of reasoning about what kind of action is
appropriate in each of the different social contexts they occupy.
There is no reason to suppose, then, that a person who affirms a

fundamentalist doctrine in her religious life is constitutionally incapable of making appropriate arguments in political discourse.[49] Of course, she may do so, but I see no reason why we should suppose from the outset that she cannot do otherwise. Further, Nancy Rosenblum's plea for psychological realism about illiberal associations is especially apropos here: there is very frequently a gap between a group's express purpose and its actual demeanor, and between its doctrine and its actual effect on individual members.[50] The concept of citizenship as identity supposes that unless commitments to critical reason, equality, freedom, and toleration are deeply inscribed into the individual's soul, the capacities for democratic citizenship are unlikely to develop. As an empirical matter, however, there are good reasons to question this supposition.

There are costs, then, to the project of citizenship as identity, in particular the risk that by labeling groups or individuals as illiberal or unreasonable we might unnecessarily or unjustly marginalize them as citizens. Defenders of this project might argue that the price is worth paying if inculcating citizen identity yields the promised fruits: a loyal citizenry, ready to make sacrifices for fellow citizens, and stable democracy.

From an empirical standpoint, however, the connection between an educational project of civic identity and national loyalty, on the one hand, and the ends of distributive justice and political stability, on the other, are highly dubious. Even advocates of civic education have acknowledged that we cannot have utter confidence that an education for critical reason, toleration, and a commitment to freedom and equality will actually produce these virtues in individuals.[51] Moreover, the historical evidence does not support a claim that a strong national identity generates a willingness to support redistribution. As Bhikhu Parekh points out, under Margaret Thatcher the British populace[52] was at its most nationalistic in decades, but this did not stem that government's radical cutbacks to social welfare.[53] Citizens of the United States have a very strong sense of national identity compared with citizens of other advanced industrial societies, but also the weakest programs of redistribution.

I am particularly sceptical of the claim that moral agreement and shared identity are the preconditions of stable democracy. What are the empirical measures of the instability, which such pluralism supposedly generates? Where is the evidence of "balkanization" and "ungovernability" as a consequence of moral and cultural pluralism?[54] It is common to claim that granting group-based requests for recognition and accommodation produces unmanageable strains on government officials. Yet nowhere have I seen evidence that links the two phenomena. Interestingly, this argument was made in the *Mozert* case, but as Judge Boggs noted in his concurrence, there had in fact been some accommodation of the parents' requests prior to the litigation, with no suggestion that the accommodation had produced a proliferation of similar claims from other religious communities.[55] Similarly, the claim that civil discord results from moral pluralism or group accommodation is never accompanied with systematic empirical evidence. To the contrary, as Macedo acknowledges, it is more likely that moderate accommodations will serve liberal purposes by avoiding the sense of alienation that can lead religious or cultural minorities to withdraw from participation in public institutions and discussions. Although I do not wish to argue in favor of indiscriminate accommodation for religious and cultural groups, and agree with liberals that policies of accommodation should maintain a steady concern for individual equality and autonomy, I think it likely that the ends of toleration and civil cooperation are better served by an openness to accommodation than by the conscious marginalization of the "unreasonable" and "illiberal."[56]

The project of a civic education aimed at citizenship as identity seeks a security for liberal democracy in the content of the individual soul. I have suggested above that this is a security that we do not need, and that it is dangerous to seek. I tend to agree with Judith Shklar in her declaration that "When the state demands loyalty it is looking for trouble, for legislated patriotism is no patriotism at all. Loyalty is either spontaneous or it is thought control, and it is very bad news."[57] It is in any event a security we can never have, since in pluralistic societies (and even in relatively homogeneous ones) human beings simply will have multiple and sometimes divided loyalties. "All selves are self-divided", Michael Walzer tells us, between multiple roles, multiple identities, and multiple ideals or principles.[58] The effort to claim "*all* of our *deepest* moral commitments" on behalf of the political community—or on behalf of any other community or cause—is destined for failure.[59] There is always the chance that, in cases of profound conflict, other human beings will disappoint our hopes and expectations about which loyalty they should prefer.

8.3. Globalization and the Shifting Boundaries of Citizenship

It is noteworthy that the current wave of interest in inculcating shared national identity as a project of civic education should arrive just at the moment when the nation-state to which such identity would attach is itself on the wane.[60] The cluster of phenomena that we call "globalization" pulls apart those spheres of human activity whose boundaries have coincided with the boundaries of the nation-state.[61] The increasing dynamism of population flows mean that the *boundaries of political and cultural identity* are no longer exclusive and singular. There is a steady rise in the number of individuals who hold dual citizenship, or who have strong bonds of membership in more than one country (what sociologists call "transmigrants" or "transnationals"), or who maintain strong cultural networks across several countries ("diasporic" communities, such as ethnic Chinese).[62] Even in quieter times, when the project of nation building advanced at the cost of suppressing social and cultural diversity, the demand for an exclusive or supreme loyalty to the nation was unreasonable. In present circumstances, the implications for citizenship of pluralism and the multiple bonds of loyalty—some of which have inescapably political dimensions—are irrepressible. The boundaries of attachment never coincided perfectly with those of the nation-state, and it seems highly unlikely that even a strong program of civic education could bring that about in an era of globalization. A conception of citizenship that fails to come to grips with this will offer little guidance in our fast-changing world.

The phenomenon of increasing population movements is related to the fact that *economic boundaries* no longer coincide with the political boundaries of the nation-state. Increasing flows of trade, the rise of multinational corporations, and the increasing importance of regional and international regulatory bodies displace the power of the nation-state to control its own economic destiny. This has obvious consequences for what, following T. H. Marshall, we may call social citizenship, the enjoyment of basic social rights such as a right to employment (a work permit); health care; welfare; unemployment insurance; etc.[63] We have already seen this each time a government cites international competitiveness as a reason for scaling back the welfare state. The security of social rights depends on some coincidence of political/administrative boundaries and those of the economic system. Such rights presuppose a system of social and economic corpora-tion that generates wealth that can, in turn, be redistributed to participants to provide for their needs. By doing so, redistribution can sustain (or reproduce) ongoing cooperation over time. This must be a *more or less closed system* in two respects. First, the wealth generated through cooperation cannot be transferred outside the system beyond a certain limit without jeopardizing the system's capacity to reproduce itself. Second, the system cannot, beyond a certain limit, contain valid claimants to social rights who are not also contributors to the production of wealth. In other words, social rights depend on boundaries that limit the *outward flow of wealth* from the system of cooperation that produces it and limit the *inward flow of non-productive claimants*. Both kinds of limits are strained by the phenomena of economic globalization and global migration: the *political systems* that control the redistribution of wealth no longer share boundaries with the *economic systems* that produce wealth. The former are territorial; the latter, increasingly, are not. This trend strikes me as a much greater threat to distributive justice than the absence of a shared national identity among citizens.

Third, *political–institutional* boundaries, understood as the boundaries of jurisdictional and decision-making authority capable of generating binding decisions, no longer coincide exactly with the boundaries of the nation-state and its institutions. The European Union, of course, is the clearest example of this trend; at present, the United States is probably the country least susceptible to it. As the now familiar critique of the "democratic deficit" in European institutions makes clear, this phenomenon also has profound implications for democratic citizenship and for democratic legitimacy. Without institutional channels for popular participation and for public accountability, particularly through institutions of representation, democratic self-governance is a sham. Jürgen Habermas has expressed this concern very well: "[T]he new elites of bureaucrats are, formally speaking, still accountable to the governments and institutions in their respective countries of origin; factually, however, they have outgrown their national context.... For the citizen, this translates into an ever greater gap between being affected by something and participating in changing it."[64]

Finally, the *boundaries of democratic participation*, in response to the foregoing phenomena, are in a process of change. Participation in national political institutions appears to be on the decline, whereas other forms of political action seem to be gaining in salience. Social movements aimed at political change on issues of gender, sexuality, indigenous peoples, the environment, and labor have an increasingly transnational dimension. The demonstrations against the WTO in Seattle and Genoa suggest that popular political resistance to policy may be increasingly focused on transnational decision-making bodies and drawn from international coalitions of activists and organizations. In addition, political participation aimed at decision makers in large cosmopolitan cities seems likely to increase in relevance relative to participation in national institutions. In other words, it is by no means clear that individuals' self-understanding as citizens will be so clearly oriented toward national governments as in the past. The changing sites of citizenship, then, also suggest that the model of citizenship-as-national-identity is obsolescent.

The changing boundaries of citizenship call for a conception of citizenship that is adaptable to new circumstances without abandoning the legacy of the democratic tradition. How can we conceptualize a meaningful citizenship that is not so closely tied to the weakening boundaries of territorially defined nation-states? I believe this to be one of the most important challenges for political theory in the coming years, and certainly do not presume to offer a definitive answer to it. However, it seems likely that a successful response will require that we abstract away from the historical institutions and practices of citizenship and focus instead on a *pragmatic* or *functional* account of citizenship.[65] What is citizenship good for? What are the most important functions it serves in the life of the individual and in collective life?

When we gaze at the Western tradition of democratic citizenship, two broad functions stand out as crucial, and likely to remain so even if the contexts and institutions of citizenship change dramatically. One of these is the legacy of classical political thought; the other is the achievement of the era of Enlightenment and the age of democratic revolutions. The first is what I will call the function of *self-rule*; the second I will call the function of *self-protection*.

Beginning with Aristotle, citizenship has been understood as an integral part of the project of human freedom. To fulfil the human potential for freedom, we must learn to govern ourselves both as individuals and as collectivities. The role of the citizen consists above all in participating with other citizens in collective self-rule by reasoning and speaking or deliberating together over what they, collectively, ought to do. Thus being a citizen means being able to recognize and affirm, through the exercise of one's own judgment, that the rules under which one lives issue from good judgments about what is just and what is beneficial to the community as a whole. Citizenship serves the function of collective self-rule, then, by giving individuals the means for exercising some *agency* over the circumstances that profoundly shape their lives, an agency they can meaningfully possess only if they exercise it in concert with others.

Let me turn now to the second function of citizenship, what I am calling the function of self-protection.[66] The central idea here is that citizenship consists in the protection of rights in which we have a prepolitical interest. These were originally conceived as universal or natural rights—like the rights to life, liberty, and the pursuit of happiness proclaimed in the Declaration of Independence. Within this view, as Jefferson wrote, "to secure these rights, Governments are instituted among Men, deriving their just powers from the consent of the governed."

Why does the security of rights depend on citizenship? In what sense is the protection of rights a kind of *self*-protection? The answer is that governments can only be trusted to protect rights when they are accountable to those who live under them; the security of rights depends upon the active vigilance and regular participation of citizens. Thus a key instrument of citizenship as self-protection is participation in the regular election of decision-making officials. The institutions of political representation, and the lines of accountability they establish between governors and governed, are critically important.

The self-protective function of citizenship, by itself, does not tell us very much about *which* rights we seek to protect, and indeed the content of these rights has gradually changed in the evolution of democratic societies. Despite the origins of the protective function of democracy in conceptions of prepolitical natural rights, few are now committed to such foundationalist understandings of rights. Instead, most contemporary theorists understand the content of rights as something that is itself worked out through political contests over time. In this way, the functions of self-rule and of self-protection intersect through the distinctive forms of constitutional politics that give substantive content and legal force to the broader concept of rights.

Whatever the future holds for the boundaries of politics, it seems clear to me that the prospects of democracy—and of political legitimacy—will depend upon practices of democratic citizenship that meet these two broad functions of self-rule and self-protection. In ways that I cannot elaborate here for reasons of space, both functions of citizenship do depend in important ways on the existence of boundaries of different kinds—moral, economic, institutional, procedural, administrative, jurisdictional—though they need not correspond precisely to the boundaries that have historically been instituted in the nation-state.[67] No matter what these other boundaries might be, however, there is one boundary that must be defined in order for either of the functions of citizenship to be met: what boundaries define the "self" of "self-rule" and "self-protection?" In other words, what defines the boundaries of *membership* in democratic communities? This question takes us back to the opening questions of the chapter. As we have seen, providing that boundary by appeal to a concept of citizenship-as-national-identity is fraught with difficulty. In the next section, I will briefly offer an alternative way of understanding the boundaries of membership, one that I hope will be reconcilable with traditional understandings of citizenship as focused on the nation-state, but flexible and expansive enough to make sense of the new sites and demands of citizenship in the global era.

8.4. *Citizenship as Shared Fate*

The core of the idea of citizenship as shared fate is that we find ourselves in webs of relationship with other human beings that profoundly shape our lives, whether or not we consciously choose or voluntarily assent to be enmeshed in these webs. What connects us in a community of shared fate is that our actions have an impact on other identifiable human beings, and other human beings' actions have an impact on us. The idea of a community of shared fate is thus quite similar to John Dewey's idea of a "public",[68] though I would emphasize the multiplicity of possible publics in which we are situated, and the variable degree to which such publics have or could have sufficiently firm institutional boundaries to sustain the two functions of self-rule and self-protection.

A community of shared fate is *not* an ethical community as such. Its members are not bound to each other by shared values or moral commitments, but by relations of interdependence, which may or may not be positively valued by its members. Our futures are bound to each other, whether we like it or not.[69] There is no plausible alternative to living together. In this way, a community of shared fate is a descriptive rather than a normative category. White slaveowners and Black slaves formed a community of shared fate. The future of one was inextricably tied to the future of the other. Black and white South Africans formed a community of shared fate before constitutional reform as much as they do afterward. In North America, Native peoples' fate was tied to that of non-Natives the moment European explorers landed on their shores. We have been thrown together by the circumstances of history, often without choosing to be thrown together.

But communities of shared fate may be more or less legitimate. Indeed, the basic account of legitimacy proffered by most contemporary democratic theorists suggests a conceptual connection between the idea of a community of shared fate and the idea of legitimacy: legitimacy consists in the ability to justify actions to those who are affected by them according to reasons they can accept.[70] We can use Rawls's language to distinguish better from worse communities of shared fate: for Rawls, a well-ordered society is one in which individuals "*agree* to share one another's fate."[71] They acknowledge their interdependence, and choose to live with it rather than fight against it. But the claim to legitimacy does not rest on mere acquiescence; it rests on the ability to justify the structure of interdependence and cooperation to those who are enmeshed in it. Since communities of shared fate entail relations of *reciprocal* interdependence and interconnection, the standard of legitimacy also entails a requirement of *reciprocal justification*.

The idea of citizenship as shared fate is implicit in many recent accounts of citizenship in multicultural societies, including some of the accounts I have criticized above for tying citizenship too strongly to an ideal of national identity. Like national identity, a conception of citizenship as shared fate requires that individuals be able to *imagine themselves* in a network of relationship with other human beings, some of whom they may never meet face-to-face. But in contrast to national identity, there is nothing in the idea of shared fate to require that it is a shared *cultural* identity or heritage that links human beings in bonds of interdependence and mutual accountability.[72] Although shared cultural identity may be *one* source of a subjective sense of shared fate, it is not the only source. *Institutional* linkages, particularly those that have hitherto secured the functions of democratic self-rule and self-protection, are another important source of shared fate. Whether or not I see myself as culturally connected to Newfoundlanders, it remains the case that the institutions of representative government that link my political representation to theirs in the Canadian Parliament also links my future to theirs. This is not irreversibly the case, but since these institutions are one of the strongest forms of political accountability we have going, I would do well to see my fate as tied to them until some equally or more effective institutional alternative is in place. *Material* linkages are also important sources of shared fate, whether in the form of economic interdependence, environmental impact, or natural resource access and use.

In conceiving of citizenship as shared fate, there is no reason *in principle* to privilege one set of linkages over others. But it is true that to be active and effective citizens—to exercise the agency to *reshape* those connections through shared political judgment and action—requires one to understand oneself as situated within networks that have some connection to one's lived experience. These networks of interdependence have a history, and we judge their legitimacy or illegitimacy well only by understanding how they have come to take the shape they have, and what possibilities we may imagine for the future. So the idea of shared fate does rest on powers of imagination, but not on an imagined *identity* as such. Nonetheless, historical imagination, clearly, is an important part of a capacity for citizenship within a community of shared fate. We can see from this that the creation of *subjective* consciousness of a community of shared fate is itself a political achievement, for it involves choosing among different histories that may privilege some structures of interconnection or interdependence and suppress others. As Burke told us, we have a "*choice* of inheritance."[73]

The idea that sharing citizenship means seeing our own narratives as entwined with those of others, and so sharing a narrative of some sort with those others, has been gaining currency in recent political theory. Jeremy Webber, for example, has emphasized the importance of conceiving the bonds of social unity in Canada in terms of an ongoing "Canadian conversation" which structures ongoing debates about principles, political players, and issues. The conversation itself has a history that is contested, and by participating in it individuals contribute to shaping its future.[74] But sharing membership in one community of shared fate by participating in its narrative is by no means an exclusive proposition. Every community is constituted by a multiplicity of narratives that intersect at some points and not at others. This holds for local communities and cultures as for political community at the level of the constitutional state. As James Tully has argued in his excellent book, *Strange Multiplicity*, contemporary constitutionalism is marked by its dialogic and pluralistic character: "There is not one national narrative that gives the partnership its unity, but a diversity of criss-crossing and contested narratives through which citizens participate in and identify with their association. Constitutions are not fixed and unchangeable agreements reached at some foundational moment, but chains of continual intercultural negotiations and agreements."[75]

This suggests that having a sense of ourselves as members of a community of fate entails telling ourselves (true) stories about how we came to be connected to particular other human beings, and believing that we are responsible for constructing that connection in a manner that is justifiable to them. Telling those stories truthfully and conscientiously, in a manner that acknowledges others' perspectives on past and future, requires effort and intentionality. So too does recognizing the danger that important narratives may have been overlooked or distorted in the construction of the collective narrative.

Although I have tried to distance the idea of citizenship as shared fate from the idea of citizenship as identity, there clearly is some connection between the former and identity broadly understood. To act as part of a community of shared fate the individual must see herself as situated within, and to a certain extent bound by, networks of relationship with others. If we define individual identity as *having a coherent sense of self*, then citizenship-as-shared-fate does constitute an element of individual identity because it is part of how individuals see themselves as political agents. But this is a much thinner sense of identity than is often suggested by those who use the language of identity in defining citizenship, and particularly among those who tend to elide the concepts of identity, nationality, and loyalty. As we saw above, these discussions ascribe a particular *substantive content* of citizen identity in terms of a commitment to certain principles or an affective attachment to the imagined community. In contrast, there is nothing in the idea of shared fate that requires a positive affect toward others with whom one is connected, no requirement of allegiance and no possibility of betrayal, no particular principles to which one must be deeply committed so long as one observes the *practice* of reciprocity.[76] All of these forms of giving substantive content to citizen identity set it up as a standard against which we can then judge the identities of actual others. And this, as I have argued, is a dangerous and limiting move. It is dangerous because it leads us to look first to the content of others' identity, judge it against the substantive standard we have devised, and then exclude them from a claim to shared citizenship when we find them wanting. It is limiting insofar as it connects identity to membership in this community—the nation—and shuts down our capacity to understand citizenship in terms that withstand the transformations which the nation-state is currently undergoing. To have a conception of citizenship that can persist through and beyond the current period of globalization, we need to be much more open to the possibility that communities of shared fate other than the nation-state might sometimes, and very appropriately, come to occupy a greater part of citizen energies than the nation-state itself.

What are the advantages of conceiving citizenship as membership in a community of shared fate? First, it does not presuppose that any *particular* community is the privileged or exclusive site of citizenship. This restraint is an advantage because of the phenomena of multiple and overlapping memberships that has always characterized even putatively homogeneous nation-states, but which is an increasingly irresistible phenomenon in the age of globalization. The functions of self-rule and self-protection may be served within the institutions of local government, within cultural communities (as in Aboriginal self-government), at the national level, or through participation in regional or transnational movements and organizations. Indeed, there is nothing, in principle, to prevent an individual participating in the activities of self-rule and self-protection at *all* of these levels, though presumably it would require a person of extraordinary energy and imagination to do so. Certainly the capacity to exercise meaningful citizenship is constrained by the institutional capacities of the relevant communities. And there may well be good arguments for limiting the number of memberships of a certain kind any particular individual may hold because of the need for some kinds of communities (e.g. communities within which redistribution is a goal) to depend upon individuals' commitment to long-term participation. Thus, although I agree with Walter Feinberg when he argues that the nation-state may well continue to be the most relevant site of citizenship for most people for the foreseeable future, the idea of citizenship as shared fate enables us to imagine other important sites of collective self-rule and self-protection—and to consider how to strengthen their legitimacy-conferring institutional features—as well.[77]

Second, although the idea of citizenship as shared fate implicitly affirms a specific set of citizen virtues (on which more below), it does not require that we inquire into the content of an individual's identity or the commitments of her conscience to know whether or not she is capable of good citizenship. Good citizenship is something we know from individuals' *acts* rather than from their *beliefs*. Citizenship as shared fate requires of individuals that they develop a capacity to see themselves as participants in a project of cooperation that includes others who are different and distant from them, and to participate in a manner consistent with the ethical norms that sustain legitimacy, including norms of egalitarian reciprocity and respect for individual freedom.

Third, the idea of citizenship as shared fate does not presuppose that all individuals' or groups' understandings of their place in a community of shared fate need be the same as those of all others. The fact that we are all players in the same story does not require that we give it the same interpretation, nor that we see it as the only or most important political story in which we are involved. Although the idea of a community of shared fate does require, as suggested above, that individuals identify with the community in *some* way, it does not require that they identify in the *same* way.[78]

Like any conception of citizenship, the idea of citizenship as shared fate implicitly affirms a certain set of virtues of the citizen. Some of these are common to other accounts of citizenship, particularly insofar as they are connected to the core functions of self-rule and self-protection. Participating in self-rule requires a capacity for shared deliberation with others, which includes a capacity for reason giving and judgment. As many political liberals emphasize, the capacity for participating in political deliberation requires skills of critical reason. Although these theorists may be right that it is likely that developed skills of critical reason will subject not only matters of public concern, but also matters of private conscience, to critical reflection,[79] I think we should be cautious about making overly strong assumptions about this connection. In particular, I think it is important to avoid the inductive logic described earlier in this chapter: that because a group or individual *declines* to affirm the principle of critical self-reflection as a good in religious life, we need not assume that this demonstrates an incapacity to exercise powers of critical reflection and shared deliberation on matters of politics. People often display remarkable capacities for compartmentalizing their moral lives, and I see no reason why this should not be the case with regard to the objects of critical reflection. Again, then, citizenship as shared fate would encourage us to focus on citizens' *performance* in public deliberation rather than on the content of their religious or other moral beliefs.

The function of self-protection also requires certain virtues. In particular, it requires that individuals have a clear knowledge of their rights and a disposition to insist upon the observance of those rights. It also requires a disposition to resist the abuse of others' rights—to avoid what Judith Shklar called "passive injustice."[80] This latter disposition is closely related to the virtue of tolerance, as it entails that we acknowledge an obligation to respect others' rights even when we disapprove of the way in which they use those rights. Finally, self-protection requires some level of awareness of and participation in institutions that secure political accountability: a familiarity with public affairs, a habit of voting, and the like.

In addition to the virtues associated with self-rule and self-protection—which I believe must be common to *any* contemporary conception of democratic citizenship—there are also certain virtues which are distinctively tied to the idea of membership in a community of shared fate.[81] One of these is a capacity to see oneself as connected in a network of mutual interdependence and mutual impact with other human beings, some of whom have very different social experiences from our own, whether those differences are traceable to "race", culture, religion, class, gender identity, sexual identity, economic role, region, etc. Another is an inclination to take some responsibility for the legitimacy of the relationships and for securing the institutional and social conditions in which they can meet at least the basic standards of legitimacy. That is, a good citizen will possess a sense of *political agency* and the responsibility for exercising it when relationships fail to meet standards of legitimacy. A third virtue, perhaps less crucial than these two, would be a capacity to see oneself as situated within *several* networks of human interdependence, and to be able to make judgments and choices among them as to when to invest one's energies of citizen participation in one network, and when to shift to a different network.

8.5. The Role of Multicultural Education within a View of Citizenship-as-Shared-Fate

Nancy Rosenblum has recently noted that "it is a long way from appreciation of liberal democratic dispositions to the view that the chief purpose of liberal democracy is to reproduce citizens, and that public policy should cultivate and motivate us to exhibit specific virtues.... Nothing provokes anxiety like the proposition that in American democracy 'statecraft is soulcraft.' "[82] I confess to some sympathy with this liberal caution, but also agree with Amy Gutmann and others that it is an important function of education in a democratic society to equip individuals with the capacities for meaningful and effective citizenship.[83] Moreover, just as it is impossible for any system of governance to be neutral with respect to culture, it is also impossible for a system of education to be neutral with respect to citizenship. Even for those who do not believe that a capacity for citizenship is the *primary* function of education in a democracy, it is clearly a necessary and unavoidable one. For this reason, we can suppose it likely that differences in accounts of the meaning of citizenship will yield differences in accounts of citizen education.

What, then, follows from the idea of citizenship as shared fate for democratic education? As I discussed above, this conception of citizenship shares with other conceptions the notion that there are two broad functions that citizenship serves, those of self-rule and self-protection. Like other programs of democratic education, education for citizenship as shared fate would include inculcating basic skills of critical reasoning, of speech and argument, an awareness of public affairs through such habits as newspaper reading, and so on. All of these skills are necessary for participation in the deliberative activities through which the function of democratic self-rule is performed.

Similarly, the function of self-protection requires that individuals learn about their civil and political rights, about the structure and process of the institutions of government, about the mechanics of political participation in the form of voting, lobbying, peaceful demonstration, petitions, grassroots organizing, etc.

As Michael Walzer has emphasized, an important part of learning about the rights and skills of democratic participation is learning about their *history*.[84] Children need to understand that these rights and practices are the product of struggles, ideas, experiments, and more struggles. In other words, they need to see democratic institutions as an *achievement* whose current form is not entirely accidental or arbitrary, and whose imperfection requires their efforts at improving upon it. In other words, a part of children's developing sense of political agency is to understand themselves as contributing to an ongoing story of democratic self-rule, a story that is not situated exclusively within the boundaries of their own countries.

Other theorists of democratic education in multicultural societies—who are much more knowledgeable about the philosophy of education than I—have offered interesting, complementary, and often very persuasive accounts of the relationship between communal education (at the level of the religious, cultural, or national community), civic education (regarding citizenship in the institutions of a federal or multicultural constitutional order), private or separate education, and common or public education.[85] I agree with many of their arguments about the desiderata of democratic education. Rather than engaging more carefully with their arguments, I will focus in the remainder of this chapter on what I see as the distinctive contributions of the idea of citizenship as shared fate to a conception of democratic education.

I have argued above that citizenship as shared fate requires that individuals see themselves as enmeshed in relationships which they may or may not have chosen, with individuals who may be very different from themselves. For most citizens of multicultural democracies, both the (partial or total) involuntariness of shared membership and pluralism are palpable realities. For those of us who were born into such societies, we obviously did not choose to become members, nor did we choose the diverse collection of human beings amongst whom we find ourselves. Even those who immigrate seldom (if ever) do so with a full consciousness of the ways in which their future lives will be shaped by their new society, nor with a full awareness of the range of diversity with which they will have to come to terms. The involuntary dimensions of shared membership are difficult to reconcile with the requirements of legitimacy, for there is a natural human temptation to avoid encounters with those who are different from ourselves in ways that make us uncomfortable. Yet democratic legitimacy in a diverse society requires that we engage in an exchange of reasons about matters that affect us jointly, and that we do not seek simply to impose our will on others. Bringing the requirements of legitimacy together with the fact of sometimes-unwelcome diversity means that citizens must learn to engage in democratic discourse through which they can come to understand (even if imperfectly or incompletely) others' experience from others' perspectives. As Seyla Benhabib and other feminist theorists have argued, following Hannah Arendt's conception of political judgment, this activity requires a capacity for "enlarged mentality", a capacity to "mak[e] present to oneself what the perspectives of others involved are or could be, and [to ask] whether I could 'woo their consent' in acting the way I do.... To 'think from the perspective of everyone else' is to know 'how to listen' to what the other is saying, or when the voices of others are absent, to imagine to oneself a conversation with the other as my dialogue partner."[86]

Since this capacity for "enlarged thought" is a critically important capacity for the conception of citizenship as shared fate, we need to consider how it develops in individual human beings and whether a program of democratic education could contribute to it. As a condition of the human capacity for judgment, the capacity for enlarged thinking is presumably something that humans as such possess, like the capacity for speech. But it is also a capacity that develops only by being exercised, which is where the role of democratic education comes in. It is here, I believe, that a conception of citizenship as shared fate offers something distinctive to our understanding of the project of democratic education in multicultural societies.

Let's begin by unpacking the conditions for enlarged thinking: (1) it is a capacity that develops only through its exercise; (2) its exercise depends on encounters with diversity—with perspectives on shared practices or concerns that are different from one's own; and (3) its emergence and development depends upon discursive *exchange* between different perspectives, that is, through *dialogue* with different others. In other words, it seems likely that the capacity for enlarged thought is most likely to develop through a mutual engagement among diverse perspectives that are *immediately present* in individuals' lives, for only such engagement can be genuinely discursive. In pedagogical terms, this suggests that we should emphasize those forms of diversity that are an immediate presence in students' lives.[87] The idea here is gradually to expand students' consciousness to encompass others' experience through exposure to the presence of that experience in their midst.

An education that begins with a focus on local diversity is also important for developing individuals' capacity to imagine themselves as part of communities of shared fate. It would include local histories, explaining how people of diverse cultural and religious backgrounds came to live together in *this* locale, and how the history of their presence and their interaction here is inscribed in the structure of everyday life—the presence of this church on the corner, of this market and the goods traded in it, of those signs in a minority language, and so on. By teaching children to connect their immediate and everyday experiences with an ongoing story about how their diverse communities came to have the shape they have, we also teach children to imagine their lives as connected to the lives of others in a more distant place or time. Just as the capacity for enlarged thought, begun in an encounter with immediate others, may be further enlarged to encompass more and more distant others, so a capacity to see one's interconnection with past, present, and future others in one's immediate locale can lead to a capacity to shift or broaden one's sense of connection to other relations of mutual dependence.

Finally, an education for citizenship as shared fate would encourage students to develop a sense of agency and responsibility for reshaping relations of interdependence so that they better approximate the ideal of democratic legitimacy. Again, it seems likely that this aspect of citizenship education will be more successful the more immediate its focus and results, at least at the outset. It is important that children learn what it is to engage in a project of cooperation aimed at promoting shared ends, whether at the level of their cultural or religious communities, local political communities, school, classroom, or in the domain of national or international citizenship. From designing a new playground to cleaning up a local park, helping with voter registration or holding a bake sale to fund a special piece of classroom equipment, learning cooperation as a *practice* is the only way to develop individuals' sense of agency to reshape the world they share with others. It teaches moderation in promoting one's own vision, and the capacity of individuals to see themselves as part of a project of collective self-rule.

In short, an education for citizenship as shared fate would stress the development of three dimensions of human agency that tend not to be stressed in other accounts of civic education: the capacity for enlarged thought; the imaginative capacity to see oneself as bound up with others through relations of interdependence as well as through shared history and institutions; and the capacity to reshape the shared practices and institutions that shape one's environment through direct participation. To illustrate, let me briefly address one practical issue in primary and secondary education to which an education for citizenship as shared fate might give a distinctive cast: what to teach children about history and literature in a multicultural society.

The history and literature curriculum for primary and secondary education is a lightning rod for debates over civic education in multicultural societies. Some advocates for an ideal of citizenship-as-identity argue that children should be taught an idealized history that will inculcate a sense of national pride and give children inspirational models of civic virtue. William Galston, for example, argues that "[c]ivic education... requires a nobler, moralizing history: a pantheon of heroes who confer legitimacy on central institutions and are worthy of emulation."[88] As Harry Brighouse has argued, the problem with this view of civic education is that it "deliberately withholds relevant information and thus distorts the development of national loyalties. The state involves itself in deliberately trying to condition consent in a way that bypasses the critical faculties of its citizens and future citizens, thus undermining its own capacity for legitimacy."[89] Moreover, in a multicultural society, the danger in teaching an idealized "patriotic history" is that we tell stories of national glory whose heroes are male and white and which ignores the presence and contributions of women and of racial and ethnic minorities.

The radical transformation of American primary and secondary curricula since the 1960s has consisted mainly in the rejection of the patriotic model of civic education. It is abundantly clear that the homogeneous and exclusivist depictions of national history that had hitherto characterized public school curricula needed to change.[90] The project of curriculum reform has been inspired by the idea that "public school... programs should be designed so that all students, regardless of ethnic or racial background, are exposed to the full range of ethnic and racial diversity in this country."[91] But this approach is fraught with its own difficulties. First, given the immense diversity of societies such as Canada and the United States, is it practicable to expose children to the *full range* of diversity? The effort to do so would lead to treating each cultural group's history and literature so fleetingly and so superficially as to contribute little to children's genuine understanding of other citizens' experiences and worldviews.[92] Yet selectivity can tend to create tensions between cultural groups about whose legacy is more valuable and whose presence is more significant. Such battles surely defeat the purpose of encouraging students to see themselves as members of a shared community.

Defenders of a patriotic history are right that children need *some* sense of a shared narrative in relation to which they can situate themselves as citizens. Robert Fullinwider expresses this idea very helpfully when he writes of the need for a "usable past", one "in which they can find values and projects to take as their own legacies. As heirs, they define their own lives around goals and commitments that build on what came before. Their moral and political identities reside in making 'more perfect' the unions and Union they are a part of. There must be, then, something perfectible in those unions", and it is the task of the educator to show students what that something might be.[93] But defenders of multicultural education are right that children's sense of agency will be diminished if they do not see themselves reflected in the narratives they are taught. Both approaches are mistaken, I believe, to the extent that they rely upon an implicit supposition that the capacity for a sense of shared citizenship must be developed through an encounter with the same curriculum. To the contrary, it seems more likely that children will have little of any sense of identification with a curriculum that does not resonate with their lived experience. Neither an idealized history—the prototype is the celebration of the heroes of the American Revolution such as Washington, Jefferson, and Madison—nor a smorgasbord of multicultural tidbits seems especially well suited to strike that resonant chord.

An education for citizenship as shared fate suggests a third alternative. I suggested above that the capacity for "enlarged thinking" and for an ability to see oneself in relation to different others requires encounters with actual and immediate diversity. From this some curriculum guidelines follow quite directly: students should first be taught the history of their local communities, and learn first about the literatures and cultures of the people who live in their midst. In my neighborhood in Toronto, for example, this would mean learning why there was a large wave of Greek immigration to Canada following the Second World War, and how they came to settle in this part of Toronto. What were the political circumstances in Greece that made emigration to Canada attractive? Raising this question could open a path to teaching about democratic institutions, human rights, and economics. Beginning with local diversity might mean learning something about the Greek Orthodox religion that is practiced in the neighborhood churches, about the cuisine that is served in the local restaurants, and about the history of ancient Greece that is reflected in the columns and statues that decorate some local buildings. It might also mean learning about the origins of democracy in ancient Athens and the connections and differences between Athenian democracy and modern representative government. But our neighborhood also borders on one of Toronto's three Chinatowns, so an encounter with local diversity would also lead to learning similar things about ethnic Chinese immigration into Canada (from mainland China, from Vietnam, and most recently from Hong Kong), about Chinese holidays and cuisine, and about Chinese literature. The gathering of women in the local park to practice Tai Ch'i every morning might be a door through which to learn about Taoism and about different ways of understanding human health. Ideally, teaching in this way leads children to see their daily experiences and encounters through a lens that connects them to others in their community, to others in the past, and to more distant others in the present (the families in Greece or China or Hong Kong to whom immigrants in this community are still linked).

It is clear that such an approach to education would lead to different curricula in different regions, especially in the early years. As Anthony Appiah has argued in offering a similar vision of education, "Because different elements [of diversity] are important to different degrees in different places today, we can assume that the balance will and should be differently struck in different places."[94] At the same time, educators must bear in mind that the purpose of an education in *local* diversity is ultimately to enable students to see themselves as having political agency in the broader communities of shared fate to which they belong. Because of the continuing importance of constitutional government at the national level, it will be important to highlight the connections between local diversity and shared national institutions of self-rule and self-protection, though not to the exclusion of local, regional, global, and transnational institutions. Ideally, then, although children will follow different paths to an education about shared political institutions and histories, they will emerge from this process with common knowledge and realized capacities that will enable them to act together as citizens.

NOTES

The author wishes to thank Joseph Carens, David Fott, Genevieve Johnson, Catherine Lu, Kevin McDonough, David Welch, and the participants in the Conference on Collective Identities and Cosmopolitan Values in Montreal, June

2000, for their helpful comments. Special thanks to Walter Feinberg, Eamonn Callan, Meira Levinson, and Glen Newey for their detailed responses to this chapter, though I am under no misapprehension that I will have satisfied all the thoughtful and challenging concerns they raised.

1. "Citizenship is not just a certain status, defined by a set of rights and responsibilities. It is also an identity, an expression of one's membership in a political community." Will Kymlicka and Wayne Norman, "Return of the Citizen: A Survey of Recent Work on Citizenship Theory," in R. Beiner (ed.), *Theorizing Citizenship* (Albany: SUNY Press, 1995), 301.

2. Joseph Carens, "Multiple Political Memberships, Overlapping National Identities, and the Dimensions of Citizenships", in *Culture, Citizenship, and Community: A Contextual Exploration of Justice as Evenhandedness* (Oxford: Oxford University Press, 2000), 166 (emphasis added). Carens goes on to emphasize, contra many conventional understandings of citizenship, that this psychological dimension of citizenship need not go hand-in-hand with the legal rights of citizenship: one can have a subjective sense of membership without the legal rights, and one can have the legal rights without the felt sense of membership.

3. Benedict Anderson, *Imagined Communities: Reflections on the Origin and Spread of Nationalism* (London: Verso, 1983), 15.

4. Jürgen Habermas, "Citizenship and National Identity: Some Reflections on the Future of Europe", in R. Beiner (ed.), *Theorizing Citizenship* (Albany: SUNY Press, 1995, 1992). For a discussion of these concepts, see Ronald Beiner, "Introduction: Nationalism's Challenge to Political Philosophy", in Ronald Beiner (ed.), *Theorizing Nationalism* (Albany: SUNY Press, 1999), 7–14.

5. And a good thing, too, Bernard Yack tells us: "Birthright citizenship can have the effect of moderating our concern about our neighbors' commitments to shared principles, thereby promoting greater inclusion and toleration," Bernard Yack, "The Myth of the Civic Nation" in R. Beiner (ed.), *Theorizing Nationalism* (Albany: SUNY Press, 1999, 1996), 118 n. 31. I think he has hit this nail squarely on the head.

6. Yael Tamir, *Liberal Nationalism* (paperback edn) (Princeton: Princeton University Press, 1995), 117–18.

7. Ibid., 121.

8. Eamonn Callan, *Creating Citizens: Political Education and Liberal Democracy* (Oxford: Clarendon Press, 1997), 96.

9. Walter Feinberg, *Common Schools/Uncommon Identities: National Unity and Cultural Difference* (New Haven: Yale University Press, 1998), 119.

10. John Rawls, *Political Liberalism* (paperback edn) (New York: Columbia University Press, 1996), 147–8.

11. Stephen Macedo, *Diversity and Distrust: Civic Education in a Multicultural Democracy* (Cambridge: Harvard University Press, 2000), 33.

12. Rawls, *Political Liberalism*, 148–9, 158–68.

13. See, for example, Ibid., 156, 160.

14. John Rawls, *The Law of Peoples* (Cambridge: Harvard University Press, 1999), 13 n. 2.

15. Callan, *Creating Citizens*, 92.

16. Macedo, *Diversity and Distrust*, 3 (emphasis added).

17. Ibid., 1–2.

18. Ibid., 164 (emphasis added).

19. Ibid., 25.

20. Ibid., 191; see also Brian Barry, *Culture and Equality: An Egalitarian Critique of Multiculturalism* (Cambridge: Harvard University Press, 2001), 38–50.

21. Stephen Macedo, "Multiculturalism for the Religious Right? Defending Liberal Civic Education", *Journal of Philosophy of Education*, 29 (2), (1995), 226. See also Callan, *Creating Citizens*, 92.
22. Callan, *Creating Citizens*, 222.
23. Macedo, *Diversity and Distrust*, 164.
24. Feinberg, *Common Schools/Uncommon Identities*, 47–8 (emphasis in original). Cf. Callan: "Induction into the role of citizen and the growth of affective attachment to fellow citizens are essentially tied to the particularity of the polity within which moral learning occurs: it is *this* scheme of just social cooperation to which the individual becomes attached, *these* fellow citizens with whom bonds of trust and affection take root." *Creating Citizens*, 93 (emphasis in original).
25. Feinberg, *Common Schools/Uncommon Identities*, 49 (emphasis added).
26. Macedo, *Diversity and Distrust*, 146 (emphasis added).
27. Ibid., 146.
28. Ibid., 164 (emphasis added).
29. Rawls, *Political Liberalism*, 54–8.
30. It remains a contested issue whether it is possible to defend an education that develops the skills and capacities of democratic citizenship without also insisting that it should shape individual identity. As I shall argue below, I think it important to try to develop such a view of democratic education.
31. See esp. Amy Gutmann, *Democratic Education* (Princeton: Princeton University Press, 1987).
32. Rogers Smith, *Civic Ideals: Conflicting Visions of Citizenship in U.S. History* (New Haven: Yale University Press, 1997), 15.
33. See, for example, James W. Walker St. G. *"Race," Rights and the Law in the Supreme Court of Canada* (Waterloo: Wilfrid Laurier University Press, 1997).
34. Tamir, *Liberal Nationalism*, 72–7.
35. Yael Tamir, "Two Concepts of Multiculturalism", *Journal of Philosophy of Education*, 29 (2) (1995), 161–72.
36. Callan, *Creating Citizens*. See esp. 189–95 and ch. 8, generally; also see Feinberg, *Common Schools/Uncommon Identities*, esp. ch. 8.
37. Macedo, *Diversity and Distrust*, 160.
38. Ibid., 24.
39. Ibid., 164 (emphasis added).
40. Judith Shklar, "Obligation, Loyalty, Exile", *Political Theory*, 21 (2) (1993), 185. See also Smith, *Civic Ideals*, 92–3, 274–7.
41. Macedo, *Diversity and Distrust*, 136, quoting Sanford Levinson, "The Confrontation of Religious Faith and Civil Religion: Catholics Becoming Justices", *DePaul Law Review*, 39 (1990), 1047–81, 1049.
42. Macedo, *Diversity and Distrust*, 59–73.
43. Susan Okin, "Is Multiculturalism Bad for Women?" in J. Cohen, M. Howard, and M. Nussbaum (eds), *Is Multiculturalism Bad for Women?* (Princeton: Princeton University Press, 1999), 13–14.
44. See, for example, John Rawls, "The Idea of Public Reason Revisited", in *The Law of Peoples* (Cambridge: Harvard University Press, 1999), 129–80, 178.
45. See, for example, Callan, *Creating Citizens*, 44.
46. Macedo, *Diversity and Distrust*, 228.
47. Macedo now suggests some sympathy for this point (see Ibid., 203), though in his earlier work on the *Mozert* case his rejection of the parents' claim to accommodation was unequivocal. *Mozert* v. *Hawkins County Bd. of Education*, 827 F.2d 1058 (6th Cir. 1987). See Stephen Macedo, "Multiculturalism for the Religious Right? Defending Liberal Civic Education", *Journal of Philosophy of*

Education, 29 (2) (1995), 223–38, 227; and Stephen Macedo, "Liberal Civic Education and Religious Fundamentalism: The Case of God v. John Rawls?" *Ethics*, 105 (3) (1995), 468–96, 485–8.

48. *Mozert*, 1075.
49. Macedo sometimes seems to rely on such a supposition. See, for example, Macedo, "Liberal Civic Education..." p. 478: "Totalistic faiths (such as [*Mozert* parent] Vicki Frost's belief in the Christian Bible as 'the whole truth') will be especially resistant to thinking about politics (or anything else) from a perspective that in any way 'brackets' the truth of their particular religious views."
50. See Nancy Rosenblum, *Membership and Morals: The Personal Uses of Pluralism in America* (Princeton: Princeton University Press, 1998), 104–8.
51. Callan, *Creating Citizens*, ch. 8; Macedo, *Diversity and Distrust*, 254. Cf. Amy Gutmann, "Civic Education and Social Diversity", *Ethics*, 105 (April) (1995), 557–79, 106–7 (who cites a study to the contrary).
52. Or at least the English populace. Justin Bates has pointed out to me that both Scottish and Welsh nationalisms, defined in opposition to English identity, were also at a peak in this period, and that Thatcher's electoral support came almost entirely from within England.
53. Bhikhu Parekh, "The Incoherence of Nationalism" in R. Beiner (ed.), *Theorizing Nationalism* (Albany: SUNY Press, 1999), 314.
54. I have criticized "balkanization" and "ungovernability" arguments at greater length in Melissa S. Williams, *Voice, Trust and Memory: Marginalized Groups and the Failings of Liberal Representation* (Princeton: Princeton University Press, 1998), 7–8, 213–14.
55. *Mozert* (1987), 1074.
56. For further discussion of these points, see Melissa Williams, "Toleration, Canadian Style: Reflections of a Yankee-Canadian" in R. Beiner and W. Norman (eds), *Canadian Political Philosophy* (Toronto: Oxford University Press, 2001), 216–31; see also Joseph H. Carens and Melissa S. Williams, "Islam, Immigration, and Group Recognition", *Citizenship Studies*, 2 (3) (1998), 475–500.
57. Judith Shklar, "The Work of Michael Walzer" in *Political Thought and Political Thinkers* (Chicago: University of Chicago Press, 1998), 381.
58. Michael Walzer, *Thick and Thin: Moral Argument at Home and Abroad* (Notre Dame: University of Notre Dame Press, 1994), 85.
59. Macedo, *Diversity and Distrust*, 164 (emphasis added).
60. For a similar argument, see Parekh, "The Incoherence of Nationalism", 311.
61. David Cameron and Janice Gross Stein, "Globalization, Culture and Society: The State as Place Amidst Shifting Spaces", *Canadian Public Policy*, 26 (Supp.) (2000), S15–S34.
62. Lloyd Wong, "Transnationalism, Diasporan Communities and Changing Identity" (Paper read at National Policy Research Conference: Analysing the Trends, at Ottawa, 1999).
63. T. H. Marshall, *Class, Citizenship and Social Development* (New York: Anchor, 1965).
64. Habermas, "Citizenship and National Identity", 266–7.
65. Despite differences in our conceptualizations of citizenship, my approach here is similar to that of Joseph Carens (Carens, "Multiple Political Memberships..." insofar as both proceed by *disaggregating* the concept of citizenship.
66. Cf. the "protective goal" of representative government as discussed in Dennis F. Thompson, *John Stuart Mill and Representative Government* (Princeton: Princeton University Press, 1976), 9 and *passim*.

67. I have made a preliminary attempt to articulate these reasons in Melissa Williams, "Democratic Citizenship in an Era of Globalization" (Paul D. Stewart Lecture, Februrary 25, at Marshall University, Huntington, West Virginia, 2000).

68. "The public consists of all those who are affected by the indirect consequences of transactions to such an extent that it is deemed necessary to have those consequences systematically cared for." John Dewey, *The Public and Its Problems* (New York: Henry Holt, 1927), 15–16.

69. In some ways, then, my aspirations for shared citizenship are more minimalist than Carens's, for whom ties of "regrettable necessity" are something we should wish to move beyond. Although I agree that sharing citizenship is easier and more inspiring when it involves a more positive psychological stance than "regrettable necessity", I believe that achieving a sense of shared membership that was perceived as *legitimate*, even if a regrettable necessity, would be a remarkable moral accomplishment. For the time being, I would be happy to set my sights there.

70. Contemporary theorists including: Jurgen Habermas, "Discourse Ethics: Notes on Philosophical Justification" in Seyla Benhabib and Fred Dallmayr (eds), *The Communicative Ethics Controversy* (Cambridge: MIT Press, 1991); Rawls, *Political Liberalism*, xlvi, 137; T. M. Scanlon, "Contractualism and Utilitarianism" in Amartya Sen and Bernard Williams (eds), *Utilitarianism and Beyond* (Cambridge: Cambridge University Press,1982); T. M. Scanlon, *What We Owe to Each Other* (Cambridge: Harvard University Press, 1998), 4–5, 148–9; Amy Gutmann and Dennis Thompson, *Democracy and Disagreement* (Cambridge: Harvard University Press, 1996), ch. 2; Joshua Cohen, "Deliberation and Democratic Legitimacy" in Alan Hamlin and Philip Pettit (eds), *The Good Polity: Normative Analysis of the State* (Oxford: Basil Blackwell, 1989), all agree on this fundamental notion of legitimacy as grounded in reciprocal justification.

71. John Rawls, *A Theory of Justice* (Cambridge: Harvard University Press, 1971), 102; (emphasis added).

72. Max Pensky uses the language of shared fate in a similar way to conceptualize cosmopolitan democracy: "[G]lobal ethical substance [would not] be adequately described as a nationally unbounded Habermasian constituitonal patriotism, in which each nation would critically rework it *own* ethical substance and national history to put some flesh on the bare bones of moral universalism. Cosmopolitan solidarity would intend something a bit different, and a bit stranger: a consciousness of the *shared fate* of global risks, of course, and of shared potentials and dangers in the decades to come as globalization processes continue to undermine older forms of identity and generate new potentials and dangers." Max Pensky, "Cosmopolitanism and the Solidarity Problem: Habermas on National and Cultural Identities." *Constellations*, 7 (1) (2000), 64–79, 77 (emphasis added).

73. Edmund Burke, *Reflections on the Revolution in France*. In *The Works of the Right Hon. Edmund Burke* (12 vols). (Boston: Little, Brown, 1871, 1790), 275.

74. Jeremy Webber, *Reimagining Canada* (Montreal: McGill-Queen's University Press, 1994), ch. 9; see also Will Kymlicka, *Finding Our Way: Rethinking Ethnocultural Relations in Canada* (Toronto: Oxford University Press, 1998), 173–7.

75. James Tully, *Strange Multiplicity: Constitutionalism in an Age of Diversity* (Cambridge: Cambridge University Press, 1995), 183–4.

76. This point tells against the notion that secularism provides an adequate standard of neutrality for public discourse in liberal democracies; instead we should

aim at the exchange of mutually comprehensible arguments, whether those arguments are secular or religious in their foundations. Veit Bader makes this point in his powerful critique of secularist versions of neutralist liberalism: "Instead of trying to limit the content of public reason by keeping all contested comprehensive conceptions and truth-claims out, one has to develop the duties of civility, such as the duty to explain positions in publicly understandable language, the willingness to listen to others, fair-mindedness, and readiness to accept reasonable accommodations or alterations in one's own view." Veit Bader, "Religious Pluralism: Secularism or Priority for Democracy?" *Political Theory*, 27 (5) (1999), 597–633, 614.

77. Feinberg, *Common Schools/Uncommon Identities*, 29.
78. Anthony Appiah makes a similar point: "[T]he institutions of democracy—the election, the public debate, the protection of minority rights—have different meanings to different subcultures... [T]here is no reason to require that we all value them in the same way, for the same reasons. All that is required is that everybody is willing to 'play the game.'" Anthony Appiah, "Culture, Subculture, Multiculturalism: Educational Options" in Robert K. Fullinwider (ed.), *Public Education in a Multicultural Society* (Cambridge: Cambridge University Press, 1996), 65–89, see 86–7. See also Veit Bader's trenchant critique of the "concentric circles" model of individuals' moral attachment to family, locale, state, and humanity that is implicit in many accounts of civic education. His argument elucidates the dangers attached to the supposition that we can articulate a proper priority of attachments, "as if there is just one throw of the pebble, and the obligations are strongest the closest by, getting weaker and weaker the farther away from this center." Veit Bader, "For Love of Country", *Political Theory*, 27(3) (1999), 379–97, 391. Yet even cosmopolitans like Martha Nussbaum, who reject the moral priority of close attachments, retain the concentric circles model, and in doing so overlook the ways in which the "multilayered ties, relations, identities, and commitments" of "multicultural, global society" disrupt its neat ordering. Bader, Ibid., 392.
79. See, for example, Gutmann, "Civic Education and Social Diversity."
80. Judith Shklar, *The Faces of Injustice* (New Haven: Yale University Press, 1990).
81. For a more general list of democratic virtues, see, for example, Veit Bader, "The Cultural Conditions of Transnational Citizenship: On the Interpenetration of Political and Ethnic Cultures", *Political Theory*, 25(6) (1997), 771–813, 787. Carlos Alberto Torres enumerates virtues that are especially relevant for multicultural civic education. *Democracy, Education, and Multiculturalism: Dilemmas of Citizenship in a Global World* (Lanham: Rowman and Littlefield, 1998), 255–8.
82. Rosenblum, *Membership and Morals*, 13.
83. Gutmann, *Democratic Education*.
84. Michael Walzer, "Education, Democratic Citizenship and Multiculturalism", *Journal of Philosophy of Education*, 29 (2) (1995), 181–9.
85. See esp. Feinberg, *Common Schools/Uncommon Identities*; Callan, *Creating Citizens*; and Yael Tamir, "Two Concepts of Multiculturalism", *Journal of Philosophy of Education*, 29 (2) 1995, 161–72. Macedo's work also addresses these relationships, of course, though his critique of multiculturalism sets him apart from these other writers. See esp. Macedo, "Multiculturalism for the Religious Right? ..." and Macedo, *Diversity and Distrust*, ch. 1.
86. Seyla Benhabib, "Judgment and the Moral Foundations of Politics in Hannah Arendt's Thought" in *Situating the Self: Gender, Community and Postmodernism in Contemporary Ethics* (New York: Routledge, 1992), 137.

See also Bickford, Susan, *The Dissonance of Democracy* (Ithaca: Cornell University Press, 1996), esp. ch. 5.

87. As Amy Gutmann argues, "children often learn to respect other human beings by first learning to respect people who are close and familiar to them." Amy Gutmann, "Challenges of Multiculturalism in Democratic Education" in Robert K. Fullinwider (ed.), *Public Education in a Multicultural Society* (Cambridge: Cambridge University Press, 1996), 175.

88. William Galston, *Liberal Purposes* (Cambridge: Cambridge University Press, 1991), 244.

89. Harry Brighouse, "Against Nationalism", *Canadian Journal of Philosophy*, 22 (Supp.) 1996, 365–405, 371.

90. Thus I agree with Veit Bader's argument that "A minimal requirement, in this regard, [is] to rethink and rewrite the history of 'nations' to include the history of conquered and oppressed *ethnicities* and nations, of enforced cultural association, of old and recent migration." Bader, "The Cultural Conditions of Transnational Citizenship", 783.

91. Sandra Stotsky, "Multicultural Literature and Civic Education: A Problematic Relationship with Possibilities" in Robert K. Fullinwider (ed.), *Public Education in a Multicultural Society*, 256.

92. As Anthony Appiah has argued: "a curriculum filled with the history of Korean-Americans and African-Americans and Anglo-Americans and Jewish Americans and so on risks being a curriculum with a shallow appreciation of them all." Appiah, "Culture, Subculture, Multiculturalism", 82.

93. Robert K. Fullinwider, "Patriotic History" in Robert K. Fullinwider (ed.), *Public Education in a Multicultural Society*, 222.

94. Appiah, "Culture, Subculture, Multiculturalism", 82.

CHAPTER 9

Civic Friendship and Democratic Education

DAVID BLACKER

Democracy requires deeper moral roots for itself than it alone can provide. The political liberalism of John Rawls recognizes this and takes it as a central problem. There exists within Rawlsian political liberalism an urgent yet underemphasized imperative to shore up the "reasonable" comprehensively grounded moral anchorings that keep secure the political terms of cooperation that constitutional democracy needs in order to function. As George Washington emphasizes in his *Farewell Address*, "Of all the dispositions and habits which lead to political prosperity, religion and morality are indispensable supports...Whatever may be conceded to the influence of refined education on minds of peculiar structure, reason and experience both forbid us to expect that national morality can prevail in exclusion of religious principle (pp. 492–3)."[1] Along with the cultivation of citizenship proper, this Washingtonian civic education concern with citizens' comprehensive groundings must therefore be recognized as a legitimate and even core aim of democratic education. Yet it also presents a particular challenge to polities as heterodox as the United States and others. Analogous to capitalism's need for extra-capitalistic virtues like loyalty and trust,[2] democracy requires extra-democratic virtues associated with the commitment to *some* reasonable comprehensive account of the good, secular or religious. For without the deeper groundings (and I emphasize "groundings", in the plural), the political cooperation is placed at unacceptable risk.

A compelling way of framing this concern is in terms of what Rawls calls "civic friendship", an idea with a long pedigree in democratic thought, extending, at least, to the semi-antagonistic Platonic and Aristotelian conceptions (p. 594).[3] Based on mutual respect and also a concern for democracy's stability, Rawlsian civic friendship enjoins us to have a certain kind of concern for one another's character, though not in the manner of the busybody who wants to scrutinize everyone's private lives. Civic friendship represents a public way of relating to one another *as citizens*, where we are not only civil in our discourse but we work positively to overcome mutual suspicion and hostility by bothering to try to understand something of our own and our fellow citizens' deepest moral motivations. I will argue that, although rightly constrained constitutionally by the Establishment Clause, the public school system can and should do a great deal more for civic friendship than it does now. My Washingtonian concern is how our public schools—presently enrolling some 90 per cent of US schoolchildren—might best advance civic friendship, both for the sake of our souls (so to speak) and also for our "national morality" and "political prosperity", that is, for democracy itself.

Civic friendship as a educational imperative encompasses two main goals: (1) securing a certain level of spiritual and/or moral and/or aesthetic depth in individual citizens' political commitments; and (2) cultivating in citizens an ability to see and tolerate the divergent (within a reasonable range) depths possessed by their fellows. Civic friendship therefore requires a deeper sort of tolerance that emanates from the very depths of the commitments themselves. There are many reasonable ways of being deeply supportive of democratic norms. What is unreasonable is to expect that these norms need no support outside themselves or that everyone must always support democratic norms in the same way. The drive toward uniformity of deep commitment will require a degree of overly intrusive and coercive state action that will become illiberal in its abridgement of individual liberty. To borrow a metaphor from evolutionary biology, with regard to the ways in which individual citizens support democratic politics, liberalism and its pedagogies must be satisfied with analogous rather than homologous commitments, that is, with those that look and function the same politically rather than with those that are identical "all the way down." But it would be equally mistaken to suppose that this required degree of moral developmental laissez-faire means that the depth of citizens' comprehensive conceptions of the Good ("CCGs") is of no concern to liberalism. Again, the concern is rooted in stability. Since political liberalism cares about democratic politics, it must also care about what is necessary to preserve and perpetuate democratic politics. Complacency on this point is excessively risky as, following the building materials metaphor, history teaches that political norms which are unsupported in the sense that they are not really believed in, have a way of eventually collapsing. There is no reason to think this less true for democracies than for other political regimes.[4] Indeed, it may be more so.

With such concerns in mind, this chapter will explore and defend civic friendship as a core aim of democratic education and what it might mean for US school policy. In doing so, I will pay particular attention to the First Amendment, most pertinently the "nonestablishment norm"[5], a legal parameter that realistic education policy prescriptions must recognize. The embrace of civic friendship therefore involves a simultaneous acceptance of the legal constraints nonestablishment places on the actual teaching of CCGs. With both the imperative and constraints in mind, then, I will describe and champion what I think are two good ideas: an extracurricular "school stamps" plan first proposed in the 1970s and a modified version of a "clergy in the schools" counseling program recently struck down by a federal circuit court.

Rawlsian political liberalism, through schooling and other appropriate means, does what it can to respect and foster the depth of commitment that our many extant CCGs can supply. For Rawls, the fact of pluralism—and not just that typically recognized by identity politics, but *all* kinds within wide boundaries of reasonableness—is not a matter for liberals grudgingly to accept, a "compromise" with a less-than-perfect world. It is, rather, an expected and welcome product of liberty itself: insofar as they enjoy political freedom, rational individuals will diverge rather than converge as they attempt to find answers about the final ends of life. (I say this fully aware of the irony that political liberalism's assumption of heterogeneity, though protective of their autonomy at the political level, is also quite contrary to what many CCGs actually believe on their own terms.) This means "that the diversity of reasonable comprehensive religious, philosophical, and moral doctrines found in modern democratic societies is not a mere historical condition that may soon pass away; it is a permanent feature of the public culture of democracy."[6] From the point of view of political liberalism, democracy must remain metaphysically humble. As Anthony Appiah elegantly expresses it, liberalism "as a political creed...does not claim to answer every ethical question, every shallow puzzle or deep mystery about how one should live."[7] The abiding conviction that no one has the final truth about the Good (and, a fortiori, how best to teach it), not even—perhaps especially not—those at the helm of government's police powers, is the lifeblood of such a system.

Consistent with this conviction, political liberalism differs in salient ways from a more staunchly comprehensive or Enlightenment liberalism, which I will very roughly define here as a liberalism confident that its core commitments (such as autonomy) matter "all the way down" and across all or most all spheres of life.[8] Political liberalism lacks this confidence in its own comprehensiveness, however, and is therefore proportionately reluctant to impose itself as a CCG on other CCGs, particularly when this imposition involves the use of police powers, as it often does and as it quite unambiguously does in US school policy (e.g. truancy laws send parents to jail if their children do not attend a state-approved school). Sensitive to such considerations, political liberalism holds those in positions of governmental power (legislative, executive, judicial) to an exacting "idea of public reason" (Rawls), where the appeal to any kind of orthodoxy, secular or religious, is to be foresworn. This applies to governmental actors involved with the basic structures of democracy; in constitutions, judicial decisions, executive orders, legislative statutes, and the like, a certain justificatory abstinence is to be observed, in the same sense as in the enumerated constraints in the Bill of Rights ("Congress shall make no law..."). A judicial opinion should not cite Scripture as a basis for a ruling, a state governor should not appeal to a view about what she believes is "natural" or not (e.g. regarding homosexuality), an elected school board should refrain from most forms of ideologically motivated, content-based viewpoint discrimination, and so on. The idea of public reason rules out certain ways of justifying governmental action, and as such it will be rejected by "those who believe that fundamental political questions should be decided by what they regard as the best reasons according to their own idea of the whole truth" (p. 579).[9] It is this insistence on the "whole" truth (a tendency of comprehensive belief) that is, from the perspective of political liberalism, "incompatible with democratic citizenship and the idea of legitimate law."[10] A "constitutional essential" depending upon *any* particular comprehensive conception—religious or secular—rather than upon, say, the political requirements of democratic citizenship, is therefore out of bounds.

If, *in my official administrative capacity* as a public school official, I create an Earth Day holiday on the grounds that the Gaia Hypothesis commands it or because I think consumerism is destroying our souls, then I have violated the idea of public reason, inasmuch as either rationale would seem to depend on some CCG. (The same would be true of having a day off for Good Friday rather than for spring break.) But if I explain Earth Day in terms not anchored to any comprehensive doctrine, perhaps appealing to the need to combat littering, promote recycling, or defeat a throwaway mentality that has deleterious environmental consequences, then I have abided by the idea of public reason. Rawls thinks individual citizens should also abide by the idea of public reason when debating matters of public policy, in effect, deciding such matters *as if* they were actual legislators. He calls this a "duty of civility": the idea that when we address one another as citizens, we should do so in ways that are not limited to the comprehensive doctrines we ourselves happen to hold. In the public square, then, there is indeed a duty either to bracket one's deepest beliefs in favor of more publicly accessible justifications, or at least to follow what Rawls calls "the proviso" that one add such a publicly accessible justification where one has spoken of the proposal exclusively in terms of one's own favored comprehensive doctrine. It is important, though, to add that, as opposed to the idea of public reason as applied to governmental actors, this duty of civility applies to citizens and is a moral duty based on respect for persons rather than a legal one. A legal duty of civility would violate free speech.[11]

Despite these legal and moral duties, however, Rawls is at great pains to counter the common criticism of political liberalism that it excessively constrains public debate by ruling out comprehensive conceptions, gagging citizens by not letting them speak their full minds, disrespecting their deepest beliefs. This criticism misses that Rawlsian public reason and attendant considerations like the proviso apply to government actors in their official capacity and only in very special situations to private citizens (again: when they are debating essential matters of public policy, and even then only as moral not legal requirements). He emphasizes how the discursive restraints do not apply to what he calls the "background culture", which comprises just about everything outside the formal political structure, including, he says specifically, "institutions of learning at all levels."[12] "The idea of public reason does not apply to the background culture with its many forms of non-public reason nor to media of any kind. Sometimes those who appear to reject the idea of public reason actually mean to assert the need for full and open discussion in the background culture. With this political liberalism fully agrees."[13] In the background culture, then, the level of comprehensiveness with which we advance our views is to be unrestricted.

Yet the notion of the background culture upon which Rawls relies is overly vague when applied to the US public school system. Because of their status as government actors who are exercising compulsion (starting with age-sensitive school attendance statutes), K-12 school personnel are subject to a host of Establishment Clause and other limitations on their basic freedoms, for example, the size of the religious trinkets they can wear, discussing their religious beliefs with students, the time off they are allowed for holidays, even the extent to which they are allowed to speak their minds (including on matters of public concern).[14] The non-establishment norm separating church and state therefore *in practice* restricts schoolteachers and other school officials to something very much like the Rawlsian idea of public reason, more so than those in other areas of the background culture such as higher education (where attendance is formally voluntary), professional and community groups, the media, and also less compulsory areas of government itself (e.g. religious displays at certain government offices, prayers at the start of legislative sessions, etc.). Political liberalism must therefore accept restrictions on school officials such as those described in my Earth Day example, thereby repositioning public schooling as a constitutional essential or, at the least, qualifying its alleged status as merely part of the background culture. Either way, non-establishment must obtain in public schools.

This raises vital questions for political liberalism as a guide to education policy. For, through its idea of public reason, political liberalism effectively *expands* the principle of non-establishment to cover the traditionally covered religious justifications as well as secular ones, including Enlightenment liberalism. Consistent with this insight, Rawls emphasizes how "[t]here is, or need be, no war between religion and democracy. In this respect, political liberalism is sharply different from and rejects Enlightenment Liberalism, which historically attacked orthodox Christianity."[15] The question then arises as to how political liberalism can uphold what appears to be its own *expanded* principle of non-establishment ("expanded" because it covers secular as well as religious doctrines) while also supervising a school system capable of sustaining the deep thinking and thoroughgoing (but diverse) commitments democracy needs in order to survive. In other words: how, given the ideological austerity imposed by expanded non-establishment, can political liberalism integrate the CCG-inspired drive to connect pedagogy to final ends with the democratic–procedural impetus toward ensuring a fair and open education system?

As if in implicit response to this question, too many "school wars" partisans have been tempted into a false choice between either orthodox Goodliness/Godliness against a soulless regulatory state or, perhaps, a litigious rights agenda posing as a heroic casting off of superstition. Political liberalism is different from either extreme because it takes seriously both liberal democracy's constitutional and also citizens' needs for a substantive moral grounding of their own choosing. Rawls provides an update of the Washingtonian sentiment quoted at the outset:

> The roots of democratic citizens' allegiance to their political conceptions lie in their respective comprehensive doctrines, both religious and nonreligious. In this way, citizens' allegiance to the democratic ideal of public reason is strengthened for the right reasons. We may think of the reasonable comprehensive doctrines that support society's reasonable political conceptions as those conceptions' vital social basis, giving them enduring strength and vigor.[16]

Understood as an expansion of non-establishment *in the service of deepening citizens' chosen comprehensive allegiances*, political liberalism imagines a compromise that would orient school policy toward both the Right and the Good(s).

But any such compromise would be delicate and very difficult to pull off in practice in the US public school system. For expanded non-establishment means that state-run schools will *not* for the most part be in a position to accomplish what even a congruent CCG would require of them; school officials would be too restrictively gagged to fully provide the needed depth dimension (religious *or* secular) to a child's education.[17] In the absence of a comprehensive system of non-public schools accessible to all students, the state-run public schools will continue to be depended upon by the vast majority—for very practical access reasons if for no other.[18] These realities suggest that if there is to be a Washingtonian-cum-politically liberal effort at deepening the comprehensive moral groundings of young citizens through K-12 education, such an effort must: (1) work largely within the framework of the existing public school system; (2) not rely on public school personnel to provide the actual direct instruction about the particular comprehensive moral groundings; and, most important and challenging of all; (3) undertake creative and large-scale experimentation involving collaboration between public schools and appropriate community groups—religious and non-religious, "faith based" and secular, "pervasively sectarian" and non-sectarian—that are oriented by some reasonable CCG.[19]

Such an agenda would doubtless cause a great deal of initial confusion and upheaval. But, I believe, the short-term turbulence would be more than made up by the long-term gains in legitimacy, creativity, and adaptability that would be won for the public education system as a whole. For all these reasons, the crucial goal of stability for that system would thereby also be aided, given that an education system so reformed would be publicly recognized as generating its own support from a healthy number of parties with otherwise divergent interests (p. 171)[20] and, in the process, going some ways toward filling the vacuum of legitimacy left behind by the dissolution of yesteryear's broad public school coalition of business, labor, and others. For the many relevant CCGs, such an education regime would be a door held wide open to their efforts to show young citizens how their everyday lives are (and ought to be) inextricable from their own and their fellows' yearning for proximity to the Good as they see it. Yet this reformed politically liberal educational regime would also respect an expanded non-establishment principle that would not allow the state directly to support religious or other comprehensive instruction. By various means, the state would play a salutary *indirect* role, one consistent with non-establishment and other relevant constitutional parameters.

How might all this work? By way of an answer, let me stress that any number of policies might be consistent with what I am suggesting. It is neither possible nor desirable for a lone theorist to lay out a detailed menu of policies and procedures that will work for every locality within our still-kicking tradition of local control of schools, some 13,000 school districts in a daunting heterogeneity of settings. Moreover, it would be implausible to suggest that any particular education policies follow deductively from the first principles—such as they exist—of political liberalism. From its meta-level perch, the prescriptive determinacy of this kind of political theory is limited. Full, detailed policy prescriptions do not spring from the head of political liberalism merely to be implemented by those "on the ground." On the contrary, one of the great strengths of political liberalism is that it provides a framework for innovation, where most of the creativity and excitement is properly relegated to the groups and individuals most directly involved, closest to the pulse of a particular practice or sphere of life.[21] It in no way implies that democracy's education policy must pursue the "one best system" of any description,[22] democratic process being best understood, in Joshua Cohen's terms, as "one kind of institutionalized process of reason giving."[23] Reason giving is quite different from dictating policy. There is a need for prescriptive modesty, then, the larger point being to defend the creation of the conditions for innovation rather than to issue directives detailing what those innovations must be.

Political liberalism aids democracy's durability by ensuring a salutary degree of moral capaciousness. It allows citizens to embrace democracy on their own terms, drawing support for democracy's requisite political conceptions from the perspectives of citizens' many different secular and/or religious comprehensive doctrines. Rawls himself is quite clear on this: "it is central to political liberalism that free and equal citizens affirm both a comprehensive doctrine and a political conception."[24] There will of course be those who do not arrive at conclusions that are in fact supportive of democracy. There can be no guarantee against this. As has long been noted, democracy stands or falls on the wager that the weight of enlightened opinion will fall on the side of the democratic political conclusions the system needs in order to survive. If things are so far gone that no sufficient overlapping consensus is sustainable, then the democracy in question is probably already dead, attention likely having turned in such a case from school policy and toward matters such as borders, treaties, and refugees.

Despite their centrifugal potential, however, as Washington emphasized, democracy also stands or falls according to the strength with which those many different comprehensive doctrines support the democratic political consensus—a point distinct from the mere existence of a consensus (e.g. there could be an anemic consensus, unsettled by the slightest disagreement). There is therefore a strong civic education imperative aimed both directly toward the political terms of cooperation themselves and also indirectly toward the multiple supports for that consensus. This in turn implies that democracy must foster in citizens a certain depth dimension in their own and their fellows' political commitments, though, as I have argued, this vital work must be done indirectly. This is the essence of Rawlsian civic friendship, through which those holding different comprehensive doctrines reassure one another (and, one might add, themselves) about their mutual commitment to democracy:

[E]ach of us shows how, from our own doctrines, we can and do endorse a reasonable public political conception of justice with its principles and ideals. The aim of doing this is to declare to others who affirm different comprehensive doctrines that we also each endorse a reasonable political conception belonging to the family of reasonable such conceptions.[25]

Pursuant to this stability-conducive "reassurance", democratic education must embrace civic friendship, even if it means exploring territory traditionally taboo for most liberals. This includes a willingness creatively to use public schools, in a manner consistent with non-establishment, as a means for shaping citizens capable of real civic friendship. Civic friendship takes from traditional liberalism its guarantees for constitutional essentials (including non-establishment). But it takes from extant CCGs the concern to anchor those guarantees in something beyond themselves. Though it thereby makes itself a more fertile field for certain kinds of principled dissent, a pluralistic democracy durably grounds itself nowhere else but in the groundedness of its individual citizens.

A balm for the wounds created by the "culture wars", a civic friendship reform agenda would embrace a wide range of school initiatives and reforms. Consistent with the foregoing discussion, I see at least two categories of these as especially relevant.

First, educators must be much more willing than they have been to teach about citizens' many different religions—and a healthy portion of other actual and reasonable secular CCGs—in the public schools, and should embrace the many recent calls from thoughtful observers toward doing just that, including those of the US Department of Education itself.[26] As the Supreme Court has repeatedly made clear,[27] teaching *about* religion per se raises no Establishment Clause worries, so long as it is done in a non-devotional manner, a requirement sufficiently clear for most pedagogical purposes.

The second area is more complex, as it involves rethinking aspects of the post-war Establishment Clause settlements as applied to public schooling, and as such is little amenable to any summary generalization. In the broadest strokes, though, and consistent with what it seems to me a civic friendship mission would entail, states and local educational authorities should be allowed to make their schools more porous and penetrable by community groups with religious and non-religious CCGs, including those one might call "pervasively comprehensive" groups.[28] Schools should continue to adhere to the non-establishment norm guarding against children being coerced into religious activity by the state, for example, in the areas of school prayer within school and as part of major activities sponsored by the school,[29] creationism (rightly adjudged as lacking a primarily secular purpose),[30] and in the extent to which schools and religious enterprises may consolidate their activities.[31] Yet the centrality of civic friendship to democratic education should direct policymakers and judges to adopt with regard to schools a looser "neutrality theory" (regarding public aid to private and religious groups performing functions coinciding with the public interest) rather than the stricter "no-aid" separationism that obtains in many areas of school policy.[32] In neutrality theory, which is the standard for public aid to competing community service providers (where the set of providers may include religious groups), public money is to be awarded according to religion-neutral criteria so that the religious or non-religious character of the applicant is to be formally irrelevant.[33] This means, among other things, that a community service group that is religious is not to be ruled out (so long as they are not determined to be pervasively sectarian). Civic friendship would furnish a compelling justification for including religious and non-religious groups operating according to comprehensive doctrines—even ones that are "pervasively" so—as potential recipients of public money for specified educational activities conducted by those groups. As I have argued, the compelling state interest supplied by civic friendship is the Washingtonian one of securing in individual citizens the deep religious and/or secular groundings necessary for anchoring their commitments to democracy.

Correlatively, it stands to reason that actual exposure to such groundings in the form of persons actually grounded by them will be the best means by which to induce these individual anchorings to occur. However, consistent with non-establishment, and as reflected in current law, school personnel must be prohibited from providing these groundings themselves (particularly the religious ones). Given these constraints, the question arises as to what, constrained as they are by non-establishment, schools might do for civic friendship, beyond what they already do (e.g. "celebrations" of the general idea of multiculturalism and freedom of conscience, neutralist dialogical, and conflict resolution techniques, etc.)? My view is that, while the schools cannot and should not *themselves* teach the comprehensive doctrines, they can and should make greater room for the many responsible parties who are not so constrained, a kind of structural-programmatic accommodation, of which I will give examples below. This is how schools should respond to mounting calls that religion and morality be taught more robustly than they currently are.

For starters, public schools should begin experimenting more urgently with ways they might responsibly delegate appropriate parts of their curriculum and/or extra curriculum to community groups that adhere to comprehensive doctrines of various sorts. As have other democracies,[34] and consistent with some of the public debate surrounding policy initiatives such as school vouchers and charter schools in our own, US democracy should begin to mature out of its persistent identification of public education exclusively with government-run education.[35] Gone are the days (if they ever actually existed) when one could confidently proclaim that CCGs are private matters in the sense that home and church alone will see to them. It is uncontroversial that the family, for one, is overextended and overburdened (witness, e.g. the decreasing amount of time parents spend with their children, the decreasing centrality of children in parents' lives and social policy generally, including the desperate need for proper day—and after school—care[36]), so it would make very little practical sense at this historical moment to add yet another burden. It is much more likely that such matters will simply go unattended. As William Galston has remarked, "the greatest threat to children in modern liberal societies is not that they will believe in something too deeply, but that they will believe in nothing very deeply at all."[37] As it has at its proudest moments in the United States—the fifty state guarantees of schooling for all, the erection of the comprehensive high school,[38] the GI Bill, racial and disability-based desegregation, to name a few—democratic education must perpetually respond to contextual demands. Commitment corroding large-scale forces of marketization and juridification comprise challenges just as formidable and action necessitating as any that have come before. In the name of liberalism, some of the older and tidier traditional liberal assumptions may need to fall.

By way of clarification, I will conclude with two concrete recommendations. One is a policy proposal that would help make public schools more porous (in the above sense) vis-à-vis community groups with comprehensive orientations, while also maintaining non-establishment and an appropriate level of oversight. The other is drawn from a recent federal circuit court case outlawing a certain kind of collaboration between a public school district and religious educators. I will argue that the outlawed practice could be easily modified to pass constitutional muster and that the resulting modified program would be consistent with non-establishment and conducive to civic friendship.

First, the policy proposal resurrects an idea first proposed in the 1970s by longtime school voucher advocate and legal scholar Stephen Sugarman, what he calls a "school stamps plan", in essence a voucher plan for *extracurricular* activities that leaves intact the compulsory part of the curriculum.[39] With a school stamps plan, families would be issued school stamps redeemable for educational services of many different kinds, particularly those most commonly found outside the regular school program. The possibilities for which the stamps could be used would be limited only by the resources of the community and the suitability of the providers (which could be certified in various ways—Sugarman suggests, e.g. that providers post a modest bond and file an affidavit with the local educational authority). Also, for feasibility and equity reasons, distribution of the stamps might be means-tested. Building on Sugarman's idea, school stamps might be used for foreign language instruction, supplementary science courses, tutoring of all kinds, athletics, piano lessons, scouting, acquiring educational material such as books and computer equipment, certain types of before and after-school programs for the youngest children, and also, pending the resolution of potential Establishment Clause difficulties, certain types of secular and/or religious moral education.[40] In the post-*Zelman* era, a school stamps plan limited to extracurriculars would seem easy to justify constitutionally (see note 33). A school stamps plan limited to extracurriculars would be rife with relevant dissimilarities. For example, such plans would be outside the ambit of state compulsory education laws (a factor typically augmenting non-establishment protections) and, so long as the criteria for approval and oversight of potential providers were religion-neutral,[41] school stamps would constitute "indirect" rather than "direct" aid to provider organizations, in that individuals are doing the provider choosing (as in the case of college student loans). Perhaps most significantly, school stamps would provide an impressive array of secular benefits not easily achievable in other ways. I would also add that such a program would be a natural site for the public service, or "service learning", proposals popular among many communitarians.[42] Sugarman elaborates some additional details:

> Many persons and groups could qualify as providers of goods and services for which the coupons could be used. The public schools themselves could offer after-school, evening, and weekend programs; but a pupil would not be restricted to the offerings of his own regular school. Other public institutions such as libraries and parks and recreation departments could also become providers. The state or district might even set up warehouses for the purpose of renting educational materials—telescopes, pocket calculators, and the like. Finally, private parties could offer programs in return for the coupons: dancing schools, photographic studios, financial institutions that could train in money management, reading clubs, and so on, as well as individual or small-group tutors of nearly every imaginable subject. Public schools have another role here: to lease space as their facilities for other offers to use. The school stamps plan could operate in the summer as well as during the school year . . .[43]

Administering a school stamps program would involve substantial resources, not only to fund the stamps themselves, but also to sort out the many logistical, clerical, governance, and liability complexities that would ensue. But it would be a worthy challenge.

From the perspective of political liberalism and its civic friendship imperative, a well-run school stamps program would stand to offer a great deal. First and foremost, it would provide greater opportunities for helping children to discover and elaborate their own moral depths, particularly insofar as they were rendered more likely to come into contact with individuals, informal groups, and organizations who are actually expressing *and tangibly enacting* their various comprehensive commitments. Perhaps they might come to understand what really motivates some citizens to care for the planet, beyond just putting out the recycling every week. They might be more likely to see first-hand how strong religiously and/or secularly based moral views sustain many citizens in physically and emotionally demanding charitable work, such as Meals on Wheels, the foster care of disabled infants, organizing the town's annual parade, becoming a Big Brother or Sister, working in a soup kitchen. Maybe school stamps will maximize their chances of experiencing directly how lively certain activities can become when animated by the deep and specific convictions rarely on display within public school walls: by participating in a church choir, working with those planning a Wiccan summer solstice festival, researching their own and others' genealogy and family history, interpreting their dreams with Freudians or Jungians, studying anti-Semitism and a trip to the Holocaust Museum in Washington DC, learning an Asian martial art and its enveloping moral and spiritual code. This kind of thing would, I think, be very far from "cafeteria-style" multiculturalism and other superficial attempts at "celebrating" diversity currently afflicting many public schools. It would enable a much more authentic encounter with diversity of all kinds (including the moral and religious kinds of diversity systematically ignored by public schools) in an environment where those involved are infinitely freer than public school teachers to discuss and exhibit their motive comprehensive underpinnings. Young citizens would thereby be less cripplingly sheltered than they are now from people with strong, passionate commitments. For this exposure seems a sine qua non of civic friendship, where one develops an ability to perceive and, where appropriate, appreciate what lies beneath and behind the politics of those who agree and, most importantly, those who do not. Political liberalism aspires to forge a citizenry depthful enough to do this.

This leads to my second example. It involves a recent case from the US Fifth Circuit Court of Appeals, *Doe v. Beaumont Independent School District* (1999), striking down a school counseling program utilizing clergy as volunteers.[44] Beaumont Independent School District (BISD), a medium-sized district in Texas, initiated in 1996 a "Clergy in the Schools" (CIS) program, where individual members of the local clergy were invited into the school to provide volunteer group counseling sessions to students at the school during school hours. CIS is part of a broader "School Volunteer Program" where BISD works with a range of community volunteer groups in order to take advantage of various types of expertise in the community so as to enhance students' education. CIS is open only to clergy, paralleling the composition of the other volunteer programs, which were also limited to individuals of the desired type (other programs utilized local attorneys, senior citizens, business persons). "The Program's stated goals are to provide (1) meaningful dialogue between the clergy and the students regarding civic virtues and morality; (2) a safe school atmosphere; and (3) volunteer opportunities for an additional group of stakeholders in the public schools."[45] School administrators and the clergy volunteers meet to discuss central aspects of the program, including relevant First Amendment constraints on the counseling sessions (e.g. no praying with students, etc.), as the clergy members plan one or two visits to the schools annually (elementary schools are to be visited once, secondary schools twice). The majority of the clergy volunteers were Protestants, but there were others, including a rabbi. (The school explains this disproportion as reflecting the pattern of religious affiliation among the local population.) When they arrive on campus, school personnel escort the clergy volunteers inside, whereupon school officials (administrators and counselors) then select students for participation,

with an eye toward assembling a group diverse in ethnicity, academic ability, and school deportment. BISD officials then remove the selected students from class and assemble them in another schoolroom to participate in the group counseling, without parental notification or consent... students who are selected have the option of declining to participate. Each counseling session is attended by the school's principal and counselor. Under the Program's guidelines, the sessions are designed to comprise approximately thirty-five students and ten to twelve volunteer clergymen; the guidelines proscribe one-on-one meetings...[46]

The District had distributed a "Fact Sheet" further explicating the aims of CIS. These are detailed in Judge Emilio Garza's dissenting opinion:

The Program sought to provide 'a positive forum which contributes to open dialogue of students discussing concerns and problems of the 21st century,' to create a meaningful dialogue between clergy and students, to make schools safer, and to give the clergy a volunteering opportunity. It included the following set of expectations for volunteers: be a positive role model for students; show concern for students' success; provide academic support for students; be aware of what is happening in the schools; provide a safe and secure atmosphere for students; provide a positive means for obtaining desired student behavior; and help students gain an understanding of the real world. It listed alcohol, peer pressure, racial issues, self-discipline, self-esteem, setting goals, stereotyping, respect, the reasons for rules, unity, and violence as possible discussion topics suggested by students.[47]

The District also stressed in the "Fact Sheet" that CIS did not concern religious issues and, in fact, explicitly prohibited discussion of them in the counseling sessions. It emphasized that clergy in particular were chosen, in the words of the "Fact Sheet", "to provide opportunities for students to dialogue with skilled resources in the community. Because the clergy has the natural skills of listening and communicating, BISD chose to tap this resource which has been previously not used to its fullest."[48]

The Doe parents filed for a temporary restraining order to halt the program on behalf of their minor children. This was denied, as was another motion to halt the program. The federal district court then granted a summary judgment in favor of BISD. Yet on appeal to the three-judge US Fifth Circuit Court of Appeals, the Does won a reversal of the district court's ruling against them. The Fifth Circuit Court struck down the CIS program as an Establishment Clause violation, therefore "invalidating the Program and prohibiting its further implementation."[49]

After deciding the Does had standing to sue (none of the Doe children actually took part in the counseling sessions, though they were present in classrooms from which participant students were drawn), the two-judge majority reasoned through the three main Establishment Clause violation tests and ruled that the CIS program flunked them all. First is the tripartite *Lemon* test. The first prong of *Lemon* requires that the policy in question have a clear secular purpose that neither "advances nor inhibits religion." *Lemon*'s second prong requires that the challenged state action have a "primary purpose that neither advances nor inhibits religion." Finally, *Lemon* also prohibits the "excessive entanglement" of church and state officials in planning, administering, evaluating, etc. the activity.[50] The majority opinion finds that the secular purpose of the CIS, the main elements of which are stated above by BISD, is "merely pretextual", largely because of a public statement made by BISD Superintendent Carroll Thomas favoring prayer in the schools and also the fact that the CIS is an "exclusive counseling arrangement afforded to the clergy."[51] Because the *Lemon* test is disjunctive, this flunking of one prong would be enough to rule CIS an Establishment Clause violation. Yet the Court continued. Turning to the second part of *Lemon*, the majority points out that not only is aid to a particular religion prohibited, but also the favoring of religion over non-religion.[52] Here the main problem also involves the exclusivity of the arrangement. Why did BISD think that only clergy were suitable for counseling on matters of civic virtue and morality? BISD, for example, failed to include lay professionals who might be equally qualified. "BISD does not select its volunteer counselors based on neutral criteria—such as listening or communication skills—but on the very fact that they are *religious* representatives."[53] In this way, BISD exhibits preference for religion over non-religion, which violates *Lemon*'s second prong. CIS also fails the third "excessive entanglement" prong, owing to the extent of planning and oversight exercised over the program by its created ensemble of religious and government officials: the selection of clergy volunteers, the preliminary planning and "training sessions", program monitoring, the fact that school administrators and counselors attended and facilitated the sessions, etc.

Second, the *Doe* majority also argues that CIS violates the coercion test laid out in *Lee* v. *Weisman* (1992) (school-sponsored prayers at graduation create "subtle coercive pressures" toward participation and so violate the Establishment Clause), which prohibits government direction of a religious exercise in which objectors are obliged to participate, even if the participation is formally non-compulsory and the obligation is generated merely by psychological or "peer" pressure. Following *Lee*, the *Doe* majority argues that the student who is pulled from the classroom but "does not wish to participate is placed in the untenable position of having to choose either to attend a session he truly wants to avoid or to decline the 'invitation' and thereby risk actual or perceived opprobrium and ostracism from BISD administrators and faculty, not to mention from his peers. This affords the student no real choice, just a 'Hobson's Choice'— either to participate in the Program against his wishes or decline at the risk of becoming a pariah."[54] *Lee* establishes that such a "choice" does not count as voluntary. As for the question of whether the counseling sessions were religious exercises, the premise from which the coercion worry proceeds, the majority again relies on the exclusivity of the selection of clergy as volunteers, which causes "the exercise to lose its secular character entirely", though "in a vacuum student counseling is not an inherently religious undertaking..."[55]

Third and finally, the "endorsement test" seeks to determine whether government is endorsing religion by means of the action in question. Here, the government should never favor religion over non-religion such that a reasonable observer might conclude that the government is taking a position on the matter, "or makes adherence to a religion relevant in any way to a person's standing in the political community."[56] "The government creates this appearance when it conveys a message that religion is 'favored,' 'preferred,' or 'promoted' over other beliefs."[57] Yet again, because of the selection and utilization of clergy to the exclusion of other qualified persons in the community capable of engaging in dialogue about morality with students, BISD officially "conveys the unmistakable message that religion is favored, preferred, and even promoted over other beliefs...Theirs is a message of endorsement that cannot possibly be lost on the young, impressionable, easily influenced schoolchildren whom the law entrusts to these very officials, *in loco parentis*, for the entire school day."[58]

From the perspective of the Establishment Clause, then, the Doe majority holds CIS in violation by every available standard. Yet Judge Garza's spirited dissenting opinion disputes the majority opinion point by point. In his view, BISD exhibited an "unwavering commitment to a secular focus" sufficient to establish (not withstanding the stray comments of the Superintendent about prayer in schools) their sincerity. He also questions how CIS, in the context of the other volunteer programs that also have a particular focus (and so limit the selection of volunteers accordingly), could really be providing a benefit to religion when, in a situation such as this, it seems more accurate to say that the clergy volunteers are the ones actually *providing* benefits to the students, not the other way around, and so any benefit the clergy volunteers end up receiving is "no more than indirect or incidental."[59] More significantly, Garza questions the majority's argument that the exclusivity of BISD's exclusive reliance upon clergy for the counseling sessions is analogous to Bible reading, prayer, or some other religious ceremony. Garza writes:

Beneath this perception lies the assumption that the clergy are incapable of expounding on civic values from anything but a religious perspective.

I reject the majority's position. That civic values bear a close relationship to certain religious beliefs proves neither that CIS lacks a secular purpose nor that its primary effect is the advancement of religion. BISD may advocate civic values that 'merely happen to coincide or harmonize with the tenets of some or all religions.'[60]

For Garza, the exclusivity of the reliance upon clergy does not render CIS unconstitutional because the clergy are not here conducting anything resembling a religious observance and are, in fact, explicitly prohibited from doing so by BISD. In the absence of any performance of anything resembling distinctly religious duties, their mere *identity* as clergy should not prohibit a public school from inviting them to volunteer. Such a prohibition would risk a non-neutral discriminatory stance toward religion, a priori singling it out and excluding it from involvement in a government program in which groups of every other kind are eligible to participate. This would begin to look like a violation of Free Exercise. To underscore the point, Garza quotes approvingly from none other than Justice William Brennan, who writes, "The Establishment Clause does not license government to treat religion and those who teach or practice it, simply by virtue of their status as such, as subversive of American ideals and therefore subject to unique disabilities."[61]

However, Garza then proceeds to diminish the rhetorical force of his dissent with the intemperate accusation that the *Doe* majority would have to rule against a school speaker such as the Reverend Martin Luther King, Jr or Archbishop Desmond Tutu.[62] That he would level this charge shows that Garza, despite his salutary caveats expressed above, does not recognize the full subtlety of the main issue. The majority rightly dismisses his mischievous inference, for, as indicated above, the salient issue is not the mere fact of the volunteers' religious identity, but the exclusivity of the selection of them according to that constitutionally singular identity. They respond by reinforcing just this point:

BISD cannot design and implement a volunteer counseling program consisting *solely* of clergy members. The opinion in no way affects BISD's ability to create a broad-based program that truly integrates the clergy with nonreligious community representatives and certainly does not mandate that BISD discriminate against the clergy or bar a high-profile public figure from advising the student body simply because such [a] figure happens to be a cleric. Civil rights leaders like King and Tutu speaking as civil rights leaders do not lose their eligibility to speak publicly by virtue of their ordination.[63]

This clarification provides rather obvious instructions for how BISD or anyone else might revise such a program consistent with nonestablishment. As we have seen, CIS fails the Establishment Clause tests largely because of the element of exclusivity inherent in BISD's somewhat blind preference for mainstream, "respectable" religion as a teacher of civic virtues, morality, and the like.

If, however, following the majority's suggestion above, BISD had designed the program such that it was at least potentially inclusive of secular persons[64] with the relevant expertise or, to use the terminology of political liberalism, if it had constructed the program as an occasion whereby those adhering to CCGs, *secular or religious*, might participate, then such a program would plainly be in much better constitutional shape. The "religiousness" of the program thereby decreased, the other Establishment Clause concerns, such as coercion and endorsement, would proportionately decrease as well.

Such a reconstruction of the program would not only be more consistent with non-establishment, it would also be more conducive to educating students toward civic friendship. For civic friendship requires citizens to be disposed and able to recognize and appreciate (in the sense at least of trying to understand) the CCGs underlying fellow citizens' adherence to the overlapping democratic political consensus. So civic education is shortchanged when citizens are limited in the range of their fellow citizens' CCGs to which they are exposed. Civic friendship pedagogues would likely face tough pedagogical choices here, quasi-utilitarian dilemmas such as whether it would be better to know, say, three or four other comprehensive doctrines in depth or a dozen of them superficially. This would be an appropriate arena for the exercise of pedagogical expertise. In any event, it is the kind of problem with which educators *should* be wrestling: surely, even in a place like Beaumont, Texas, there is bound to be a wider range of comprehensive doctrines upon which to draw than simply those represented by the town's mainstream religions. It is likely that the real reason not to reach beyond the mainstream—and for a school district like BISD to equate virtue and morality with religion—resides in the moral parochialism and consequent lack of ability for civic friendship found in many of the local government officials themselves, along with a large dose of prudent timidity regarding the preservation of school–community relations. As has been the case historically, school administrators are not typically known for their brazenness over and against their local communities.[65] This is largely because "we the people" have wanted it this way: the US's staunch commitment, relative to other democracies, to the local control of schools has in this respect reaped exactly what it's sown. Far from being a matter of fuzzy "niceness" or etiquette, then, civic friendship will often present something of a challenge to school administrators and local school boards, sometimes compelling them to confront elements of their local communities just often as they "partner" with them. When fundamentalist parents complain about environmentalist volunteers, atheist parents about clergy, and the whole lot of them about who-knows-what, school officials should have something justifiable to say to them all. The teaching of civic friendship gives them a compelling *educational* reason to overcome curricular (and extracurricular) narrowness by both affirming and challenging their constituencies' comprehensive views, the latter accomplished by the school's pedagogical attention to multiple CCGs. The democratic educator's commitment to civic friendship therefore always gestures beyond itself, toward to a wider world than is dreamt of in any single "philosophy."

NOTES

For her helpful comments, thanks to Meira Levinson, and also to Walter Feinberg, Kevin McDonough, and the other participants at "Collective Identities, and Cosmopolitan Values: Group Rights and Public Education in Liberal Democratic Societies", Montreal, Quebec, June 2000.

1. George Washington, "The Farewell Address, September 17, 1796" in *The People Shall Judge: Readings in the Formation of American Policy, Volume I*, selected and edited by the Staff, Social Sciences 1, The College of the University of Chicago (Chicago: University of Chicago Press, 1949), 486–95.
2. See Francis Fukuyama, *Trust: The Social Virtues and the Creation of Prosperity* (New York: The Free Press, 1995).
3. John Rawls, "The Idea of Public Reason Revisited" in Samuel Freeman (ed.), *John Rawls: Collected Papers* (Cambridge, MA: Harvard University Press, 1999), 573–615. For some historical background, as well as an argument that civic friendship is inclusive of feminist concerns, see Sibyl A. Schwarzenbach, "On Civic Friendship", *Ethics*, 107(1) (1996), 97. On the Greek conceptions, including a good overview of Plato and Aristotle (and later followers of both) on this point, see Horst Hutter, *Politics as Friendship: The Origins of Classical Notions of Politics in the Theory and Practice of Friendship* (Waterloo, Ontario: Wilfrid Laurier University Press, 1978), and also the relevant chapters in John Cooper, *Reason and Emotion: Essays on Ancient Moral Psychology and Ethical Theory* (Princeton: Princeton University Press, 1999).
4. Though we have disagreements about it, I thank Meira Levinson for pressing me on this point.
5. Michael Perry, *Religion in Politics: Constitutional and Moral Perspectives* (Oxford: Oxford University Press, 1997). It is, of course, a separate endeavor to examine the moral desirability of the non-establishment norm.
6. Rawls, *Political Liberalism* (New York: Columbia University Press, 1993), 36.
7. See Chapter 2 of this volume.
8. Important examples of strongly autonomy-centered views include Eamonn Callan, *Creating Citizens: Political Education and Liberal Democracy* (Oxford: Oxford University Press, 1997), 39–42, which also argues that "Rawlsian political liberalism is really a kind of closet comprehensive liberalism"; and Meira Levinson, *The Demands of Liberal Education* (Oxford: Oxford University Press, 1999), which endorses a high degree of state regulation of even private schools— substantially higher than the current legal status quo—of private schooling in the name of liberal autonomy (161 ff). Ultimately, my "thinner" political liberalism would have to answer more completely to these "thicker" liberal views.
9. Rawls, "The Idea of Public Reason Revisited" in Samuel Freeman (ed.), *John Rawls* (Cambridge, MA: Harvard University Press, 1999), 573–615.

10. Ibid.
11. Ibid., 577.
12. Ibid., 576, n.13. Rawls does imply some distinction between K-12 and higher education when he adds that the notion of background culture applies "especially" to "universities and professional schools, scientific and other societies."
13. Ibid., 576.
14. Even when speaking out about a matter of public concern (e.g. a letter to the editor), the so-called "*Pickering* balance" weighs teachers' freedom of speech rights against other factors involving any potential serious disruption of the educational process. *Pickering* v. *Board of Education of Township High School District 205*, 391 U.S. 563 (1968).
15. Rawls, "The Idea of Public Reason Revisited", 611.
16. Ibid., 592.
17. Some argue that all teaching is necessarily normative and hence non-neutral. This is true but trivial. For it is perfectly imaginable and even, arguably, an accurate description of many current practices, for a school to teach non-controversial "moral" values such as politeness, honesty, and the like, without touching upon anything deeper about why anyone should bother to be polite, honest, etc., in the first place.
18. For this reason, friend and foe alike overstate the significance of the school choice debate. Even under imagined conditions of full-blown public–private school choice, little would change, except perhaps in the inner cities where such experiments are already being tried in many places. Wealthy suburbanites are for the most part content with their public schools and would be unlikely to compromise their fiscal base, so there would be correspondingly little incentive for a large network of non-public voucher recipients to arise in the suburbs. Simple geographical reality and the lack of economies of scale (e.g. school transportation over large distances) renders most choice systems unfeasible in most rural areas. That leaves the inner cities, where school choice is feasible and attractive to "escaping" parents. This is, of course, an absolutely essential arena, but even if US inner cities become islands of choice, they would likely remain just that: islands.
19. I have discussed in some detail parameters for identifying which kinds of groups should count as "reasonable" for these purposes and which should not. See my "Fanaticism and Schooling in the Democratic State", *American Journal of Education*, 106(2) (1998), 241–72. In short, I think there should be an extremely capacious interpretation of which groups should be allowed, though omissions must be recognized forthrightly in extreme cases.
20. "A conception of justice is stable if, given the laws of human psychology and moral learning, the institutions which satisfy it tend to generate their own support, at least when this fact is publicly recognized (171)." John Rawls, "Distributive Justice: Some Addenda" in Samuel Freeman (ed.), *John Rawls* (Cambridge, MA: Harvard University Press, 1999), 154–75.
21. In this I follow Michael Walzer, *Spheres of Justice: A Defense of Pluralism and Equality* (New York: Basic Books, 1983).
22. David Tyack, *The One Best System: A History of American Urban Education* (Cambridge, MA: Harvard University Press, 1974).
23. "Pluralism and Proceduralism", *Chicago Kent Law Review*, 589 (1994), 601.
24. Rawls, "The Idea of Public Reason Revisited", 608.
25. Ibid., 594.
26. See Warren Nord, *Religion and American Education: Rethinking a National Dilemma* (Chapel Hill, NC: University of North Carolina Press, 1995), and

Robert Nash, *Faith, Hype and Clarity: Teaching About Religion in America's Schools* (New York: Teachers College Press, 1999). The widely disseminated "Joint Statement", reissued in 1998, is available from the US Department of Education, along with their several official publications advocating greater (careful) collaboration between religious individuals and organizations and public schools.

27. "... it might well be said that one's education is not complete without a study of comparative religion or the history of religion and its relationship to the advancement of civilization. It certainly may be said that the Bible is worthy of study for its literary and historic qualities. Nothing we have said here indicates that such a study of the Bible or of religion, when presented objectively as part of a secular program of education, may not be effected consistently with the First Amendment." *School District of Abington Township* v. *Schempp*, 374 U.S. 203 (1963).

28. This echoes the 'pervasive sectarian' notion used to distinguish between permissible and impermissible religious group recipients of public monies, as developed, *inter alia*, in *Hunt* vs *McNair*, 413 U.S. 743 (1973), and *Roemer* v. *Board of Public Works*, 426 U.S. 755 (1976). See Stephen V. Monsma, "The 'Pervasively Sectarian' Standard in Theory and Practice", *Notre Dame Journal of Law, Ethics and Public Policy*, 13 (1999), 321.

29. *Engel* v. *Vitale*, 370 U.S. 421 (1962); *School District of Abington Township, Pennsylvania* v. *Schempp*, 374 U.S. 203 (1963); *Lemon* v. *Kurtzman*, 403 U.S. 602 (1971); *Lee* v. *Weisman*, 505 U.S. 577 (1992).

30. *Epperson* v. *Arkansas*, 393 U.S. 97 (1968) and *Edwards* v. *Aguillard*, 482 U.S. 578 (1987).

31. That is, the third 'excessive entanglement' prong of the *Lemon* test.

32. I am relying on the analysis of Carl Esbeck, "A Constitutional Case for Governmental Co-operation With Faith-Based Social Service Providers", *Emory Law Review* 46(1) (1997), 1–41.

33. See *Bowen* v. *Kendrick*, 487 U.S. 593 (1988) (upholding federal grants under the Adolescent Family Life Act for teenage counseling, including faith-based centers for such counseling). See Carl Esbeck, "A Constitutional Case for Government Co-operation with Faith-Based Social Service Providers", 7–15. Something like the neutrality principle as applied to school policy has recently been embraced by a plurality of the US Supreme Court in *Mitchell* v. *Helms*, 000 U.S. 98–1648 (2000), which upholds certain forms of state aid, such as computer equipment, to private religious schools. Most recently–and dramatically–the Court has apparently embraced the neutrality idea in the area of government vouchers to private religious schools. See *Zelman* v. *Simmons-Harris*, No. 00–1751 (2002).

34. The United Kingdom and Holland are two examples. For a comparison among the United Kingdom, United States, and France in this regard, see Meira Levinson, "Liberalism Versus Democracy? Schooling Private Citizens in the Public Square", *British Journal of Political Science*, 27(3) (1997), 333–60.

35. I have mostly avoided the voucher and charter debates because they raise distributive concerns outside this chapter's scope. As they pertain to vital matters of school policy, though, those concerns and my own present concerns of course intersect. Generally, I would argue that political liberalism does not need to take a specific position on vouchers, because there are plans both pro and con that would seem within its scope. I would submit, though, that the public debate over these policies has thus far been salutary for civic friendship, in that it has directed public attention to some of the basic normative assumptions

undergirding our education system generally. An excellent example of how school choice might bring philosophical considerations to the fore is found in Harry Brighouse, *School Choice and Social Justice* (Oxford: Oxford University Press, 2000). In addition to much else, Brighouse presents a compelling and clear critique of the identification of public education with state-run schools.

36. See Penelope Leach, *Children First: What Our Society Must Do—And Is Not Doing—For Our Children Today* (New York: Alfred A. Knopf, 1994).

37. William Galston, "Civic Education in the Liberal State" in Nancy L. Rosenblum (ed.), *Liberalism and the Moral Life* (Cambridge, MA: Harvard University Press, 1989), 101.

38. This process was largely completed by the 1960s. See Robert L. Hampel, *The Last Little Citadel: American High Schools Since 1940* (Boston: Houghton Mifflin Company, 1986).

39. Stephen Sugarman, "Education Reform at the Margin: Two Ideals", *Phi Delta Kappan* (November 1977), 155–6.

40. Some of these examples are mentioned by Sugarman; some I am supplying myself.

41. This would be to embrace "neutrality theory" à la *Bowen*, supra, where there are criteria neutral among religious providers and neutral between religious and non-religious providers. These programs would also need to take steps to avoid any serious entanglement situations that might run afoul of *Lemon*.

42. Foremost among these has been Amitai Etzioni, for example, in his *The Spirit of Community: The Reinvention of American Society* (New York: Touchstone Books, 1994). The Clinton Administration's Americorps program embodies some of these ideas. Service activities within the context of school stamps would also have the advantage of removing some of the more objectionable features of 'forced' public service by making it voluntary. Public service in the context I am recommending, however, is potentially more equitable than, say, a blanket high school graduation requirement, in the sense that the service requirements might not be as crucial for poorer kids as wealthier ones. It probably makes a lot more sense for the rich kid to work in the soup kitchen, while the poor kid (who may be in the soup line!) gets ballet lessons he or she might otherwise not get. Both children benefit, but in different ways. One might even designate some of the components as "service learning experiences" and officially encourage students to take a certain proportion of those (though I would encourage the service experiences rather than require them, again, forced public spiritedness being a difficult pill to swallow).

43. Sugarman, "Education Reform at the Margin", 156.

44. *Doe v. Beaumont Independent School District*, 5th Circuit Court of Appeals, No. 97-40429 (1999).

45. Ibid.

46. Ibid.

47. Ibid., J. Garza, dissenting, at 17.

48. Ibid.

49. Ibid.

50. *Lemon v. Kurtzman*, 403 U.S. 602 (1971).

51. *Doe v. Beaumont Independent School District*, at 8.

52. *Everson v. Board of Education of Education of Ewing*, 330 U.S. 1, 15–16 (1947).

53. *Doe v. Beaumont Independent School District*, at 9.

54. Ibid., at 10.

55. Ibid., at 11.

56. *Doe*, quoting *Ingebretson*, 88 F.3d at 280 (5th Cir. 1996).
57. *Doe*, Id., quoting *Allegheny*, 492 U.S. 593 (1989).
58. *Doe*, at 12.
59. *Doe*, J. Garza, dissent, at 24.
60. Ibid., at 25, quoting *McGowan*, 366 U.S., at 442.
61. Ibid., J. Garza, dissent, at 32–3, quoting from *McDaniel* v. *Paty*, 435 U.S. 618, 641 (1978) (J., Brennan, concurring in the judgment).
62. Ibid., J., Garza, dissent, at 25.
63. Doe, at 14.
64. I say "potentially inclusive" rather than de facto inclusion because it would seem permissible if it made eligible and treated equally both religious and non-religious volunteers, but through no omission, misdeed, or bias on the part of BISD. It might happen that no non-religious volunteer would apply, or those who did might happen to be ineligible for some requisite non-religious reason, such as having a criminal record, insufficient experience working with children, or the like.
65. See Raymond Callahan, *Education and the Cult of Efficiency* (Chicago: University of Chicago Press, 1962).

CHAPTER 10

Schooling and Cultural Maintenance for Religious Minorities in the Liberal State

J. Mark Halstead

Groups come in all shapes and sizes, with all kinds of crosscutting memberships. By birth, choice, or chance, citizens live much of their lives within groups, and groups contribute significantly to their identity and self-concept. Some groups involve only a loose form of attachment, but others may make bigger demands on the loyalty of citizens than does the state itself. Groups can have both beneficial and harmful effects on individuals: they can protect and advance individuals' interests and help to satisfy their needs, but they can also exert excessive and oppressive control over individuals, thus inhibiting their freedom to direct the course of their own lives. Generally, however, individuals need the social contact which groups provide, and they value the sense of belonging which comes from sharing the goals and aspirations of other members of the group. It may also be argued that belonging to a group provides an essential part of the emotional security and guidance that children need as they develop toward moral maturity and personal autonomy.

However, not all groups are of equal significance, either personally or politically. In this chapter, the term "minority group" is used to mean a sizable and politically significant collectivity or community of people who have shared, over a substantial period of time, a distinctive cultural identity differing from that of the majority or dominant group in the state. The sense of belonging and loyalty which is typical among members of any such minority group results from their sharing at least one (and often several) of the following: a distinctive language, religion, nationality, ethnicity, history, race, or set of cultural traditions, or values, or lifestyles, or other fairly permanent defining characteristics which have a significant impact on their way of life and which help to define their identity in both their own and other people's eyes. The significance of these defining characteristics is socially constructed, but they are generally perceived as "given" rather than a matter of choice (though of course religion is sometimes a matter of choice, and the "givenness" of other characteristics such as sexual orientation is still a matter of debate).

Even on this definition, however, there is wide variation in the political significance of different minority groups. Some, such as religious orders of monks or nuns, may have little political impact and be happy to leave things that way. Others have disproportionately high levels of political influence; for example, the small Jewish community in the United Kingdom has for many years been able to make a highly important contribution to public life. Other groups act as effective political pressure groups on specific ethical issues; for example, Roman Catholics are able to ensure that their voice is heard on issues to do with abortion and matters of sexual morality. Other groups again—and these form the focus of the present chapter—are significant for more negative reasons: they share a sense of being denied some of the freedoms or some of the recognition that members of the majority or dominant group take for granted. It is this perception of discrimination or disadvantage which gives the group some of its distinctive identity and leads it to make demands of the state, including demands for recognition and demands for freedom to pursue its own cultural goals and ways of life. As we shall see shortly, such demands frequently include an educational dimension.

The main concern of this chapter is one particular set of politically significant disadvantaged minority groups in liberal societies: non-Western fundamentalist religious minorities. Typically, philosophical debate in the West makes reference to such groups only in connection with attempts to define the limits of tolerance or in order to illustrate a failure to match up to liberal ideals. However, I believe it is dangerous for liberals to close off dialogue with such groups; in this chapter I therefore make some attempt initially to see the liberal world as if through the eyes of someone belonging to such a minority, and to explore what it is like to live as a member of such a group in a liberal society. I ask, for example, how true is their perception that they systematically lose out in liberal societies, particularly in terms of being required to surrender any real chance of passing on their cultural heritage and most cherished values to their children in an uncompromised form. In the early part of the chapter, therefore, attention is focused mainly on the experiences and demands of minority groups, so that these can be balanced more fairly with the needs of liberal societies as the chapter proceeds.

The chapter falls into three sections. In Section 1 an attempt is made to distinguish non-Western fundamentalist religious minorities living in the West from other minorities that may experience disadvantage of various kinds in liberal societies. Section 2 explores some of the educational and other difficulties encountered by such religious minorities in more detail, and typical liberal responses. Section 3 contains some proposals which are designed to meet the educational needs of both the liberal state and the religious minorities at the same time.

10.1. *Four Types of Disadvantaged Minority*

Politically significant disadvantaged minority groups generally lack the power and resources to urge their cause against entrenched interests, especially when positive discrimination and compensatory programs are resisted by the dominant group. They also do not generally belong to crosscutting networks of groups which would facilitate interaction with members of other groups. On the contrary, they are likely to live most of their lives within their own group, separated from others by language, religion, nationality, ethnicity, or whatever.

However, when we look more closely at disadvantaged minority groups in liberal states, it becomes clear that there are significant differences between groups in terms of goals and aspirations, and this makes it very unlikely that a single approach or policy will satisfy the demands of all such groups equally. Indeed, one of the biggest mistakes made by some proponents of pluralism[1] is to assume that minority groups are all more or less of a kind. Among the many criteria that may be proposed for distinguishing different kinds of disadvantaged minority groups (such as whether membership is a matter of choice or not), I shall argue that two are of particular significance. The first factor is whether the primary aspiration of the group is greater social acceptance and integration within the broader society, or greater freedom to preserve the distinctive elements of its cultural identity across the generations. Clearly the former is more in harmony with the values of the liberal state than the latter. The second factor is whether or not the group generally shares the same values and beliefs, and has internalized the same legal system and broadly the same cultural heritage as the dominant cultural group. This is most likely to be the case with autochthonous groups (i.e. those whose cultural roots are within the state itself) and groups from other Western democracies, and least likely with those whose cultural roots are outside the Western world. It is often the case that where people have migrated to Western states from former colonies of those states, the colonial pattern of living separately from the "ruling class" may be replicated, so that the migrants end up living their lives largely within their own group, meeting members of other groups only "in the market place." Other things being equal, the liberal state will find it easier to deal with those originating within its own territories or within other liberal states, who share a wide range of values and beliefs with the dominant group, rather than with those whose cultural roots and values originate outside the Western world.

Putting these two sets of distinctions together, we can identify four types of disadavantaged minority groups:

Type 1. Western cultural values/social integration (e.g. gay/lesbians; disabled people).
Type 2. Non-Western cultural values/social integration (e.g. Black-British; Chinese-Americans).
Type 3. Western cultural values/cultural preservation (e.g. the *Québécois*; the Basques).
Type 4. Non-Western cultural values/cultural preservation (e.g. French Muslims; British Sikhs).

Each type of group presents different issues to the liberal state and requires different responses. My main concern in the remainder of this chapter is Type 4, since it is clear that this group represents the biggest problem for the liberal state, and it is also the group which has traditionally received least attention from philosophers. But before turning to focus exclusively on Type 4 groups, I shall briefly review the other three types, in order to clarify both the distinctions themselves and the reasons why each type of group has different needs.

Type 1 groups have their cultural roots within their country of citizenship, but have a key defining characteristic which unites them with other members of their group. The key defining characteristic may, for example, be age, disability, sexual orientation, social class, gender, or skin color. The demands of such groups are typically twofold. The first is equality of opportunity, such as the right of gays to be employed in the armed forces, or the right of disabled people to have access to public buildings. The second is the right of the group to represent its own cultural identity publicly as a source of pride and personal identity and as something to be recognized and celebrated as part of the broader society. From a liberal perspective, the claims of Type 1 groups are comparatively unproblematic: equality of opportunity is the right of each individual citizen, even if it involves differentiated treatment or "changing the way things have always been done"; and in any case the members of such groups are as likely as other citizens to share fundamental liberal values, with the result that the diversity of their cultural identities can be seen as part of the rich tapestry of the liberal state.

Type 2 groups have cultural or ethnic roots not only outside the territory of the state in which they have citizenship but also outside the Western world, and their identity is often described in hyphenated form, as in Black-British or Chinese-American, where the second element refers to their citizenship and the first to the cultural minority to which they belong. I am not concerned here with the problems of guest workers, temporary residents, and refugees who have not gained the equal rights of permanent citizens in their country of residence (important though these issues are), but only with the problems of non-Western cultural minorities aspiring to greater social integration in the state of which they are citizens. Such minorities face two main difficulties. The first is an unwillingness on the part of the dominant cultural group or of longer established cultural groups to change existing structures in the light of new circumstances of cultural diversity. The second is an overt or hidden sense of cultural superiority on the part of the dominant cultural group, leading to various forms of prejudice, racism, discrimination, social avoidance, and inferior treatment, and also to paternalistic or condescending attitudes, including treating minority cultures as quaint or exotic. The first aspiration of Type 2 groups therefore is to break through the barriers of discrimination and institutional racism and achieve parity of respect and recognition with members of other cultural groups. This may best be achieved by full social integration within the institutions of the state and by the adjustment of these institutions to take account of the cultural diversity in society. Thus in a system of common schooling it would be necessary to find a way of including elements of African history and culture, for example, in a new curriculum for all, or including both Christian and Muslim perspectives in lessons on the Crusades. In this respect the aspirations of Type 2 groups, and the ways the state can respond to these aspirations, are similar to those of Type 1, though they may be more difficult to fulfil.

However, Type 2 groups are also anxious to ensure that their children are not denied the chance to continue their own cultural traditions. This kind of cultural maintenance for a minority group cannot be achieved without some special provision. Let us imagine a hypothetical state with a common school system, in which 96 per cent of the population share broadly the same cultural background and aspirations, and in which there are two distinct ethnic minorities each making up 2 per cent of the total population. If we accept that education can never be culture free, how should the cultural influences within the curriculum be distributed? An initial response suggests that the proportion of cultural influence should correspond to the actual size of the cultural groups involved. The percentage of input for each of the minority cultures could probably be increased to 5 per cent without too much argument, but if it were increased much further, then the likelihood of a backlash from the dominant cultural group would correspondingly increase. But while a cultural input into the common curriculum of 5 per cent would be sufficient to give the majority group a taste of another culture, it would hardly be sufficient to support the distinctive cultural identity of the children from the minority group. Some supplementary provision (whether supplementary classes within the common school or supplementary schooling run by the minority community outside normal school hours) would be necessary for the minority group but not for the majority, so that the former could have an equal opportunity to maintain their cultural identity. The demand for such differentiated or additional provision would be justified on the basis of the right to recognition and equality of respect, and it may be the only way in which the kind of hyphenated identity refered to above could be developed or maintained. The aim of such provision would not be to close off the cultural options of children from such minority groups, but the opposite: it would equalize their exposure to the minority culture of their parents and the majority culture of the broader society, so that they would be in a very strong position to make autonomous choices in the future. The use of public funds for such provision in a liberal state would seem no less just than allowing increased public expenditure for the education of differently abled pupils. All this seems to be consistent with the account of common schooling which Terry McLaughlin provides elsewhere in this volume.

Type 3 groups are autochthonous minorities (i.e. national minorities or aboriginal peoples) anxious to preserve the distinctive elements of their cultural identity and prevent it from becoming submerged in the culture of the majority. The danger to the culture of such groups might arise not from a failure on the part of the state to treat its native minorities on equal terms with all other citizens, but precisely as a result of such equal treatment. If all the citizens of a state are equally free to work and settle in any part of the state, then over time a territory associated with a particular cultural minority may be settled by other citizens and the territory's distinct cultural identity may not survive. In such circumstances it may be possible to maintain the cultural integrity of a minority group within a particular territory only by restricting the freedom of other citizens of the state to settle permanently or change the original character of the territory. What is at issue here is the claim that a minority's right to cultural survival should sometimes take priority over some of the rights a liberal democratic state usually guarantees to all its citizens. This claim has received a lot of attention from philosophers in the last decade or so, with Charles Taylor[2] suggesting that cultural membership is a primary good, an essential factor to take into account in judgments about the good life, and Will Kymlicka[3] arguing that a cultural community can justifiably be protected by a liberal state if it provides a necessary context for choice for its members, but not if it simply seeks to preserve its distinctive *character*. These arguments are debated more fully elsewhere in this volume, and will not be discussed here, except to point out that however appropriate Kymlicka's latter claim may be with regard to Type 3 groups, it is clearly at odds with the arguments I wish to develop in connection with Type 4 groups.[4]

Type 4 groups are mainly religious minorities originating outside the Western world, whose primary goal is not greater social integration within the institutions of the state, but greater freedom to preserve and maintain the character of their religious beliefs, values, and traditions, and transmit these intact to the next generation. The shared identity of these groups depends not so much on a shared national or cultural heritage—indeed, such religious minorities may be multiethnic groups with more than a smattering of autochthonous converts—but on a shared framework of fundamental beliefs and practices. I have in mind in particular certain sections of the Sikh, Muslim, Hindu, Jewish, and Black Christian communities living in Western states, though many of the features of Type 4 groups are also shared by indigenous fundamentalist Christian groups as well. What such groups have in common is that they choose to identify themselves in terms of a distinctive religious faith and set of practices, rather than according to their nationality, ethnicity, or land of origin.

Type 4 groups are similar to Type 3 in that their primary goal is to seek structural change in order to accommodate and preserve their distinctive identity, but differ in that their culture is not associated with a particular territory within their state of residence, and also in that the preservation of their distinctive culture does not involve significant restrictions being placed on the rights of the majority. They are similar to Type 2 groups in that they generally have cultural roots outside the Western world, and they typically suffer political, economic, and cultural disadvantages on account of prejudice and exclusion (though the degree of disadvantage may vary from country to country: in Europe e.g. most Muslims are at the bottom of the socioeconomic scale, but this is not the case in the United States or Hong Kong). However, they differ from Type 2 groups in four crucial respects. First, they are not claiming equity of treatment as such with other cultural groups within the state; for example, the withholding of public funds from all religious schools in a liberal state would be equitable, but would not satisfy this group's goal of freedom to educate their children in accordance with their own beliefs and values. Second, it is their religious and cultural commitments, rather than their citizenship, which determine their primary identity. This distinction may be seen by comparing the hyphenated identity of such groups (e.g. British-Muslim) with that of Type 2 groups (e.g. Chinese-American); in each case, what comes after the hyphen appears to indicate the primary loyalty. Third, they have a quite different agenda from Type 2 groups, in that they prioritize freedom to preserve and maintain their distinctive religious beliefs and values across the generations more highly than overcoming political and economic disadvantage. Fourth, the religious identity of such groups is not of a form which can be tacked on as an extra component to their citizenship, as supplementary schooling may be tacked on to the experience of the common school for children from Type 2 groups anxious to retain their cultural identity. On the contrary, their religious identity is something which they believe should permeate the whole of life, and they do not want their children to be exposed to alien influences which might undermine their faith at a vulnerable or impressionable age.

The remainder of this chapter focuses exclusively on Type 4 groups, since their demands, which represent a serious challenge to the core values of the liberal state, have received comparatively little philosophical attention. For convenience, I shall take all my examples from the United Kingdom, and mainly from the British Muslim community.

10.2. Religious Minorities in the Liberal State

The kind of religious minority with which I am concerned here, and which I have called Type 4, treats religion as a whole way of life and has a framework of values which is coherent in its own terms but is at odds in several crucial respects with the liberal framework. For example, individual freedom is not a primary value, and individuals within the group may not be free to opt out easily or to question the foundations of the religion; equality is understood differently from the liberal concept of equality, and may not be thought incompatible with differentiated social roles for women; and human rationality is not the only source of knowledge, for "revealed" knowledge plays a crucial part in the religion. However, there are three key features of such religious minorities which are of particular relevance here.

First, such minorities engage in practices which differ from those current in the broader liberal society in which they live, and which liberal citizens may sometimes find offensive. In an important article discussing the way a liberal society should evaluate such practices, Parekh[5] offers a useful list of examples: female circumcision; polygamy; arranged marriages; physical mutilation (such as the scarring of children's cheeks during an initiation ceremony); Muslim and Jewish methods of slaughtering animals; Sikh insistence on wearing turbans rather than helmets when riding motorcycles or working on building sites; Muslim girls' insistence on wearing the *hijab* in schools and on covering their bodies during physical education or sporting activities; Hindu requests for permission to cremate their deceased on a funeral pyre and scatter the ashes in rivers, or to drown rather than cremate the corpses; Amish refusal to send their children to school after a certain age; and Muslim demands for time off work for prayer. Listing practices like this is of limited value, however, for it is important to note that such practices cannot be separated easily from the fundamental beliefs and values which underpin them. Indeed, it is those fundamental beliefs and values which give the practices meaning. Looking at them in isolation from the wider way of life of which they are a part can make them seem odd and fail to indicate the way they may be perceived as binding by the community concerned. From the community's point of view, it may seem that if the state disallows these practices, it is failing to respect the entire way of life of which the practices are a part.

Second, such religious minorities may have an ambivalent attitude to citizenship. On the one hand, they may be model citizens in terms of being law-abiding and having a sense of social responsibility. On the other, they may have a very different set of loyalties (e.g. Muslims may view their citizenship of *dar al-islam* as far more important than citizenship of any nation state), and a different understanding of the central concepts involved in citizenship. Thus they may not feel comfortable with the notion of rights (which is after all rooted in a framework of liberal values) and may use rights talk only as a second language. This may explain why such religious minorities have not always been willing to grant the same freedoms to other groups, such as gays and lesbians, as they have demanded for themselves; because they do not present their arguments and claims in terms of rights, they do not see any necessary inconsistency in such a position.

Third, such religious minorities may have a conception of education which is opposed in several key respects to liberal education. For them, the primary purpose of education is to strengthen children's commitment to the faith and thus preserve the faith and its associated cultural identity across the generations. Other purposes, such as preparation for citizenship and employment, and for enjoying the benefits of modern scientific and technological progress, are secondary. Yet other purposes, such as preparing pupils for personal and moral autonomy, are simply not accepted; for example, many British Muslims consider sex education as currently practised in state schools to be in serious conflict with Islamic teaching.[6] Such groups may prefer separate schooling for their children as the best way to pass on their central beliefs and values to their children in an uncompromised form and to preserve their cultural and religious identity from being unduly influenced, and thereby significantly diluted, by contact with the majority.

How should the liberal state respond to such groups? Let us look first at two extreme responses. One possible response is to say simply that the existence of such groups within a liberal state is intolerable because they support fundamentalist values which are not open to challenge and change, because they violate basic human rights and freedoms, and because they wish schools to offer an uncritical presentation of a particular version of the good in which children are not free to distance themselves from the culture of their parents or to make autonomous decisions about their own commitments, values, and life plans. The central values of such groups are thus in conflict with the foundational values of the broader liberal society. As Raz points out, "Since they insist on bringing up their children in their own ways they are, in the eyes of liberals like myself, harming them."[7] On this view, therefore, no steps should be taken to support the continued existence of such groups; perhaps active steps should even be taken to discourage their continued existence. One such active step might be to ensure that parents are not free to bring their children up in the faith or to use education to preserve and maintain the faith. Though Raz somewhat reluctantly accepts toleration of communities whose culture does not support autonomy, so long as they are "viable communities", he also claims that if the life they offer their young is too impoverished and unrewarding by liberal standards, "assimilationist policies may well be the only humane course, even if implemented by force of law."[8] The so-called "French model"[9] finds it intolerable for minorities to express their religious characteristics outside their private lives and requires them to assimilate not only the liberal values but also the linguistic and cultural norms of broader society.

However, to dismiss such groups as intolerable and to take active steps to undermine their continued existence appears oppressive from the perspective of group members, as I have argued elsewhere:[10] if they cannot use education to maintain their distinctive beliefs and values, then their culture is vulnerable either to gradual corrosion as a result of sustained exposure to liberal values or to a more direct assault by liberal laws and social policy. Such an approach appears to undermine the claim of the liberal state to be based on the values of pluralism, tolerance, and respect for diversity, and it is a counterintuitive response to groups which are made up (as we have seen) of people who are in some respects model citizens. In addition it seems to involve (a) a degree of injustice by denying them the recognition accorded to other groups—roughly, what Taylor[11] calls the "politics of equal respect"; (b) a denial of the groups' freedom to preserve intact across the generations what seems to them the most central part of their cultural identity, namely, their religion; and perhaps (c) an attempt to require them to acquire knowledge, beliefs, and values and engage in practices which conflict with their own most fundamental commitments.

A more subtle way of imposing the values of the majority on such religious minorities is to insist on open dialogue and the democratic negotiation of core values, as proposed by White[12] and also supported by Parekh.[13] This goes some way to limiting the harm set out in (a) above, by recognising and respecting the minorities as legitimate groups, while at the same time wrong footing them if they refuse to take part. But such democratic dialogue may do little to resolve (b) or (c). White assumes that the democratic negotiation of values will result in a "gradual merging of outlooks" and "a further decline among religiously based values"[14]—a conclusion hardly likely to endear the process to religious minorities. Indeed, the democratic negotiation of values presupposes certain shared liberal values, forces minorities to justify their beliefs and practices using unfamiliar concepts, and commits them to an outcome agreed by the majority, all of which put non-liberal religious minorities at a disadvantage.

Democratic participation can thus become merely a cover for majoritarianism in which the weak go to the wall.

At the opposite extreme, Lustgarten suggests that any minority cultural group should be allowed "unrestricted freedom to follow their own customs and religious practices, be governed by their personal law and receive education in their language and cultural tradition."[15] This freedom would be subject to just two limitations, according to Lustgarten: any practice leading to severe physical abuse would be disallowed, and impractical institutional accommodations to minority beliefs and values would not be required.[16] On this view (which is roughly the Danish model), groups would be free to organize their children's education in line with their own religion, culture, or ideology with a substantial state subsidy. The main problems with this response are (i) that it may contribute to the fragmentation of the liberal state and make integration more difficult; (ii) that it may not prepare children for citizenship of a multicultural society (e.g. it may promote intolerance or a lack of respect for others); and (iii) that by reinforcing the cultural attachments of children from minority groups, it may fail to respect their right to grow up as autonomous individuals.

What is needed is a system of educational provision between these two extremes which avoids both the potential harm to the religious minority set out in (a)–(c) above and the potential harm to the liberal state set out in (i)–(iii) above. In fact, most liberal states in their educational policy toward religious minorities occupy some area of middle ground between the extremes of the French model and the Danish model. However, there are certain aspects of liberal education that remain non-negotiable. As Dworkin[17] points out, one of the key features of liberal societies is that they do not adopt any particular substantive view about the ends of life; hence education in such societies cannot support the uncritical presentation of any concept of the good. Liberal education is also based on the claim that children need to be free to distance themselves from the culture of their parents and to make autonomous decisions about their own commitments, values, and life plans.[18] In this sense the needs of children do not vary according to the commitments of their parents, and thus education can and should become a common enterprise for the children of all groups in a culturally diverse society. The provision of public funds for separate schools for religious or other cultural minorities is thus opposed on the grounds that such schools are unnecessary, socially divisive, and educationally harmful. Typically, therefore, liberal states will adopt a neutral approach to the religious minorities under discussion. Such neutrality might take one of two forms.[19] In America it is seen in the separation of church and state and the exclusion of religion of any kind from the state's institutions such as public education, though it should be noted that the American constitution guarantees religious minorities certain freedoms (such as the right of Muslim girls to wear the *hijab* in public schools) for which they have had to fight strenuously in many European countries. In the United Kingdom, on the other hand, state neutrality takes a more self-consciously multicultural form, involving attempts to include all major faiths and cultures in the state's institutions (e.g. in Religious Education all children in state schools in the United Kingdom are taught about six different world religions). This neutral approach satisfies problems (a) and (i)–(iii), but does not satisfy (b) or (c) because it denies the group the freedom to ensure that the beliefs and values of their children's schooling are in line with those of the home, and leaves the group with the impression that liberal values which undermine their distinctive beliefs are being imposed on their children. Effectively it involves treating Type 4 groups as if they were Type 2. Current practice in many liberal states provides an alternative option for those religious minorities who cannot accept liberal education for their children by allowing them to pay for private education more in line with their own beliefs and values. The number of private Muslim schools and schools for other religious minorities in both the United Kingdom and the United States is growing rapidly. This option satisfies problems (b) and (c) but not the others.

Because of the apparent injustice to religious minorities under discussion resulting from the ongoing failure to satisfy problems (b) and (c) within the state-funded educational system, several European states, and particularly states such as the Netherlands and the United Kingdom with a tradition of state funding for religious schools, have begun to explore different ways of providing financial support to minority religious groups for the education of their children—in spite of the commitment of liberalism to a common education for all. Such financial support may take the form either of grants to private religious schools and supplementary religious schools, or of incorporating schools run by the religious groups into the state system of education. The latter initiative, which has been the subject of a lengthy campaign by large sections of the Muslim community in Britain in particular,[20] resulted in the establishment in 1999 of the first two state-funded Muslim schools in the United Kingdom (as well as state-funded Sikh, Jewish, Seventh Day Adventist, and Greek Orthodox schools).[21]

However, such schools (which incidentally cater to less than 1 per cent of Muslim pupils in the United Kingdom) do not seem to be part of a carefully thought out policy toward religious minorities, but rather an ad hoc response to a protracted campaign. What I shall argue for in conclusion is for a much more carefully grounded approach to educational provision for religious minorities, taking account of the need to protect both the integrity of the liberal state as defined in points (i)–(iii) above and the needs of the religious minorities set out in (a)–(c).

10.3. Rethinking the Liberal Response

My proposals in this concluding section take as their starting point a particular strand in recent political thinking about value pluralism and the multicultural state, drawing particularly on authors as diverse as William Galston,[22] John Gray,[23] Chandran Kukathas,[24] John Rawls,[25] and Charles Taylor.[26] Responding to an earlier statement by Rawls to the effect that only unworthy ways of life lose out in a just constitutional regime,[27] Galston points out that the line between ways of life that can flourish in a pluralist context and those whose viability depends on a more hospitable homogeneity "does not easily divide valuable from worthless, or generous from repressive, conceptions of the good."[28] He further clearly argues (though Macedo elsewhere in this volume accuses him of holding an ambivalent attitude toward non-liberal minority groups) that "the liberal state must allow the fullest possible scope for diversity"[29] and that liberal freedom entails the right to live unexamined as well as examined lives.[30] Rawls himself in his more recent writings acknowledges that "political good, no matter how important, can never in general outweigh the transcendent values—certain religious, philosophical, and moral values—that may possibly come into conflict with it."[31] Minority groups, Rawls proposes, should have the maximum freedom consistent with individual freedom of conscience. Thus they may be free to establish their own educational system, or even to withdraw from the modern world in accordance with the injunctions of their religion, so long as they "acknowledge the principles of the political conception of justice and appreciate its political ideals of person and society."[32] Finally, there are Taylor's arguments that we need to approach "all human cultures that have animated whole societies over some considerable stretch of time" with a presumption of their equal worth;[33] this implies that until such cultures can be appropriately evaluated in an unbiased, unprejudiced way, they should be presumed to have the right to take steps to ensure their own continuation.

On the basis of this rather more open liberal thinking, I have elsewhere begun to explore the possibility of a compromise involving the development of a set of educational structures within a liberal democratic state which would generate an equality of dignity and respect for all cultural minorities, including religious ones, enabling them to retain their specific identity and preserve this across the generations, while at the same time allowing them to participate fully as citizens and developing the qualities necessary to make this possible.[34] In this final section I shall attempt to summarize these proposals.

The argument here involves the claim made by Rawls and others that liberalism has a cultural as well as a political dimension, and the related claim that it is only through careful regard to this distinction that cultural dominance within education can be avoided. Cultural liberalism manifests itself in two ways. First, political liberalism inevitably overflows into the cultural domain, even where the state does not formally align itself with a nation or with the culture of the majority. For example, there are enormous advantages if a state has a common language which all citizens can use when participating in democratic activities. But the identification of one language as the official language of the state has cultural implications both for the privileged majority who speak it as their mother tongue, and for the cultural minorities with a different mother tongue, who are correspondingly disadvantaged. The search for a substantial set of shared values in a liberal society (on which to construct a common educational system) is also likely to move beyond the political and encroach on the cultural domain.[35] Second, the claim to cultural neutrality, which, as we saw in Section 2, is a feature of educational policy in both the United Kingdom and the United States, is itself a cultural stance. For example, liberalism is hospitable to a wide diversity of sexual lifestyles, but is less hospitable to any cultural group wishing to exert a high level of control over the sexuality of its members. Cultural liberalism is perhaps best understood as a framework of conditions within which certain cultures might thrive, particularly those which emphasize autonomy and individuality, but which is inhospitable to other cultures, for example, to those which emphasize group interests at the expense of individual freedom. In many cases when cultural minorities object to liberal practices and claim to find liberalism oppressive, it is cultural rather than political liberalism which presents the problem.[36]

Insofar as the distinction between political and cultural liberalism is accepted (and of course the distinction can never be absolute, for liberal politics and liberal culture are intimately intertwined and interdependent), it opens the way for the suggestion that while political liberalism provides the foundation for citizenship education for all the children within a democratic state, cultural liberalism must take its place alongside other cultural ways of life, whose members have an equal moral right to make provision for children's primary cultural development.[37] All the children in a democratic state have in one sense a shared fate, as Melissa Williams points out in this volume: they will all grow up to be citizens of that state and will therefore all equally need to learn about the principles of democracy and about the privileges and responsibilities of citizenship. That part of the curriculum can be common for all children. However, not all children in a democratic state will grow up to be members of the same cultural community. If it is true that education cannot be culture free, then to provide a common liberal education for all children regardless of religion, ethnicity, nationality, or mother tongue is likely to tip the scales in favor of cultural liberalism and against nonliberal cultures. Such inequality of respect could be avoided by allowing all cultural communities the right to set up their own schools which would offer common provision with regard to citizenship education, but distinctive cultural education. Schools with a liberal cultural perspective would thus exist alongside a wide variety of denominational schools and schools for pupils of different mother tongues, national origins, or other cultural affiliations, and parents would be able to choose freely among the diversity of schools.[38] All schools which provided education for democratic citizenship would receive public funding, and would be accountable to the funding agencies for such provision.

The structure being proposed here thus involves two key elements: education for democratic citizenship (which is common across all schools), and education for a specific cultural attachment (which is different in different schools). Both elements give rise to a number of important and complex questions, and further questions are raised by the relationship of the elements to each other in a unified curriculum. I shall also shortly mention a third core element—education for cross-cultural understanding—though this may be considered to be implicit in the notion of democratic citizenship.

Education for democratic citizenship is an education in those political beliefs and values on which the very existence of a liberal state is based. These values include the recognition of all citizens as equal in respect of fundamental rights and freedoms, the rejection of racism, prejudice, and discrimination as an affront to individual dignity, and the duty of all citizens to support and uphold institutions that embody a shared conception of justice and the rule of law. As Rawls points out, a strong sense of citizenship is needed to sustain the political virtues of "reasonableness and fairness, a spirit of compromise and a readiness to meet others halfway."[39] Education for citizenship thus potentially involves much more than an unreflective initiation into the existing political structures of the state; it may include reflection on principles and values and the critical appraisal of prevailing political structures in the light of these values, as well as encouraging political involvement and participation and developing a sense of obligation and responsibility to the wider political community. In McLaughlin's terms, therefore, the kind of education for citizenship under discussion here is not limited to a "minimalist kind of interpretation."[40] However, since modern liberal democracies are characterized by conflicting conceptions of the good, it is important that education for citizenship should not be seen as promoting any particular cultural conception of the good. Each cultural group must be free to pursue its own conception of the good within a framework of justice and equal respect. The freedom guaranteed to citizens by political liberalism includes the freedom to pursue non-liberal cultural goals within that basic framework.[41] Education for citizenship would as far as possible exclude cultural issues from its agenda and focus solely on political matters,[42] though there remains the danger, as Rawls is aware,[43] that initiating children into "political liberalism" will predispose them to accept "a comprehensive liberal conception." As Macedo points out elsewhere in this volume, the "public virtues" which would be promoted through education for democratic citizenship can be justified without summoning up some comprehensive philosophical ideal of autonomy; but autonomy might still be a by-product of such education. In liberal schools, this predisposition toward autonomy would be reinforced by the teaching of cultural liberalism, but in non-liberal schools it would be challenged by the teaching of cultural values which questioned the value of autonomy.

Education for a specific cultural attachment would thus be what differentiated the schools within a state and would therefore be one important consideration by which parents made their choice of school. It would be justified on three grounds: first, a recognition that citizens may have "affections, devotions, and loyalties that they believe they ... should not stand apart from and objectively evaluate from the standpoint of their purely rational good";[44] second, the presumption of the equal worth of different cultures, as expounded by Taylor;[45] and third, the belief that children need a secure and stable environment, at least in their formative years, where the cultural values of the school are broadly in line with those of the home.[46] Schools providing an education in what I have called cultural liberalism would therefore be competing with a variety of other schools offering education based on more specific national, religious, linguistic, or other cultural values. Cultural groups might sometimes form alliances in order to provide a viable school (as already happens on a very limited scale in the United Kingdom with joint Catholic and Anglican schools, and in the Netherlands with joint Christian and Muslim schools).

The concept of education for a specific cultural attachment raises several important questions. Would any cultural groups be barred from establishing their own schools? Could a school have a democratic ethos (as required by education for citizenship) and a specific cultural ethos at the same time? Would prejudice be reinforced or an unhealthy rivalry or animosity develop between schools with different cultural attachments? Would the loyalties engendered by the school tend toward divisiveness rather than social integration? Although I cannot discuss the complexities of these questions here at any length, I will indicate possible approaches to them. With regard to the first question, there would undoubtedly be a debate between those who wished to restrict the right to establish schools to "cultures that have provided the horizon of meaning to large numbers of human beings ... over a long period of time"[47] and those who wished to extend the right to any group whose fundamental beliefs and values were not in conflict with the political values underpinning democratic citizenship. Some cultural groups holding sexist, racist, or homophobic beliefs would exclude themselves because they would be unable to promote the public virtues which as we have seen are embodied in the concept of education for democratic citizenship and for which they would be accountable to the funding bodies. There would undoubtedly be other groups who claimed to accept the public virtues but who interpreted them in non-liberal ways; my own view is that such groups should not be barred from establishing their own schools, for it is only through open dialogue, once the differences between (say) a liberal and non-liberal interpretation of gender equality have come to the surface in an institutional context, that the hardening of attitudes and closed versions of culture can be prevented. Of course, there may still be some situations, as in a case raised by Galston[48] and discussed in detail by Susan Okin in this volume, where the differences can only be resolved by recourse to the courts. With regard to the second question, it might be argued that schools have a duty to help pupils to learn to balance their civic and cultural commitments. With regard to the third and fourth questions, Giraud[49] reminds us that where people share a common territory but have quite different cultural norms, this can be a recipe for conflict. However, I would argue that it is the perception of inequality and disadvantage which is most likely to generate conflict: rivalry and divisiveness are less likely to thrive in a state which shows an equality of respect toward diverse cultural groups. Suspicion and resentment between groups could be further diminished by education for cross-cultural understanding.

Education for cross-cultural understanding would seek to encourage mutual understanding, tolerance, and respect between groups with different cultural values. It has much in common with what Blacker elsewhere in this volume calls civic friendship. It would require a variety of pedagogical approaches, including actual contact and interaction with other groups wherever possible, not just formal teaching about different cultures, and Blacker's proposed revival of the "school stamps plan" would enable pupils from different schools to have authentic interactions with other groups in a wide variety of extracurricular activities. The focus of attention for younger children would be the development of tolerance and understanding of other groups, but as they grew older they would be in a strong position to engage in rational deliberation about different cultural beliefs and values and different conceptions of the good life. In fact, different groups might understand and justify education for cross-cultural understanding in different ways. Liberals might see it as a precondition to autonomy, so that while children are not *encouraged* to leave their own community, they are at least aware of alternatives. At the other extreme, Muslims may see it as a fulfilment of the Qur'anic injunction to "know one another" and the *hadith* of the Prophet Muhammad to "go in search of knowledge, even to China." Education for cross-cultural understanding might guard against the danger that too strong an emphasis on cultural or religious identity could lead, as Hall warns, to the adoption of "closed versions of culture or community" and "the refusal to engage with the difficult problems that arise from trying to live with difference."[50] It might also provide a safety valve for those who find the culture of their parents and cultural group suffocating, by increasing their awareness of alternatives; this would go some way to making the formal "exit right" demanded by most liberals (the exercise of which, as Okin has shown in this volume, is beset with practical difficulties, for women in particular) into more of a reality. All groups might also see education for cross-cultural understanding as a way of encouraging gradual change and development within the cultural community as a result of interaction with others. The identity of Muslims in the West, for example, is undoubtedly influenced by contact with the surrounding cultures, but may nonetheless remain true to core Islamic values.[51]

The distinction between the three elements (education for democratic citizenship, education for a specific cultural attachment, and education for cross-cultural understanding) can be illustrated by reference to teaching a controversial issue such as homosexuality. Within education for democratic citizenship, children would be taught that homophobic bullying is always wrong, an affront to individual dignity, and a failure to respect fundamental rights and freedoms. Within education for a specific cultural attachment, children would be taught the attitude of their own cultural group toward homosexuality. Within education for cross-cultural understanding, children would be introduced to and learn to respect worldviews other than their own; thus Muslims would learn about gay and lesbian values and lifestyles, and vice versa. The combination of these three elements would result, I believe, in a fairer approach to teaching about homosexuality than any approach current in schools today.[52]

The proposals sketched out here (which are of course in need of a much fuller discussion than I am able to provide in a single chapter[53]) involve compromises on all sides—between parents and the state, between liberals and non-liberals, and between all kinds of cultural groups. However, the proposals go a long way toward recognizing the legitimate interests of parents, minority groups, and the broader society in the education of children. They also imply that all parties have much to learn from each other. They seek to protect the integrity of the liberal state while at the same time taking account of the needs of religious and cultural minorities. They largely satisfy problems (a)–(c) and (i) and (ii) as set out in 10.2 above, and go some way toward meeting (iii) as well. The ultimate aim of citizenship education on this approach is to help the minority group to develop an internalized commitment to the laws and values of the broader society, so that these are accepted as guides in their social, political, and economic life (though not, of course, their cultural, personal, or religious life, where they would be free to pursue their own goals). It is clear that education for a specific cultural attachment must be balanced by education for democratic citizenship to counteract its divisive tendencies and that education for cross-cultural understanding will contribute further to the development of toleration and respect within society. The effect of these proposals overall would be to help to transform the religious minorities under consideration from disadvantaged to respected groups who could not only hold their own in, but also make a significant positive contribution to, the broader liberal society.

NOTES

1. cf. D. Nicholls, *Three Varieties of Pluralism* (London: Macmillan, 1974); and D. Nicholls, *The Pluralist State* (London: Macmillan, 1975).
2. C. Taylor, *Multiculturalism and "The Politics of Recognition"* (Princeton: Princeton University Press, 1992).
3. W. Kymlicka, *Multicultural Citizenship: A Liberal Theory of Minority Rights* (Oxford: Clarendon Press, 1995).
4. cf. W. A. Galston, "Two Concepts of Liberalism", *Ethics*, 105(3) (1995), 516–34, 523.
5. B. Parekh, "The Logic of Intercultural Evaluation" in J. Horton and S. Mendus (eds), *Toleration, Identity and Difference* (Basingstoke: Macmillan, 1999), 163–97.
6. J. M. Halstead, "Muslims and Sex Education", *Journal of Moral Education*, 26(3) (1997), 317–30.
7. J. Raz, *The Morality of Freedom* (Oxford: Clarendon Press, 1986), 423.
8. Ibid., 424.
9. M. Giraud, "Cultural Identity and Migrations" in R. Hudson and F. Reno (eds), *Politics of Identity: Migrants and Minorities in Multicultural States* (Basingstoke: Macmillan, 2000), 61. See also M. Levinson, "Liberalism versus Democracy? Schooling Private Citizens in the Public Square", *British Journal of Political Science*, 27 (1997), 333–60.
10. J. M. Halstead, "Voluntary Apartheid: Problems of Schooling for Religious and other Minorities in Democratic Societies", *Journal of Philosophy of Education*, 29(2) (1995), 257–72, 267.
11. C. Taylor, 1992.
12. J. White, "The Quest for Common Values" in G. Haydon (ed.), *Education for a Pluralist Society* (London: University of London Institute of Education, 1987).
13. B. Parekh (1999). See also J. M. Halstead, *Education, Justice and Cultural Diversity: An Examination of the Honeyford Affair, 1984–85* (Lewes: Falmer Press, 1988), 217–19.
14. J. White, "The Quest for Common Values", 15, 21–2.
15. L. S. Lustgarten, "Liberty in a Culturally Plural Society" in A. Phillips Griffiths (ed.), *Of Liberty* (Cambridge: Cambridge University Press, 1983), 101f.
16. cf. C. Kukathas, "Are There Any Cultural Rights?" *Political Theory*, 20(1) (1992), 105–39; and C. Kukathas, "Cultural Toleration" in I. Shapiro and W. Kymlicka (eds), *Ethnicity and Group Rights* (New York: New York University Press, 1997) 69–104.

17. R. Dworkin, "Liberalism" in S. Hamphire (ed.), *Public and Private Morality* (Cambridge, Cambridge University Press, 1978), 113–43.
18. J. M. Halstead, "Liberal Values and Liberal Education" in J. M. Halstead and M. J. Taylor (eds), *Values in Education and Education in Values* (Lewes: Falmer Press, 1996), 17–32.
19. cf. M. Levinson, "Liberalism versus Democracy?"
20. J. M. Halstead, *The Case for Muslim Voluntary-Aided Schools: Some Philosophical Reflections* (Cambridge: Islamic Academy, 1986).
21. J. M. Halstead, "Faith and Diversity in Religious School Provision" in L. Gearon (ed.), *Education in the United Kingdom: Structures and Organisation* (London: David Fulton, 2002).
22. W. A. Galston, *Liberal Purposes: Goods, Virtues and Diversity in the Liberal State* (Cambridge: Cambridge University Press, 1991).
23. J. Gray, *Isaiah Berlin* (Princeton: Princeton University Press, 1996).
24. C. Kukathas, "Are there Any Cultural Rights?" and C. Kukathas, "Cultural Toleration."
25. J. Rawls, *Political Liberalism* (New York: Columbia University Press, 1993).
26. C. Taylor, *Multiculturalism and "The Politics of Recognition."*
27. J. Rawls, "Fairness to Goodness", *Philosophical Review*, 84 (1975).
28. W. A. Galston, *Liberal Purposes*, 275. See also Rawls' reply in *Political Liberalism*, 198, footnote 33.
29. W. A. Galston, "Two Concepts of Liberalism", 523.
30. W. A. Galston, "Civic Education in the Liberal State" in N. L. Rosenblum (ed.), *Liberalism and the Moral Life* (Cambridge: Harvard University Press, 1989), 100.
31. J. Rawls, "The Priority of Right and Ideas of the Good", *Philosophy and Public Affairs*, 17(4) (1988), 251–76.
32. J. Rawls, *Political Liberalism*, 200.
33. C. Taylor, *Multiculturalism and "The Politics of Recognition"*, 64–73.
34. J. M. Halstead, "Voluntary Apartheid."
35. cf. T. H. McLaughlin, "Citizenship, Diversity and Education: A Philosophical Perspective", *Journal of Moral Education*, 21(3) (1992), 235–50, 240ff.
36. cf. S. Burtt, "Religious Parents, Secular Schools: A Liberal Defense of an Illiberal Education", *Review of Politics*, 56 (1994) 51–70.
37. cf. J. Gray, *Isaiah Berlin*, 168.
38. cf. D. Hargreaves, *The Mosaic of Learning: School and Teachers for the Next Century* (London: Demos, 1994).
39. J. Rawls, *Political Liberalism*, 163.
40. T. H. McLaughlin, "The Ethics of Separate Schools", 238.
41. cf. W. A. Galston, "Civic Education in the Liberal State", 100.
42. cf. J. Rawls, *Political Liberalism*, Lecture IV.
43. Ibid., 199–200.
44. J. Rawls, "Justice as Fairness: Political not Metaphysical", *Philosophy and Public Affairs*, 14(3) (1985), 223–51.
45. C. Taylor, *Multiculturalism and "The Politics of Recognition."*
46. cf. T. H. McLaughlin, "Parental Rights and the Religious Upbringing of Children", *Journal of Philosophy of Education*, 18(1) (1984), 75–83.
47. C. Taylor, *Multiculturalism and "The Politics of Recognition"*, 72.
48. W. A. Galston, "Two Concepts of Liberalism", 532–3.
49. M. Giraud, "Cultural Identity and Migrations", 77.
50. S. Hall, "Our Mongrel Selves", *New Statesman and Society Supplement*, 19 (June, 1992), 6–8, 8.

51. cf. J. M. Halstead, "Between Two Cultures? Muslim Children in a Western Liberal Society", *Children and Society*, 8(4) (1994), 312–26.
52. cf. J. M. Halstead, "Should Homosexuality Be Taught as an Acceptable Alternative Lifestyle? A Muslim Perspective", *Cambridge Journal of Education*, 28(1) (1998), 49–64.
53. For a fuller discussion of these issues from an alternative perspective, see M. Levinson, *The Demands of Liberal Education* (Oxford: Oxford University Press, 1999).

Part III

LIBERAL CONSTRAINTS ON TRADITIONALIST EDUCATION

CHAPTER 11

Multicultural Accommodations in Education

ROB REICH

Multicultural theorists unite in the conviction that a blanket reliance on difference-blind individual rights and public institutions does not suffice for justice when considering the inevitable partiality of the liberal state to some of the cultural groups contained within it. More often than not, multiculturalists argue, difference-blindness will favor majority cultures and disadvantage smaller ethnocultural or national minority groups. For many, the appropriate remedy is to defend a slate of group rights or multicultural accommodations that duly recognize the significance of cultural membership in the lives of individuals and attempt to compensate for unfair disadvantages suffered by minorities. A significant literature has evolved on the appropriate kind and scope of group rights and accommodations for a multicultural theory.[1]

Among the most important of these multicultural accommodations is the right of minorities to exert far greater control over the education of their children. Such control comes in two general forms, either via the right to separate schools or culturally-centric curricula, sometimes at state expense, or via the right to exemptions from educational requirements, such as compulsory attendance laws.

It is easy to understand why in culturally diverse states control over education is so important. First, schools are a central vehicle of cultural transmission, perhaps the most important vehicle next to the family. Beyond socialization within the home, schools often play a crucial role in initiating children into the norms, beliefs, and rites of the larger group, forming and deepening their cultural identities in the process. For this reason, historically as well as presently, many parents choose a school for their children not (only) on the basis of academic quality but (also) on what the child in the seat next to their son or daughter looks like or believes in. Second, when children of ethnocultural, religiocultural, or national minority groups attend common schools, they have often been discriminated against as a matter of state policy, or marginalized within the curriculum. Schools in many parts of the world, and especially in the United States, have historically attempted to strip away cultural attachments and beliefs in an effort to assimilate children of the adult members of minority groups to the majority culture. More subtly, schools have often failed in their curricula to recognize the existence and history of many minority groups, leading minorities to feelings of invisibility, inferiority, and second-class citizenship. And third, control over schooling also means that those in charge can decide who gets an education at all. Schools often restrict attendance to certain children, reinforcing particular norms about those who are considered educable or worthy of education. Consider the shameful history in the United States of preventing African-Americans from attending schools, or forcing them to attend impoverished schools, or the current practice in many parts of the world of educating only boys.

In multicultural states, control over the education of children has therefore always been contested territory. Within the United States, one thinks back to the evangelical Protestantism of the common school founders and their antipathy toward Catholics, who responded by creating a parallel system of Catholic schools.[2] One thinks back to the efforts to remake Indian children into good Americans by sending them to boarding schools in order to take the Indian out of them.[3] And one thinks back to the many publicly funded German-language schools for German immigrants at the end of the nineteenth century, which were resisted and outlawed by many states in the following years.[4] Resistance to difference-blind education is not a new phenomenon, and efforts to secure all variety of educational accommodations for ethnocultural and national minority groups predate the contemporary debate about multiculturalism.

But my focus here is not on the very interesting history of multicultural accommodations in education. I intend rather to argue that the current defense of multicultural accommodations in education tends to neglect the potential perils of accommodation. I do not wish to press the typical fear, however, that extending cultural rights to ethnocultural and minority groups threatens the value of common citizenship and leads to balkanization. My sense is that, at least in the US context, such fears are greatly exaggerated. My concern is that accommodation policies meant to promote or preserve cultural groups potentially place the integrity of the group above the freedom and equality of the individuals within, especially children. In particular, multicultural accommodation policies in education that grant rights to separate schools or wholesale exemptions from state regulations amount in some circumstances to sanctioning the oppression of children.

Because schools are a central site of cultural transmission, a place where the norms of group life are passed on to the youngest members of the group, education can be used to shape children in very deliberate and illiberal ways. Schools can reinforce norms—of gender inequality, racism, or homophobia, for example—that are unjust when considered from the point of view of equal citizenship. They can shield children from exposure to, and engagement with, the possibly conflicting norms of other individuals or groups. And those in control of schools can restrict certain children from even attending, thereby undermining the opportunities of such children to secure employment. Schools can be, and often are, used to insure the perpetuation of the group and to discourage or disable the capacity of children to exit the group. Education, in short, is not always a tool of liberation; as the history of schooling repeatedly demonstrates, education is also a possible tool of oppression.

This points to a clear tension in multiculturalism. When the state relinquishes or delegates control over the schooling of minority children, thereby attempting to be difference-conscious and compensate for unfair disadvantages suffered by minority groups, it can undermine the freedom and equality of children within the groups. We can express this point more generally: when the state seeks through collective rights to improve the status of minority groups and their members with respect to the larger society, it can also undermine the status of the weaker members—namely children, sometimes women, and internal dissenters—within the group. Susan Moller Okin has pointed to this phenomenon in her critique of multiculturalism, arguing that group rights often reinforce the subordination of women within the groups.[5] In resisting the delegation of authority over issues of family law, Ayelet Shachar notes a similar dynamic, labelling it the "paradox of multicultural vulnerability."[6] Neither, however, focuses on those who are the most vulnerable and the least powerful: children.

In this chapter, I aim to examine two prominent defenses of multiculturalism, showing how each pays insufficient attention to the tension described above. Avishai Margalit and Moshe Halbertal argue that, because individuals have a "right to culture", the state must grant groups a status that may flout the rights of some individuals, conditioned on the ability of those individuals to exit.[7] Will Kymlicka, in a far more sophisticated version of multiculturalism, defends cultural rights, and accommodations, but only for those cultural groups that are themselves internally liberal (except in rare circumstances) and that take seriously the value of personal autonomy.[8] While the freedom to exit from a group is indeed important, I shall contend that the group rights supported by Margalit and Halbertal may serve to disable or severely impoverish the ability of children to exit from groups. And while personal autonomy is indeed important, I shall contend that Kymlicka's conception of autonomy is unsatisfactory and that, moreover, his defense of rights to separate schooling for national minorities and to educational exemptions for some polyethnic groups leaves him open to the same critique about exit that I levy against Margalit and Halbertal. Along the way, I shall comment on the odd fixation of multiculturalists on rights of exit.

11.1. A Right to Culture?

Margalit and Halbertal articulate a basic claim of almost all multicultural theories: individual freedom and flourishing depend crucially on a person's cultural attachments. This rather unobjectionable claim leads to what, at bottom, is a strikingly elementary argument: if culture matters to individual freedom and flourishing, then liberals, who seek to guarantee freedom and facilitate individual flourishing, should also concern themselves with culture. Margalit and Halbertal thus begin their argument with the simple but dramatic assertion, "Human beings have a right to culture—not just any culture but their own."[9]

Note here, however, that the key assertion is not that cultural attachments are important per se, but rather that attachments to *one's own* culture are important. Now it is trivially true that people need cultural attachments in order to lead satisfying lives, but it is another question entirely whether or not people need to be attached always to their own cultural groups in order to lead satisfying lives. And prior to this question, we must ask a host of others about the meaning of "one's own culture": how will one's own culture be identified? who shall be the identifying agent(s)? are multiple cultural attachments possible or, perhaps, common? can people change cultural allegiances?

These familiar questions raise some initial problems for Margalit and Halbertal, but it is important first to ask what follows from their notion of a right to culture. Margalit and Halbertal believe that "...the right to culture may involve giving groups a status that contradicts the status of the individual in a liberal state" and that "[p]rotecting cultures out of the human right to culture may take the form of an obligation to support cultures that flout the rights of the individual in a liberal society."[10] Moreover, they say that the liberal state must "abandon its neutral position and actively assist needy cultures" not because this is in the interest of the majority, but because it is necessary "to make it possible for members of minority groups to retain their identity."[11] Thus the motivating force behind the right to culture is an interest in protecting the existence of minority cultural groups.

For Margalit and Halbertal, then, cultural identification, or more precisely, identification with one's own culture, is so important that it generates a right that overrides other traditional liberal beliefs in freedom of choice, association, and movement. Minority cultural groups may be allowed to impose certain restrictions on their members as well as certain regulations on outsiders. Margalit and Halbertal say, for example, that the right to culture will permit groups to recognize only arranged marriages, or to forbid outsiders from entering or living in a particular geographical area. Moreover, using as an example the Ultra-Orthodox Jews in Israel, they assert that defending a right to culture issues in a defense of the subordinate status of women within the group.[12]

The most significant implications of a right to culture, in my view, regard schooling. Margalit and Halbertal, at least in their assessment of Ultra-Orthodox Jews, seem to agree, calling education "an issue of central importance."[13] The right to culture justifies for Margalit and Halbertal the right to publicly subsidized separate schooling. They argue that the right to culture and the privileges that follow from it are not meant merely to protect cultures in danger of disappearing, but also to aid a minority group that finds it difficult to "maintain specific aspects of its culture without these privileges."[14] Thus for those groups whose ability to transmit their cultural values and beliefs to children may be compromised or undermined by attendance in public schools, the state ought to provide public assistance for separate educational institutions. Margalit and Halbertal say that, within the Israeli context, both Ultra-Orthodox Jews and Arab Israelis should be permitted to establish and maintain separate schools at public expense.[15] Should the state continue to regulate or oversee the structure and content of the separate educational institutions desired by each particular cultural group? Referring to Ultra-Orthodox society, Margalit and Halbertal note that "the school curriculum is controlled exclusively by the community, and there is a clear discrimination between the education of girls and of boys."[16] Boys engage in life-long study of the Torah, learning almost no secular subjects; girls receive a different curriculum and complete their studies before age twenty. Summing up their position, Margalit and Halbertal contrast the *conditional* right to control access to a community's neighborhood, based on a balance of the community's interest and the burdens that restricted access place on outsiders, with the apparently *absolute* right to maintain separate educational institutions. A right to culture, for Margalit and Halbertal, means that cultural groups, without state oversight but with state financial support, ought to be permitted to direct and control the education of their youngest members.

Given this list of implications regarding marriage, geographical access, and education, it is not difficult to discern how establishing a right to culture leads directly to potential conflicts. If the liberal state takes the freedom and equality of individuals seriously, it cannot permit a cultural rights program of the sort suggested by Margalit and Halbertal. The reason is that in the interest of preserving the culture, the rights extended to groups may sanction illiberal treatment of group members, not to mention the potential neglect of the development and sustenance of civic or political virtues in children.

Permitting, as Margalit and Halbertal do, "judicial autonomy in marital and family matters"[17] might qualify as a prima facie case against the supposed liberalism of their theory.[18] But consider their stance on separate education and their own example of the Ultra-Orthodox. By extending multicultural accommodations in education, the state implicitly sanctions an educational system where not only are girls denied equal educational opportunity[19] to study the same subjects as boys, but boys are denied the opportunity to study anything secular. Given, as Margalit and Halbertal admit, that "Ultra-Orthodox culture is essentially illiberal" and that "there is no aspect of its members' lives in which it does not actively interfere, sometimes to the extent of compulsion",[20] schooling that perpetuates a second class status may go far in preserving the character of Ultra-Orthodox culture, but from the standpoint of equal citizenship we need at least to consider the likely effects on children. Group rights of the sort described by Margalit and Halbertal allow for illiberal treatment of individuals within groups.

Margalit and Halbertal might reply in two ways. First, they say that cultural rights are valuable only insofar as they are in the interests of individuals. Or more precisely, they say that "the individual's right to culture stems from the fact that every person has an overriding interest in his personality identity—that is, in preserving his way of life and the traits that are central identity components for him and the other members of his cultural group."[21] But the notion of personality identity as the grounds for a right to culture seems to me controversial at best and incoherent at worst, considering what Jeremy Waldron has called the "cosmopolitan alternative."[22] Do all individual adherents of a culture have similar personality identities? Must personality identities derive from the cultural unit into which a person is born? Do they alter over time? Can a person construct a personality identity out of multiple cultural materials?

Second, reminding readers that "the right to culture is based on its contribution to the basic interests of individuals", Margalit and Halbertal argue that each individual must always retain the right to exit a culture if he or she wishes to do so.[23] The right to culture does not, they write, "justify coercing those who wish to leave the culture to remain within it on the pretext that if people begin to leave, the culture will be destroyed."[24] Consistent with the value of personal autonomy, they aim to honor the capacity of individuals to examine their lives and preserve freedom of association by denying cultural groups the right to forbid exit.

But are the group rights they endorse themselves consistent with a meaningful right of exit? Given the restrictions Margalit and Halbertal are willing to tolerate even among self-described illiberal groups, this hardly seems the case. It is one thing simply to announce that cultural groups may not forbid their members from exiting; it is an entirely different matter to create the capacity for individuals to exercise this right. The distinction here is a familiar one, namely between formal liberties and the actual worth of liberties. Margalit and Halbertal are all too willing to sacrifice basic conditions for exercising a right of exit in the name of ensuring the continued existence of the group, all in order to preserve an individual's personality identity.

Think about the (absolute) right of cultural groups to separate educational institutions that Margalit and Halbertal defend. The Ultra-Orthodox education they describe—in its effort to shield students from secular society, in its reinforcement of gender inequality—seems unlikely to play a role in creating the conditions where students might be capable of revising or rejecting their religious attachments.[25] Indeed, the Ultra-Orthodox education is designed to prevent exactly that. But we can imagine still less attractive scenarios. If the norms of a cultural group were continually to reinforce a message that girls and women are sources of evil, sexual temptresses, or merely unequal in all respects to men, would Margalit and Halbertal defend schools that taught these lessons? If the norms of a cultural group aim systematically to disable the ability of boys to think critically except with relation to the Talmud, or teach them to accept unerringly the dictates of elders, would Margalit and Halbertal defend an educational system designed to further this end? If the answer is no, Margalit and Halbertal offer no criteria by which to distinguish acceptable from unacceptable aims and forms of separate education. On their own admission, the relative liberality or illiberality of group practices would *not* count as such a criterion. In fact, far from distinguishing between liberal versus illiberal educational practices, they suggest that the state must not only tolerate separate schools, but actively support them financially. Yet when cultural groups are deeply illiberal in their educational practices, it is hard to believe that the right of exit Margalit and Halbertal guarantee individuals will have any real substance. Rights of exit are meaningless without the capacity to exercise them.

Margalit and Halbertal are not alone in their reliance on the right of exit strategy. Multicultural theorists often seem to condition the justice of proposed group rights or accommodations on the right of individuals to exit. Yet, as Cass Sunstein and Jon Elster have argued, a person's preferences often adapt to the environment in which they form, all the more so when the environment puts up barriers to exposure to diversity. As a result, people's preferences, Sunstein writes, "need not be respected when they are adaptive to unjust background conditions; in such circumstances it is not even clear whether the relevant preferences are authentically 'theirs'."[26] We may wonder, therefore, about the expressed preferences *not to exit* of adults who have received exceptionally illiberal educations; we may wonder, essentially, whether they have been indoctrinated. It is hard to see how a liberal state could justify multicultural accommodations in education that permitted indoctrination. But unless an education is provided that does not indoctrinate, that does not systematically adapt one's preferences and, over time, one's very character to uphold cultural norms, the right of exit strategy inevitably fails. If the right of exit strategy is even to be coherent, individuals must acquire the capacity to question the value of continued allegiance to cultural norms and practices, and ultimately to the group itself. This is necessary simply to begin the process of deciding for oneself whether deserting the group is, all things considered, a desirable pursuit.

In fact, we might express another concern about the right of exit strategy precisely because, even if one is capable of it, exiting one's group is, in the real world, a momentous and highly consequential decision. Since children are still dependent on their families for care, it is highly unlikely that many children would ever avail themselves of the exit option, even were they able to consider it. The costs of exit for children—possibly forgoing the continued love and support of one's parents and family, of suffering shame and ostracism, and so on—are so great that even those with the wherewithal and courage to leave will have powerful reasons to stay. Moreover, as for adults, those who would consider exiting are likely to be those already subject to illiberal and unjust treatment—internal dissenters or women, for example. To the extent that multicultural accommodations come conditioned on the ability of persons to exit, the burden of such accommodations is often borne by minority group members who are already most vulnerable. As Ayelet Shachar notes, if a state extends collective rights to a minority group and tensions then arise between an individual and the group, it is the individual who must resolve the tension by deciding whether or not to stay. "By turning a blind eye to differential power distributions within the group hierarchy and ignoring women's heightened symbolic role in relation to other group members, the right of exit rationale forces an individual member into a choice of penalties: either accept all group practices, including those that violate your fundamental citizenship rights, or (somehow) leave."[27] Thus, even if education were to provide children a substantive, as well as formal, ability to exit, we might worry about the overall justice of the right of exit strategy.[28]

Returning, then, to Margalit and Halbertal, I conclude that the group rights and multicultural accommodations they defend, especially the allowance for separate and publicly subsidized illiberal educational systems, seem to undermine the very possibility of exit from the start. At a very minimum, we can say without any controversy that, given separate schools, the capacity to exit a group will be distributed differentially amongst citizens.[29]

11.2. Kymlicka's Liberal Defense of Minority Rights

In contrast to the almost blanket endorsement for state support of cultural groups given by Margalit and Halbertal, Will Kymlicka offers a far more sophisticated "liberal theory of minority rights."[30] Unlike Margalit and Halbertal, Kymlicka emphasizes the value of personal autonomy and applies his theory only to groups whose internal practices are themselves liberal. In doing so, Kymlicka attempts to avoid the problem of placing cultural purity and integrity above individual freedom. In my view, Kymlicka has convincingly shown how difference-blind rights and institutions are not neutral to culture, but rather partial to dominant cultural groups. In many respects, I agree with Kymlicka's overall project and would endorse many of his practical recommendations. Nevertheless, I argue here that his theory suffers from two problems that serve to obscure the signal importance of education, especially with respect to who controls it and what its aims are. The first problem concerns his defense of rights to separate schooling as a form of protection for national minorities from the broader society; the second problem concerns his confusing conception of autonomy.

Before explicating these problems, a few comments on Kymlicka's overall project are in order. Like other multiculturalists, Kymlicka connects freedom with culture. Membership in a secure, rich, and stable culture is a precondition for freedom of choice and individual flourishing.[31] With this argument, Kymlicka provided the basic framework of multicultural theory which many others have since followed. Kymlicka's sophistication owes in large part to the number of important distinctions he makes in the course of his argument. Three are worth mentioning here. First, Kymlicka distinguishes between political communities and cultural communities, arguing that people are owed respect both as citizens and as members of their cultural groups.[32] A political community (i.e. a state) is not necessarily coextensive with a cultural community (i.e. a nation or people), and in fact most political communities are composed of multiple cultural communities. Cultural diversity within countries is the norm. Yet not all countries are diverse in the same way. This leads to Kymlicka's second distinction, that between multinational states and polyethnic states. Multinational states are those composed of national minorities, peoples incorporated by conquest or agreement into a single political unit. Polyethnic states are those composed of various ethnic groups, peoples incorporated via voluntary immigration.[33] Switzerland is an example of a multinational state, a consociational arrangement among four different cultural groups. The United States is an example of a polyethnic state, a country of immigrants from across the globe who are permitted, even encouraged, to retain a sense of their ethnic identity. Of course, a country may be at once multinational and polyethnic. The United States fits this bill; Kymlicka cites American Indians, Puerto Ricans, descendants of Mexicans in the southwest, native Hawaiians, and the Chamorros of Guam as examples of national minorities in the United States.[34] Kymlicka argues that both national minorities and ethnic groups should receive certain group rights, though national minorities lay claim to stronger and more substantial rights, possibly including territorial sovereignty, than do ethnic groups. Finally, Kymlicka distinguishes between two kinds of group rights that either kind of cultural group may receive. He supports what he calls external protections, which refer to the right of a group to limit the power of the larger society to regulate the group. He rejects what he calls internal restrictions, which refer to the right of a group to limit the liberty of its own members for the sake of cultural solidarity or purity.[35] On the basis of these three distinctions, Kymlicka builds an impressive case for why liberals, without sacrificing a commitment to individual autonomy, can and should promote some group rights (those that are external protections) for cultural minorities.

When considering rights to separate education, however, the distinction between external protections and internal restrictions breaks down. Kymlicka says that "we should aim at ensuring that all national groups have the opportunity to maintain themselves as a distinct culture, if they so choose."[36] Control over education is central to this task; it is necessary, Kymlicka argues, in order to ensure that the assimilative pressures of larger society, and especially of public schools, do not undermine the ability of such groups to survive.[37] Cultural minorities whose survival is threatened by exposure to larger society will often seek to educate their children in restrictive ways. But whereas separate schooling in these cases does indeed provide a form of external protection for the adult members of a cultural group, it can also create an internal restriction for the children of the group.

Kymlicka makes clear that he supports rights over schooling for national minorities. But he also supports exemption rights for isolationist religious groups, at least when they are rooted in historical agreements and when their numbers are not so large as to threaten liberal citizenship generally.[38] Adherents of minority religious groups who seek to shield their children from the modern secular world and do not participate in civil society, on Kymlicka's view, might best be considered "partial citizens" and be permitted therefore to educate their children according to the norms and values of their particular religious culture.[39] But consider the now all-too-familiar cases of the

Amish (*Wisconsin* v. *Yoder*) and the Fundamentalist Christians (*Mozert* v. *Hawkins*).[40] As the testimony in each court case detailed, the purpose of separate education or exemption from parts of the public school curriculum was to protect children from the allegedly baleful influences of secular society. Engagement with diverse ways of life was said to threaten the existence of the Amish way of life and condemn fundamentalist children to eternal damnation. The stated educational aims of the Amish and fundamentalists were not to enhance the autonomous choice-making capacities of children, but rather to diminish them. Speaking generally, the more that separate schooling increases the likelihood that children will not come into contact with the broader environment, the less the chance that children will ever be able reasonably to assess their own way of life, much less other ways of life.[41] Anthony Appiah rightly warns that cultural rights designed to ensure the survival of minority groups may seem desirable and just insofar as they apply to adults who are free to endorse, choose, or reject membership in a group and enjoy the capacity to examine critically the ends of that group. But children neither choose membership in a group nor naturally have the capacity to examine their ends critically. Respecting cultural groups, in short, may not respect the autonomy of future adults born into the group.[42] In this way, external protections slide into internal restrictions. In promoting multiculturalism at the level of society and extending group rights such as separate schooling, Kymlicka potentially sanctions a form of cultural compulsion at the level of individuals. The development and exercise of autonomy, which Kymlicka says he cares about, may be sacrificed to the external protections afforded the minority group into which he or she is born.

To be fair, Kymlicka says often that all children must get a liberal education.[43] He writes, for example, that a liberal society "not only allows people to pursue their current way of life, but also gives them access to information about other ways of life (through freedom of expression), and indeed requires children to learn about other ways of life (through mandatory education)..."[44] But if this is so, Kymlicka's defense of rights for national minorities and some isolationist religious groups stands in tension with his support of liberal education. Historically, one of the first desires of cultural minorities— national minorities more than polyethnic groups—is to exert at least significant, if not exclusive, control over the educational experiences of their children. Even amongst polyethnic groups, the impulse to direct the education of the community's children is not uncommon.[45] The form of this education is often illiberal. As Amy Gutmann says,

"To save their children from future pain, especially the pain of eternal damnation, parents have historically shielded their children from diverse associations, convinced them that all other ways of life are sinful, and implicitly fostered (if not explicitly taught them) disrespect for people who are different."[46]

Kymlicka asserts an "unrelenting commitment to individual autonomy", the consequence of which is a refusal to defend group rights for cultures that do not seek to develop the autonomy of their members.[47] He also writes that: "To learn public reasonableness, students must come to know and understand people who are reasonable and decent and humane, but do not share their religion."[48] But insofar as Kymlicka defends either special subsidies for culturally centric forms of education for cultural minorities (think of the demands of the Ultra-Orthodox) or broad exemptions from any form of education (think of the demands of the Amish or of gypsies), he falls into the same problem for which I criticized Margalit and Halbertal: a right to separate education potentially undermines the very conditions of autonomy or of a meaningful right of exit. Possibly one may interpret Kymlicka as rejecting any form of education that restricts social and intellectual interaction with other ways of life. (His main concern, in fact, often appears to be the right of minority groups to an education in their own language.) But Kymlicka defends rights for at least some cultural groups to exercise control over the scope and content of education. Kymlicka must be clearer about whether his liberal theory of minority rights includes rights to separate education or broad exemptions from educational requirements that are otherwise binding on other citizens, and, if it does, the extent to which the theory can accommodate culturally-centric, illiberal forms of education. At the very least, it seems to me, Kymlicka must grant that multicultural accommodations in education should be approached on a case-by-case basis, rather than deciding at the level of theory that national minorities *tout court* should have rights to separate schooling or exemptions from schooling.

Perhaps Kymlicka's ambiguity about education is merely accidental; he might simply rule out illiberal forms of education and insist that all children, regardless of cultural affiliation, must be educated so as to develop their autonomy. But I suspect that the ambiguity is not simply accidental. It may be related to the second problem with Kymlicka's theory, namely, a confusing and ultimately unsatisfactory conception of autonomy.

Kymlicka offers an emphatic and unabashed endorsement of individual autonomy.[49] For him it is an essential feature of liberalism:

> Liberals are committed to supporting the right of individuals to decide for themselves which aspects of their cultural heritage are worth passing on. Liberalism is committed to (perhaps even defined by) the view that individuals should have the freedom and capacity to question and possibly revise the traditional practices of their community, should they come to see them as no longer worthy of their allegiance.[50]

Kymlicka in fact criticizes Rawls's refusal to endorse anything beyond political autonomy.[51] Kymlicka believes that the exercise of political autonomy has important consequences for one's private commitments and beliefs. He believes, moreover, that autonomy is defensible on its own terms, regardless of its application to public or private identities. Simply put, "We must endorse the traditional belief in personal autonomy", writes Kymlicka.[52]

Because of Kymlicka's commitment to autonomy and his rejection of minority rights for illiberal cultures, some people find his theory to be *insufficiently* multicultural and not respectful enough of cultural differences. Chandran Kukathas, for example, criticizes Kymlicka for his intolerance of groups that do not cherish the capacity for autonomy; for Kukathas, promoting autonomy limits diversity instead of protecting it.[53] Similarly, William Galston says that Kymlicka's insistence on attempting to liberalize autonomy-retarding groups amounts to the "cultural equivalent of the Vietnam-era principle of 'destroying the village in order to save it.' "[54] For these theorists, Kymlicka's multicultural theory is not permissive enough.

I have criticized Kymlicka from the opposite direction. I share his commitment to autonomy, yet I believe that the provision of group rights for separate schooling potentially denies the educational conditions necessary for developing autonomy and exercising a meaningful right of exit. My question concerns not whether Kymlicka is too permissive, but his peculiar understanding of autonomy, an understanding that is intimately tied up with his entire theory of minority rights. The basic issue is this: most often Kymlicka views autonomy in terms of its value in giving individuals the ability to choose among significant and diverse options *within* a cultural group. But it is questionable whether this is the sort of autonomy liberals should defend. Why must the autonomous choices of individuals be hemmed in by cultural boundaries? On some occasions, Kymlicka himself seems to uphold autonomy in terms of its value in giving individuals the ability to choose among significant and diverse options *among* cultural groups. The difference here is worth underlining, for the respective understanding of autonomy affects the scope of minority rights, especially concerning education, in absolutely critical ways.

Recall that Kymlicka justifies a concern for cultural rights precisely on the basis that membership in one's own culture is a precondition for intelligent choice-making. "Cultures are valuable, not in and of themselves, but because it is only through having access to a societal culture that people have access to a range of meaningful options."[55] To understand this fully, it is important to ask specifically what is meant by "societal culture." Societal cultures, Kymlicka tells us, are equivalent to a nation or people, a culture "which provides its members with meaningful ways of life across the full range of human activities, including social, educational, religious, recreational, and economic life, encompassing both private and public spheres."[56] He emphasizes that societal cultures are usually "institutionally complete."[57] This is an atypically broad definition of culture, and this is significant for at least two reasons. First, it excludes many groups we typically think of as defining a meaningful way of life, groups based on class, gender, disability, sexual orientation, religion, etc.[58] Second, and perhaps more importantly, it means that immigrant ethnic groups either do not have their own societal cultures or should not be permitted to recreate their societal culture in their adopted country.[59] On Kymlicka's theory, immigrants are expected to (or conceived of as expecting to) integrate into mainstream society; only national minorities and nations have societal cultures.[60]

The unusual capaciousness of Kymlicka's definition helps us to understand, however, what he means when he says that "freedom involves making choices amongst various options, and our societal culture not only provides these options, but it also makes them meaningful to us."[61] Kymlicka says that cultural membership is a precondition for autonomous decision making within cultures. Secure location in, and identification with, a societal culture is said to provide a horizon of choices, a menu of possible roles to assume. Most succinctly: "The freedom which liberals demand for individuals is not primarily the freedom to go beyond one's language and history, but rather the freedom to move around within one's societal culture, to distance oneself from particular cultural roles, to choose which features of the culture are most worth developing, and which are without value."[62] Freedom and autonomy for Kymlicka therefore refer to the capacity to examine and revise one's ends, *but first and foremost insofar as these ends are contained within and made available by one's societal culture.*

It is instructive to contemplate the educational implications of this understanding of autonomy. I have already argued that a policy of supporting external protections in the form of separate schools may in practice result in internal restrictions. But now we are well placed to tease out of Kymlicka's theory its deeper educational implications. Paradoxically, Kymlicka's politically progressive multicultural theory seems to require a politically conservative educational theory. That is, insofar as Kymlicka values primarily the freedom to move around one's culture (and not amongst cultures), the corresponding education to facilitate such movement will be an education that teaches children the skills for intra-cultural navigation. Learning about the variety of roles and values within a societal culture, and acquiring the skills necessary to adopt one or some among these, will be a fundamental aim of education. The educational companion to Kymlicka's multicultural political theory, therefore, becomes something like E. D. Hirsch's program of cultural literacy. Hirsch's book by the same title makes the argument that for children to become free and equal adults they must receive an education that teaches them about their cultural traditions and symbols.[63] Cultural illiteracy is, on Hirsch's analysis, the cause of much social injustice, for it narrows the scope of options available within a culture, preventing social and economic mobility. Indeed, echoing my conclusions here with respect to Kymlicka's argument, Hirsch writes, "the goals of political liberalism require educational conservatism."[64]

Can educational conservatism be the necessary companion of a progressive multicultural political theory? Kymlicka's conception of autonomy as free choice making within the scope of a societal culture leads in this direction. Yet is this the sort of autonomy that liberals should value? I want to suggest that it is not. The value and importance of autonomy lies in enabling not only choice within culture, but also choice beyond one's culture. Moreover, I wish to suggest that the exercise of autonomous choice making within or outside of one's culture is promoted by, and may in fact require, learning about the values and practices of other cultures.

Kymlicka himself appears at times to waver on the conception of autonomy he upholds, and this is most evident when he discusses education. Kymlicka would resist the conclusion that the educational complement of his multicultural theory is a pedagogically conservative program of cultural literacy. When Kymlicka discusses the proper aims of education, he champions a more progressive theory of education. But on this more progressive theory, Kymlicka seems to suggest that autonomy is not merely the capacity to move within one's societal culture, but also among other societal cultures. In reaction to the objection, for example, that cultural rights may be invoked to prohibit cultural interaction, Kymlicka says that "liberals cannot endorse a notion of culture that sees the process of interacting with and learning from other cultures as a threat to 'purity' and 'integrity', rather than an opportunity for enrichment."[65] Elsewhere, indicating his support for cultural change, he notes that "people should be able to decide what is best from within their own culture, and to integrate into their culture whatever they find admirable in other cultures."[66] Finally, in his most direct comment on this matter, Kymlicka writes that though autonomy is dependent on membership in a culture, "Over time, individuals can put these cultural contexts themselves into question and choose which culture they wish to live in."[67]

Given these comments on education, Kymlicka evinces uneasiness with autonomy conceived as choice making within culture. Of what value is mutual learning unless it is meant to contribute to an individual's freedom to question, revise, and even move beyond one's societal culture?[68] Kymlicka's uneasiness is warranted. There are several problems, from a liberal perspective, with understanding autonomy as choice making only within culture.

First, Kymlicka notices only half of what it means for a societal culture to be a context of choice. Cultures do indeed provide a range of choices and a variety of roles to assume; they establish horizons of possibility for their members. But horizons also have limits; they indicate the boundaries of choice and circumscribe the roles that a person can adopt. Cultures constrain as well as enable. Importantly, societal cultures are not all equivalent in their capaciousness. Despite the fact that societal culture is defined broadly, some societal cultures provide for much narrower ranges of options than others; some have more restricted menus of sanctioned roles than others.[69] If a culture sets the context of choice for individuals, beyond which it would be difficult if not impossible to choose, then horizons of opportunity are always limited by the relative vastness or narrowness of one's culture. In emphasizing the way in which cultural membership enables choice, Kymlicka overlooks the way in which membership also constrains choice. Though it is plain that not all societal cultures are equal in the choices they make available, they are all of equal standing for Kymlicka. For Kymlicka focuses not on the particular range of choice offered, or the substance of the actual choices; instead his concern is simply that the societal culture *is* the context of choice. We need not argue against this claim, but why does it follow that this is the context of choice that matters? Put differently, Kymlicka argues that liberals should care about cultures because freedom is connected with culture. But from this premise it does not follow that liberals should concern themselves only with the cultural group into which one is born. With a broader conception of autonomy, liberals might wish to protect choice making among cultures or allow a person to cobble together a life whose values derive from multiple cultures.

Second, to say that liberals should protect cultures because they provide a context of choice presumes in fact that cultural groups are easily identifiable. Given Kymlicka's broad definition of culture, is it true that societal cultures are so easily distinguished from one another? Are cultures unified? Part of what defines a culture, after all, in addition to a shared history and language, is a shared commitment to a particular conception of the good, or to a narrow range of these conceptions. Cultures are said to develop particular ways of life.[70] But the broader the range of roles and ends that cultures offer their members, the more difficult it becomes to mark cultures off from one another, and the more difficult it becomes to say what members share in common. Kymlicka notices this himself, saying that as various cultural communities have become more and more liberal, they have become more and more similar, blurring the boundaries where one culture begins and another ends.[71]

Third, even presuming that cultures are readily distinguishable, is it true that each person belongs only to one? Some people, as Jeremy Waldron suggests, are "cosmopolitan" and grow up with multiple societal cultures providing the relevant context of choice.[72] Think too of a child born to parents who belong to different societal cultures, say of a Native American mother and a Euro-American father or of a French-Canadian mother and a British-Canadian father. What will be the relevant societal culture for this child? The increasing number of mixed race and multinational children poses a de facto challenge to Kymlicka's theory, and certainly to the educational implications that he believes follows it.

Kymlicka's response to these objections might be to reemphasize that, although the context of individual choice is passed down by each person's culture, the right of each person to assess, criticize, and revise these choices remains absolute. Individuals may never transcend the societal culture of their birth, but they may engage in critical appraisal and revision of it. "It is of fundamental importance", as Kymlicka says, "that we be able rationally to assess our conceptions of the good in light of new information or experiences, and to revise them if they are not worthy of our continued allegiance."[73] But without exposure to and engagement with other cultural beliefs and practices, the scope of this new information and experience must already be contained within the structure of a societal culture. I submit that the kinds of information and experience most likely to be of value in assessing one's conception of the good (or the range of roles within one's societal culture) are precisely those to be found *outside* one's own culture.[74] To assess whether particular conceptions of the good or whether particular roles are worthy of our allegiance we require for comparison some other, rival, conceptions of the good. These rival conceptions may conceivably be found within one's societal culture, but for the purpose of rational assessment and comparison we may need to look beyond the scope of the familiar. For the purpose of actual revision, wherein new elements are incorporated into the culture, interaction with other cultures is probably a necessity.

It would take a detailed psychological and sociological argument to substantiate this claim. But the basic idea is that only the superhuman self-generate cultural criticism; for the rest of us, it is encounters with foreignness and novelty (through literature, friendship, travel, and so on) that spur us to assess or revise what we take as given. Reflect quickly upon your own experience: do not the moments in which the limits of the possible are most thrown into question—the moments when novel possibilities of how to lead a life present themselves most vividly, the moments that inspire us to call into question the way we have led our lives—occur most often when we experience something utterly foreign? Kymlicka insists that individuals must "have the conditions necessary to acquire an awareness of different views of the good life, and an ability to examine these views intelligently."[75] One of these conditions, I suggest, is not only *intracultural* learning and comparison, but *intercultural* learning and comparison.

But if intercultural learning and comparison is valuable, then why should the context of choice or range of options of another societal culture remain closed off to an individual? Insofar as mutual learning between cultures is valued, so too should a conception of autonomy that permits choice among cultures be valuable. And as previously suggested, we need not conceive of intercultural choice as binary—either we belong wholly to one societal culture or we reject it and affiliate with another. Autonomous choice among cultures may mean simply the freedom to be a cosmopolitan hybrid, appropriating the values of other cultures for oneself, renegotiating the values of the culture(s) one is born into, asserting shifting allegiances and affiliations, and, in the end, constructing for oneself a context of choice that extends beyond the culture of one's birth.

Kymlicka's theory of multiculturalism is therefore problematic in two respects. First, though he firmly endorses autonomy, his support

of rights to separate schooling for national minorities and some isolationist religious groups potentially undermines its development and
exercise. Second, his conception of autonomy as choice making within culture may be found to be too limited. Kymlicka is right to connect autonomy and freedom with cultural membership, but it should
not (need not) follow from this that the scope of autonomy is properly limited by cultural membership. Nor should it follow that the
liberal state should enforce this limitation through its institutions.
Liberals typically wish to defend the widest possible freedom for
individuals; this is consistent not with predetermined cultural horizons but with autonomous choice whose bounds range beyond one's
own culture. Such autonomous choice does not imply encouraging
individuals to revise or reject their cultural affiliations; it implies
instead that education must not be culturally-centric, if the possibility
of assessment and revision is to be made real.[76]

11.3. Conclusion

Multiculturalists often promote multicultural accommodations in
schooling as central to achieving justice for cultural minorities. I
have endeavored to show in this chapter why there is good reason to
be concerned about the blanket extension of rights to separate
schooling or exemptions from schooling. Education is essential to
cultural transmission, but it is for this very reason that group rights
or wholesale exemptions cannot, in my view, be justified as a matter
of principle. Because in the modern world school attendance is often
mandatory, schools, as Kymlicka himself notes, may represent the
only institutional vehicle that larger societies have at their disposal
to ensure the freedom of its citizens and to transmit civic or political
virtues. It is clear, for example, that direct state intervention in the
socialization that parents give their children in the home, or that cultural groups give their members in their associational lives, will often
be found to be too intrusive. The liberal state itself acts illiberally
when it intrudes too directly or too deeply into family life. In other
words, it is philosophically undesirable, and, in addition, impossible
in practice, for the liberal state to prevent parents from socializing
their children in deeply illiberal ways, or to block cultural groups
from promulgating norms of gender inequity, for example. But it is
not impossible for the state to require an education of a certain sort
for children. What this means, in my view, is that the liberal state
should be reluctant to grant rights to separate schooling or to permit

broad exemptions from educational requirements such as mandatory attendance. The liberal state should maintain, at the very least, regulatory authority over schooling and attempt to provide an education that aims, among other things, to foster the development of autonomy in children, as well as some civic virtues, such as tolerance and civility. (The promotion of autonomy by the state is itself a controversial issue, and while I do not have the space here to defend the claim, autonomy should neither be construed so robustly as to mean individual self-creation or constant Socratic skepticism, nor so anemically as to suggest that any expression of agency or preference would count as autonomous.[77]) In the end, multicultural accommodations in education in the form of multicultural curriculua, bilingual education, and many other things that typically fall under the rubric of "multicultural education" are justifiable; accommodations that mean the state may no longer regulate schooling are not.

NOTES

For helpful comments on this chapter, I would like to thank Walter Feinberg, Kevin McDonough, Eamonn Callan, and Meira Levinson.

1. For a descriptive overview, see Jacob Levy, "Classifying Cultural Rights" in Ian Shapiro and Will Kymlicka (eds), *NOMOS XXXIX: Ethnicity and Group Rights* (New York: New York University Press, 1997).
2. See David Tyack, *The One Best System: A History of American Urban Education* (Cambridge: Harvard University Press, 1974) and Carl Kaestle, *Pillars of the Republic: Common Schools and American Society*, 1780–1860 (New York: Hill and Wang, 1983).
3. See David Wallace Adams, *Education for Extinction: American Indians and the Boarding School Experience*, 1875–1928 (Lawrence, KS: University of Kansas Press, 1995).
4. See Tyack, *The One Best System*, 107–8. Of course, the Supreme Court found in Meyer v. Nebraska in 1923 that states could not forbid instruction in a foreign language, thereby laying the groundwork for the modern use of bilingual education.
5. Susan Moller Okin, "Feminism and Multiculturalism: Some Tensions", *Ethics*, 108(4) (1998), 661–84. See also Okin, *Is Multiculturalism Bad For Women?* (Princeton: Princeton University Press, 1999).
6. Ayelet Shachar, "On Citizenship and Multicultural Vulnerability", *Political Theory*, 28(1) (2000), 64–89. See also Shachar, "The Paradox of Multicultural Vulnerability" in Christian Joppke and Steven Lukes (eds), *Multicultural Questions* (Oxford: Oxford University Press, 1999).
7. Avishai Margalit and Moshe Halbertal, "Liberalism and the Right to Culture", *Social Research*, 61(3) (1994), 491–510.
8. Will Kymlicka, *Multicultural Citizenship* (Oxford: Clarendon Press, 1995).
9. Margalit and Halbertal, "Liberalism and the Right to Culture", 491.
10. Ibid., 491.

11. Ibid., 492.
12. Ibid., 491–2.
13. Ibid., 493.
14. Ibid., 506.
15. Ibid., 493, 507.
16. Ibid., 493.
17. Ibid., 507.
18. Ayelet Shachar's criticism of multicultural accommodations is aimed directly at issues of family law. See Shachar, "The Paradox of Multicultural Vulnerability", 95–9.
19. I mean equal educational opportunity in the simple sense of having equal access to schools and curriculum.
20. Margalit and Halbertal, "Liberalism and the Right to Culture", 492–3.
21. Ibid., 505.
22. The cosmopolitan alternative suggests that individuals craft, or if one prefers language conveying less agent-directed activity, develop identities from diverse cultural materials. See Jeremy Waldron, "Minority Cultures and the Cosmopolitan Alternative", *The University of Michigan Journal of Law Reform*, 25(3, 4) (1992). Also, see Waldron's essay in chapter one of this volume.
23. Presumably this would imply the conscious rejection of one's personality identity and subsequent adoption of a new one, although Margalit and Halbertal never make this clear.
24. Margalit and Halbertal, "Liberalism and the Right to Culture", 508.
25. It seems equally unlikely to teach children the civic skills and behavior they need to be informed and active citizens.
26. Cass Sunstein, "Should Sex Equality Law Apply to Religious Institutions?" in Okin 1999, 88. See also Jon Elster, *Sour Grapes* (Cambridge: Cambridge University Press, 1983).
27. Shachar, "On Citizenship and Multicultural Vulnerability", 80.
28. For a detailed discussion and criticism of the right-of-exit strategy, see Brian Barry, *Culture and Equality* (Cambridge, MA: Harvard University Press, 2001), 149f.
29. Certainly the capacity for exit will be distributed differentially even in societies in which all persons receive the same education, or even in the most liberal of societies. My point here is not that unequal capacity to exit is unjust, but that a theory of group rights that institutionalizes the discrepancy in exit capacities may not be called a liberal one.
30. Kymlicka's argument has evolved over the past decade, beginning with *Liberalism, Community, and Culture* (Oxford: Clarendon Press, 1989) and culminating in *Multicultural Citizenship* (Oxford: Clarendon Press, 1995). Among multicultural theorists, he is exceptional both for the impressive scope of his theoretical contributions (in addition to provoking the debate between liberals and multiculturalists, Kymlicka has offered a passionate defense of liberalism against communitarian critics), and the globe-spanning range of practical examples upon which he draws. The phrase "liberal theory of minority rights" is the subtitle of Kymlicka's *Multicultural Citizenship*.
31. Kymlicka offers a lengthier argument for the connection of freedom and culture in his earlier book. See Kymlicka, *Liberalism, Community, and Culture*, chs 7–9. The form of his argument there would be followed by many others, including Margalit and Halbertal. Note the familiar ring to this passage: "Liberals should be concerned with the fate of cultural structures, not because

they have some moral status of their own, but because it's only through having a rich and secure cultural structure that people can become aware, in a vivid way, of the options available to them, and intelligently examine their value" (165). Kymlicka takes more care to protect people's options than do Margalit and Halbertal.

32. Kymlicka, *Multicultural Citizenship*, 151.
33. The sociologist John Ogbu made a similar distinction years earlier, calling attention to voluntary versus involuntary immigrants. The situation of African-Americans and Native Americans can be better understood, he argued, once theorists and social scientists view them apart from an immigrant model. See, for example, Ogbu's, *Minority Education and Caste: The American System in Cross-Cultural Perspective* (New York: Academic Press, 1978).
34. Will Kymlicka, *Multicultural Citizenship* (Oxford: Clarendon Press, 1995), 11.
35. Ibid., 7, 35, 152.
36. Ibid., 113.
37. Thus Kymlicka discusses separate schooling for Native Americans and French-Canadians (*Multicultural Citizenship*, 12, 28, 38, 78). He also writes, "If a national group has full language rights and control over immigration, education, and resource development policy, then its long-term viability is secured" (Kymlicka, "Misunderstanding Nationalism", *Dissent* (Winter 1995), 137.) It is less clear whether such rights would apply to ethnic minorities, though Kymlicka certainly indicates support for rights to public schooling in the language of any minority group (*Multicultural Citizenship*, 111). Whether he means by this entirely separate public schools or bilingual education programs within common schools is left unclear.
38. See Will Kymlicka, *Politics in the Vernacular* (Oxford: Oxford University Press, 2001), 306; see also Will Kymlicka, "Comments on Shachar and Spinner-Halev: An Update from the Multiculturalism Wars" in Christian Joppke and Steven Lukes (eds), *Multicultural Questions* (Oxford: Oxford University Press, 1999), 125.
39. Kymlicka is here following an argument made by Jeff Spinner-Halev. See Spinner-Halev, *The Boundaries of Citizenship*; and Spinner-Halev, "Cultural Pluralism and Partial Citizenship" in Christian Joppke and Steven Lukes (eds), *Multicultural Questions* (Oxford: Oxford University Press, 1999).
40. The Amish are a tiny sect, and the Yoder decision made much of the exceptional nature of the ruling. Fundamentalist Christians, however, are not tiny and there has been a large but mostly unnoticed shift to educate fundamentalist Christian children separately. Consider the booming enrollment in Christian Fundamentalist academies, or the rocketing number of home-schooled children, the vast majority of whom are Fundamentalist Christians. For an extended discussion of the Yoder and Mozert cases, see my "Opting Out of Education: *Yoder*, *Mozert*, and the Autonomy of Children", *Educational Theory*, 2002.

   Home-schooling, in my view, raises especially sharp questions of parental and group authority over schooling because, as practiced in the United States, it is essentially unregulated. I examine the home-schooling question in "Testing the Boundaries of Parental Authority Over Education: The Case of Homeschooling" in Stephen Macedo and Yael Tamir (eds), *NOMOS XLII: Political and Moral Education* (New York: New York University Press, 2002).
41. For an argument in this vein concerning Catholic schools, see Jim Dwyer, *Religious Schools v. Children's Rights* (Ithaca, NY: Cornell University Press, 1998).

42. See K. Anthony Appiah, "Identity, Authenticity, Survival: Multicultural Societies and Social Reproduction" in Amy Gutmann (ed.), *Multiculturalism and the Politics of Recognition* (Princeton: Princeton University Press, 1994), 157.
43. Will Kymlicka, *Multicultural Citizenship* (Oxford: Clarendon Press, 1995), 92, 102, 204, n. 11.
44. Will Kymlicka, *Multicultural Citizenship* (Oxford: Clarendon Press, 1995), 82.
45. Consider, in an American context, the connection between the ethnic revivalism and the 1960s community schools movement.
46. Amy Gutmann, *Democratic Education* (Princeton: Princeton University Press, 1987), 31.
47. Kymlicka, *Politics in the Vernacular*, 304.
48. Will Kymlicka, *Multicultural Citizenship* (Oxford: Clarendon Press, 1995), 154.
49. Will Kymlicka, *Multicultural Citizenship* (Oxford: Clarendon Press, 1995), 94, 105, 164–5.
50. Ibid., 152.
51. Ibid., 231, n. 8.
52. Ibid., 163.
53. Chandran Kukathas, "Are There Any Cultural Rights?" in Will Kymlicka (ed.), *The Rights of Minority Cultures* (Oxford: Oxford University Press, 1995), 242ff.
54. William Galston, "Two Concepts of Liberalism", *Ethics*, 105(3) (1995), 523.
55. Will Kymlicka, *Multicultural Citizenship* (Oxford: Clarendon Press, 1995), 83.
56. Ibid., 76, cf. 18.
57. Ibid., 78, 98.
58. Ibid., 18.
59. Ibid., 78, 101.
60. Kymlicka emphasizes throughout the book that, despite recurrent revivals in ethnic identity, immigrants should not be viewed as rejecting the notion of assimilation. On the contrary, immigrants seek full inclusion, claims Kymlicka. For a vigorous, occasionally strident, defense of this view, see Kymlicka, "Ethnic Associations and Democratic Citizenship" in Amy Gutmann (ed.), *Freedom of Association* (Princeton: Princeton University Press, 1998), 177–213. By explaining away assertions of ethnic particularity among immigrants, and by avoiding the allegedly anomalous situation of African-Americans, Kymlicka winds up in a position where the Chamorros of Guam generate more theoretical interest and attention than do immigrants and blacks. Within the context of the United States, this is an odd source of multicultural concern. Nathan Glazer, in fact, sees the energy behind multiculturalism in the United States as driven by the frustrations of the African-American community over the failed promise of the Civil Rights era. After many years of fighting for full equality and inclusion, assimilation and integration have been called into question (see Glazer, *We Are All Multiculturalists Now* (Cambridge: Harvard University Press, 1997), 93ff. Indeed, many versions of multiculturalism can be seen as rejecting assimilation into one mainstream society and instead embracing some form of cultural pluralism. Kymlicka has a more plausible view when, following John Higham and Jeff Spinner-Halev, he calls recent assertions of ethnic particularity an attempt to establish "pluralistic integration" (see Kymlicka, "Ethnic Associations and Democratic Citizenship", 206). For more on this view of multiculturalism in the US context, see John Higham, "Multiculturalism and Universalism: History and Critique", *American Quarterly*, 45(2), esp. pp. 206ff; David Hollinger, *Postethnic America: Beyond Multiculturalism* (New York: Basic Books, 1995); and Todd Gitlin, *The Twilight of Common Dreams* (New York: Metropolitan Books, 1995).

61. Will Kymlicka, *Multicultural Citizenship* (Oxford: Clarendon Press, 1995), 83.
62. Ibid., 91–2.
63. E. D. Hirsch, *Cultural Literacy* (New York: Vintage Books, 1988).
64. Hirsch, *Cultural Literacy*, xii. See also Hirsch, *The Schools We Need and Why We Don't Have Them* (New York: Doubleday, 1996). He writes there that "the only practical way to achieve liberalism's aim of greater social justice is to pursue conservative educational policies" (p. 6).
65. Kymlicka, *Multicultural Citizenship* (102; 204n. 11).
66. Ibid., 108. Still elsewhere Kymlicka endorses a very Rawlsian view of public reason that implies an education beyond one's own cultural horizon: "Because reasonable people disagree about the merits of different religions and conceptions of the good life, children must learn to distinguish reasons based on private faith from reasons that can be publicly accepted in a diverse society. To develop this capacity, children must not only learn how to distance themselves from beliefs that are taken for granted in their private life, but they must also learn how to put themselves in other people's shoes..." (*Politics in the Vernacular*, 309).
67. Kymlicka, "Misunderstanding Nationalism", *Dissent* (Winter 1995), 134. I should note that it is somewhat unclear whether or not Kymlicka is speaking for himself here or summarizing the view of another writer. I have interpreted him as speaking for himself.
68. Seyla Benhabib criticizes Kymlicka on similar grounds, rejecting first the very coherence of the notion of societal cultures, and complaining second that "The goal of any policy for the preservation of cultures must be the empowerment of the members of cultural groups to appropriate, enrich, continue as well as subvert the terms of their own cultures. The right to cultural membership entails the right to say 'no' to the various cultural offers made to one by one's upbringing, one's nation, one's religious or familial community. The exercise of autonomy is inconceivable if it does not only entail cultural reproduction but also cultural struggle and rejection, through which the old is transformed and new cultural horizons are articulated" (Benhabib, "The Liberal Imagination and the Four Dogmas of Multiculturalism", *Yale Journal of Criticism*, 12(2) (1999), 406–7).
69. It is important to emphasize here that even the most capacious societal cultures also constrain. This is true not just as a hermeneutical insight, but also as a reflection of the history of intolerance and discrimination in even egalitarian and liberal societies. Take, for example, the position of homosexuals or disabled persons in the United States. The point is that promoting liberal forms of education is not something that liberal states should do just for cultural minorities; it is something the liberal state needs to promote for itself.
70. Another way of describing the normative space in which members of cultural groups live is to say that cultural groups provide for their members a nomos. See Shachar, "On Citizenship and Multicultural Vulnerability", citing Robert Cover and Abner Greene, 65.
71. *Multicultural Citizenship*, 88.
72. See Waldron, "Minority Cultures and the Cosmopolitan Alternative" and Waldron's essay in Chapter 1 of this volume.
73. *Multicultural Citizenship*, 81.
74. Martha Nussbaum provides a host of examples about how this might happen. She writes, for instance, of the importance of studying human sexuality in Ancient Greece, where gender norms were very different from those common today. When we do so, "we begin to see our own norms and practices as ours

rather than as universal and necessary. In that way we learn something about ourselves and the choices our history and culture have made. We also begin to ask questions that we did not ask before, such as whether we have good reasons for the distinctions and judgments we make.... Cross-cultural history, by showing us the variety of norms that have been endorsed by a species sharing a common biological heritage, prepares us to inquire further into the morality of our own sexual choices", *Cultivating Humanity: A Classical Defense of Reform in Liberal Education* (Cambridge, MA: Harvard University Press, 1997), 237.

75. *Multicultural Citizenship*, 81.
76. Although my argument here has emphasized the centrality of choice making and the possibility of revising one's conception of the good, I want to make clear that a defensible conception of autonomy should not over-valorize the availability of options in one's life, as if autonomy were discernible to the extent that a person "chose" his or her ends from a menu of diverse choices. I would fully endorse Eamonn Callan's claim that liberals should pay attention as much to autonomous adherence to the good as to autonomous revision of the good. That is to say, an autonomous character is marked by the manner in which a person cleaves to the good, not by whether a person chose this good from an array of life options. See Callan's "Autonomy, Child-Rearing, and Good Lives" in David Archard and Colin Macleod (eds), *The Political and Moral Status of Children* (Oxford: Clarendon Press, 2002).
77. I defend a conception of "minimalist autonomy", and describe the educational implications that follow from it, in *Bridging Liberalism and Multiculturalism in Education* (Chicago: University of Chicago Press, 2002).

CHAPTER 12

"Mistresses of Their Own Destiny": Group Rights, Gender, and Realistic Rights of Exit

Susan Moller Okin

Many recent arguments for rights or exemptions for religious or other cultural groups that may not themselves be liberal are based on liberal premises—whether the central liberal value be individual autonomy or tolerance for diversity of ways of life.[1] Any consistent defense of group rights or exemptions that is based on liberal premises has to ensure that at least one individual right—the right to exit one's group of origin—trumps any group right. What this entails will be explored later in the chapter but, for several reasons, the claim itself seems prima facie incontrovertible. Not to be able to leave the group in which one has been raised for an alternative mode of life is a serious violation of the kind of freedom that is basic to liberalism. Indeed, advocates of the rights of groups that do not espouse or practice liberal principles with regard to their own members frequently justify these rights provisionally: any group to which such rights are accorded must (at least) allow its members the right of exit. It seems, moreover, that any liberal defender of the rights of groups should recognize that individuals must be not only formally free, but substantively and more or less equally free, to leave their religions or cultures of origin; they must have *realistic* rights of exit.

Given this, it is surprising that so little attention has been paid in the literature about multicultural group rights to the fact that persons in different subgroups within most cultural and religious groups have very different chances of being able to exit from them successfully. As I shall argue here, in many cultural or religious groups on whose behalf liberal theorists have argued for special rights or exemptions, women are far less likely than men to be able to exercise the right of exit. They need not even be formally discriminated against in the public sphere, though they often are, for this to be so. For sex discrimination of various kinds is more likely than other forms of discrimination to occur out of public view, within the domestic sphere. Wherever it occurs, the unequal treatment of girls and women can mean, as I shall show, that by the time they reach young adulthood, in many cultures and religions they are effectively far less able to exit their respective groups of origin than are men. Any liberal group rights theorist—especially any who is concerned to defend the claims of illiberal groups to rights or exemptions—should be concerned about this inequality. For some individuals not to be able to choose an alternative mode of life, when others in the group are far more likely to be able to do so, is a serious violation of the equality of persons that is basic to liberalism.

My argument has three main parts. First, I show, looking at three examples, that liberal defenders of group rights tend not to take gender inequality as seriously as other forms of morally arbitrary inequality (e.g. such as that of race or caste) when considering group rights and the limitations that should be placed on them by anyone starting from liberal premises. Second, I specify and discuss a number of reasons that contribute to women's being, in many cultural contexts, significantly less able than men to chart their own courses of life—outside of their community of origin if they should so choose. I then return to the three theorists discussed earlier, looking at their arguments for why religious or cultural groups—whether liberal or illiberal in their internal practices—must permit their members the right to exit the group. Each of the three calls on the right of exit at least in part to lessen the effect of illiberal or oppressive internal group practices. I show, drawing on Section 12.2, that the option of exit is, in the great majority of cases concerning group rights, considerably less likely to be available to female than to male members of the group.

I conclude that the theories I examine thus contain several problematic elements. If girls and women are treated unequally in various important ways within their cultural groups, it cannot but affect their capacities to exercise the right of exit that is of crucial importance to each theory. Moreover, having an unequal capacity to exit cannot but affect women's potential to influence the directions taken by the group. Thus they have less chance of being able to change the group's norms and practices—including being able to remedy their status and to achieve gender equality within the group. To call on the right of exit as a palliative for oppression is unsatisfactory for another reason, too, for in many circumstances oppressed persons, in particular women, are not only less able to exit, but have many reasons not to *want* to exit their culture of origin. Rather, they want, and should have the right, to be treated fairly within it. Thus, I conclude, the right of exit, while no doubt important, does not have the clout it is often thought to have in arguments defending the rights of illiberal groups within liberal contexts. Instead, it is inherently problematic. Those most likely to need it are those least likely to be able to employ it. Neither may they see it as a desirable or even an imaginable option.

12.1. Gender and Other Forms of Inequality in Group Rights Theories

As I have argued elsewhere, tensions exist between the feminist project of achieving equality between the sexes and the multicultural project of recognizing minority religious or other cultural groups by granting them special group rights.[2] Both the neglect of significant groups, whose interests may differ *within* groups, and the lack of attention to the private sphere have resulted in a widespread failure to recognize that, in cases where groups with more patriarchal beliefs and practices exist as minorities within contexts that are generally less patriarchal, women may well be harmed rather than benefited by special group rights. Some defenders of group rights pay more attention to the issue of inequality between the sexes than do others. Even those—such as Will Kymlicka—who explicitly deny rights to cultural or religious groups that overtly discriminate against women are insufficiently attentive to private sphere discrimination, which often has serious impacts on women's well-being and life opportunities.[3] Not surprisingly, though, liberals who defend the right of illiberal, overtly discriminatory groups to regulate the lives of their members pose greater problems from a feminist point of view.

While working on gender issues in the context of arguments for group rights, I have noticed that discrimination against women and girls is not only overlooked or mentioned briefly, only to be passed over, in such discussions. Not infrequently, it is given special status in a negative sense—by being perceived as somehow not really discrimination or at least absolved from the scrutiny that is given to other types of discrimination. It is, of course, in one sense not surprising that gender inequality is less or differently scrutinized—even often ignored—by liberals arguing for group rights. For, as I have argued, since virtually all cultures are to some degree patriarchal, it is exceedingly difficult to reconcile the claim that women be treated equally with the practices of many religions and other cultural groups, including many of those claiming special rights. But gender inequality is nonetheless a problem that any liberal theorist needs to understand and address since, despite the common tendency to forget the fact, women *are* more than half of those individuals who constitute the world's population, and any theory based on the liberty or well-being of individuals cannot afford to ignore them, or to pay relatively little attention to discrimination against them. First, then, let us look at three examples in which discrimination between the sexes is treated less seriously than other forms of discrimination.

The first is Joseph Raz's essay, "Multiculturalism: A Liberal Perspective."[4] Raz argues for the recognition of multicultural group rights, though he does not specify clearly just which rights he would defend. He claims generally that "multiculturalism requires a society to recognize the equal standing of all the stable and viable communities in that society."[5] His argument is based on the fact of "value pluralism" in contemporary societies and, in line with his general emphasis on autonomy, on the rights of individuals to freedom and well-being or prosperity—for which he claims that "unimpeded membership in a respected and prosperous cultural group" is a prerequisite.[6] While arguing for such rights, Raz does not think that all cultural groups merit them. One dimension on which cultures can be judged for this purpose is "obvious," he says. "Some cultures repress groups of either their own members or of outsiders. Slave cultures, racially discriminatory cultures, and homophobic cultures are obvious examples." He states: "Such cultures may be supported only to the degree that it is possible to neutralize their oppressive aspects, or compensate for them . . ." (e.g. by permitting exit, which point I shall discuss below).[7]

It is striking that Raz does not include sexist or patriarchal cultures in his list. Rather, he discusses them separately. Having already mentioned the "treatment of women" as one of those reasons, along with "decadence . . . vulgarity, [and] lack of sense of humour," that make cultures in general tend to disapprove of each other, he seems already to have given it a different, less serious, valance.[8] He reintroduces it in order to illustrate the point that what is not oppressive in one context may become oppressive in another—more multicultural—one. He first says: "Set aside the various cultures which repressed women." (A feminist reader may wonder why he uses the past tense here, and may also wonder how many, and which, cultures this set aside leaves us with.) He then goes on to say: "Probably all cultures known to us, even those which did not repress women, distinguished between men and women in that a large array of social relationships, occupations, leisure activities, educational, and cultural opportunities, and the like were gender-specific." But provided such separation "does not carry with it the implication of an inferior status" and neither men's nor women's "full development and self-expression" are stunted, "there is nothing wrong with such gender-sensitive cultures so long as they succeed in socializing the young to a willing acceptance of their ways." (Again, given the first two conditions, and that gender specificity and separation are typically coupled with claims of female inferiority, one wonders which cultures he has in mind.) However, Raz goes on to say that, if transplanted to a different cultural context, in which "gender determination of opportunities" is a rarity, "the transplanted group is transformed into an oppressive one." What results in this transformation? Precisely, he says, the culture's failure to continue to be able to socialize "all its young to accept its ways and reject the ideas prevalent in the general culture." The latter's "prevailing notions of gender non-discrimination and the debate about feminism is [sic] bound to filter across the cultural barriers", affecting the minority culture's members' perceptions of their own practices, which many will come to understand "as consigning women to an inferior status."[9] The new setting can not only, according to Raz, "lead to a change in the meaning of some of its practices"; but also it can "make them oppressive."

This is a strange and unconvincing story, not only because the pervasively "gender sensitive" but acceptably egalitarian societies Raz invents bear little relation to the real world. If the practices of such hypothetical cultures did not imply female inferiority, and if indeed, as he specifies, they "provided the opportunities available to either men or women...adequate for their full development and self-expression", then why and how would the feminism and the prevailing non-discrimination of the new context cause them to be understood so differently? If they were not previously oppressive, how could the move to a new cultural context "make them oppressive?"[10] Raz's own definition of "oppression" is an objective one: he says that it is "a result of a structural feature of [a] culture which systematically frustrates the ability of people, or groups of people, to fulfill or give expression to an important aspect of their nature within that society."[11] But according to the story he tells about gender and culture, the key to what makes the previously non-oppressive practices oppressive depends on the *subjective* perceptions of its members: the young women are now unable to be successfully socialized to accept them. Would it not be truer to Raz's own definition to acknowledge that, so long as the culture existed in relative isolation, its socializing techniques prevented its people—most importantly, its young women—from perceiving the oppressiveness of oppressive practices? For if such practices come to be seen as systematically frustrating the fulfillment of an important aspect of their nature, in the new setting, how could it be that they did not do so in the old? Perhaps Raz might respond that the women's "nature" has been significantly changed, by their move to a new cultural setting. If so, however, Raz gives no account of why we should expect greater human plasticity in the case of gender than in other, seemingly similar, cases? As we saw, he is unwilling to extend the advantages of group recognition to slave cultures, racially discriminatory cultures, and homophobic cultures. Yet such cultures, too, not infrequently succeed in successfully socializing their oppressed members into not recognizing their oppression.[12] But Raz does not even raise the possibility that slave holding, racist, and homophobic cultures are not oppressive until they come to be perceived as such by their oppressed members. Women and their treatment, it seems, are different. The fact that women are successfully socialized into their various degrees of inferior status in virtually all of the world's cultures means, Raz implies, that they are less oppressed.

The second example I shall discuss of lesser scrutiny's being given to sex discrimination than to another form of discrimination—racial—occurs at a fairly pivotal point in William Galston's defense of group rights in "Two Concepts of Liberalism."[13] Galston tests his theory of "the Diversity State" which, as he has argued, should cede considerable liberty to minority cultural groups, including religious groups, that do not respect the value of individual autonomy, though they must meet certain other conditions. He tests it by considering two cases.[14] While I think the two cases are extremely similar, Galston does not. In the first, Bob Jones University sought to keep its tax-exempt status while forbidding its students from dating interracially, on religious grounds. Galston thinks, as I do, that the Supreme Court decided right in denying this request. His reasoning is that the free exercise of religion protected by the First Amendment—though it may in many conflictual cases require the non-prohibition of "conduct judged obnoxious by public principles"—does not properly extend to "associations conducting their internal affairs in a manner contrary to core public purposes", which include the government's "fundamental, overriding interest in eradicating racial discrimination."[15] In the second case, a fundamentalist religious school in Dayton, Ohio terminated the employment of a (married) pregnant teacher because of its religious belief that mothers with young children should not engage in paid work outside their homes. The Ohio Civil Rights Commission ordered full reinstatement with back pay, but its decision was reversed by a court. The Supreme Court, which Galston says "ducked the issue" of religious freedom, heard the case and reversed again, stating that "[w]e have no doubt that that the elimination of prohibited sex discrimination is a sufficiently important state interest to bring the case within the ambit of the cited authorities" and that "[e]ven religious schools cannot claim to be wholly free from some state regulation."[16] However, Galston voices disagreement with the Court in this case, unlike the other, saying: "I believe a reasonable case can be made in this instance for giving priority to free exercise claims."[17] Strangely, while he acknowledges that "the teacher unquestionably experienced serious injury through loss of employment on religious grounds",[18] Galston does not even mention sex discrimination in the context of this case. He presents the Civil Rights Commission's finding that the school had "impermissibly...discriminated on the basis of religion", without mentioning the Supreme Court's reference to sex discrimination.[19]

But surely the Dayton case is clearly no less a case of sex discrimination than the Bob Jones case is one of racial discrimination. After all, if the young teacher involved had been a man about to become a father, the school would have had no objection to his continued employment. Moreover, its policy in the actual case seems unrelated to the expected child's well-being, since leaving the mother unemployed could have undermined an intention on the part of the parents-to-be to have the father take care of the baby. As Galston says, the reason for the school's ending her contract was so that it could not only preach but also practice its "distinctive religious views" (by which he means, but does not say, its sex-discriminatory views about the roles of parents) and to disallow this would have "forced [the religious community] to conform to majoritarian beliefs and practices concerning gender."

How and why is this different from the Bob Jones University case? There, the religious institution was not, and should not have been according to Galston, permitted to enforce racial discrimination. Here, the religious institution was not, but should have been according to Galston, allowed to practice sex discrimination. Implicit in his analysis, clearly, is the belief that it is less offensive for a religion to enforce its views about sex roles than its views about race relations on its dissenting members. But he does not explain what justifies this belief. His stated reasoning on the matter is unconvincing. He argues that, since the religious community was not coextensive with the political community, the Dayton teacher had the secure and available right of exit, since she had outside of the religious community "a wide array of other employment options."[20] There are two major problems with this reasoning. First, the Bob Jones students who wanted to date interracially also had plenty of exit options, if prepared to go outside of the particular religious community. They could have opted for a non-racist religious college, of which there were surely many, or for a secular one. Yet Galston does not apply this reasoning to their case. Second, by forcing exit in the one case and not the other, he radically reduces the opportunities for change within the religion in the one case and not the other. Let us speculate that both the students at Bob Jones who wanted to date interracially and the teacher in Dayton who wanted to share the care of their baby with her husband, though in general religious fundamentalists, objected, respectively, to the racism and the sexism of their religion and aimed, by their choices, to try to initiate change within it. Galston's analysis and solution would give only the former any chance of effecting change from within.

Here, we are reminded that important aspects of exit rights reach far beyond the interests of the particular individuals involved. If the existence of such rights is held to justify oppression or the silencing of dissent within a group, on the grounds that dissenters or those who consider themselves oppressed can leave, this is likely to reinforce conservative tendencies within the group. For it clearly tends to disempower potential reformers and thus to empower those who are likely to want to preserve the group's hierarchy and prevent its beliefs and practices from changing. On the one hand, as Albert Hirschman famously argued, having the meaningful and substantive opportunity of exit is likely to enhance one's ability to exert influence on both the general direction and specific decisions taken by one's group, since one—and those like oneself—can, whether overtly or, more often, implicitly, plausibly threaten to leave.[21] On the other hand, having only the purely formal right of exit, without any real capacity to exercise it, tends to eviscerate such capacity for influence. But being subject to *involuntary* exit, in order to practice one's dissent, as the Dayton teacher was, is even worse than merely having the formal right of exit, since it utterly eliminates one's potential influence. These aspects of exit rights are clearly relevant in any analysis of group rights that is concerned with the kinds of intra-group inequalities often faced by women.

My final example of gender inequality's being taken less than seriously comes from Chandran Kukathas's arguments that any truly tolerant liberal society should leave alone religious or cultural groups to live by their own ways. (He argues that even worse forms of treatment of children than of women should be permitted, as I shall also mention.) Although not an advocate of *positive* group rights, Kukathas is the most extreme defender of tolerance for the internal practices—even extremely coercive and harmful ones—of diverse groups within liberal contexts. His position seems to have hardened over time, so that by 1997 he claimed that the tolerant liberal state was justified in interfering with almost no illiberal practices of groups within it. However, since he does not retract the positions somewhat more restrictive of group practices that he took in a 1992 paper, it seems reasonable to consider them alongside his more recent statements. In the earlier paper, Kukathas set certain limits on the practices of cultural or religious groups that should be protected against interference by the wider society. He writes: "In recognizing the right of exit, they would also have to abide by liberal norms forbidding slavery [including "voluntary slavery"] and physical coercion. More generally, they would be bound by liberal prohibitions on "cruel, inhuman or degrading treatment."[22] It is unclear just how Kukathas thinks such norms can justifiably be enforced. Does he mean, given his initial reference to the right of exit, simply that members who objected to such treatment must have the right to leave the group? Or does he mean that the liberal state can intervene so as to curtail any such group practices? He seems to mean the former only, since the passage concludes with the statement that "[c]ultural groups that persisted in violating such norms would *therefore* disappear as their dissident members exercised their enforceable claims against the community."[23] However, this is often neither a viable nor a desired option for persons treated badly by their groups; it is a particularly unfeasible route to offer to dissenting (but helpless) children; and it is, as we shall see, an option often far less available to a group's female than to its male members.

Moreover, in his more recent paper, Kukathas takes a more extreme position, arguing that a whole range of practices that "could count as intolerable" by liberal standards *should* be tolerated by liberal states. Some of the most extreme of such practices affect children of both sexes, whose parents or group Kukathas thinks should be permitted to limit their socialization so as to restrict their opportunities to prepare for life outside their group of origin, subject them to high risk initiation rites, and even to deny them conventional medical care in life-threatening situations. A number of the other practices he argues groups should be allowed to practice seriously affect girls and women. They include "denying them the right to hold property, or limiting their access to education, or 'forcing' them into unequal marriages", as well as mandatory "operations (performed with or without the fully informed consent of the subject) which are physically harmful . . . [including] clitoridectomy."[24] It is not at all easy to reconcile Kukathas's position regarding these to-be-tolerated though seemingly intolerable practices with the minimal restrictions he argued could rightly be placed on groups, in his earlier paper. If slavery—even voluntary slavery—and physical coercion are beyond the pale, then how can forcing women into unequal marriages (in which they can become quasi-slaves, including sexual slaves, of their husbands) be sanctioned? If physical coercion and cruel, inhuman, or degrading treatment are ruled out, then how can clitoridectomy (which Kukathas agrees with Amy Gutmann in calling a form of torture) be tolerated?[25] Again a double standard seems to be operating, as with the other theorists I have discussed, though here it is even more antifeminist as well as dismissive of the rights of children in some cultural groups to life and physical integrity.

12.2. Cultural Factors Affecting Women's Realistic Rights of Exit

Clearly, defenders of cultural group rights or exemptions are often relatively insensitive to issues of gender, and sometimes explicitly differentiate sex inequality from other forms of morally arbitrary inequality such as racial inequality. Not surprisingly, as we shall see, this tendency to neglect issues of gender or treat them less than seriously continues into their discussions relevant to, or their conclusions about, the issue of exit rights. However, because of the general tendency of most cultures to try to control the lives of girls and women more than those of boys and men, women's capacities to exit their cultures of origin are usually considerably more restricted than men's.[26] There are at least three major reasons this is so, which are often closely linked. I shall focus on education, practices concerning marriage and divorce, and socialization for gender roles and gender hierarchy.

In many of the world's cultures, girls receive far less education than boys. This is especially likely to be so in poorer countries, where education is not freely provided, many families cannot afford much education, and in cultural contexts where girls, but not boys, are expected to play a major role in taking care of younger siblings and performing other domestic work.[27] However, it is also the case in a few much more affluent societies, mostly Muslim ones. Factors affecting girls' educational deprivation include specific religious or other cultural beliefs that women's only significant role in life is to bear and rear children, and marital practices in which girls are married very young and/or become part of their husbands' families once married. The education of daughters, in such cases, may be considered a luxury, or even a waste of their parents' money. When only some children can stay in school, often boys are given preference. The World Bank's figures on adult illiteracy by sex and by country reveal some of the results of such practices. Illiteracy rates are much higher for women in many countries, especially poorer countries.[28] The rates of female to male illiteracy in the world's two most populous countries, China and India, in which the prevalent culture or cultures are still in their various ways highly patriarchal, are 27:10 and 62:35 per cent, respectively. Clearly, many factors, including poverty, affect women's lesser chances of becoming educated. However, cultural factors are clearly significant, since among both the poorest and the richest countries, those with highly patriarchal traditions and cultural heritages have some of the highest discrepancies between female and male literacy.

It is not only the *lack* of education that can disproportionately affect girls' future potential to exit their cultural groups of origin; what is imparted to them in the course of their education can also have far-ranging effects.[29] In the United States, fundamentalist Christians, as in the case of *Mozert* v. *Hawkins*,[30] have claimed the right, even in public schools, to shelter their children from any alternatives but enculturation into strict gender roles, claiming these as in accordance with religious truth. But for the exceptional case of *Wisconsin* v. *Yoder*, the courts have not allowed religious exemptions within public schooling. However, according to James Dwyer, approximately 1.5 million children in the United States are in private fundamentalist Christian schools and about 2.6 million are in Catholic schools. In both cases, but especially in the former (since there is great variation amongst Catholic schools, though all are ultimately accountable to a male-only hierarchy), the message often given to girls is that they are less than fully equal to boys, and that their proper role in life is to care for their families and to obey their husbands. Dwyer relates that teachers in some fundamentalist schools "openly tell their students that a woman must submit to a subordinate, obedient role in the home; if she does not, 'the doors are wide open to Satan.' "[31] That the belief in hierarchical marriage extends further than fundamentalist fringes was confirmed in June of 1998 by a vote of the leadership of the largest Protestant denomination in the United States, the Southern Baptist Convention, that wives should "graciously submit to the servant leadership of their husbands."[32] Dwyer argues strongly and persuasively that it is a violation of children's rights to subject them to this and other forms of indoctrination. But a number of liberal defenders of group rights, even though they claim that illiberal groups should be required to allow their members to exit, think that parents should be free to thus define and restrict their children's education.

Other cultural practices that can radically affect a woman's capacity to exit her culture of origin are early or involuntarily arranged marriage, and other practices that result in significant inequalities in marriage, including lesser rights to exit from a bad marriage. In many cultural groups girls are married early (sometimes even as children, though cohabitation does not usually begin until after puberty), and marriages are often arranged for them, regardless of their preferences about either the timing or the husband.[33] Commonly cited reasons for these practices are to ensure the wife's virginity at the time of marriage, to accustom her to her husband's family while she is still malleable, and, of course, to enable parents to have a very large say, if not the only say, in whom their children can marry. The frequent results of early marriage for girls include interruption of their education, very long years of childbearing with accompanying depletion of their health, and age differences between themselves and their husbands that augment the latter's already often significant power over them.[34] But in addition to this, of course, arranged and early marriages preempt young women's choices about the kinds of lives they might want to lead, including the choice to exit their cultural group. Once married within it, especially since such marriages are unequal in many ways, a woman is far more encumbered by its requirements of her than a man is, has far less power than her husband (and often his family, especially his mother) to make decisions about her life, and in most cases has little room to maneuver her destiny.[35] Uma Narayan's moving essay "Contesting Cultures" and the powerful short stories of Chitra Banerjee Divakaruni pay testimony to the burdens often borne by women expected to submit to arranged marriages and, once within them, to submit to their husbands and their husbands' families.[36]

In many of the cultures with these marriage customs, divorce is also much more difficult for a woman to attain than for her husband, and she often has far less chance of gaining custody of their children, though she has usually altered her life far more than he has for the sake of the marriage. These factors too, of course, restrain her options of exiting an unhappy or abusive relationship, let alone changing the course of her life or her cultural membership.

The overall socialization that girls undergo and the expectations placed on them in many cultures also tend to undermine their self-esteem—a necessary quality for persons to plan their own lives and pursue such plans, including, if they wish, choosing a different mode of life from into which they were born. Even in our prevalent North American culture, where most young women's opportunities are relatively expansive, eating disorders show up in far more women than men, as a symptom of self-esteem problems in a society obsessed with female beauty that is focused on thinness. In many other cultures, the more extreme and pervasive inequality between the sexes surely cannot fail to damage many women's self-esteem. One of the young Indian brides interviewed in a recent *New York Times* article explained that no woman in her family had ever called her husband by his first name, since "[f]or a wife, your husband is God."[37] And Martha Nussbaum has recently spoken and written of women in South Asia's SEWA (Self Employed Women's Association) who are so accustomed to modesty and humility that their first training in the program consists of learning to stand up, look someone in the eye, and say their names. Without a cultural context that allows one to develop a sound sense of self, it is difficult to imagine a woman's being able even to conceive of exit as an option.

Such cultural practices concerning girls and women affect the relationship between gender, group rights, and the realistic capacity for exit in the context of a number of liberal states. In multicultural liberal states where group rights exist, sexist biases within the various cultures can seriously affect girls' and young women's access to education, choices about and status within marriage, and socialization for subordinate status. In the case of India, the existence of "communalism", in particular, the rights of the country's various religious groups to rule their members entirely in the realm of personal law—which regulates such crucial matters as marriage, divorce, child custody, and inheritance—is clearly detrimental to women's status, including their opportunities to be educated.[38] Many aspects of the religious group rights system in India, and the custom of arranged marriage, certainly make it even more difficult for women than it is for men to exercise the right to exit the religious group into which they were born, should they want to do so, or even be able to conceive of doing so.

In the context of liberal states whose majority cultures are less patriarchal than those of most immigrant groups and other indigenous ethnic or religious groups that are actual or potential claimants of group rights, such rights would be likely to affect adversely the education and the marriages of girls, as well as other important aspects of their lives relevant to this discussion. In many of the cultural groups that now form significant minorities in the United States, Canada, and Europe, families place their daughters under significantly greater constraints than their sons. A recent study by Laurie Olsen of first-generation immigrant adolescents in an urban California high school focuses particularly on the experiences of the young women. Olsen shows that, even in the absence of group rights, tight controls are often exerted on them. The young women are expected, far more than the young men, to perpetuate their parents' cultures—thus being expected to negotiate their way between that and the surrounding US culture, often at considerable cost to themselves. Like the boys, they go through the traumas of being different and of having to learn English as fast as possible. Like the boys, too, they often experience racism and exclusionary treatment from the majority culture. But unlike the boys, they carry the added burdens of both the patriarchal attitudes of their own cultures and the expectation that they are responsible for the preservation of these cultures. As Olsen writes:

[T]he Vietnamese or Chinese girls handle the dilemmas differently from Mexican Catholic girls, and the young Hindu and Muslim women still differently. Meanwhile, each hears the clock ticking in terms of cultural expectations about marriage, having children, and assuming female roles. The young women are unsure if or when their parents will expect, allow, or arrange their marriages, require help in assuming responsibility for siblings or arrange to send them back to their homeland to help with family responsibilities there or to begin a process of traditional marriage.[39]

Clearly, the girls—unlike their brothers—are very rarely allowed to decide how to combine the surrounding majority culture with their own culture of origin, or to choose between the two. They are expected to maintain and to reproduce in their own marriages and children their original cultural identity. To this end, their parents frequently restrict or dictate their mode of dress, their participation in extracurricular and social activities, and their choices of further education, future employment, time of marriage, and, in some cultural groups, not only the ethnicity of their husband but their actual husband. Many spoke of marriage within their cultures as "a state of isolation and constriction", and they feared they might be assigned to husbands who would control them strictly or even abuse them. It was largely in order to prevent such power imbalances in marriage that they were concerned to further their educations and gain employment skills.

For those who want to become "American" the constraints can be harsh, and Olsen was told by some that they often lie to their parents, risking severe penalties if found out. But many, not surprisingly, are extremely attached to their cultures and religions, as well as to their families. They chafe against, and are sometimes severely distressed by, the restrictions placed on their lives, but are very far from considering the option of leaving their cultural or religious group. The words of a seventeen and a half year old Indian student from Fiji capture the dilemma such young women face. Suddenly faced with a coerced marriage that would not allow her to graduate high school, she said: "I don't know what to do now. My dreams and plans are all messed up.... I am tormented." But when a teacher suggest that she need not, perhaps, go through with the marriage, she responded indignantly: "In our religion, we have to think of our parents first. It would kill them if I ran away or disobeyed them.... For me, I couldn't marry someone who wasn't a Muslim. I will do it the Muslim way. And I would never go against my parents!"[40] A young woman like this has a formal right of exit, since as a resident of the United States she could legally change her religion. So also could she appeal to the law in order to prevent the unwanted marriage. But clearly neither of these options is thinkable to her for, given the manner in which she has been raised, by doing either she would lose much of what she most values in life. As we shall see, theorists who look to exit rights in order to counterbalance or mitigate discrimination or oppression within groups do not often seem to consider the depth of acquired cultural attachments, which can render the exit option not merely undesirable, but unthinkable.

12.3. Rights of Exit and Realistic Rights of Exit for Women

All liberal defenders of group rights, as I have mentioned, insist that such rights cannot be justified unless individuals have the right to exit their cultures or religions of origin. Those who reject the centrality of individual freedom or autonomy in favor of toleration, and are more concerned that the state not interfere with the internal lives of groups than that groups not restrict their own members' beliefs or behavior, nevertheless express the view that individuals must have the right of exit.[41] Disagreement does not begin until the question arises of what such a right requires, and here, as we shall see, views diverge widely. Let us now turn back to the theorists discussed above—Raz, Galston, and Kukathas—in order to examine what they say about the right of exit in the light of their own treatment of gender inequality and the points I have just made about its strong links with many cultures and religions. Specifically, I shall bring to bear on their arguments both the fact that various cultural practices concerning women are liable to effectively nullify or severely restrict their rights of exit, and the point that even a realistic right of exit is by no means always a satisfactory solution to the forms of culturally reinforced discrimination women often experience.

Raz raises the issue of the individual's right of exit from his or her cultural group explicitly in the context of groups that oppress at least some of their own members. "Such cultures", he says, "may be supported only to the degree that it is possible to neutralize their oppressive aspects, or compensate for them (e.g. by providing convenient exit from the oppressive community to members of the discriminated-against group)."[42] Later, he reinforces this connection between the likelihood of repression and the individual's right of exit, saying:

Moreover, the opportunity to exit from a group is a vital protection for those members of it who are repressed by its culture. Given that most cultures known to us are repressive to a lesser or greater degree, the opportunity of exit is of vital importance as a counter to the worry that multiculturalism encourages repressive cultures to perpetuate their ways.... [While] groups should be encouraged to change their oppressive practices...this is a very slow process. Opportunities of exit should be encouraged as a safeguard, however imperfect, for members who cannot develop and find adequate avenues for self-expression within their native culture.[43]

While Raz is clearly aware of some of the difficulties of leaving one's cultural group, he does not specify what conditions he thinks must obtain to ensure that opportunities of exit as a "viable option" are available.[44] As we have seen, however, for girls and women especially, formal rights of exit are a less than satisfactory palliative for oppression, for several reasons. First, as I pointed out above, and as Raz himself implies in his example, girls are often successfully socialized into the acceptance of practices that, in a less sexist cultural context, they would be likely to come to regard as oppressive. Second, as we have seen, many cultures are far more inclined to shortchange girls than boys educationally. But having an education that prepares one for alternative modes of life is surely an essential prerequisite for a realistic or substantive right of exit. Third, in many cultural or religious groups, families control their daughters' times of marriage and choices of husbands far more than they do their sons'. Once a young woman is married within a culture, especially if she bears children early (as is often expected of her, to prove her fertility and ensure the continuation of the male line), and especially if the terms of marriage and divorce are biased against her (as is also often the case), her capacity to exit even her marriage, let alone her cultural group, is severely restricted. Furthermore, the right of exit from one's cultural group is, surely, often not at all desired as the sole option to such modes of female deprivation or oppression. As accounts such as Olsen's make clear, young women, not surprisingly, often value their cultural and familial ties extremely highly, even though they suffer from and chafe against their oppressive aspects. Thus, for example, for an adolescent girl to be faced with the choice of either giving up her education and marrying against her will, or leaving her family and her culture of origin, may be very far from a convenient opportunity to exit. It may well be such an unbearable "choice" as to be, in practice, no choice at all.

Galston raises issues pertinent to exit early in his discussion of group rights, in the context of Justice Douglas's dissent in *Yoder*. He quotes Douglas on the right of students to be "masters of their own destiny" and also his ensuing statement that "[i]f he is harnessed to the Amish way of life by those in authority over him and if his education is truncated, his entire life may be stunted and deformed."[45] While Galston disagrees with Douglas's position, he acknowledges that there is "obviously something to Douglas's distinction between the interests and standing of parents and those of children." He continues: anyone who wishes (as Galston does) to deny Jehovah's Witnesses or Christian Scientists the right to let their children die for lack of conventional medical treatment, yet to allow the Amish to deny their children an education adequate for other ways of life "must either find some principled way of distinguishing these cases or treat them similarly."[46] While distinguishing himself from liberals primarily focused on individual autonomy, and claiming that "properly understood, liberalism is about the protection of diversity, not the valorization of choice", he aims to show that "respect for diversity, and especially group diversity, does not improperly disregard individual autonomy claims."[47] As we saw earlier, however, Galston recognizes that there can be significant tension between individual autonomy and commitment to a wide diversity of ways of life. Since "many cultures or groups do not place a high value on choice and (to say the least) do not encourage their members to exercise it" and that membership in such a group may be among "the deepest sources of...identity", throwing state power behind the promotion of individual autonomy can "weaken or undermine" such groups.[48]

Given this, however, Galston is adamant that individuals should retain the right of exit: the liberal state "must defend...the liberty not to be coerced into, or trapped within, ways of life", and must "[a]ccordingly...safeguard the ability of individuals to shift allegiances and cross boundaries."[49] As well as ensuring that groups protect human life, protect and promote the "normal development of basic capacities", and develop "social rationality (the kind of understanding needed to participate in the society, economy, and polity)" in their members, the liberal "Diversity State" Galston favors must "enforce strong prohibitions" against coerced entrance into and exit from such groups.[50] He concludes that "in circumstances of genuine pluralism, individual freedom is adequately protected by secure rights of exit coupled with the existence of a wider society open to individuals wishing to leave their groups of origin."[51]

However, Galston's defense of illiberal groups that do not value autonomy, and his position on the Dayton case in particular, are incompatible with any kind of realistic or meaningful right of exit, especially for women. Neither is the right of exit sufficient to justify the kinds of restrictions on individuals that his theory permits. He himself acknowledges that his position is "hardly unproblematic." On the one hand, there are "entrance problems", since people are born into groups which they do not choose for themselves. On the other hand there are "exit problems, especially if exit is understood substantively as well as formally." And thus Galston acknowledges, in conclusion, that a "meaningful" right of exit seems to require a number of conditions: the awareness of alternatives to one's current mode of life, the ability to assess these alternatives if one wishes, freedom from brainwashing and from other than physical forms of coercion, and the ability to participate effectively in at least some other ways of life. As he says, this protection of a meaningful right of exit "brings us back some distance toward policies more typically associated with autonomy concerns."[52]

Undoubtedly, Galston's conditions for the existence of a meaningful right of exit bring us back very far toward autonomy-based policies.[53] Moreover, the issue of sex-role indoctrination can illustrate well just how far. If parents are permitted to educate their children in sheltered settings in which they are taught by example, doctrine, and the content of their curriculum, that it is the will of an omnipotent and punitive God that women's proper role in life is to be an obedient wife and a full-time mother, how can the girls be said to be "aware of...alternatives" in any meaningful way, to be able to "assess these alternatives" (or even to think it desirable to do so), or to be able to "participate effectively" in other roles or ways of life? As I briefly indicated above, many fundamentalist religious schools and other institutions of cultural groups do socialize their children into the inevitability of sex roles and sex hierarchy, and the godlessness of any departure from them. By thus limiting their autonomy, most especially in the case of girls, they clearly do not meet the specific requirements Galston sets out for meaningful exit, without which his argument loses its claim to being liberal. Also, as I pointed out earlier, the right of exit is insufficient to justify illiberal practices, especially if it is the kind of involuntary exit that Galston does not object to in the case of the Dayton woman who wanted to continue teaching after the birth of her child. For this kind of forced exit, especially, prevents those within the group who might want to liberalize it from the inside from having any chance of doing so. Even the bare availability of exit for such practical dissenters, though, is insufficient to gain them what others may take for granted: the choice between exerting a fair share of influence within their cultural group and exiting from it if they should find any of its beliefs or practices unduly constraining. Rights of exit provide no help to women or members of other oppressed groups who are deeply attached to their cultures but not to their oppressive aspects. It is likely to be far preferable, from their point of view, to have the wider society address the discrimination they suffer from, just as it would for its other citizens.

Kukathas, who, as we saw earlier, defends the right of religious or cultural groups to be left alone even to the point of allowing children to die preventable deaths, paradoxically also claims that the members of such groups have "the inalienable right to leave—to renounce membership of—the community."[54] Later, in the context of addressing the problem of various injustices that might occur within groups, he adds: "What is crucially important here...is the extent to which the individual does enjoy a *substantial* freedom to leave."[55] The right of exit is of considerable importance in Kukathas's argument, for three reasons. First, an important basis for his argument against positive group rights is his liberal attachment to individual rights, and not to be captive in a group one wishes to leave seems fundamental among such rights. Second, like both Raz and Galston, he thinks that the right of exit mitigates the harm of group injustice or oppression. Third, unlike these other theorists, he notes that "the nature of his community is transformed" by the individual's freedom to leave, "particularly if the formal right comes with substantive opportunities."[56] Thus, implicitly, at least, he acknowledges the important relationship between exit and voice.

On the other hand though, in several ways, Kukathas both recognizes the limitations of and significantly dilutes the exit rights he insists on. First, he acknowledges (but fails to respond to) the point that the exit option is "insufficient to ensure any kind of freedom from oppression since it is precisely the most vulnerable members of such communities who would find exit most difficult and costly."[57] This is a valid and important point, which, as we have seen, is particularly pertinent to women and children in many cultural contexts. It badly needs a response. But instead, later, apparently discounting this point, he claims that if persons or subgroups who seem to be being treated unjustly by their group do not leave it, this mitigates the injustice: "If an individual continues to live in a community and according to ways that (in the judgment of the wider society) treat her unjustly, even though she is free to leave, then our concern about the injustice diminishes."[58] This, however, is one of the passages in which he stresses that the freedom to leave must be "substantial"—must have "considerable substantive bite"—and that certain conditions must hold, for this to be so. However, the only condition he mentions, which he regards as the most important, is the existence of a wider liberal society that is open to those wishing to leave their groups. For freedom of exit to be "credible", he says, there must exist, in such a society, "a considerable degree of individual independence."[59] But while Kukathas is clearly aware that substantial freedom to leave depends in part in having somewhere to go, he largely ignores another important prerequisite: that one must have to capacity to get there. Given many of the group practices Kukathas claims must be permitted by a tolerant society, it is impossible to see how some members—a child who has been allowed to die, for example—could leave; and it is hard to see how others could leave without enormous difficulty, including persons of both sexes deprived of the education required for alternative modes of life, and girls and women who had, in addition, no access to property, had undergone clitoridectomy, or had been forced into unequal marriages (especially if at an early age, without access to contraception, or with little or no possibility of initiating divorce). It is perhaps not surprising that Kukathas does not elaborate what capacities individuals must have in order to have a "substantial" right of exit, since such requirements would run into serious conflict with many of the group practices he thinks should be permitted.

12.4. Conclusion

As I have argued elsewhere, in the case of groups that have emigrated from cultures which are more patriarchal to a more liberal majority culture, as well as in other multicultural states, rights to maintain cultural practices that discriminate against women are frequently among those sought after by group leaders.[60] Raz, Galston, and Kukathas seem prepared to concede such rights to minority groups, whether immigrant or not. Each tries to mitigate the rights or exemptions by specifying that individuals must have the right of exit, but in no case is the argument convincing. Raz, to be sure, would rather the wider society successfully discourage the repressive practices of groups, but sees the right of exit as a safeguard while this lengthy process takes place. However, he neither specifies what having a realistic right of exit would entail, nor considers the substantial obstacles that are likely to impede women's exit from such groups. Galston clearly does not put overt sex discrimination in the same serious category as overt racial discrimination, the elimination of which he does think overrides group rights. It is fine with him, apparently, if girls in Christian schools learn from who is and who is not allowed to teach them, as well as from what they are directly taught in class, that it is divinely ordained that the mothers of young children should not be employed outside of the home. But this runs directly contrary to his stated requirements for a person's having a "meaningful right of exit." And Kukathas thinks that groups should be allowed, within tolerant liberal states, to continue even practices that harm or restrict women (as well as children) seriously, as he has recently made clear. He too states that persons must have "substantial" rights of exit from such groups, but the only condition he specifies is the existence of a wider liberal society that is willing to take them in. He takes no account of the extent to which many of the practices he advocates permitting groups to practice would make some of their members' exercise of their exit options extremely difficult or even impossible.

In proposing that the right to exit one's cultural or religious group of origin somehow makes the repressive practices of some such groups more tolerable to liberals, the three theorists whose arguments I have discussed seem insufficiently aware of the impossible position this is bound to put some persons in. To be sure, Kukathas mentions, though he does not respond to, the objection that often the most repressed are the least able to exit. Neither Raz nor Galston even mentions this relevant fact. And none of the three takes seriously enough the problem that, even if it were feasible or even possible in a practical sense, exit may not be an option at all desirable, or even thinkable, to those most in need of it. But this is not infrequently the case, which partly explains why women put up with some of the practices they do. Only by neglecting such pertinent facts could one argue, in the name of tolerance or in the name of individual freedom and well-being, for group rights that might give no recourse at all to a seventeen year old girl forced to choose between not finishing high school in order to marry a virtual stranger and losing her ties with not only her family but also her religion. What kind of a choice is one between total submission and total alienation from the person she understands herself to be? Is this a choice that a group within a liberal state should place some of its members in the position of having to make? The liberal state, I conclude, should not only not give special rights or exemptions to cultural and religious groups that discriminate against or oppress women. It should also enforce individual rights against such groups when the opportunity arises, and encourage all groups within its borders to cease such practices.[61] Not to do so, from the point of view of a liberal who takes women's, children's, and other potentially vulnerable persons' rights seriously, is to let toleration for diversity run amok.

NOTES

I would like to thank Rob Reich, as well as various participants at the Montreal Conference on Citizenship and Education, June 2000, for their helpful comments on an earlier version of this chapter. This chapter has previously been published in *Ethics* 112 (January 2002): 205–30, © University of Chicago Press, 2002, reproduced by kind permission.

Justice William Douglas wrote: "If a parent keep his child out of school beyond the grade school, then the child will be forever barred from entry into the new and amazing world of diversity that we have today. The child may decide that that is the preferred course, or he may rebel. It is the student's judgment, not his parents', that is to be essential if we are to give full meaning to the Bill of Rights and of the right of students to be masters of their own destiny. If he is harnessed to the Amish way of life by those in authority over him and if his education is truncated, his entire life may be stunted and deformed." (*Wisconsin* v. *Yoder*, 406 U.S. 245–46, Justice

Douglas dissenting.) Converting the phrase into "mistresses of their own destiny" has an unavoidable irony, since there is no apparent way of making it apply specifically to young women without using a word that both has sexual connotations and makes reference to them in relation to men.

1. The autonomy-based argument I focus on here is that of Joseph Raz in "Multiculturalism: A Liberal Perspective" in *Ethics in the Public Domain* (Oxford: Clarendon Press, 1994), 155–76; those based on tolerance for diversity are that of William Galston, in "Two Concepts of Liberalism", *Ethics*, 105(3) (1995), 516–34, and that of Chandran Kukathas, in "Are There Any Cultural Rights?", *Political Theory*, 20(3) (1992), 105–39 and "Cultural Toleration" in Ian Shapiro and Will Kymlicka (eds), *Ethnicity and Group Rights*, Nomos XXXIX (New York: New York University Press, 1997), 69–104. Subsequent references to the first two essays will be to "Raz" and "Galston" respectively, and those to Kukathas's will be indicated by the brief titles "Cultural Rights?" and "Cultural Toleration."

2. Okin, "Is Multiculturalism Bad for Women?" *The Boston Review*, XXII(5) (1997), 25–8, and "Feminism and Multiculturalism: Some Tensions", *Ethics*, 108(4) (1998), 661–84. The former, with comments by twelve scholars and a response by me, was subsequently published as Joshua Cohen, Martha Nussbaum, and Matthew Howard (eds), *Is Multiculturalism Bad for Women?* (Princeton: Princeton University Press, 1999). See also the rich and interesting discussions in Ayelet Shachar, "Group Identity and Women's Rights in Family Law: The Perils of Multicultural Accommodation", *Journal of Political Philosophy*, 6 (1998), 285–305 and "On Citizenship and Multicultural Vulnerability", *Political Theory*, 28(1) (2000), 64–89. Shachar and I discern similar tensions between the goals of multiculturalism and women's equality, attribute them to similar causes, and propose similar ways to lessen them, but she presents my position as problematic and unacceptable to her (e.g. cf. "Feminism and Multiculturalism" and "On Citizenship"; but see n. 48, p. 86 of the latter).

3. Will Kymlicka, *Liberalism, Community, and Culture* (Oxford: Clarendon, 1989) and *Multicultural Citizenship: A Liberal Theory of Minority Rights* (Oxford: Oxford University Press, 1995).

4. Raz, "Multiculturalism..."

5. Ibid., 159. This requirement is rather vague. What would it mean, for example, to give a group whose membership numbered in the hundreds "equal standing" with one whose membership numbered in the tens of millions?

6. For his arguments about autonomy, see Raz, *The Morality of Freedom* (Oxford: Clarendon Press, 1986), passim but esp. ch. 14. The quotation is from Raz, "Multiculturalism", 169.

7. Ibid., 169.

8. Ibid., 179.

9. Ibid., 171.

10. I do not mean here to deny that a new social context can make some of a cultural group's practices worse for women. This has clearly been the case for immigrant women in polygynous marriages now living in France. As some said when interviewed, what was a barely tolerable institution in their North African countries of origin is an unbearable imposition in the French context. However, the main reason for this was clearly the change in living conditions: whereas in Africa, each wife had her own hut, and some privacy, living in a French apartment designed for a nuclear family made polygynous marriage in practice much worse. It was clearly by no means principally a change in the

women's *perception* of the practice. *International Herald Tribune*, 2(2) (1996), News Section.

11. Raz, "Multiculturalism", 169.
12. See, for example, Elinor Burkett, "God Created me to be a Slave", *New York Times Magazine*, (12 Oct. 1997), 56–60.
13. Galston, "Two Concepts of Liberalsm."
14. Though he briefly mentions several other cases, he gives little indication of his views about them, except to note of the earlier race cases, but not the more recent gender ones, that they "have significantly reshaped our understanding" (Ibid., 531).
15. Ibid., 532. The second quotation is from *Bob Jones University* v. *United States*, 461 U.S. 574 (1983), at 604.
16. Ibid., 533; *Ohio Civil Rights Commission* v. *Dayton Schools*, 477 U.S. 619 (1986), at 628.
17. Ibid., 533.
18. Ibid., 532.
19. Ibid., 532.
20. Ibid., 533.
21. See Albert O. Hirschman, *Exit, Voice, and Loyalty: Reponses to Declines in Firms, Organizations, and States* (Cambridge: Harvard University Press, 1970).
22. Kukathas, "Cultural Rights?", 128 (see note 1 above).
23. Ibid., 128 (emphasis added).
24. Kukathas, "Cultural Toleration", 70.
25. Ibid., 88, citing Gutmann, "The Challenge of Multiculturalism in Political Ethics", *Philosophy and Public Affairs*, (1993), 171–206, 116.
26. For more detail on cultural controls on women, see Okin, "Feminism and Multiculturalism", esp. 667–70 and references, esp.n. 17; also *Is Multiculturalism Bad for Women?* passim.
27. In many cases, the costs and unavailability of education have risen due to the Structural Adjustment policies enforced on indebted countries since the 1970s by the World Bank and the IMF. It is well documented that this and other cuts in social spending have had considerably worse impacts on women and girls in these countries than on men and boys. See, for example, Haleh Afshar and Carolynne Dennis (eds), *Women and Adjustment Policies in the Third World* (New York: St. Martin's Press, 1992); Mariarosa Dalla Costa and Giovanna F. Dalla Costa (eds), *Paying the Price: Women and the Politics of International Economic Strategy* (London: Zed Books, 1995).
28. Of the forty poorest countries for which data is available for 1995, the illiteracy rates for women are non-trivially higher—in most cases much higher—than those of men in all but three. In nineteen cases—India, Pakistan, and sixteen African countries—the illiteracy rates for women are between 150 and 200% of men's, and in four others—Tanzania, Zambia, Cambodia, and China—they are more than twice as high. In the lower middle and middle income economies, the discrepancies between the sexes are still high. In only seven out of the twenty-six such countries with data available are the figures equal or almost so; in ten the rate of women's illiteracy is between 150 and 200% of men's; in four it is between twice and three times as high; and in another three it is three times as high or more. Of the last seven countries, four are predominantly Muslim. In the upper middle and high income countries, where illiteracy is in general much lower, for obvious reasons, there are still wide discrepancies between the sexes in a few countries where it is high, most notably Saudi Arabia, Malaysia, and Gabon, but much less discrepancy in

others where it is also quite high, including the most affluent Muslim countries, Kuwait and United Arab Emirates. *Human Development Report* (Oxford: Oxford University Press, for The World Bank, 1997), 220–1.

29. For a more general discussion of the importance of education for substantive rights of exit, see Rob Reich, *Liberalism, Multiculturalism, and Education* (Chicago: The University of Chicago Press, forthcoming, 2002).

30. *Mozert* v. *Hawkins County Bd. of Education*, 827 F.2d 1058 (6th Cir. 1987).

31. James G. Dwyer, *Religious Schools* v. *Children's Rights* (Ithaca, NY: Cornell University Press, 1998), 26.

32. *The New York Times*, June 1998.

33. In a recent *New York Times* story about Indians in the United States who practice arranged marriage, it was fairly evident that the men involved had more choice about the marriage's being arranged for them, about the marital partner, and about the timing. One twenty year old woman, a student at Barnard—who had obviously put much effort into her education—clearly did not want to terminate her education, as she was being required to do by her parents, but she saw herself as having no choice. She said: "I wish it didn't have to be this way, but I can't really do anything about it." (Celia Dugger, "In India, an Arranged Marriage of Two Worlds", *New York Times*, 7(20) (1998), A1,10, and 11. The quotation is from p.11.)

34. Neera Kuckreja Sohoni, *The Burden of Girlhood: A Global Inquiry into the Status of Girls* (Oakland, CA: Third Party Publishing, 1995), ch. 3.

35. Another anecdote in the *New York Times*'s story is about a young, though fully adult, married woman who has to wear what her mother-in-law decrees, even while at home, and to await her mother-in-law's permission to resume her education. Dugger, "In India", A.11. See Shachar, "On Citizenship", 73–7 for discussion of how and why women are often given the role of bearers of their cultures.

36. Uma Narayan, "Contesting Cultures" in *Dislocating Cultures: Identities, Traditions, and Third World Feminisms* (Routledge: New York and London, 1997), 3–39; Chitra Banerjee Divakaruni, *Arranged Marriage* (New York: Doubleday, 1995); see also *The Mistress of Spices* (New York: Doubleday, 1997).

37. Dugger, "In India", A1.

38. Obviously, communalism in India—given the country's history of violent religious conflict—has important virtues, but these do not include the promotion of women's equality in most Indian states, with a few exceptions, such as Kerala, where women's status is notably higher than average. On the effects of religious group rights on women, see Kirti Singh, "Obstacles to Women's Rights in India" in Rebecca J. Cook (ed.), *Human Rights of Women: National and International Perspectives* (Philadelphia: University of Pennsylvania Press, 1994), 375–96, esp. 378–89.

39. Laurie Olsen, *Made in America: Immigrant Students in our Public Schools* (New York: The New Press, 1997), 124.

40. Olsen, *Made in America*, 136, 138.

41. For example, Galston, "Two Concepts...", 553–4.

42. Raz, "Multiculturalism", 184.

43. Ibid., 187.

44. Ibid., 185, 190.

45. *Wisconsin* v. *Yoder*, 406 U.S. 245–46, quoted in Galston, "Two Concepts", 517.

46. Galston, "Two Concepts", 518.

47. Ibid., 523, 518.

48. Ibid., 521–2.

49. Ibid., 522.
50. Ibid., 525, 528.
51. Ibid., 533.
52. Ibid., 534.
53. See Kimberly A. Yuracko, "Enforcing Linberalism: Liberal Responses to Illiberal Groups" in Stuart S. Nagel (ed.), *Handbook of Global Legal Policy* (New York: Marcel Dekker, 2000), 485–509, for an insightful discussion of the relationship between toleration-based and autonomy-based arguments for group rights.
54. Kukathas, "Cultural Rights?" 117.
55. Ibid., 133.
56. Ibid., 128.
57. Kukathas, "Cultural Toleration", 87. He responds to the charge that the extent of tolerance of group practices he advocates would make society into a "mosaic of tyrannies" by citing examples of the persecution of groups by the wider society and claiming that "islands of tyranny in a sea of indifference" are to be preferred to more centralized tyranny. Most of his examples, however, have little or nothing to do with the control of groups in order to protect their members; one is the twentieth century persecution of Jews, for example.
58. Kukathas, "Cultural Rights?" 133.
59. Ibid.
60. Okin, *Is Multiculturalism Bad for Women?* passim; Parekh, "Minority Practices."
61. These guidelines should, of course, apply equally to old groups as to newly arrived ones. For example, religious groups such as the Catholic Church and Orthodox Judaism should be denied tax-exempt status as long as they discriminate against women.

CHAPTER 13

Multinational Civic Education

KEVIN McDONOUGH

13.1. Introduction

The main purpose of this chapter is to develop a justification for a conception of what I shall call multinational civic education. This conception of civic education addresses the particular circumstances and problems of political stability and justice in multination states, which incorporate more than one nation within the borders of a single country—the larger, federal nation along with one or more minority national groups. Membership in each of these nations usually entails a sense of national loyalty—a particularistic attachment on the part of individuals to a group, its laws, and institutions. In most multination states, a majority of citizens identify most strongly with the federal nation, while some citizens identify most strongly with a minority nation (e.g. Québécois or Aboriginal peoples within Canada, the Catalans in Spain, the Flemish in Belgium, the Scots in the United Kingdom). As such, they often identify with the federal nation only weakly and provisionally. Sometimes these different national loyalties do not conflict and can be nicely nested together. However, conflicts can and sometimes do arise, and an adequate conception of multinational civic education needs to address problems that arise when they do.

Problems of political instability and justice in multination states are therefore unique in a couple of important ways. First, unlike civic education in most nation-states, the predicament facing multinational civic education is not that an existing, established, and robust national identity is now threatened and needs to be reinforced (and perhaps redefined) in light of new forms of diversity, for example, those that follow in the train of new patterns of immigration. Rather, in the first place, multination states typically lack a strong overlapping national identity based on mutual trust and solidarity, and there are powerful historical forces that are likely to interfere with educational attempts to create such an identity. Past attempts by the majority nation to colonize and repress minority national movements, sometimes brutally, have given rise to feelings of mutual suspicion and distrust that are now firmly imprinted on political discourse in multination states. While these feelings are perhaps understandable in light of the abysmal historical record, they now entail immense costs for social justice in multination states. Citizens from the majority national group may respond listlessly or with indifference when members of other national groups are treated unjustly. When members of minority national groups are victims of injustice within their minority national groups, they often lack confidence in the federal institutions of justice that might offer them alternative recourse. In Section 13.2 of this chapter, I suggest a way in which multinational civic education might justify the aim of promoting a shared federal identity of solidarity and justice that addresses such problems.

A second and related problem arises because minority national groups demand the right to self-government and national self-determination, and as a result the political instability of multination states is especially acute. Liberalism's commitment to tolerance and cultural respect demands that multination states accommodate the right to national self-determination for minority national groups. However, the limits of liberal tolerance and respect are tested when the minority national culture is pervasively illiberal. In this case, the illiberal culture and political principles of the minority nation conflict sharply with the liberal principles and civic culture of the federal nation. Questions arise in this context about the circumstances under which the liberal federal state may act to force illiberal minority nations to respect liberal principles, or to support efforts from within to liberalize the national culture. In Section 13.3, I justify a multinational civic educational aim of promoting cultural respect as respect for the minority national right to self-determination.

Ultimately, the conception of multinational civic education I defend in this chapter seeks to foster conditional identities at both the federal and minority national levels. The justification for promoting a shared federal civic identity depends on the need to secure conditions for justice at the federal level when members of minority national groups are subject to grievous injustices within their group, and particularly when they require recourse for justice outside of their group. This requires that members of minority national groups develop capacities and dispositions that enable them to see their minority national loyalties as conditional. The justification for cultural respect as respect for minority national self-determination depends on the need to ensure that the aim of promoting a shared federal identity does not undermine the legitimate demands of minority national groups to govern themselves. I argue that this requires an education that fosters an affirmative understanding of the conditional nature of both federal and minority national identities. In Section 13.4, I briefly outline some practical difficulties related to issues of feasibility and implementation, and argue that while there are significant obstacles to realizing multinational civic education in practice, the project is not hopeless.

Throughout the chapter I draw heavily on examples from the Canadian context in order to illuminate more general features of multinational civic education. Canadians have recently become polarized around opposing and uncompromising declarations of national identity, and many have lost faith in the ability of the federal and provincial governments cooperatively to develop a coherent and cohesive vision of the nation at all.[1] Much of this lack of confidence and incoherence arises from confusion surrounding issues related to Canada's multinational character. Some argue that the federal state has a strong obligation to accommodate minority national identities through the recognition of special rights to national self-determination and self-government, including extensive control over education and schools. Contrastingly, many others believe there is something deeply wrong with the idea that some groups should have powers of self-government that are denied to other groups. Instead, they argue that liberal commitments to equality require the federal nation to grant equal powers to all provincial and territorial governments within the federation, even though some of these governments represent groups who define themselves as distinct nations and others do not. People in this camp sometimes also regard policies that assign special recognition and rights to minority national groups as somehow demeaning to members of the rest of the nation. As one prominent Canadian recently put it: "If Quebec is a distinct society, then what are the rest of us—so much chopped liver?"[2] In any case, the result of this polarized debate is that few people are satisfied with the status quo and many are deeply confused as to what the status quo should be. The fact that constitutional issues are now largely dormant in Canadian political discourse does not necessarily reflect the emergence of a more confident, coherent, and stable sense of Canada's multinational character; and there is little understanding of how civic education should address issues of political stability, justice, and diversity when it comes to transnational relations in the multination state.

Amid the recent explosion of scholarly literature on the issue of civic education and diversity in liberal democratic societies, the question of how civic education should be specifically structured and justified in order to address issues of national stability, justice, and diversity in multination states has not received sustained critical attention. One reason for this may have to do with the shameful history of civic educational practices in multination states. To mention just one example, agents of the federal government in Canada near the turn of the twentieth century often withheld food and other necessary rations so that Indian parents would part with their children and allow them to attend industrial schools. Once under the jurisdiction of these schools, Indian children were subjected to an education that "was intended to be the culmination of an education designed to sever young Indians' connections with their ancestral culture."[3] Thus, according to Indian commissioner Hayter Reed, "every effort should be directed against anything calculated to keep fresh in the memories of children habits and associations which it is one of the main objects of industrial schools to obliterate."[4] Due in part to this history, contemporary policies of multinational civic education that seek to foster a strong sense of solidarity across national lines are likely to be condemned by many on the grounds that they are oppressive and imperialistic. Nevertheless, multination societies need to address problems of justice, political instability, and conflict that traverse national borders and, so long as they do, there are powerful reasons to seek a justification for some form of civic education that can develop capacities and dispositions citizens need in order to address these issues through common citizenship in the federal nation.

13.2. Multinational Civic Education for Shared Federal Identity

Underpinning the justification for multinational civic education that I seek to develop in this chapter is an important distinction between instrumental justifications for promoting national identities, on the one hand, and intrinsic justifications, on the other. Liberal theorists who would justify civic education's role in promoting a shared national identity do so on instrumental grounds. They argue that having a shared national identity reinforces liberal principles of justice and helps rectify injustices. For example, standing up when another's right to freedom of association or freedom of conscience is threatened often takes courage and requires sacrifice, and I am more likely to act courageously and make the required sacrifices if I see myself and others as part of a larger shared community. As Will Kymlicka puts it: "We know that people are more likely to make sacrifices for others if these others are viewed as 'one of us,' and so promoting a sense of national identity strengthens the sense of mutual obligation needed to sustain liberal justice."[5] In contrast, republican theories of citizenship and civic education assign intrinsic value to civic participation, and hence to the identity citizens share as participants in national political debate and decision making.[6] On this view, the state has good reason to tilt the playing field of civic education so that citizens will view their civic identities as intrinsically valuable components of their overall conception of the good life.[7] What matters for republicans is just that I come to see myself as a citizen of this particular territory, shared with this particular group of people and their ancestors, which provides "continuity between their own lives and the lives of their ancestors."[8] As Kymlicka points out, an intrinsic civic identity expresses something like the "essential nature" of a people; and the identity matters for its own sake, regardless of the ways in which it might breach the requirements of liberal justice.

These two views are not strictly incompatible because there is no obvious reason that there cannot be intrinsic value to civic participation in liberal-civic nations. Some liberal citizens may see their identity as civic participants as valuable for its own sake, while also recognizing that liberal principles set important limits to the ways in which shared civic identity can be promoted or pursued. Notably, contemporary republican theorists do not express (at least explicitly) a taste for promoting intrinsically valuable civic identities even when doing so comes at the expense of liberal justice. Rather, they tend to frame their arguments for republican citizenship in ways that implicitly or explicitly acknowledge liberal constraints on promoting republican civic identities. For example, Kymlicka points out that Michael Sandel's recent defense of republican citizenship does not contain a single instance in which he approves of promoting civic identities when doing so comes at the expense of liberal justice.[9] I could find no such cases in David Miller's or Richard Dagger's recent defenses of republican civic virtue either.[10] In any case, neither Miller nor Sandel provide arguments to defend such measures, while Dagger explicitly defends liberal constraints on the promotion of republican civic virtues.[11] When Miller does criticize liberal theories of citizenship he presents his argument for republican citizenship in opposition to a "purely political" view of liberal citizenship, in which citizens are bound together solely by their allegiance to liberal principles of justice.[12] Similarly, Miller contrasts his republican conception of national identity, which is "committed to non-neutrality where the national culture itself is at stake" in contrast to a liberal view that is committed to a policy of "cultural neutrality."[13] However, no such contrast exists when these two considerations are applied to the liberal-instrumentalist view, because that view is committed neither to cultural neutrality nor to promoting civic bonds based solely on shared principles. Rather, it advocates promoting a shared, non-neutral civic identity whose value is judged ultimately by how well it serves liberal principles of justice, not by how much it promotes republican political participation. The point I want to emphasize, therefore, is that there are good reasons to believe that there is considerable overlap between contemporary republican and liberal-instrumentalist justifications for promoting shared civic identities.[14]

Nevertheless, it makes an important difference whether the civic educational aim of promoting an overarching national identity is justified on instrumental or intrinsic grounds. In multination states, people can presumably engage in intrinsically valuable projects of political deliberation both at the level of the minority nation and at that of the federal nation. To this extent, the republican model can be coherently applied to multinational civic education. However, in some cases national identities at the minority and federal level conflict, and the idea of an intrinsically valuable civic identity cannot by itself tell us how to resolve such conflicts. If both federal and minority nations promote intrinsically valuable identities, the notion of an intrinsic national identity provides no way of determining the limits to the ways in which a federal civic identity can be promoted in multination states. For example, sometimes the best or most efficient way of promoting intrinsic civic identities at the federal level may involve undermining and even destroying minority national identities. I mentioned one such example of Canadian educational attempts to "obliterate" the ancestral identities of Indian children by assimilating them to the cultural habits and associations of the dominant national culture. Kymlicka cites the example of colonialist project of conquering, displacing, and colonizing American Indians by westward expansion in the United States. He also points out that governments sometimes invent threats (e.g. illegal immigrants, gays and lesbians, drug users, terrorists) in order to promote civic participation.[15] The more general problem these examples are meant to illustrate is that when national identities conflict, sometimes promoting intrinsically valuable activities of civic participation at one level entails imposing injustice, either within the nation itself or upon another nation. Consequently, when conflicts arise between different intrinsically valuable civic identities, we need some way of evaluating such conflicts and determining how they are best resolved.

The liberal instrumentalist justification suggests an argument for multinational civic education that addresses the problem of conflicting federal and minority national identities, which, given the overlap between liberal and republican views noted above, should be attractive both to liberals and to republican theorists with liberal scruples. That argument is that multinational civic education should seek to promote a shared civic identity so long as doing so respects core liberal commitments such as freedom of conscience, association, and expression. This argument is perhaps more complex than it initially appears to be. I now want to examine this complexity by looking at some not so obvious difficulties in establishing a credible justification for civic educational policies aimed at promoting civic solidarity in multination states.

Liberal civic education seeks to foster a range of virtues and attitudes that demand critical self-examination in deliberating with others on issues of significance to the nation. Furthermore, the civic educational project of fostering a shared, federal civic identity is likely to have significant "spillover" effects on other spheres of life. Stephen Macedo points out that liberal civic education has the effect of "promoting certain broad patterns of life" that are likely to powerfully influence (some would say manipulate) the way in which individuals understand and orient themselves to the minority nation as well.[16] Thus, even if a theory of civic education is carefully circumscribed to foster such patterns only with respect to issues directly relevant to issues of political debate and justice at the level of federal citizenship, any competent execution of that theory will effect that spillover and potentially undermine or threaten minority national cultures. These effects need not be undesirable. Some cultures may be so pervasively indecent and unjust that they are worthy of being undermined. In this case, it may be best to educate citizens for solidarity and justice at the federal level even if this undermines the minority nation. But in many cases minority national cultures, including illiberal ones, can and do provide a variety of substantial benefits to individual members who value their national identity. Nationalist education within the minority group may seek to ensure that these benefits are available for future members of the group by reinforcing and strengthening the loyalty members feel toward the nation, its institutions, and its traditions. If these groups are culturally illiberal, they may be deplored from a liberal point of view. However, given the benefits that illiberal national cultures provide for their members, enforcing any conception of civic education that may undermine or radically transform another culture cannot be undertaken lightly or recklessly.

A further difficulty in establishing an instrumental justification promoting federal loyalties through civic education involves recognizing that minority national groups have a right to national self-determination, and the project of national self-determination cannot be realized in practice unless a group has a significant degree of self-government. For example, national cultures almost always have a public dimension that is expressed, for example, in the way a particular group understands its relationship to the landscape, its distinctive art forms, architecture, and, notably, the content of national education. Furthermore, as David Miller points out, in order for these aspects of a national culture to flourish, they must be subject to a significant degree of collective control.[17] This is probably particularly true of minority national cultures that are always vulnerable to the greater power of the dominant majority culture of the larger multination state within which it resides. If cultural expressions are completely left to the whims of competitive markets, especially in this context, it is perhaps especially likely that the national culture will be overwhelmed and taken over to a large extent by the more inexpensive cultural products of large scale, mass market economies.[18] As Miller says, under these conditions, "national cultures can decay without anybody intending that this should happen."[19] The best, and perhaps only, way in which this sort of cultural decay can be prevented, or at least the best possible way of safeguarding minority national cultures against the corrosive effects of mass global culture on minority national groups, is to give control of it to those who share it.[20]

Thus, proponents of such multinational civic education must be able to tell a realistic and convincing story about the substantial benefits civic educational policies aimed at promoting a federal identity can promise, and why these benefits outweigh those offered by the existing national culture. Furthermore, the story must include an account of how these benefits can be promoted in ways that respect what is legitimate in minority national groups' demands for the right to national self-determination and self-government. To the extent that such a story can be told, multinational civic education is justi-fied in educating for loyalty to the federal nation. However, I have suggested that in some cases it will be possible to develop such argu-ments, but in other cases it will not. In some cases, the best available arguments will tell us that policies of civic education aimed at fos-tering loyalty to the federal nation will backfire, with profoundly illiberal consequences. Or they may be able to determine only tentat-ive or minor achievements for liberal principles at the federal level. To this extent, attempts to justify civic education at the federal level on liberal grounds will be correspondingly unimpressive, and will instead smack of the sort of cultural arrogance and insensitivity that has often characterized the history of relations between federal and minority nations in multination states. It does not follow from this point that liberal—instrumental arguments must fail to provide an adequate justification for multinational civic education's role in pro-moting federal civic loyalties. However, it does require that the best arguments will justify only a conditional and provisional role for civic education in promoting federal civic loyalties.

This argument for a "conditionalist" conception of multinational civic education obviously stands in need of further justification and, in the remainder of this section, I develop in more detail the argument for a conditionalist conception of multinational civic education. A conditionalist view says that multinational civic education can foster a shared civic identity at the federal level, and it can teach that cit-izens are sometimes obliged to give priority to their loyalty of the fed-eral nation. However, it cannot teach that members of minority nations are always obliged to do so when their national identities con-flict. In what follows, I develop this justification against the backdrop of a particular liberal objection to the conditionalist alternative.

Justifying the Conditionalist Conception of Multinational Civic Education

In order to understand the liberal objection to the conditionalist con-ception of multinational civic education, we need to take a closer look at the distinction between civic and ethnic nationalism. A famil-iar way of drawing this distinction highlights contrasting views about what gives a nation its cohesion. Accordingly, ethnic nationalism is a tribal, strongly communalist phenomenon that is thoroughly at odds with Western, liberal individualist principles. Ethnic nations seek cohesion based on shared descent and common blood, or shared reli-gion. People who share in the relevant ethnicity, race, or religion can have citizenship, while others cannot. Alternatively, civic nations seek cohesion on the basis of shared political principles, and citizenship is open in principle to anyone who wants to live within their borders, regardless of race, religion, or ethnicity, and who willingly endorses the nation's constitutional principles.

Some liberals have thought this distinction rules out the conditionalist option for multinational citizenship because they assume that minority national identities are necessarily "ethnic" nations, and any policy that accommodates minority nationalism ensures that individuals are tied to ethnically exclusive, oppressive, and freedom restricting cultures. They argue that liberal-democratic norms are not organic to, and thus cannot be effectively fostered within, many minority national cultures. As such, minority national loyalties are impervious to, and incompatible with, the teachings of liberal civic education, including respect for the values of personal autonomy, reciprocity, mutual respect, and freedom of association.

If we accept the assumption that minority nationalism is an inherently illiberal, ethnic phenomenon then the conditionalist position becomes considerably less alluring from a liberal point of view, because liberal purposes will always, or nearly always, be best served more straightforwardly, by reeducating members of minority nations so that their loyalties to the minority nation are weakened or eradicated and those to the federal nation strengthened. According to this view, civic education for loyalty to the federal nation represents the hope of individual freedom and growth, equality and cross-cultural dialogue, and peace, while education for allegiance to the minority nation represents the danger of communal oppression, nationalist violence and conflict, and cultural parochialism.[21] In what follows, I refer to this as the liberal assimilationist alternative to the conditionalist argument.

However, there is no reason to accept the assimilationist alternative because there is no reason to accept the assumption that minority nationalism is an inherently ethnic phenomenon. In fact, it is crucially important to stress that nations, including illiberal minority nations, have a civic dimension.[22] For example, minority national groups like the Québécois clearly define their culture predominantly in liberal and "civic" terms, as involving membership in a societal culture committed to liberal principles of free association, free speech, and freedom of conscience. Citizenship in these societies is open to all regardless of ethnic descent, religious belief, or race. Of course, even predominantly liberal and civic minority national cultures contain some illiberal, exclusive, and "ethnic" features. Some Quebec nationalists articulate their nationalist aspirations in "ethnic" or racial terms, employing terms such as Québécois *"pure laine"* to distinguish authentic from inauthentic Quebecers, such as ethnic immigrant groups.[23] It is worth noting that in this respect, Quebec is no different from many civic nations, such as the United States, Canada, and the United Kingdom, that contain extremist minority groups who would define the nation in racially or religiously exclusive terms. Quebec also famously legislates restrictions on freedom of association by setting up strong barriers restricting access to English language schooling within the province, and such laws may ultimately be unjustifiable from a liberal point of view. Nevertheless, it would be a serious distortion to suggest that accommodating Quebec's nationalist aspirations necessarily serves "ethnic" and pervasively illiberal purposes, simply because it incorporates certain illiberal minority groups, or because it incorporates certain laws that are suspect from a liberal point of view. In fact, the national culture of Quebec is predominantly both civic and liberal.

This example may seem falsely tendentious because many minority national groups, unlike Quebec, emphasize their cultural distinctness by explicitly rejecting Western liberal values and by defining themselves in ethnic terms. Kymlicka, for example, cites some "spokespersons" for indigenous groups who argue that liberal-democratic principles violate the "cultural integrity" of indigenous cultures.[24] However, even these minority nations may in fact be more liberal (or less illiberal) and civic than they initially appear or claim to be. For example, Kymlicka points out that minority national groups seek exemptions from the Bill of Rights in the United States or Canada's Charter of Rights not because they or their cultural traditions reject the underlying principles of human rights, but for other, less obviously illiberal, reasons. More specifically, minority national groups may seek the same rights that other, established, majority nations have to restrict the rights of outsiders to settle on tribal territories. They may do so not in order to deprive individuals of liberal rights, but because unrestricted settlement can be (and often is) used as a tool of political and cultural dominance, by ensuring that aboriginal people become a minority within their own territory.[25] Similarly, aboriginal peoples reject federal control over tribal institutions, including schools. But they need not do so because they are antipathetic to the liberal and democratic cultural values that the federal nation claims to stand for. They may do so because federal control has traditionally been a tool of colonization and imperialism— forces that aboriginal groups have resisted and in the face of which they have reasserted their independence as nations. As such, the apparent parochialism and exclusiveness of minority national groups may reflect a strategic response to issues of power and dominance that underwrite relations between federal and minority nations in multination states, and may provide little indication by itself about the extent to which a minority nation's culture and identity is in fact illiberal.[26]

As these examples illustrate, it is important to keep in mind that the terms "liberal" and "illiberal", or "civic" and "ethnic", when used as descriptors of actual national cultural groups, are not absolute, but refer to degrees of cultural openness, individual freedom and political participation, cultural pluralism, and hetero-geneity.[27] Different minority national cultures are scattered at various points along these spectra. They are not purely liberal or illiberal, ethnic or civic. Cultures are impure, complex, and fragmented when viewed from the perspective of liberal principles.[28] Once we recognize this, it becomes possible to see the demand by minority nations for the right to political autonomy and national self-determination as expressing an aspiration to create conditions of political and cultural security so that minority national groups can better determine for themselves how and on what terms to interact with the federal nation, and to enable members of the nation to better decide for themselves what elements of other cultures to incorporate into their own.[29] This may or may not be a liberal nationalist enterprise. In any case, liberals cannot simply assume beforehand that minority national cultures are illiberal, even if their own self-descriptions explicitly say so. As Kymlicka says, "the balance between liberal and illiberal strands is something that can only be determined empirically, not pre-supposed in advance."[30]

Nevertheless, suppose we can, after careful examination of the empirical evidence, be reasonably certain that a particular minority national culture is deeply illiberal. This is clearly true of some groups. These groups may have governments that have long non-democratic traditions; they may have cultural traditions that expli-citly or implicitly reject liberal commitments, for example, to gender equality. They may seek to foster a closed and exclusive culture that may restrict individual autonomy and freedom. To this extent, lib-erals have powerful reasons to undermine such loyalties. However, there are also powerful liberal reasons to restrict the extent to which the political and educational policies of the federal state can seek to undermine minority national identities. Some of these reasons become clear when we explicitly distinguish the question of determining the illiberal identity of a particular nation from the question of determining the likely consequences of educational policies that attempt to undermine or weaken that identity.

First, suppose civic educational policies aimed at promoting attachments to liberal principles and to the federal nation initiate a process of reflection that leads children from a minority national group to question the illiberal and exclusive foundations of their culture. It does not follow that this process of reflection will lead to a secure and stable identification with the liberal federal state. Part of the reason for this is that it is unlikely that there will be a ready made, secure, or stable federal cultural identity waiting to replace the former attachment to the minority national culture. To a significant extent, in fact, the prevailing culture of the federal nation likely contains substantial threads that are hostile to members of minority national groups. It may be a racist or otherwise discriminatory culture that threatens to undermine the self-respect and autonomy of members of minority national groups. At the same time, the economically more powerful and technologically advanced societal culture of the federal nation offers numerous alluring opportunities that are unavailable in the minority culture. Under these circumstances, many aboriginal children in North America will grow up with a striking sense of ambivalence toward both their traditional aboriginal identity and their emerging identification with the federal nation. On the one hand, their ancestral culture may be deeply cherished, as the culture of parents, grandparents, and other loved ones, but also carry a stigma as a culture doomed to failure in the face of the overwhelming dominance of the Western culture that underwrites the larger multinational society. On the other hand, the federal nation may be both an oppressive threat and a potentially exciting arena for growth and opportunity. In this context, it needs to be emphasized that, in multination states, the project of building loyalty to the federal nation is rarely one of strengthening an already deeply entrenched and stable common federal–national identity. It is more often a project of building a common national identity that exists only feebly and precariously. In some cases, a minority national culture may have become so degraded, and entail such atrocious injustices, that the culture may not be worth saving. Here the only option may be for the federal nation to do the best it can to promote justice by educating for a stronger national identity at the level of the federal nation. However, in other cases, it may be best from a liberal point of view to try to support efforts to strengthen children's sense of self-respect and autonomy by accommodating or even supporting efforts to reinforce the child's minority national identity, even if this means that children may be slow or unlikely to soon develop a pervasive commitment to liberal principles, and even if it comes at some expense to educational efforts to promote loyalty to the federal nation. Under these circumstances, civic educational policies that aim to promote federal loyalties, and that undermine national loyalties and attachments, must be provisional in the sense that when they are sensitive to their own potentially harmful effects, they will recognize that sometimes the project of promoting federal civic loyalties must be delayed or suitably abridged.[31]

The process of strengthening liberal federal loyalties can have a number of other illiberal consequences as well. First, attempts by a majority nation to forcibly assimilate minority nationalist groups can and does provoke conflict, sometimes violent, between majority and minority nations. Despite the best liberal intentions of liberals, assimilationist policies are likely to be resisted by members of minority nations as projects of colonization and oppression. One of the results of this is that illiberal minority national cultures become radicalized and militant, more parochial and more illiberal than they already are. Such policies can trigger dormant illiberal tendencies in the minority national culture, or stifle the development of liberal tendencies in the culture, and perhaps defuse opportunities for cooperative dialogue between the liberal federal nation and the illiberal minority nation.[32] In any case, I have argued that liberals must balance the potential harms and benefits from a liberal point of view on both sides of the equation. When they do, they cannot be presupposed in advance that the outcome of such judgment will favor policies that promote loyalty to the federal nation over policies that recommend accommodating illiberal minority national loyalties. Most importantly, I have argued, even after close examination of the best available arguments and evidence shows that a particular minority national culture is pervasively illiberal, multinational civic education may need to condition its aim of developing federal civic loyalties in ways that accommodate minority national groups and their educational aims.

There is still another crucially important consideration for which multinational civic education must account in justifying the aim of promoting federal civic loyalties. Minority national groups may reject multinational civic education by appealing to the right to national self-determination. The liberal commitment to this right is not absolute, and may be overridden in certain circumstances; but it cannot reasonably be defeated simply by the fact that civic educational policies in multination states can be credibly shown to avoid problems having to do with the problems highlighted above—the provision of conditions for self-respect and autonomy, and the threat of nationalist conflict and radicalization, etc. For the rest of this section, I further develop the justification for multinational civic education by taking up the issue of the conditions under which federal governments in multination states are justified in restricting the minority right to national self-determination, by imposing coercive measures designed to force minority national governments to respect liberal principles. In particular, I argue that such measures are justified especially when the rights of children are involved and when dissidents and reformers within the minority nation invite or demand such measures.

The Case of Lester Desjarlais

I introduce this justification by discussing a concrete example, involving the case of an aboriginal child named Lester Desjarlais. In 1992, at the age of 13, Desjarlais committed suicide at the Sandy Bay Ojibway Reserve in Manitoba, after a history of sexual and physical abuse at the hands of a series of foster parents. In the aftermath of this incident, aboriginal feminist groups strongly and successfully advocated federal government intervention into the administration of aboriginal child welfare agencies, who had mishandled the Desjarlais case and others like it. These women were concerned that Ojibway political leaders had conspired with members of the Manitoba provincial government to keep the matter secret and hence exempt from public scrutiny. They also charged that male aboriginal leaders had attempted to silence aboriginal feminists who had initiated the inquiry.[33] The report arising from the hearings over the case—known as the Giesbrecht Report after the judge who headed the inquiry— supported the feminist aboriginal groups by recommending that the federal government impose strong disciplinary measures against provincial government officials, as well as impose strong restrictions on the authority of aboriginal controlled child welfare.[34] Following the report, the leader of the Aboriginal Women's Unity Coalition strongly praised the judge's report and actions, while expressing reservations at the report's recommendation that aboriginals should be excluded from membership in child welfare agencies altogether.[35] Ojibway leaders who disagreed with the report's findings reacted quite differently by warning the provincial government "not to curtail the powers of aboriginal child welfare agencies", on the grounds that "Those days of having governments impose their will on First Nations are over."[36]

This question presents a case in which the practices of a minority nation clearly violate liberal principles.[37] However, it does not automatically follow that federal governments are justified in coercively *imposing* liberal principles.[38] In *Multicultural Citizenship*, Kymlicka argues that intervention is justified only rarely, in cases of "gross and systematic violation of human rights, such as slavery or genocide or mass torture and expulsions."[39] This exacting standard would probably prohibit federal intervention in cases like that of Lester Desjarlais since the injustices at stake in that case cannot reasonably be interpreted as gross and systematic violations at the same level as slavery, genocide, or ethnic cleansing. However, Kymlicka provides no independent arguments to justify this standard for federal intervention in the affairs of minority national groups and, in any case, this standard seems arbitrary. Injustices can be gross and systematic violations of human rights even if they are less severe than those involved in slavery and genocide. Furthermore, liberal citizens have strong reasons to support intervention in the affairs of the minority nation in cases like that of Lester Desjarlais. First, even if most adults in the minority nation express a preference for living in a fully autonomous, self-governing, but pervasively abusive national culture, it hardly follows that they should be allowed to force children, who have had no say in what their national identity is or should be, to live in such a culture. Importantly, the individual rights most severely violated here are those of children and particularly their right to individual autonomy and their right to exit the group. Furthermore, there is no question of whether or not children's rights are being violated here since nothing violates a person's rights so much as the fact of being driven to suicide by pervasive abuse. Second, it is important to note that in this case some adult members of the minority nation objected so strongly to their government's countenance of pervasive child abuse that they initiated the call for federal intervention. The case for federal intervention in the affairs of a minority national group is surely especially strong when internal dissidents from the minority group in question demand it, when the injustice in question is a clear and grievous one, and when the victims are children.

Cases like that of Lester Desjarlais cannot safely be ignored by civic education in multination states. In order to see why, it is worth taking a closer look at what sort of dispositions are required in order for members of minority nations to seek assistance from the federal government in order to rectify injustices that cannot be addressed within the group itself. First of all, they can do so only if they have developed dispositions and capacities that enable them to recognize their minority national identities as at least partially contingent and conditional. However, some forms of nationalist education will seek to forge a strong loyalty to the minority nation that forestalls the development of such dispositions and capacities. Indeed, this is perhaps particularly likely within minority nations given their history of colonization and oppression. As David Miller notes, in colonial contexts, it "was not absurd for people to expect that they would have a greater sense of control over their destinies when ruled by local oligarchies than when ruled by imperial powers, even if in many cases these expectations have been frustrated."[40]

Suppose a minority national group, given its history of colonization by the majority federal nation, seeks to foster an unconditional national loyalty such that individual members come to see federal intervention as necessarily oppressive and hence never justified. The result of such an education, if it is successful, is not just that individual members will be prevented from seeking outside assistance when conditions within the nation become intolerable. It will also severely limit the capacity of individuals to exercise their right to exit the nation. Not all minority national groups will foster, or attempt to foster, such an absolute sense of allegiance, and to this extent members of the nation may develop a sufficiently contingent sense of their loyalty to the nation to meet the requirements of citizenship at the federal level. But when minority nations do foster a strong sense of national loyalty, there is a strong prima facie case for civic education at the federal level to claim a substantial role in developing at least a conditional national allegiance. In any case, if civic education in multination states cannot or does not play such a role, then the conditions under which the federal state is clearly justified in intervening in minority national affairs on behalf of members of the minority group cannot be enforced. When this happens, members of minority national groups, especially children, will be deprived of the sort of education that enables them to seek outside assistance, or to exercise their right to exit, when they are treated unjustly within the group.

At least as importantly, the Desjarlais case helps to illuminate an important role for multinational civic education for citizens of the majority federal nation. A distressing feature of the Desjarlais case is the apparent lethargy and reluctance of provincial politicians in reacting to the pervasive child abuse within the Ojibway culture. There is no way to determine the precise reasons for this reluctance in this case. However, the mere fact that it occurred raises the question of what sort of education is required in order to enable and favorably dispose citizens of the majority federal nation to support and enforce principles of justice when the need arises to support oppressed individuals and groups within minority nations. Clearly, a conception of civic education that fosters an understanding of, and appreciation for, liberal norms is part of what is needed, but it is also far from sufficient. Citizens also need to be taught how such norms should be applied in particular cases. However, in cases of national conflict, there is a great deal of indeterminacy in the application of liberal principles to particular cases. Part of the reason for this is that in multination states there is usually no stable and entrenched tradition of mutual trust and democratic cooperation involving the treatment of issues of justice across national boundaries. The lack of trust and cooperation on the part of members of previously colonized minority nations is perhaps more often recognized than the absence of trust on the part of members of the majority nation. If boundaries of minority national loyalties are perceived as invioble and absolute, then members of the majority nation will be accordingly reluctant to intervene when injustices occur within minority national groups. To the extent that citizens of the federal nation are educated to see the borders between majority and minority nations as viable only on pain of oppression, they will be disinclined to develop the sort of national solidarity that might serve justice when it is needed. Attempts to offer help or to answer pleas for assistance from members of minority nations may be avoided not because of callousness or disregard, but because there it will be difficult for well meaning citizens to imagine their possible acts of intervention as potentially aiding justice for members of minority national groups, rather than as necessarily dominating and repressing them.

It might be objected that the argument I have advanced provides no educational justification for promoting something so strong as a shared national *identity* at the federal level. So long as citizens of multination states develop a federal disposition, they will share adequate moral resources for upholding principles of justice when circumstances require it. However, this distinction between disposition and identity strikes me as a false one in this context. In particular, it strikes me as psychologically implausible in the context of multination states. Part of the reason has to do with the particular nature of political relations between minority and majority nations in multination states like Canada. Individual members of historically oppressed and colonized minority national groups may reasonably evince suspicion and distrust of federal institutions and the liberal principles they support. Nevertheless, these same institutions may be their only recourse when the institutions of the minority nation violate values and liberties they cherish. Here, obviously, I have in mind individuals such as the children and women in the Desjarlais case. In such cases, it is not clear how individuals can develop a reliable and stable federal disposition under these circumstances, given the powerful current of distrust and suspicion that characterizes political relations in multination states. Such feelings hinder the disposition to appeal for justice at the federal level, and they also powerfully inhibit members of the majority federal nation from offering help. In this case, cultivating a shared federal identity, conditional though it may be, will help to offset or reduce the force of such inhibitions that arise from mutual suspicion and distrust, even if it cannot or should not completely eliminate them. It will do so by seeking to foster a conditional but sufficiently strong affective attachment to the federal nation, such that one can feel that, when necessary, one is welcome to seek assistance when justice requires it. In this way, multinational civic education's role is to seek ways to build traditions that moderate the sense of mutual distrust that currently characterizes relations in many multination states, and that seek to develop an overlapping federal national narrative, in which members of minority nations can come to see themselves as having a voice in reshaping the existing federal liberal identity, and that their voice is welcome within the context of federal politics.

13.3. *Accommodating Illiberal Minority Nationalism*

When nationalists demand the right to self-determination they often have in mind complete autonomy and self-government, and as a result they reject any role for the federal government in matters having to do with educating members of the nation. From this perspective, the conditionalist view of multinational civic education will seem preposterous because there is no way multinational civic education can pretend to give minority nationalists everything they want, given the commitment to promoting a shared federal–civic identity based on solidarity, mutual respect, and democratic cooperation. However, in addressing the question of accommodating the right to minority national self-determination, it is important to ask not just what minority nationalists demand of the federal state. We also need to ask under what circumstances and on what grounds, if any, the state is legitimately entitled to circumscribe the scope of this right. If the best answer to this question favors an approach to multinational civic education that accommodates the demands of minority nationalists for unrestricted control over nationalist education, it will be devastating to the conditionalist argument. However, I shall argue that the best answer in fact supports a more restrictive and conditional form of accommodation for minority national groups.

One way of approaching the issue of liberal accommodations for illiberal minority national groups is by examining the notion of cultural respect that citizens owe each other in multination states. An initial argument for cultural respect says that it makes sense to respect the dominant culture of a nation, and not dissenters from it. After all, the whole point of being a dissenter is to put oneself overtly against the popular culture of one's group, and so it is foolish to show respect for a culture by privileging dissenters from it.[41] This is an admittedly fast and loose argument for cultural respect, but it is as good a place to start as any because it nicely captures the sort of strong accommodations members of many minority nations demand. It is also supported by arguments offered by some liberals in support of strong accommodations for minority national groups. For example, Yael Tamir argues that a liberal society should "place at its core a commitment to equal concern and respect for individuals, their preferences and interests . . . regardless of whether these were formed autonomously or were forced upon individuals by their culture or tradition."[42] According to Tamir, liberals should be "constantly ready to make efforts to allow members of [illiberal] cultures to retain their ways of life", even if this means enabling those groups to make sure that children in the culture are educated in ways that deny them the conditions for personal autonomy.[43] Similarly, Chandran Kukathas argues that the liberal principle of freedom of association guarantees "the wider society has no right to require particular standards or systems of education within such [illiberal] cultural groups."[44] If the prevailing culture of a minority nation rejects any form of civic education that educates for civic solidarity at the federal level, and if minority nationalist education attempts to stifle or minimize political dissent by depriving children of the conditions for personal autonomy, or by failing to educate some of its members altogether, then cultural respect requires that the liberal state accommodate these demands, or so this liberal line of argument suggests.

The strong accommodationist position can be and is challenged on a number of grounds from a liberal point of view. For example,

Kymlicka argues that liberal conceptions of tolerance and freedom of association are shot through with commitments to personal autonomy,[45] and so these principles cannot be employed to justify accommodation of illiberal groups that prevent children from developing a capacity for personal autonomy.[46] In a similar vein, others have argued that strong accommodationist arguments betray the very principle of freedom of association that is supposed to guarantee accommodation to illiberal groups, because those groups fail to provide the conditions for a substantial right of exit from the group by denying the conditions of personal autonomy to children and other group members.[47] I think these objections are devastating to the accommodationist position. However, they do not address what is distinctive about accommodating minority national groups as opposed to other minority ethnic, religious, or cultural groups. Rather than pursue these objections further, I want to develop a different but related objection, namely that the strong accommodationist argument turns on a morally dubious interpretation of cultural respect. In particular, I shall argue that it provides a strikingly distorted and morally corrupt foundation for the civic virtue of cultural respect, and hence for civic education, in multination states.

Cultural Respect

Imagine, first, what is involved in showing respect for another. Bernard Williams has said that respect involves an "effort at identification" that we owe other people. According to Williams, in making this effort, another person "should not be regarded as the surface to which a certain label can be applied, but one should try to see the world (including the label) from his point of view."[48] We can plausibly assume that most members of minority national groups have a self-understanding that is deeply rooted in a sense of loyalty and affiliation with their own particular nation. For example, they will see themselves primarily as Quebecers or Cree or Ojibway. These labels matter for many people, but at a deeper level of self-understanding they do not necessarily matter to everyone in the same way. In general, some individuals will express their national identity through loyalty to the dominant culture of the nation, while others will express their identity by dissenting from the dominant culture. What is important here is that in asking what is involved in cultural respect, we need to ask not just how respect can be given to individuals as members of national cultures, but how respect can be given to individuals who cherish their national identities in different and sometimes divergent ways.

The example of the American abolitionist movement is instructive here. Abolitionists argued that American principles of freedom and equality actually oppose the dominant cultural practice of slavery. In doing so, they were explicitly setting themselves against the racially exclusive popular culture, and arguably the national culture, of America in the early 1800s, since slavery was not banned even in all the northeastern states until the first or second decade of the nineteenth century. Abolitionists were engaged in a civic national debate that aimed to transform the prevailing culture so that it could become more closely aligned with, and supportive of, what they took to be the nation's fundamental political principles.[49] Abolitionists defied the dominant interpretations of the nation's civic principles, and expressed a national identity that challenged the prevailing national identity. However, they did so not by rejecting their national identity or by exiting the national culture. They did so by participating in the civic culture of the nation, and by supporting unorthodox interpretations of the nation's civic principles.

Now, imagine how a nineteenth century abolitionist in the United States might have responded to a Canadian who purported to show his respect by saying: "As a Canadian, I deplore the practice of slavery as a grievous violation of the principles of freedom and equality that your nation stands for. However, I am also obliged to respect you as a member of your prevailing national culture, which supports slavery." It is hard to see how most abolitionists could, upon reflection, see this as anything but a baffling expression of ignorant contempt. Eamonn Callan points out that contempt "does not always take the shape of hostility or even explicit disagreement; it can be registered in the smiling faces of those who find us perfectly agreeable but cannot or will not take seriously our own self-understanding."[50] At the very least, the expression of "respect" by my fanciful example of the Canadian certainly fails to take seriously the self-understanding of most US abolitionists, who saw themselves as American patriots, but detested the dominant culture's endorsement of slavery. Nor is the imaginary Canadian's attempt to show respect likely to do justice to the self-understanding of many non-abolitionist Americans who saw themselves as patriots engaged in a debate about the future of the nation. The same point applies to expressions of cultural respect between members of majority and minority national groups in multination states. It makes little sense to say that Canadian citizens show due respect to aboriginal feminists, such as those in the Desjarlais case, by treating them as if their identity depended upon the prevailing culture of the nation. To do so would be to treat them as if attitudes of approbation, or at least lenience, toward child abuse were central to their national identity when in fact their self-understanding of the national identity makes central the condemnation of such attitudes. In this light, expressions of "cultural respect" that recognize only the dominant culture of a nation quickly and perhaps subtly mutate into expressions of condescension by outsiders who sanguinely accept one-dimensional caricatures of another national culture.

Jeremy Waldron has pointed out the dangers of treating people as "mere artifacts of the culture...to which we think they ought to belong."[51] Given the fact that different individuals understand the meaning of their national culture and identity in radically different and conflicting ways, when we respect only the prevailing or dominant interpretations of the national identity we are treating them as "mere artifacts" of the culture, and not as individuals who have the right to voice for themselves what it means to be a member of the nation. It is foolish to say that respect involves treating another nation according to some caricaturized version of it that we outsiders have constructed or accepted, perhaps unduly influenced by the dominant representations of the culture. In short, a liberal state cannot adequately show respect for another nation just by asking about the prevailing culture of a minority national group. It also needs to ask what it might mean to respect individual members of the nation.

The distinction between cultural respect for the prevailing culture, on the one hand, and cultural respect for individuals depends on circumstances of moral pluralism, political dissent, and disagreement that do not apply when members of a nation share a robust and tightly defined cultural identity. Furthermore, the accommodationist argues that it is precisely when a tightly defined cultural identity exists that cultural respect requires respect for the prevailing culture of the nation. When members of a group, or at least members of the group who have reached the age of moral maturity, share such an identity, the identities of individuals are likely to closely coincide with the prevailing culture of the group, and so the distinction I have drawn may therefore seem fatuous from the accommodationist point of view. However, even under favorable conditions, minority groups are likely to have a difficult time promoting this sort of snug fit between individual and group identities, and minority national groups face particular difficulties in this respect. More importantly, I shall argue, there are particular considerations having to do with the right to national self-determination that vigorously mitigate the limited moral force of cultural respect for the prevailing culture of minority national groups. Thus, I shall argue that we are especially apt to be badly misled about what cultural respect entails in discussions of multinational citizenship if we confuse different versions of cultural respect.

Underwriting this argument is an appreciation of the normative relationship between the right to national self-determination and the democratic and deliberative function of the civic dimension of national cultures. David Miller notes that national identities, including minority national identities, are importantly shaped through "a complicated picture in which the ambitions and interests of particular subgroups jostle with cultural beliefs and values to create identities that are always impure when measured against the hypothetical standard of a group of people sitting down together to think out what it means to them to be Jewish or black."[52] Furthermore, national identities, in contrast for example to minority ethnic identities, are influenced in a particularly intense way by this element of impurity in the civic national culture because "they are shaped more deliberately by political discussion in the course of which, in democratic states, each smaller group can make its voice heard."[53] Thus, as Miller says, "the historical association between ideas of democracy and ideas of national self-determination is hardly accidental: only a democratic state can ensure that the self-determination we are talking about is genuinely national, as opposed to the self-determination of a class or governing clique."[54] This will seem like a patently romanticized description of the politics of minority national self-determination in actual multination states. Nevertheless, it is important to keep in mind that the purpose of drawing attention to the connection between democratic deliberation and national self-determination is not to illustrate the conditions of civic debate within actual minority national groups, but rather to clarify the normative grounds for the sort of cultural respect that is owed by members of the wider multination state to members of minority national cultures.

In order to see this more clearly, consider the fact that the democratic function of the national civic culture is often imperfectly realized in actual national groups. In some cases, democratic civic debate can be degraded when the prevailing culture of the nation is pervasively illiberal. When we view cultural respect as respect for democratic national self-determination, the putative fact that a minority nation's prevailing illiberal culture undermines the deliberative and democratic function of the national civic culture provides no support for a view of cultural respect that privileges the prevailing culture of the nation. Sharply to the contrary, a view of cultural respect that licenses the prevailing national culture clearly and powerfully threatens to undermine the nation's right to self-determination, by supporting conditions under which political and economic elites can potentially deprive the wider national population of any significant influence over national political debate.

Accuracy demands that we acknowledge the fact that cultural respect as respect for the right to national self-determination does not strictly require recognizing the democratic dimension of minority national cultures. It is at least conceivable, as Miller points out, that there are cases in which "there is indeed a genuine convergence in the aims and interests between the population at large and those making decisions on their behalf", the nation's interest in self-determination can be satisfied by non-democratic forms of governance.[55] In this case, the minority nation will be equivalent to a purely "ethnic nation" since the dominant interpretations of the national identity will be endorsed or at least accepted by all individual members of the nation. As such, it will be impossible to distinguish the civic national culture from the prevailing culture of the nation. All members of the nation will agree upon, or at least voluntarily consent to, a single dominant interpretation of the national culture. Perhaps the best a liberal state can do in such cases is as the accommodationist recommends, which is to educate citizens to show respect for other cultures by acknowledging the prevailing culture, subject to constraints having to do with cruelty, slavery, etc.

However, minority national groups rarely fit neatly into this picture of complete cultural homogeneity and political consensus. If respect for actual minority national groups is adequately attuned to a minority national culture's right to national self-determination, in most circumstances citizens must appreciate the national culture as a civic culture of democratic deliberation and disagreement about the political future of the nation and its identity. The notion of cultural respect for the right to national self-determination therefore encourages us to imagine citizens of minority national groups in a particular way, as citizens who share a civic space and national identity even when interpretations of what that identity means differs markedly among individual citizens. I now want to explore in more detail what civic education for cultural respect in multination states entails when set against this moral-cum-political background.

Multinational Civic Education, Accommodation, and Distrust

It is perhaps easiest to begin to develop this point by examining what multinational civic education entails for members of the majority federal multination state. Consider the attitudes that underwrite sentiments that members of the majority nation sometimes express when they say that the demands of minority national groups express a disdain for, or somehow humiliate, citizens of the majority nation. This is the point of the comment, quoted much earlier in this chapter, that Quebec's claim to be a distinct society implies that "the rest of us" (i.e. Canadians) are "so much chopped liver." If multinational civic education is to be capable of making headway in cementing an affirmative understanding of the minority right to national self-determination, it must certainly be able to address this sense of distrust.

Even sophisticated liberals like Kymlicka, who are keenly attuned to the politics of multination states, do not always see quite clearly enough what the moral and psychological basis for such attitudes might be. Kymlicka argues that, in Canada, members of the majority nation assume the right to national self-determination and self-government for themselves even as they deny such rights to members of minority national groups. The only way they can overlook this contradiction, he says, is by wrongly assuming that members of minority nations are "really" Canadians first and foremost, and not Québécois or aboriginal or Inuit. Thus, members of the majority nation need to appreciate the fact that members of minority national groups see their primary national identity as Québécois, aboriginal, or Inuit. Once citizens recognize this, and once they see that maintaining a national identity requires significant measures of self-government and educational policies that teach citizens to affirm the nation and its institutions, they will be able to see the ethnocentrism that underpins their rejection of rights to minority national self-determination. Recognizing this right is not a matter of complying with demands for privileged status by some citizens over others. Rather, it is a matter of granting the *same* rights of national self-government to members of all the constituent national groups that share a multination state. Once citizens appreciate the importance of the fact that members of minority national groups are the same as those of majority national groups in the relevant sense that they are members of different *national* groups, they should be able to recognize that accommodating minority nationalist demands for national self-determination "does not involve any disrespect or invidious discrimination."[55] Rather, civic education should teach that such accommodations are sometimes necessary in order to rectify and eliminate discriminatory policies that accord the right to national self-determination for one group (Canadians) but deny it to others. According to this analysis, the linchpin of multinational civic education should be the aim of fostering a greater appreciation for national diversity within the multination state. For example, children will need to learn to identify and appreciate the value and meaning of having a national identity, both for themselves and others. They will also need to grasp the ways in which sustaining a national identity depends on self-government, and how national identities differ from immigrant–ethnic identities in this respect. Understanding these ideas is important because such understanding is a precondition for superseding discriminatory attitudes and for creating dispositions and capacities of cultural respect for minority national rights in multination states.

This account strikes me as important and valuable. However, I think a better and more complete account of the kind of cultural respect that multinational civic education needs to foster needs to tell a somewhat more complex story about the sort of civic distrust to which minority nationalist demands often give rise. I have in mind an account of civic distrust that begins from the point of view that the demand for minority national self-determination looks like a self-indulgent demand to have one's cake and eat it too. The demand for minority self-government siphons the resources of the federal nation, both in terms of financial as well as social capital, for example, by relying on the sacrifices that non-aboriginal Canadians make when tax money is distributed by the federal government to pay for minority self-government. However, members of minority national groups are unwilling to repay these sacrifices by showing their allegiance and doing their fair share as Canadians first. Instead, they respond by relegating their identity as Canadians to inferior status, or by seeking to disown their affiliation with Canada altogether. Thus, from the perspective of many Canadians, the demand for minority national self-government is not merely a demand that treats some citizens more equally than others; it is a demand that seeks privileges for those who disdain their citizenship in the nation, and who wish to use the resources of the nation to create conditions by which they can reject their citizenship as soon as possible. Given this assessment of minority national demands, it is not surprising that some members of the majority nation express feelings of humiliation and resentment when such demands are made.

There is much that is wrong-headed with this story. For example, it ignores the historical debts that Canadians may owe to members of minority national groups as the result of past oppression and discrimination. It also ignores the fact that strong and securely autonomous minority national groups may make numerous and valuable contributions to the multination state. Federal support for measures that strengthen aboriginal education and health care, for example, contribute to a stronger and more just Canada as well as to a stronger minority national identity. It also ignores the fact that citizenship in the multination state has both benefits and costs for members of minority national groups that are not borne by members of the majority nation. For example, members of minority national groups inevitably give up a significant measure of political autonomy and self-government that members of the majority nation take for granted. To the extent that civic education can foster a greater appreciation for the benefits that national diversity may have for the larger multination state, and for the burdens that members of minority nations bear by virtue of their membership in the multination state, it may be able to diminish the force of some of the distrustful attitudes Canadians express when minority national groups demand special powers of self-government. However, fostering an appreciation for such points cannot be achieved simply by fostering an appreciation for national diversity within the multination state. Ultimately, it must address the ways in which Canadian attitudes of distrust and discrimination toward minority nationalists often arise from the deeply entrenched idea that citizenship in the federal nation is an all or nothing affair.

To many Canadians, the demand for minority self-government seems, at best, to reflect a half-hearted commitment to Canada, and, at worst, a purely instrumental and self-interested use of the Canadian state as a prelude to abandonment and secession. Of course, sometimes this is true and it is important to recognize this point. However, it is also important to recognize that when Canadian citizenship is presented as an all or nothing affair, the accommodations offered to minority national groups also appear halfhearted and appear to be, and often in fact have been, instruments of policy that aim to gradually assimilate members of minority national groups into the larger nation. In order to address attitudes of mutual civic distrust that emerge in this context, multinational civic education needs to foster an appreciation on the part of members of the majority nation for the conditional and partial nature of majority and minority national civic allegiances. It needs, therefore, to teach that it is possible for citizens who feel a strong and primary attachment to a minority national group need not thereby demean their attachment to the majority multination state. It also needs to foster an appreciation for the sacrifices as well as the benefits that membership in the multination state entails for members of minority national groups. Such an approach to multinational civic education thus addresses feelings of mutual distrust and suspicion by fostering a larger and more encompassing sense of multinational citizenship, which incorporates a greater sympathetic understanding of the conditional nature of both majority and minority national affiliations.

13.4. Conclusion: From Principle to Practice

So far I have justified a conditionalist conception of multinational civic education by illuminating the ways in which such an education might help to promote justice, political stability, and transnational respect. However, I have largely ignored daunting problems having to do with the feasibility of such an approach. The most obvious and important practical problems, I think, have to do with institutional design and structure. A system of common schools that houses children from a variety of national backgrounds provides the most obvious vehicle for the kind of conditional shared federal identity I have been defending, and for promoting attitudes and dispositions of transnational respect. However, it is often unfeasible and sometimes morally undesirable to develop such a system of common schools in any comprehensive way for reasons other than concerns about national identity. Part of the problem is practical. Some minority national groups are territorially concentrated in remote areas (e.g. the Inuit), and thus the possibilities for genuinely common schools are slim. But these difficulties do not always arise. In some cases, children from aboriginal groups live in close enough proximity to other Canadian children that common schooling is a possibility. However, in these cases discriminatory and racist attitudes may be an obstacle. Members of aboriginal groups may welcome children from all backgrounds into existing aboriginal schools, but find themselves rebuffed by their white neighbors.[56] Here the liberal state might play a role in helping to create conditions whereby common schools become a more attractive option for non-aboriginal citizens, for example, by providing funding for extra programs or resources. Also, Québécois schools restrict school access according to language, and hence in this way and others attempt to foster an attitude of partiality toward Quebec. However, French schools in Quebec do not exclude on the basis of ethnicity, race, etc. Common schools in Quebec are multicultural and pluralistic. Furthermore, many children from immigrant families attend French speaking schools and members of these groups are likely to have and retain affirmative attitudes toward Canada. The same is true for children of many anglophone parents who attend French schools. Thus, overall, while Quebec's system of common schools may do little to promote a shared identification with the larger multination state, they may do little to impede or destroy that identity either.

Aside from these practical difficulties, there are other, moral considerations that need to be considered in implementing a program of multinational civic education. First, common schools and a common education for a shared loyalty to the multination state may impede or weaken minority national loyalties and thus undermine the conditions for national self-determination. This may happen not because children receive an education that enables them freely to choose their culture on the basis of reason and reflection. Rather, it may happen simply because in a common school context the culture of the federal nation, or the mass global culture that has overtaken it, will overpower minority national affiliations. As such, minority national groups have good reason to worry that when young children from the group attend common schools, their national identity will be undermined even before it has been achieved. In these cases it might be possible to address such concerns through a system of separate schools that focus on establishing a commitment to the minority nation in the early years of schooling. After this, children from the minority nation may attend common schools with children from other backgrounds.[57]

Here difficulties arise because national self-determination is closely connected to self-government, including control over schooling. In federal multination states like Canada, powers of educational governance are completely decentralized so that each province controls its own schools and has its own standards for curriculum, teacher training, etc. Most of these provincially controlled education systems are not engaged in projects of provincial self-determination or in promoting a separate provincial identity. Thus, the civic and moral educational project of these schools is not inherently in tension with the project of promoting a shared federal identity. The same is not obviously true of most minority national systems of education that do seek to foster a national identity different from, and potentially in conflict with, the federal nation. Minority national groups are not likely, especially under the sort of conditions of mutual distrust I have discussed, to voluntarily adopt the aims of multinational civic education. Nor can the federal state impose such a project without risking undermining the nation's right to self-determination.

Overall, the prospects for a system of common schooling that might serve as the vehicle for multinational civic education seem dim under present circumstances. Nevertheless, this does not mean that the multinational civic educational project is hopeless or pointless. Most importantly, if members of the majority nation are educated in ways that foster forms of cultural respect that are more attuned to the rights of national minority groups, and to the benefits and burdens of multinational citizenship, then attitudes of distrust and suspicion that currently beset political relations in multination states might be moderated; and eventually new and morally more desirable attitudes and dispositions might be able to fill in the gaps.

The difficulties here are daunting, and I do not want to underestimate them. Nevertheless, I want to end by pointing out one small reason for hope. The commonly held assumption that minority nations are inherently *ethnic* nations obscures one of the reasons that multinational civic education's aim of promoting a shared federal identity is not completely hopeless. The most serious and potentially damaging feature of this assumption is that it makes it necessary to ignore the fact that, in many cases, members of minority national groups already participate to a significant extent in the Western liberal institutions, and traditions of the federal civic nation. Aboriginal and Québécois politicians are elected to the Canadian Parliament, are appointed as judges, etc. And, importantly, members of minority national groups sometimes appeal for justice to Canadian legal institutions when oppression cannot be addressed within the nation. The interactions between members of majority and minority national groups in politics, law, and civil society may not offer the same sort of educational crucible that a well functioning system of common schools might. But these are educational contexts nonetheless. If such relations are characterized by mutual respect and a concern for justice, then those values may have a better opportunity of taking root and growing into something broader and more pervasive. Such a result might be too much to hope for. However, the likelihood of this result would be increased if multinational civic education were competently implemented in common schools that serve members of the majority nation.

Multinational civic education, understood in this light, is obviously a long-term project fraught with risk and the possibility of failure. Its success must be hoped and fought for if we are to have a chance of creating just and stable multination states. However, it must also be fought for even if it is ultimately doomed to fail. The failure of multinational civic education may be ultimately substantiated by the secession of minority national groups. Nevertheless, the prospect of secession does not obviate the need for creating and sustaining virtues of transnational respect and solidarity for justice. Ultimately, a genuine commitment to multinational civic education now may be an important way of laying the groundwork for international peace and democratic cooperation in the future.

NOTES

Thanks to David Blacker, Eamonn Callan, Walter Feinberg, Rob Reich, and Meira Levinson for generous and detailed criticism of previous versions of this chapter. I gratefully acknowledge the support of the Social Sciences and Humanities Research Council of Canada for a research grant that assisted me in writing this chapter.

1. Jeremy Webber, *Reimagining Canada: Language, Community and the Canadian Constitution* (Montreal: McGill-Queen's University Press, 1994), 7.
2. Webber, *Reimagining Canada*, 199.
3. E. Brian Titley, *A Narrow Vision: Duncan Campbell Scott and the Administration of Indian Affairs in Canada* (Montreal: McGill University Press, 1986), 78.
4. Ibid., 78.
5. Blacker's point in Chapter 9 of this volume is salient here: liberal democracy cannot by itself provide the motivational roots needed to secure its own success. For Blacker, the needed roots are to be found in the particular comprehensive conceptions of the good life citizens endorse. But liberal instrumentalists follow a different path, seeking these roots at least partly in a shared national identity.
6. David Miller, *On Nationality* (Oxford: Oxford University Press), 194.
7. Ibid., 195.
8. Ibid., 184; see also Michael Sandel, *Democracy's Discontent: America in Search of a Public Philosophy* (Cambridge: Cambridge University Press, 1996).
9. Will Kymlicka, "Liberal Egalitarianism and Civic Republicanism: Friends or Enemies?" in Anita L. Allen and Milton C. Regan, Jr (eds), *Debating Democracy's Discontent* (Oxford: Oxford University Press, 1998), 141.
10. Miller, *On Nationality*. Richard Dagger, *Civic Virtues: Rights, Citizenship and Republican Liberalism* (Oxford: Oxford University Press, 1997).
11. Dagger.
12. Miller, 189. I take it he has in mind something like John Rawls's idea of a political community as a morality of association.
13. Miller, 195.
14. A further, noteworthy advantage of the liberal-instrumentalist justification is that it addresses Ken Strike's concerns about the dangers of "identity talk" in Chapter 3 of this volume. Strike's main concern is that liberal scholars often employ "identity talk" in a way that leads to a (perhaps unintentional) emphasis on communitarian concerns about group solidarity and unity, and that obscures the importance of liberal principles of justice. This emphasis is importantly mis-leading because a shared identity is oriented to a different sort of thing than are liberal principles like freedom of conscience. One seeks to reinforce a sense of one's "essential identity" with and loyalty to a particular group of people while the other protects individuals and their groups from threats to their being able to live according to their most cherished convictions. The liberal-instrumentalist justification, however, justifies shared identities precisely because a sense of

shared membership to the nation is needed to support liberal principles of justice. In contrast, republican–intrinsic justifications for promoting shared civic identities obscure the role that national loyalty plays in protecting these values, and therefore make it difficult to understand some crucially important reasons why having a shared civic identity is worthwhile. Thus, liberal principles such as freedom of association, freedom of conscience, and freedom of speech have a point that is not easily captured by talk of the intrinsic identities, but is fully and richly captured by talk of instrumental identities.

15. Will Kymlicka, *Politics in the Vernacular: Nationalism, Multiculturalism and Citizenship* (Oxford: Oxford University Press, 2001), 140–1. Here Kymlicka cites Michael Ignatieff's *Blood and Belonging: Journeys into the New Nationalism* (New York: Farrar, Strauss and Giroux, 1993), William Pfaff, *The Wrath of Nations: Civilization and the Furies of Nationalism* (New York: Simon and Schuster, 1993).
16. Stephen Macedo, *Democracy and Distrust: Civic Education in a Multicultural Democracy* (Cambridge: Harvard University Press, 2000), 179.
17. Miller, *On Nationality*, 87.
18. See Joseph Dunne's discussion of this point in Chapter 5 of this volume.
19. Miller, *On Nationality*, 87
20. Ibid., 88.
21. Something like this view seems to underlie recent analyses of nationalism by Ignatieff, in *Blood and Belonging*, Pfaff, *The Wrath of Nations*, and David Hollinger, *Postethnic America: Beyond Multiculturalism* (New York: Basic Books, 1995). Ignatieff, for example, laments the fact that minority national groups "are often more loyal to the ethnic units that compose them than to the federation and the laws that hold the state together," 243.
22. Kymlicka, *Politics in the Vernacular*, 242–8.
23. See, for example, Esther Delisle, *The Traitor and the Jew: Anti-Semitism and the Delirium of Extremist Right-Wing Nationalism in French Canada from 1929–1939* (Montreal-Toronto: Robert Davies Publishing, 1993). See also the interesting documentary film, *Je Me Souviens*, Eric Scott, Productions Quatre Jeudis.
24. Kymlicka, *Politics in the Vernacular*, 131.
25. Ibid., 74–7.
26. See, for example, Avigail Eisenberg, "Individualism and Collectivism in the Politics of Canada's North" in Joan Anderson, Avigail Eisenberg, Sherril Grace, and Veronica Strong-Boag (eds), *Painting the Maple: Essays on Race, Gender and the Construction of Canada* (Vancouver: University of British Columbia Press, 1998).
27. Ignatieff now acknowledges this point when he concedes that "no nation is ever only ethnic or civic in the principles of its cohesion." See Ignatieff, *The Rights Revolution* (Toronto: Anansi Press, 2000), 128.
28. See Jeremy Waldron's discussion in Chapter 1 of this volume.
29. Kymlicka, *Politics in the Vernacular*, 126.
30. Ibid., 246.
31. Ibid., 230–2.
32. Ibid., 248.
33. Ruth Telchroab, "Native Women, Glover Feel Vindicated: 'The Judge Saw the Truth and Had the Courage to Tackle it' ", *Winnipeg Free Press*, (5 Sep.) A10. The opposition of aboriginal leaders to the aboriginal feminists is evident in this passage from a newspaper story on the tragedy, which describes the leaders' reaction to Sandy Glover, a native child care worker who first publicly exposed

the tragedy: "Glover . . . was the target of repeated attacks by DOCFS officials during the inquest. They were angry at her because she had publicly complained that political interference had hampered child abuse investigations at the Sandy Bay Reserve."

34. Ruth Telchroab, "Province Warned Off Native Turf: Fontaine Takes Exception as Judge Urges Tighter Reign on Care Agency", *Winnipeg Free Press*, (5 Sep. 1992), A1.

35. Telchroab, "Native Women, Glover Feel Vindicated", *Winnipeg Free Press*, (5 Sep. 1992) A10.

36. Ibid.

37. I do not mean to suggest that children's rights to freedom from sexual and physical abuse can be derived only from liberal principles. Obviously, they can be derived from a wide range of decent political principles, of which liberal principles are only one set. However, here I stress the distinctive reasons that liberals might have for supporting interventionists measures.

38. Kymlicka, *Multicultural Citizenship* (Oxford: Oxford University Press, 1995), 165.

39. Ibid., 18.

40. Miller, *On Nationality*, 90.

41. Meira Levinson helpfully articulated this argument in her comments on a previous draft of this chapter.

42. Yael Tamir, "Two Concepts of Multiculturalism" in *The Journal of Philosophy of Education*, (1995), 168.

43. Ibid., 167.

44. Chandran Kukathas, "Are There any Cultural Rights?" *Political Theory*, 20: (1), 117.

45. Kymlicka argues that tolerance and autonomy are "two sides of the same coin." See *Multicultural Citizenship*, 155–8.

46. See, for example, the essays by Susan Okin and Rob Reich in this volume (Chapters 11 and 12, respectively).

47. Williams, cited in Callan "Discrimination and Religious Schooling" in Will Kymlicka and Wayne Norman (eds), *Citizenship in Diverse Societies* (Oxford: Oxford University Press, 2000), 60. My discussion of cultural respect is indebted to Callan's discussion in Ibid., 58–63.

48. I do not mean to suggest that all abolitionist activists necessarily understood their project in precisely these terms. It is an apt description of their aims, nonetheless.

49. Callan, "Discrimination and Religious Schooling", 57.

50. Waldron, "Multiculturalism and Melange" in Robert K. Fullinwider (ed.), *Public Education in a Multicultural Society: Policy, Theory, Critique* (Cambridge: Cambridge University Press, 1996), 114.

51. Miller, *On Nationality*, 135.

52. Ibid.

53. Ibid., 89–90.

54. Ibid., 90.

55. Kymlicka, *Politics in the Vernacular*, 105.

56. Boyd Richardson, *People of Terra Nullius* (Toronto: Douglas and MacIntyre, 1993).

57. For this argument see McDonough, "Can the Liberal State Support Cultural Identity Schools?" *American Journal of Education*, 106 (4) (1998), 463–99. In that essay I defend a right to public support for "moderate" separate cultural identity schools for aboriginal peoples.

CHAPTER 14

Religious Education in Liberal Democratic Societies: The Question of Accountability and Autonomy

WALTER FEINBERG

14.1. Introduction

In this chapter I ask what level of accountability a liberal state should expect from sectarian education. I argue, along with Macedo, that educators in liberal societies are justified in tilting the playing field in favor of liberalism and that they can do this while respecting the rights of those who object to liberal educational practices.[1] I argue that the liberal policy maker has tools available for mitigating the tension between parents' right to direct their children's education in a non-liberal way and the state's educational obligation to its future citizens. I argue that a child's autonomous development within a tradition is but one consideration for the policy maker. Another is the education required in reproducing a liberal pluralist society across generations.[2]

I allow with Burtt that autonomy is possible to develop within orthodox, even non-liberal traditions, although I remain unconvinced that this is necessarily an important goal of many orthodox non-liberal traditions. However, I believe that one mistake of those who reject Burtt's point is to assume that autonomy is an all or nothing affair, that we are either autonomous or we are not. Autonomy is in fact a relative matter; we critically choose parts of our lives while we leave many others unexamined and unchallenged. Moreover, the development of autonomy may require different things at different stages of childhood. At the early stages a loving parent who is supported by a close and caring community, whether liberal or not, may go along way in developing a stable self, and thereby may well serve an important role in the child's development.[3] Later on, however, great degrees of autonomy may well require the intentional development of reflective critical skills.

Granting that individuals may develop some level of autonomy within orthodox traditions, even those in which broad critical thinking is discouraged,[4] there are additional considerations that the liberal educational policy maker must take into account. Educational practices in liberal democracies must also be evaluated by whether they are an appropriate and effective way to reproduce the intersubjective understandings and the institutional practices that are needed to sustain a liberal democratic society in which a plurality of different conceptions of the good will be allowed to flourish. Educators representing the interests of such a society must be concerned not only with the future autonomy of one child, but with producing the kind of social understanding in which future adults have developed the political skills required to maintain autonomy at acceptable levels for all.

There are a few points that need to be kept in mind as the background for this discussion. Most important is that the tension that I discussed above is not a tension between religious and public education per se. Many religious schools share the concerns to develop autonomous individuals and to maintain the political structures through which autonomy is nurtured. When these schools fail to develop reasonably autonomous adults, they have, like non-religious liberal schools, failed on their own terms. Moreover, there are all too many public schools that have failed to promote autonomy in an adequate way or to nurture a concern for the kinds of political and cultural institutions through which autonomy may flourish.

Thus the discussion that follows about the different interests of citizens and congregates addresses idea types. It is intended to focus on different forms of accountability, and in some cases on the different interests they entail. In real life these interests often overlap, but not always. Some church schools do not see their mission as the preparation of democratic citizens, and they would not shy away from being called non-democratic. However, for public schools such a label, if it meant that they were failing to provide adequate education in democratic living, is a damning criticism. To be called a public school entails the idea that this is a place where one should learn the skills and attitudes required for living together in a democracy. A public school must aim to reproduce a public. This is not an idea that is entailed by the label "religious school", as such.

One additional preliminary point: liberal democratic countries differ in their treatment of religious education. Some, such as The Netherlands, use public funds to support devotional schools while others, such as the United States, draw a rather strict line between public and religious education, providing funds only for the former.[5] This situation both raises a critical question for all liberal societies and provides constraints for any policy framework that is to be adequate to all liberal democratic societies. The critical question is what constraints on religious education and what degree of support is compatible with the main tenets of liberal democracy, and under what conditions might support of different kinds be allowable. The constraint requires that the framework respect the different histories of each country while taking into account any relevant cultural and demographic factors. Once these are in place, the policy framework may be implemented differently in each country, but there should always be a bias toward education that promotes autonomy across generations and social groups. The rest of this chapter is an elaboration of this point.

In Section 14.2 I discuss some of the potential lines of conflict between religious liberal education and public education. I do this by looking at two different educational roles, that of the citizen and that of the congregant. In Section 14.3 I examine, and find wanting, a number of arguments that have been advanced recently in support of public funding for religious schools. While Section 14.3 finds no single reason derived from liberal educational theory that is sufficiently compelling to require support of religious schools, it does not find that such support must be rejected. Rather it allows that there may well be local considerations that may tilt the decision for support one way or the other.

The proper conclusion up to this point in the argument is that citizens in liberal democracies are not illiberal if they choose to deny public support to religious schools, and that those who complain about a government monopoly when funds are denied to religious schools are wrong to suggest that such denial is illiberal. I do not argue in this section, however, that such support must be rejected or would necessarily be illiberal, and I do not think that it need be. I treat this question in Section 14.4 where I look at a potentially more fundamental reason for denying such support—that it would be tyrannical to take tax funds from one believer in order to advance the beliefs of another. I show that this is a serious criticism, one that served as part of the motivation for the First Amendment to the United States Constitution. I argue, however, that this issue was not fully settled by the First Amendment and that a creative tension still exists. I allow that a democratic consensus could decide to support religious schools, but that this support should always be conditional. In Sections 14.4 and 14.5, I suggest, by way of example, some of the conditions that need to be satisfied. I argue that any support for religious schools must be predicated on the school advancing individual and social autonomy, and that this would require accountability to public as well as to religious bodies. In Section 14.6 I briefly suggest what such an arrangement might entail for the traditional way in which we conceive of the public/private divide.

For citizens of the United States, there are First Amendment issues involved in these considerations, but because these are specific to one country I address them only briefly, and cannot pretend to speak to the many complex legal issues involved. I do point out one situation in which the religious clauses of the First Amendment may well be in conflict with one another. Moreover, in this chapter I do not ask a more fundamental question—whether it is a good idea educationally to provide public support for religious schools. To address this question we would need to examine three additional issues—first, whether religious instruction adds significantly to moral education, as is often claimed; second, whether the various conceptions of the good that are represented by religions would not be better sustained without public support; third, whether support would improve or detract from the quality of non-sectarian public education. Thus, for example, if religion were to add some significant dimension to moral education that other forms of education could not provide, as some religious educators have claimed, then there would be positive reasons for providing support to religious schools. However the task of this chapter is not to address these issues. It is to consider whether, and the conditions under which, liberal states can allow public support for religious instruction without compromising their liberal ideals.

14.2. Congregants and Citizens

Congregants and the Character of Religious Schools

I define a congregant as a person who belongs to a congregation that collectively advances a set of religious beliefs, adheres to a set of religious practices, and expresses and furthers those beliefs and practices. One reason that congregants set up religious schools is to reproduce their practices, beliefs, or attitudes in subsequent generations.

Thus, one important purpose of many religious schools is to raise children into adults who will have the outlook, points of view, beliefs, and affiliations of one group of congregants rather than another. A religious school may, of course, do other things. It may teach young students to read and write; it may teach vocational skills; it may provide a safe haven to escape a dangerous public school; it may provide more discipline, or more kindness, than a student could find in a public school, etc. It may isolate children from the influence of peers that their parents disapprove of. Yet none of these functions require a religious school per se, although many congregants may choose to provide them for religious reasons. For many congregations, however, religious schools serve to pass on the beliefs and practices of the faith.[6] Many congregants support religious schools as a way to extend their religious mission, and for many this includes developing children who become religiously committed adults of a certain kind.

Citizens

A citizen is an officer in a democracy. Citizens have the obligation to reproduce the objective and subjective conditions of democracy. Citizens reproduce the objective conditions by paying taxes that are used to maintain social stability, support the general welfare, and provide the judicial, military, administrative, electoral, and educational institutions required to maintain the society. Citizens reproduce the subjective conditions through practices and institutions that foster positive attitudes toward basic liberal democratic principles in the young. Among these principles are: (1) equality—citizens are supposed to be judged on their merit and not on the basis of race, creed, sexual orientation, gender, etc.; (2) freedom—citizens have the right to act on the principles dictated by their own conscience; (3) mutual well-being—citizens have rights to conditions that will enable them to flourish.

Public schools need to be evaluated in part by how well they reproduce the subjective conditions required for the fulfillment of these principles and on how effectively they teach children to value these ideals and practices. They are to provide children with the skills and outlook that are the necessary conditions of individual and collective flourishing. Public schools are accountable, directly or indirectly, to a political body that is ultimately elected by the citizenry. When schools fail to perform these basic functions, then this body is expected to take note and to institute corrective measures.

14.3. Four Fallacies

In this section I test the claims in support of public funds for religious education by examining four arguments that are used by congregants to advance state support to religious schools, and I show some of the difficulties that they entail. In the following section I explore the basic principles that are at stake in this issue.

The Fallacy of the Minimum

A number of countries that provide state support to religious schools also have a national curriculum, thus assuring that certain topics are covered by each school. This is the case, for example, in The Netherlands and, now, in Great Britain. Advocates of state support for religious education will sometimes claim that the national curriculum together with an adequate state testing policy is sufficient to meet the requirements of the citizenry that students learn the skills required by the society. Moreover, it is argued that since religious schools are providing the rest of us with a service by teaching reading, writing, etc., that the state should provide funds to support this education.

However, for many citizens it is not the just the minimum that is a problem for state supported religious schools. A minimum speaks to the issue of accreditation, *not* state support. The issue that is relevant for state support is not minimal, but excess meaning. It is the meaning that is attached to the minimum that is of concern. A fundamentalist school, for example, may prefer not to teach about Darwinian evolution, but if there is a state standard that requires Darwin be taught, then it must do so. However, the national standard does not state the context in which instruction about Darwin is imbedded. While many religious schools may make a strong effort to meet the spirit as well as the letter of the law, fundamentalist schools often drill their students on the most effective creationists' response to scientific evolution, with the purpose of inoculating students from evidence supporting evolution.

The problem is not that students cannot answer questions about evolution correctly if they are asked to do so on a test. The problem is that they have been taught to assume that the answers that evolution gives to the question of species development are wrong and that those provided by creationism are right. The students are not scientifically illiterate, but they are scientifically misinformed.[7] The citizenry should be concerned that the school has taught as true and scientific a belief that scientific evidence and the scientific *consensus does not support.*[8]

The Fallacy of Public School Tyranny

Congregants argue that it is unjust to single out so-called religious schools for exclusion because it is as unfair to favor non-religion as it is to favor religion, and when it comes to issues of belief, we are all congregants—creationist and evolutionist alike. Schools that teach certain doctrines of science as if they were the truth without providing the religious alternative, if supported exclusively by public funds, are being favored. This is the force of the charge that schools are the "Churches of Secular Humanism." However, this defense rests on confusion between the non-religious and the anti-religious.

The confusion allows some critics of the present arrangement to conclude that to force religious parents to pay taxes to support public schools is a form of tyranny. If the claim that schools teach the "religion" of secular humanism were accurate, then the schools would be teaching the doctrines of one religion over those of others and, at least in the United States, would be in violation of the Establishment Clause. Nord, for example, uses such an argument to support his claim that public schools are hostile to religion and to conclude that, in order to mitigate this hostility, creationist "science" should be taught along side of evolution.[9]

The charge of public school tyranny is inadequate in at least two counts. First, public schools are (or should be) accountable to all citizens, and their programs are (or should be) open to inspection, challenge, and debate through the political process. In the end a particular parent may well object to the conduct of the schools, but there are avenues for collective citizen change. Second, public schools do not teach the doctrines of Secular Humanism. They teach, or should teach, biology, chemistry, etc. Secular Humanists believe that these subjects leave little, if any room, for the supernatural. Others, however, believe the complexity and order revealed by such subjects are a sign of divine intervention.[10] The fact that public schools may be silent about such issues is neither an endorsement of a secular humanistic nor of a theistic understanding of nature. It is teaching students what scientists understand about their natural world and how they go about gaining such an understanding—through the methods of science.

To defend the public school against a blanket charge of tyranny should not be confused with the acts of individual teachers or administrators, which may in fact be inadequate, incompetent, unprofessional, or tyrannical. If a teacher belittles a child's belief, whether that belief be based in religion or not, it is a form of professional tyranny and should be seen as unprofessional. Yet public school teachers can use their positions inappropriately to advance a religious tradition, such as when Christian teachers join with Christian students to meet before school to pray around the flag post, signaling a commitment that non-Christians often find offensive and unwelcoming.

The blanket charge of public school tyranny, however, is not addressed to individual violations of professional responsibility. The charge is that public education as an institution serves to discourage or belittle religious belief. The only valid basis on which to judge this charge is in terms of policies that affect student rights within state supported schools, and which impact on their ability to express their beliefs, religious or otherwise. Students should be allowed, as the US Supreme Court has noted, to protest government policies[11] or to absent themselves for religious reasons from patriotic exercises.[12]

It may be debated whether or not these decisions are sufficient. Some may object to having any patriotic displays in schools[13], while others might believe that parents should have more authority to remove their children from classes that they find religiously offensive.[14] Granted there have been Court decisions that some congregants object to because they believe that they create an environment that is hostile to religion. These include prohibiting a football team from praying together publicly before a game or not allowing a valedictorian to invoke Jesus as his personal savior. Those who oppose these decisions argue that they serve to silence religion and to create a hostile environment.[15] Yet these are decisions that other congregants agree with, and the practices are banned not out of hostility to religion as such, but because they are perceived as using a school platform to advance a particular set of religious beliefs.

The Fallacy of the Exclusive Stakeholder

In the United States the idea of vouchers to private and religious schools has been advanced on the grounds that public funds are being provided to support parental choice, not religious schools. Should the parents choose religious schools, then the support is only indirect and unintentional. One of the reasonable concerns about an argument that provides parents with the ultimate authority over their children's schooling is that it may marginalize the democratizing mission of publicly supported education. In other words, it leaves to parents the decision whether or not to advance the inter-subjective understandings and the institutional practices needed to sustain a liberal democratic society. Yet if public funds are to be used to support education, there is an implicit understanding that other citizens, and not just the child's parents, need to have a stake in that education. Moreover, these citizens do not have a stake in education in general, but in advancing specific kinds of education and in discouraging other kinds of education.

In a liberal society the public has a stake in advancing education in which students learn the basic norms of the society, including the norms that call for respecting people who differ from themselves. Parents with strong religious commitments may or may not share such an interest, and the basic principles of liberal society require that their own beliefs and attitudes must be respected. It does not, however, require that public support be provided to help them pass these beliefs and attitudes on to their children. This may be construed as an argument to support not just public schools, but also support for private schools, including religious ones, that advance democratic ideas.[16] If private and religious schools were willing to undergo serious monitoring along these lines and to be accountable for the reproduction of democratic practices, as public schools should be, then this implication might well be acceptable. However, as things now stand, there are practical as well as philosophical problems with the state monitoring religious institutions this closely.

Regardless of how the above implication might work out in practice, the need to respect illiberal parents does not entail the requirement that society aid them in transmitting, through publicly supported church education, their illiberal views to their children. Even the question of whether to allow self-supporting schools that promote illiberal values is not just a matter of freedom of conscience. It is also a question of the rights that children have to an education that extends beyond the views of the parents. And certainly whereas freedom of conscience applies to the development and expression of one's own beliefs, it does not apply, except indirectly, to the transmission of those beliefs to one's children in publicly supported institutions. Children have a right to grow up with a reasonable possibility that they will have opportunities to develop beliefs that are different from their parents[17], and the liberal state does not compel students to attend school—private or public—so as to reproduce the views of their parents.

The question of support for private and religious schools is complicated by a number of factors. Among these is a preference on the part of most religious schools to hire teachers who belong to the faith. This means that public funds are expended on selected hiring practices.[18] This preference is perfectly understandable given the desire to maintain the specific denominational flavor of the school. However, it presents serious problems when public funds are concerned.[19] It should provide considerable hesitation to those who are considering whether or not to extend public funding to religious schools, and it should also lead to considerable hesitation on the part of religious educators who are thinking of requesting such funding. Were religious schools to be publicly funded, then pressure to require open hiring on the basis of academic qualifications would surely materialize.

Frequently those who wish support for religious schools are not happy about the public monitoring that such support entails, and express concern that professional standards limit religious diversity.[20] Yet this begs the question about what to do about illiberal private and religious schools that, should support to some religious schools be advanced, would likely argue that support for one religious school but not another is discriminatory. The answer is that the liberal state has a right to treat religious schools differently on the basis of the quality of their education and the extent to which they serve the needs and requirements of liberal democratic societies. Under this guiding principle, illiberal religious schools should not be supported by state funds.

The larger question is not that of support, but whether there may be other reasons for allowing such schools to exist. Since parents do not have a right to deny their children an autonomy developing education, they do not have a right to send their children exclusively to an autonomy retarding school. Yet the liberal state must allow parents a lot of leeway. Liberalism does not, except under extreme circumstances, allow a government agency to enter a person's home to reconstruct the politically incorrect or autonomy retarding education of their children.[21] This is not because it approves of such teachings, but because it is aware that other rights are also at stake and an overly intrusive state, even one acting in the name of one liberal principle, can threaten other liberal principles, in this instance the right to privacy. However, the school is not just an extension of the home, a mistake that some states make in terms of inadequate monitoring of parents who home-school their own children.[22] The inhibitions on state interference in parent/child relations does not mean that a parent has exclusive rights over a child's educational experience.

Because the commitment of liberalism entails a commitment to the coexistence of many different comprehensive doctrines and ways of life, the liberal state must exercise caution before it interferes with a parent's educational preferences. Schools that advance a preferred way of life must be distinguished from those that teach intolerance for any way of life other than their own. The former must be allowed; the latter should not be. When addressing religious schools a certain amount of chauvinism is to be expected and, as long as the schools are not receiving public funding, should be tolerated. According to some Christians, Jews and Muslims do not get into heaven; according to one fundamentalist teacher, Unitarians allow Hitler into their heaven; according to a Muslim teacher, Christianity is polytheistic; according to some Jews, Jews have a God-given right to Israel.[23] While these claims may seem odd to those who do not share the belief system, they do not, by themselves, constitute a threat to democratic pluralism.

While there are reasons to object to such teachings, they are part of the signature curriculum of some religious institutions, and may even serve to ease the ideological pressure on public schools.[24] Regulation of these institutions is problematic because state regulation of religious teachings is a serious problem for liberal democracies.[25] Hence, a significant burden of proof is placed on the state when it comes to monitoring religious schools, and private religious schools have often been allowed to operate outside of the social consensus.[26] This burden, however, is on the side of tolerance, not support. Whether such teachings should be interfered with is a delicate matter, but it is certainly one that should not be off the agenda of a wider public discussion.

Moreover, intensity of commitment should not be confused with indoctrination. One important test is whether students are provided with the skills required to exit a tradition should they later choose to do so. These skills involve both the academic and vocational education needed to take up work in the larger society and the capacity to evaluate different traditional practices. Policy makers need therefore to distinguish between schools that reflect parents' intensity of commitment from schools that use psychological manipulation, selected skill training, or intimidation to inhibit future adults from considering factors that might lead them to exit the tradition.

However, should such schools function to deny a minimal level of autonomy, to advance significant intolerance, or to retard the development of a reasonable capacity to exit, the presumptive right given to parents should not be sufficient to prevent the closing of the school. A less drastic measure would be to allow the school to remain open during the afternoon or weekend as a supplement to the public schools that the child would be required to attend. As Brighouse, a supporter of choice, notes: "Parents have a fundamental right to have intimate relationships with their children, which are conditional on the protection of certain of the children's interests. Failure to protect those interests amounts to forfeiture of the right, in the same way that failure to obey the laws amounts to a forfeiting of one's right to freedom of association."[27]

The Fallacy of Recognition

One argument for religious recognition is an extension of the recent concern about cultural recognition put forth by Taylor, Kymlicka, and others. It addresses the need of the individual to have the collectivity to which he or she belongs appropriately recognized by the larger society. For Taylor, misrecognition or non-recognition may constitute a real harm to the individual, whereas for Kymlicka it places the individual at a disadvantage when it comes to material and psychological development and flourishing. To recognize a culture is to provide special incentives to maintain or enhance it. For example, choosing as individuals alone, parents in Quebec have a strong incentive to send their children to English speaking schools given the opportunity structure of greater Canada. This incentive is present even if, everything else being equal, they would choose to send the children to French speaking schools. However, the opportunity structure means that everything else is not equal and the collective result of these individual decisions would be to erode the French language and to increase the incentive to choose English schools. Thus, noting the tendency of unchecked individual choice to bring about undesirable results, Taylor provides an argument for developing laws that give French culture a special status in Quebec.[28]

However, the case for providing incentives to promote a belief of a certain kind, such as the case with religious recognition, is much harder to make because it involves an interference with freedom of conscience of those who, not necessarily sharing the belief, are taxed to support it. Moreover, to deny such support is not an infringement of the rights of the believer. Freedom to believe is not conditioned on recognition in the thick sense that Taylor suggests for culture. Rather, it is conditioned on respect for uncoerced choices and requires a safe climate in which people may practice their religion. The state does not fail to give respect if it refuses to support a religious school. It fails to give respect if it does not assure a safe climate in which congregants can practice and express their beliefs and involve their children in them. Granted, this is a minimal conception of respect. It allows beliefs of many kinds to flourish without requiring those who do not believe in a certain way to support those beliefs. This conception of respect is consistent with the rejection of tyranny that underlies the First Amendment of the United States Constitution.

14.4. The Problem of Meeting the Requirements of Non-tyranny

There are two features of tyranny that the First Amendment of the United States Constitution rejects.

First, citizens should not be taxed to support congregants or their opponents. This feature is violated under the following condition: if tax funds are provided to:

(1) schools that are not accountable to the public for their instructional programs, and where;
(2) instruction takes place within a positive or negative religiously charged environment, and;
(3) is delivered to children in a way that will likely inhibit the development of the capacity to freely assent to a belief system, and;
(4) where it is intended to and will have the likely consequence of directing ultimate commitment and devotion toward one religion rather than another, or to religion over anti-religion or anti-religion over religion.

Second, citizens should not control the beliefs of congregants. Parents have rights to freedom of speech and association and, as an extension of these rights, and as a part of the practical conditions of raising children, parents may exercise strong, although not absolute, guidance over the religious beliefs of their children.

Under many circumstances these two aspects of tyranny can be rejected simultaneously. However, there are situations in which support for one places a strong tension on the support for the other, and this is the case with many proposals for public support to religious schools, including various voucher proposals. This conflict can be seen in the problems involved in making sense of a recent Wisconsin Supreme Court ruling[29] upholding legislation that provides vouchers for parents to pay tuition to private and religious schools.

Benson v. Jackson *and the Voucher Issue*

In *Jackson* v. *Benson*, the Wisconsin State Supreme Court upheld a parental choice program in which state funds were granted to Milwaukee parents to send their children to private, including religious, schools. In doing so, the Court overruled a 2 to 1 opinion of The Wisconsin Court of Appeals against the law. A few restrictions are placed on the schools participating in the program. They have to comply with antidiscrimination provisions as well as with the health and safety codes applicable to public schools in the state. Moreover, children, upon the request of their parents, have a right to opt out of devotional services should they choose to attend a religious school. Prior to the inclusion of religious schools, the participating private schools were required to submit to performance and financial audits of the Superintendent of schools, but this requirement was dropped when the law was amended.[30]

From the Wisconsin Court's point of view the program was constitutional because: (1) Since non-sectarian private schools were also supported, in its eyes, the legislation did not favor religion over non-religion; (2) Since state monitoring was reduced to a minimum, the Court noted that the state was not interfering with the free exercise of religion; (3) Since the law required religious schools to allow any student supported by public funds to be excused from religious activity upon a written request from a parent or guardian, the Court felt that it did not violate the Establishment Clause; (4) Because the aid is restricted on the basis of income, the Court held that its primary intent is not to aid religion, but to help poor children receive a better education. (The program has an income limitation that restricts participation to students whose family income does not exceed 1.75 times the federal poverty level.)

Thus the Court found the law constitutional, arguing that it does not violate the Establishment Clause ("Congress shall make no law respecting an Establishment of religion") and is consistent with the constraints developed by the US Supreme Court—it had a "secular purpose", "will not have the primary effect of advancing religion and will not lead to excessive entanglement between the State and participating sectarian schools." The purpose of the law, the court noted, was not to advance religion, but rather "to provide low-income parents with an opportunity to have their children educated outside of the embattled Milwaukee Public School system." Thus, in the Court's eyes, the state is supporting parental choice and religious schools benefit only as an indirect consequence of that choice.

Public Funds without Public Control

When religious schools were added to the voucher program in 1995, the legislation eliminated the state performance evaluation and the

Superintendent's authority to conduct financial or performance evaluation audits. On the traditional interpretation of the First Amendment, and the Free Exercise Clause, the elimination of these requirements enables the state to avoid interference in the activities of religious institutions. The Court cited this as one of the reasons it felt the legislation in its amended form was Constitutional, "the State is not given the authority to impose a 'comprehensive, discriminating, and continuing state surveillance' over the participating sectarian private schools."[31] In other words, the law is constitutional in the eyes of the court because the State of Wisconsin will not be able to monitor how its funds are used with regard to the performance of the children that they are intended to benefit. Yet, given the traditional interpretation of the First Amendment and the balance between non-support/non-interference, this tips the balance to the side of non-interference.

The Wisconsin Court understood correctly that were it to *require* religious schools to be monitored in the way that public schools are, it would be in danger of violating the Free Exercise Clause of the Constitution, the Clause that guarantees the right to worship without government interference. Just as we do not want government agents monitoring our churches, so we should not want them, uninvited, monitoring our children's religious education. However, the Court wrongly assumed that it is possible to disentangle academic instruction from religious instruction. Yet a religious school may have a different set of academic priorities from a public one and academic subjects will often be taught to illustrate religious messages. However, this creates a bind that seems to place the Free Exercise Clause in direct conflict with the Establishment Clause.

On the one hand, if religious schools are not subject to the same monitoring as public ones, then they are enjoying an advantage which is clearly counter to the Establishment Clause and must be corrected. They are allowed to indoctrinate children into discriminatory ideologies and to do so with the use of public funds. On the other hand, if such monitoring is not waived and government agents sit in religious classrooms, or set the standards and evaluate the outcomes, then the Free Exercise Clause is violated. Is there any way to avoid this conundrum? In responding to this question I want to go somewhat beyond the legalistic issues involved in interpreting the US Constitution, and look more deeply at the issue of tyranny that motivated the religion clauses.

14.5. *Conditions for State Support of Religious Schools*

I want to suggest that there are four conditions that have a bearing on the question of under what conditions support to religious schools is allowable in liberal democratic societies. They are as follows: (a) Growth in autonomy of the child and the primacy of the educational mission; (b) Political equality; (c) True availability of education to all; (d) System legitimacy. I treat these below.

Autonomy and Growth and the Primacy of the Educational Mission

Tyranny has more than one object. Forcing one person to support activities which are intended to advance the religious beliefs or non-beliefs of another is one of them, and this is especially so in the case of children who have little autonomy in the matter. Socializing children in such a way that they maintain their dependency on their parents or teachers is another. Here children's destinies are manipulated so that they have no other choice but to live the lives that their parents and teachers have laid out for them. The use of this power by parents is one reason why the case for parental rights must be a limited one. Parents may in their own mind have the best interest of the child at heart without an awareness of their own self-serving motivation for defining their child's interest in a certain way, or without an accurate understanding of what constitutes the child's best interest.

Autonomy refers to the developing capacity of a child to choose a life in accordance with her own critically developed conception of the good. Autonomy requires the ability to reflect upon one's own socialization process, and to eventually take greater control over that process. Growth refers to the capacity of a child to incorporate new information and influences into that life as her interaction with her physical and social environment becomes more deliberate and goal directed.

This growth requires adult guidance, but the aim for liberal society is to develop independence of purpose and control. A parent, for the first time, guides her toddler's hands on the computer mouse. The toddler has no idea of the parent's intent, but enjoys the physical contact and lets her hand be guided. After some months the parent can feel her intention being taken over by the child. The parent's hand plays a smaller and smaller role in controlling the mouse and the child's hand takes over more and more of the work. Soon the child goes to the computer by herself, opens up the game alone.

Then, after some time has passed, she selects her own games. Later, she uses the computer to communicate with others, and even forgets the original game and the pleasure gained by contact with her parent's hand on hers as they worked to guide the mouse. In this way she becomes free from her earlier dependence on her parent's hand and intentions.

Educating children in a way that intentionally maintains the initial dependency, and reproduces uncritically the parents' goals in the child, is a type of tyranny. It is not necessarily that the child is being forced to do something against her will, as in the case of the reluctant tax-paying citizen. It is rather that the child is being denied the opportunity to develop a will of her own.[32] The citizenry of liberal democracies have a stake in discouraging this kind of tyranny because it has a stake in reproducing the subjective conditions that are essential to its own reproduction as a liberal society.

It is sometimes a judgment call whether schools that foster non-autonomy and non-growth should be allowed control over children's education, a judgment that will depend on weighing the effects of parental educational tyranny against the consequences to the child's development of governmental intervention in the parent–child relationship. However, as the earlier citation of Brighouse notes, a parent's right to educate children is not an absolute one and can be removed when it seriously harms the child.[33]

Categories such as manipulation and best interest are open textured, and standards are not easily or precisely set. It is often in the interest of children, even those whose parents are not particularly wise in the way of understanding their own motivation or their child's interest, that caution be exercised in asserting state control over a parent's authority to educate her child in a specific school. The tragedy of the education of Native American children in state run boarding schools should be sufficient evidence that the government is not necessarily wiser than a parent. However, that was a case in which the primacy of the educational mission was subordinated to a larger social goal of total assimilation, and children were removed from the nurturing home environment and placed in the total institutional environment provided by the state.

Religious schools that refuse to hire people from other religions, or that structure the school so that the viewpoints of other religions are blocked out of consideration, should be understood as schools where the educational mission is not primary. In these cases support is not warranted. However, the issue of whether a religious school of the parent's choice should be *allowed* is quite different from that of whether it should be supported. A condition for supporting religious schools in liberal democratic society is that they not subvert the subjective conditions necessary for reproducing liberal democratic citizens, and that they thus provide the educational requirements for children to grow into reflective autonomous citizens. One of these conditions is that at age appropriate times children are allowed to gain intellectual and emotional distance over the form of life with which they are most familiar, and to understand that there are many reasonable forms of life.

Political Equality

One of the features of many religious schools is that they provide students with a disposition to favor those who share their devotional orientation over those who do not. The fundamentalist message that atheists and members of other religious faiths will not go to heaven; the Muslim view that Mohammed was the last and the greatest prophet with a more complete version of God's message than the others, including Moses and Jesus; the Jewish belief that Jews are God's chosen people; all are, in one way or another, exclusionary beliefs. The exclusionary effect may be even more penetrating when delivered to young children who have not yet had much contact with members of other faiths, and who do not yet comprehend the metaphorical functions of language.

Because members of the citizenry belong to many different faiths as well as to no faith, they have an interest in mitigating the effect of these exclusionary messages and enhancing the cooperative possibilities of people from different groups in the larger society. This can be done by both religious and non-religious schools. For example, regardless of the religious message, schools can advance a message of political equality in which students learn to separate their self-defined religious standing from their political standing and where they learn that their political voice, even when informed by their faith, should count no more than that of any other citizen. One might teach this in a number of ways in a religious context. In some religions it might be seen as the manifestation of the respect that arises from the moral worth of each individual. In others, it might be understood as one of the implications of self-fallibility arising from original sin. In advancing this distinction, religious educators would need to encourage students to become critically reflective of the doctrinal errors made by past leaders of the faith. For example, Southern Baptist schools might have units on their Church's erroneous defense of slavery and the belated retraction. Mormons, following lessons about their own persecution, could explore the church's failing in refusing black people membership. Catholic Schools could study the behavior of the Church during the Inquisition and the Crusades. And Jewish schools could encourage students to reflect upon the relationship between Jews and Palestinians and the issue of social justice. In all religious schools the distinction between the disposition to favor believers like oneself could be mitigated by appeals to humility and the ever present possibility that anyone, religious leaders included, can be wrong about God's will. Such programs within religious schools could go some way in furthering what Blacker, in this volume, refers to as civic friendship. However, without such mitigating messages there is little to advance the idea of civic friendship across congregations.

Religious schools could acknowledge the humanity of everyone, believers and non-believers alike, and the obligation each of us has to enable others to participate in the determination of our collective and individual futures. Loving one's neighbor as oneself allows self and neighbor to participate together without fear or hatred in mapping their joint futures in a liberal democratic society. As one Talmudic scholar put it:

The sanctity of life is not a function of national origin, religious affiliation, or social status. In the sight of God, the humblest citizen is the equal of the person who occupies the highest office... 'Heaven and earth I call to witness, whether it be an Israelite or pagan, man or woman, slave or maidservant, according to the work of every human being doth the Holy Spirit rest upon him.'[34]

Welcoming Factor

Liberal democratic societies require informed and knowledgeable people able to participate in political discussions, to listen to the point of others, and to defend and amend their own point of view when reason and wider considerations suggest they do so. Liberal democratic societies also need citizens able to participate in the economy, capable of taking advantage of the opportunities it offers, and of defining new opportunities and setting new economic priorities.

Religious schools often provide these services equally as well as, and sometimes better than, do public schools. However, there is more to the economic side of education than the services a school provides for its own students. Citizens in liberal democratic societies need to have the freedom to move from one part of their country to another, and such mobility requires that education be seen as available for their children.

Availability requires not just that a school exist in the new location but that the school is one that a child could attend without discrimination and with a reasonable expectation that she will be accepted. Given a highly mobile population, citizens in liberal societies have to assure that all areas of the country have schools that are able to provide a hospitable atmosphere for children from different backgrounds.

This requirement provides a special problem in some societies for those who wish to support religious schools. One way in which religion is used (or interpreted as being used) is as a welcoming signal for believers in a faith and a hostile signal for non-members. Thus the presence of a publicly supported religious school of only one or two denominations can serve as a signal to those from other denominations that they would have a difficult time in this place.[35]

In societies with highly dense populations, or in those with very limited possibilities for mobility, this may not pose a large problem. Hence, The Netherlands, a small and densely populated nation, can provide many different kinds of religious schools within a small area. If a student feels unwelcome in one, she may choose to attend another. How well such an approach works depends on the reasonableness of the population and its ability to develop avenues of cooperation across religious faiths.

Larger countries with areas where the population is sparse may have more difficulty with this kind of arrangement. People in liberal societies need to be free to move wherever their situation requires or wherever they might like, and when doing so they need to have assurances that their children have available to them schools that do not discriminate because of race, creed, or color. Moreover, they need to be assured that the available schools will not assault their children's identity by requiring that they remold their lives to conform to a certain image of goodness. Gay students cannot expect to hear that we love the sinner, but hate the sin. Jewish and Muslim students must be allowed to worship without having Jesus thrust upon them in the classroom, and Catholic students should not have to listen to teachings that reject Jesus' divine status or that hold that a belief in Jesus violates the First Commandment.

When a community has only a few public schools, it is important that they signal a welcome to anyone who might have a reason to move into the community, and this is unlikely when schools carry a strong religious message. The fact that such schools may not engender significant protest is not a sufficient reason to support them, since possible protestors may have understood their presence as a message of unwelcome. This may be difficult for some countries that have been dominated by a single religious tradition. Nevertheless, full membership requires that people from many different faiths and non-faiths feel that the entire country, and not just parts of it, belong to them, and this may well require changes in the way religious schools are supported.

Legitimacy, Accountability, and Coherence

One of the critical issues in public support for religious schools does not involve individual rights, but rather the degree of social cohesion and solidarity that a nation requires in order to function. Historically this has been one of the critical reasons that some nations have given priority to one religion or another. They wanted to provide the emerging citizen with the outcome and the loyalties of the settled ones and it was assumed that connecting public schools to a religious agenda was an effective means of doing this. This is one reason why, until the latter part of the twentieth century, many schools in the United States began the day with a prayer to God and a salute to the Flag.

As global populations become increasingly mobile and as religious affiliations within any one nation widens, as questions are raised about the hegemony of the dominant group, the link between national solidarity and religious commitment cannot be taken for granted. Reducing the tie between national loyalty and religious affiliation may promote solidarity more than linking the two. Loyalty can be developed in children to the principle that the liberal state enables everyone to worship as they wish and that they can be assured that another form of belief will never be privileged over their own. This means that any support will be conditional on the promotion of the surplus loyalty required for liberal multireligious societies to continue to function.[36] Under some circumstances this might best be accomplished by providing support to religious schools. In others it might be accomplished by withholding support for them.

If religious schools are to be supported by public funds, however, then they should be accountable to a public body. This would require some changes in the way in which we conceptualize the distinction between the public and the private, and the boundaries between the religious and the non-religious. In the United States, for example, the two clauses of the First Amendment are designed to give maximum freedom to religious bodies in conducting their own affairs and educating children into the faith. However, the price of such freedom has been the absence of government support. If this were to change, and greater support provided, then some groups might well experience a curtailment of freedom as their educational practices would become a matter for public consideration. The problem would be to find ways to accomplish this while still maintaining the uniqueness of different religious orientations.

There are at least four possible ways in which this might be accomplished: (1) Standardized tests to assure that achievement meets minimal standards; (2) Providing funds to support that part of education that is secular, while requiring the religious congregation to support that part that is devotional and sectarian; (3) Require participating schools to include members of the general public on their governing board. This possibility can be interpreted it two ways—the outsiders could be appointed by the congregants or they could be appointed by the citizenry; (4) Providing inspection and accreditation teams drawn from the larger society. These alternatives are not mutually exclusive, but some are preferable to others.

Before exploring these different possibilities, one important qualification needs to be addressed. In the discussion below I am addressing the issue of religious schools that might choose to participate in such a scheme. However, I want to leave open the possibility that some religious schools may not want to adopt the controls that public accountability requires. For example, imagine a school that held that standardized tests fostered unhealthy competition and pitted student against student in a way that was disruptive to the entire community. If such a school wishes to remain self-supporting and to also opt out of state assessment, then the state has a burden to show why it should not do so or to provide less competitive means for assessing student achievement. If, however, the school wishes to be supported by public funds the state could decide that standardized tests are a condition for such support. Given this qualification, I turn to the different ways in which educational accountability of the congregant to the citizenry might develop.

As we have seen, a number of people argue that standardized tests in a few basic subjects are sufficient to evaluate the merits of an individual school, whether public or private. I have already addressed this view in my critique of the minimum. Moreover, while standardized tests have become more common as states exert greater control over schools, they tell us only a very little about the climate of the school and its merits or demerits. To the extent that standardized tests provide some guidance in evaluating the success of a school in preparing students for the world of work, they have a certain usefulness. The burden will be on any individual school that wishes to disregard them to show: (1) either that some other purpose is defensible and that standardized tests hinder this purpose; or (2) that the school has a better way of assessing the qualities that standardized tests claim to measure.

The second possibility, supporting only that part of education within a religious school that has a secular purpose, presents similar problems, for in many devotional schools it is not possible to separate the devotional from the secular because the entire climate of the school is intended to encourage commitment to a certain faith. Hence when children read math books, they read them in a classroom that has a large cross on the wall or in front of a teacher wearing a yarmulke, or with the boys separated from the girls according to Islamic tradition. Lessons in English may concentrate on religious virtues, and social studies may emphasize the importance of certain religious heroes, while much of the taken for granted discourse of the school assumes a certain religious orientation as the following examples from a Catholic school in Ireland indicate:

I sent my four year old to the local school for one year. Unfortunately, the responsibility lay with me to remove the child from the school during the daily 'religion' class. [which she did not want him to attend and from which the law allows removal] This would have meant someone going to school at noon hour every day to take him out ... And when it came to issues such as trips to Church, which occurred outside of regular religion class, I was not informed.[37]

Religious schools carry with them certain expectations. They form the premises from which other discussions flow. For example:

A priest came into my ... son's class and stated, 'I presume everybody is going to be confirmed.' At this point some pupils jokingly pointed to my son saying that he wasn't religious. The priest asked him why he was not being confirmed. My son said that he didn't do religion. 'Why not?' asked the priest. 'That's none of your business and I don't wish to answer any more questions.' There was a long and stony silence.[38]

Thiessen, one of the strongest proponents of Christian education, criticizes McLaughlin, a more liberal advocate, for failing to understand that "every part of the curriculum will serve a religious end within a Christian school."[39] The difficult task then is to provide a system of accountability in which the inner workings of the school can maintain its religious character in a way that does not subtly discriminate against those who may, for whatever reason, wish to attend the school, but do not share its religious orientation.

14.6. *Public and Private Reconsidered*

Part of the problem arises because of the way in which we continue to conceptualize public and private as two completely separate spaces with a strong boundary between them. Thus on one side are public schools, supported by public funds, with administrators accountable to an elected body and funding dependent on the will of the electorate. On the other side of the boundary are private schools, many of which are religious, in which the state has only a minimal interest in their activity. Here safety and other minimum regulatory requirements must be met, but beyond that they are free to go their own way. The state neither supports nor encourages them. The need to minimize state intrusion in religious affairs may leave little choice but to allow wide freedom to religious schools.

Where states believe that it is desirable to provide some support to religious schools, they could develop public bodies to which participating religious schools could voluntarily submit themselves for continuous monitoring and on site inspection. Participating schools might be provided the opportunity to appoint, perhaps on a rotating basis, a reasonable portion of the supervising body, while the rest would be appointed by elected representatives of the citizenry at large. Schools that chose to participate would then be granted a certain degree of state support and it would be understood that the schools are allowed to express their religious identity in non-discriminatory ways. The body might want to provide certain incentives for maintaining a religiously plural teaching staff, but where religious schools are supported, participating schools should be allowed to hire people who will advance a given orientation. However, schools would be required to admit students from other religious and non-religious orientations, and would be required to hire teachers in non-religious courses on the basis of their subject matter competence, allowing that they are not hostile toward the religious orientation of the group. Religious instruction and devotional activities would be supported by the denomination itself.

Schools that did not wish to participate in such a program would be subject to minimum certification requirements, would receive no state support, and would have no representation on the body that supervised state supported schools. They would be allowed to maintain independent status as long as students showed evidence of sufficient factual knowledge and skills to make informed judgments about their lives. The difference between the supported and the non-supported schools would be largely a difference in the burden of proof. To maintain their support religious schools would be expected to demonstrate that they serve to advance democracy and autonomy, and monitoring procedures would be in place to assure that they did so. In order to close down a non-supported school the state would have the burden to show that it actively promotes antidemocratic means.

Glenn suggests that peer review could serve as an adequate accountability measure and I tend to agree with him.[40] However, he is unclear about who should constitute a group of peers and, given his enthusiasm for religious schools, it is likely that he would exclude representatives from outside a denominational group. However, such exclusion should be unacceptable because it would provide public funds without any effective public controls. Another possibility, one that is more promising, would include representatives of other view points—both religious and non-religious—on such review teams.

In my own view such reviews should never be a condition for a school's existence, but it should be a condition for any public support to instructional programs. Schools that do not wish such support should be able to opt out of this inspection process, except where evidence exists that they are violating the law. This should reduce any concerns about violation of the Free Exercise Clause in the United States.

Glenn largely objects to this kind of arrangement, arguing that it leads to compromise and to a reduction in the distinctly religious flavor of the school, and would prefer support with minimum controls. Yet his attempt to ease temptation and to make religious education easy only addresses the autonomy requirements of the school. It does not address the autonomy requirement for the child and fails to address the education required for reproducing the practices and understandings required in liberal pluralistic societies. Religious schools that wish to receive state support should be willing to have their programs monitored by groups that represent the public, and members of those groups must also be appraised of the religious nature of the school.

14.7. Conclusion

I have argued in this chapter that congregants who wish to pass on their beliefs, practices, and understandings to children through religious schools have a right to do so. However, liberalism provides no inherent right to demand that the state support such schools. The state only has an obligation to assure that there is a safe and secure environment for religious beliefs to be expressed and taught to others. However, to argue that congregants do not have a right to demand public support for religious education is not to say that public support for religious education is inherently undemocratic or that it need be avoided at all costs. A number of liberal democratic states do support religious schools without seeming to compromise their liberal democratic character.

Nevertheless, liberal democratic societies do have a stake in reproducing the intersubjective understandings and practices that will assure their continuation across generations, and should a state find reason to support religious schools, it also has an obligation to monitor those schools in terms of democratic pluralistic values. Non-supported schools should be provided considerably more freedom from state control than ones supported by public funds.

In this chapter I have not addressed the question whether or not support for religious schools is a good idea. However, I have shown that certain arguments for support need to be rejected out of hand. This would include the argument that schools teach "the religion of secular humanism" or that parents should have an exclusive right to determine their children's education and to have it supported by the state. There are, however, other arguments that should be investigated more closely. Some of these have to do with the relationship between religious instruction and academic achievement or moral development, while others have to do with history and national character of particular nations. At this point, we need to remain open as to whether support for religious schools is a good idea in any particular situation. However, we can conclude that religious schools do not have a right to such support but that, if it is granted, voluntary public monitoring should be a critical component of any such support.

NOTES

Appreciation to Kevin McDonough, Harry Brighouse, Tyll Van Geel, Jason Odeshoo, King Alexander, Larry Parker, Nick Burbules, Meira Levinson, and the students in my seminar on Religious Educational Policy for their comments on earlier drafts.

1. See Chapter 15 in this volume.
2. Walter Feinberg, *Understanding Education* (Cambridge University Press, 1982) and Amy Gutmann, *Democratic Education* (Princeton: Princeton University Press, 1987).

3. Jonathan Glover, *I: The Philosophy and Psychology of Personal Identity* (London: Penguin, 1991), 197.
4. This argument is sometimes given by those who argue that orthodoxy gives children rules to rebel against or to reconsider, as opposed to what they see as wishy-washy liberalism.
5. Charles L. Glenn, *The Ambiguous Embrace: Government and Faith-Based Schools and Social Agencies* (Princeton: Princeton University Press, 2000).
6. There are notable exceptions to this. In one of her comments on this chapter Meira Levinson noted that very few Friends or Episcopal schools take religious affiliation into account in student selection, and less than half of these schools rated religious development as one of their three most important goals. However, my own interviews with Muslim, Jewish, Catholic, and Lutheran educators all expressed a strong preference for teachers of their own faith.
7. This is not to suggest that public schools do not turn out students who are also scientifically misinformed. The issue is whether standardized tests are adequate to address teaching that is intentionally biased against evolution.
8. Some Evangelical Christians have begun to understand this issue and a few have begun to argue that rejection of evolution in its scientific Darwinian form is not only harmful to their cause, but also wrong and, indeed, ungodly. See Mark A. Noll, *The Scandal of the Evangelical Mind* (Grand Rapids: William B. Eerdmans, 1995).
9. Warren A. Nord, *Religion and American Education: Rethinking a National Dilemma* (Chapel Hill: The University of North Carolina Press, 1995), 138–60.
10. Noll, *The Scandal of the Evangelical Mind*, 177–210.
11. *Tinker v. Des Moines Independent School District*, 393 U.S. 503 (1969).
12. *West Virginia State Board of Education v. Barnett*, 319 U.S. 624 (1943).
13. See Brighouse's essay in Chapter 6 of this volume.
14. See the essays by Williams (Chapter 8) and Burtt (Chapter 7) in this volume.
15. Appreciation to Meira Levinson for these examples. See *Cole v. Oroville Union High Sch. Dist.*, 228 F.3d 1092 (9th Cir. 2000) and *Santa Fe Independent School District v. Doe*, 530 U.S. 290 (2000).
16. Levinson considers an option like this in Meira Levinson, *The Demands of Liberal Education* (Oxford: Oxford University Press, 1999). Levinson, however, largely focuses on the development of individual autonomy, and pays considerably less attention to the need to reproduce democratic practices and institutions.
17. Harry Brighouse, *School Choice and Social Justice* (Oxford: Oxford University Press, 2000), 92. Walter Feinberg, "On Public Support for Religious Schools", *Teachers College Record*, (Aug. 2000).
18. My ongoing research in religious schools supports this observation. Interviews with administrators in eight separate schools involving four major religious groups—Muslim, Lutheran, Catholic, and Jewish—all expressed a preference to hire their own and usually did so. Given two similarly qualified people, strong preferences were shown for those in the same religion, regardless of the subject.
19. Glenn deals with many of these issues in detail and believes that there are ways to protect the specific character of the school while also providing government funds. However, his belief that this should be done with a minimum of government oversight would favor religious schools over non-religious ones.
20. Glenn, *The Ambiguous Embrace*.
21. This observation needs to be modified in the case of home schooling which, if such practices are to be allowed, needs to be predicated on parents giving up some of this authority to allow the state the same monitoring privileges that it assumes for any school.

22. See the opinion in *Runyon* v. *McGrary*, 427 U.S. 160 (1976) where, even though the Court denied that the practice of excluding racial minorities was protected by the Constitution as Freedom of Association, it allowed that parents have a right to send their children to schools that advance the belief that racial segregation is desirable. The opinion neglects to consider the role that schools have in reproducing the subjective conditions of democracy, and to other groups.

23. These are all beliefs that I have heard expressed by religious educators in my ongoing research.

24. Alan Peshkin, *God's Choice* (Chicago: University of Chicago Press, 1986).

25. Brighouse believes that by providing public support for such institutions they can be brought under greater public control. Yet this is an empirical issue and will likely differ from country to country depending on historical and cultural factors. Nevertheless, as I argue later, the possibility for such control should certainly be a factor when considering whether public funds should go to support religious schools. See Harry Brighouse, *School Choice and Social Justice* (Oxford: Oxford University Press, 2000).

26. David Blacker, "Fanaticism and Schooling in the Democratic State", *American Journal of Education*, 106(2) (1998), 241–72.

27. Brighouse, *School Choice and Social Justice*, 17.

28. Charles Taylor, *Multiculturalism*, A. Gutmann (ed.) (Princeton: Princeton University Press, 1994), 52–72.

29. At this moment, the US Supreme Court has refused to review the Wisconsin decision hence allowing it to stand, at least for the time being. Both supporters and critics believe that the Wisconsin decision may serve to open the floodgates for vouchers. However, there are at least three obstacles that stand in the way of this happening immediately. The first is the US Supreme Court, which will eventually rule on some voucher case, and which is rather evenly divided at this time. The second is individual state constitutions which differ considerably in their attitude toward public support for religious and private schools, with some explicitly forbidding it. The third is the view of political and educational leaders about whether such support is politically sound and educationally wise. Whether the decision in Wisconsin leads the nation down the path to choice, or whether it turns out to be a legislative and judicial dead end, will depend on just how well the implications of choice are understood, both for the relationship between church and state and for the improvement of education.

30. The Supreme Court of Wisconsin, case No. 97-0270, *Jackson* v. *Benson*, June 10, 1998, www://courts.wi.us/html/sc/97/0270.htmp. p. 11 of 46.

31. *Jackson* v. *Benson*, 22.

32. See Jessica Benjamin, *The Bonds of Love* (New York: Pantheon, 1988), 11–50.

33. Brighouse, *School Choice and Social Justice*.

34. Bokser and Bokser, "Introduction: The Spirituality of the Talmud" in *The Talmud: Selected Writings*, 7 (1989), 30–1. Quoted in Michael Perry, *Love and Power* (New York: Oxford University Press, 1991), 40.

35. While non-religious public schools would continue to exist in most urban areas, it should not be assumed that this would be the case in smaller towns where religion pervades all activities. See, for example, "School Prayer: A Community at War", *Frontline*. PBS.

36. Feinberg Walter, *Common Schools/Uncommon Identities* (New Haven: Yale, 1998).

37. David Alvey, *Irish Education: The Case for Secular Reform* (Dublin: Church and State Books, 1991), 16.

38. Ibid., 15–16. It should be mentioned that not all the incidents are so negative. One very religious teacher used the taunting of a non-religious boy to teach the class how fortunate they were to have a child who was different from them in the classroom. While there is a positive message in this episode, we should not forget the climate that promotes such taunting nor its effects when an enlightened teacher is not present. (Ibid., 16).

39. Elmer John Thiessen, *Teaching for Commitment: Liberal Education, Indoctrination and Christian Nurture* (Montreal: McGill-Queens University Press, 1993).

40. Glenn, *The Ambiguous Embrace*, 279.

CHAPTER 15

Liberalism and Group Identities

Stephen Macedo

What stance ought liberal democrats to take toward educational policies and other political measures designed to recognize and affirm group identities? Does the traditional liberal concern with equal individual freedom counsel hostility toward group rights, group identities, and group inequalities? Or do liberal educational values support the sympathetic engagement with a wide array of group identities in the curriculum?

Liberal democratic values provide, I shall argue, strong *support for recognizing, affirming, and celebrating group identities* where groups suffer political, economic, and cultural disadvantages on account of prejudice and arbitrary exclusion. Moreover, basic liberal values also *accommodate and permit* all sorts of educational measures that involve the celebration of the wide array of group identities that coexist peacefully within modern pluralistic communities. Liberals will be hostile to groups only when they seek—in their educational policies and elsewhere—to oppress group members or to deny some individuals or classes of persons equal access to basic opportunities. There are some hard cases involving tensions and conflicts between group identities and equal individual freedom. These hard cases merit the sort of scholarly attention that they receive elsewhere in this volume. It would be a mistake to conclude, however, based on an examination of hard cases involving illiberal groups, that liberal societies and liberal educational values are hostile to group identities; quite the opposite is the case.

This chapter has three parts. I first rebut the charge that a liberal public philosophy embraces a narrow individualism that is incompatible with tackling group-based forms of inequality. I survey some of the myriad liberal reforms of the 1950s, 1960s, and 1970s which promoted more equal respect for differing group identities, especially in schools.

The second part of the chapter focuses on the difficulties raised by "traditionalistic" groups that seek special accommodations in part because they reject liberal values of equal freedom for all. A liberal regime should not seek to be equally hospitable or accommodating to groups that accept and those that reject educational policies designed to promote the equal freedom of all persons, including women, gays, and others subject to arbitrary discrimination. Liberal educators should not celebrate "diversity" uncritically.

The third part of the chapter takes up some recent controversies on college campuses involving Christian student groups that refuse to allow homosexual members to serve in leadership positions: should such groups be denied a portion of the university's student activities fee because they discriminate against gays, or should this mild form of discrimination be tolerated and accommodated because it is based on sincere religious beliefs? More broadly, should private schools that teach that homosexuality is sinful be excluded from publicly funded voucher schemes because they discriminate, or accommodated because their views are part of a traditional way of life grounded in sincere religious convictions?

15.1. Liberalism, Education, and Group Identities

The fundamental liberal value is equal basic freedom for all individuals irrespective of differences of race, religion, gender, creed, or any other particular "identity." It would be wrong, however, to join those who believe that pursuing the liberal ideal entails a posture of blindness or even hostility to group-based identities and categories.[1] In the United States, for example, public schools and public educational policy more generally have been important vehicles for the pursuit of liberal political and social reconstruction. There is much about American public schools that may be criticized, but there can be no doubt that they became in the latter half of the twentieth century, repositories of profound liberal efforts to promote greater respect for groups long excluded from full participation in the political mainstream. Schools and education policy were at the center of a liberal social revolution for blacks, women, ethnic minorities, and others. These liberal reforms did not deny group identities in the name of rootless individualism, but rather promoted more equal respect for groups long excluded from the mainstream. Liberal reforms also combated the unfair dominance of whites, males, and others.

It is worth recalling that liberal judges were at the forefront of several related efforts to promote greater fairness among religious, racial, ethnic, and other groups in the United States. First, liberal judges sought to recognize and rectify unfair and disabling group inequalities. Second, liberal judges sought to limit the ability of dominant cultural groups unfairly to imprint public institutions with their particular values and messages, thus helping to make common institutions more truly common. And third, liberals have tended to be more open to various forms of group-based accommodation.

Group-based Remedies for Group-based Inequalities

Let us consider, first, the pursuit of greater equality among groups. The promotion of liberal equality among individual rights holders does not require the suppression of group-based identities and categories. Quite the contrary, it is typically the most reactionary *opponents of liberal reforms*—on the Supreme Court, Justices Clarence Thomas and Antonin Scalia—who insist most vehemently that fairness among individuals requires resolute "color blindness." It was conservative judges and politicians who opposed court-ordered busing to overcome the effects of residential segregation on public school attendance, and conservatives continue to oppose race-conscious remedies of all sorts, including affirmative action programs and race-conscious legislative redistricting. As Justice Thomas puts it, "In my mind, government-sponsored racial discrimination based on benign prejudice is just as noxious as discrimination inspired by malicious prejudice. In each instance, it is racial discrimination, plain and simple."[2] Justice Scalia is equally unequivocal:

In my view, government can never have a 'compelling state interest' in discriminating on the basis of race in order to 'make up' for past racial discrimination in the opposite direction. Individuals who have been wronged by unlawful racial discrimination should be made whole; but under our Constitution there can be no such thing as either a creditor or a debtor race. This concept is alien to the Constitution's focus upon the individual ... To pursue the concept of racial entitlement—even for the most admirable and benign of purposes—is to reinforce and preserve for future mischief the way of thinking that produced race slavery, race privilege and race hatred. In the eyes of government, we are just one race here. It is American.[3]

These views are explicit reactions against liberal policies, such as affirmative action and race conscious legislative redistricting, that are designed to try and remedy the current group-based inequalities that are the result of malign discrimination. As Justice Blackmun said in *Regents of California* v. *Bakke*, the famous affirmative action case, "In order to get beyond racism we must first take account of race. There is no other way. And in order to treat some persons equally, we must treat them differently." A hallmark of contemporary liberalism is the conviction that there is all the difference in the world between using racial categories to overcome inequality, and using them to perpetuate inequality.[4]

It would be wrong, moreover, to assert that the liberalism we inherited from the revolutionary era of the 1960s and 1970s was alert only to racial and economic inequalities, and blind to gender and other forms of inequality. In *A Theory of Justice*, Rawls emphasized the broad application of liberal equality:

Justice as fairness appraises the social system from the position of equal citizenship and the various levels of income and wealth. Sometimes, however, other positions may need to be taken into account. If, for example, there are unequal basic rights founded on fixed natural characteristics, these inequalities will single out relevant positions ... Distinctions based on sex are of this type, and so are those depending on race and culture. Thus if men, say, are favored in the assignment of basic rights, this inequality is justified by the difference principle only if it is to the advantage of women and acceptable from their standpoint. And an analogous condition applies to the justification of caste systems, or racial and ethnic inequalities ... [T]hese inequalities are seldom, if ever, to the advantage of the less favored ...[5]

Liberal values support sympathetic engagement with group identities, in the first instance, by seeking group-conscious ways of remedying the current effects of past discrimination. Liberals insist, against increasingly dominant conservative majorities, that courts should be permissive rather than restrictive when states or the federal government use racial categories to *promote greater equality* in pupil assignment within public school systems, in college admissions, and in the awarding of government contracts and the drawing of legislative district lines. Where, on the other hand, laws and government policies accord *unequal* treatment to traditionally disfavored groups—especially where these group identities rest on some "immutable" characteristic, such as race, ethnicity, gender, age, or illegitimacy—liberals do indeed insist on the *strictest* judicial scrutiny and the highest level of suspicion. And liberals on the Supreme Court have argued for expanding the list of groups who should qualify for protective forms of special scrutiny to include, for example, illegal aliens and the poor.[6]

The second way in which the liberal revolution promoted greater equality of respect among majority and minority cultural and religious groups has led to the charge, ironically, that liberal judges and policy makers are bent on denuding the public educational system and the public square more broadly of shared values.[7]

The cases that struck down public school prayer and devotional Bible reading raised a firestorm of controversy, leading to wide-spread calls for the impeachment of Chief Justice Earl Warren. These cases, however, along with others, such as those concerning the display of religious symbols at Christmas time and the invalidation of a Louisiana law mandating equal time for the teaching of evolution and "Creation Science" in public schools, have done a great deal to make the public schools and public squares of America less sectarian and more truly public: the shared property of all Americans. As a matter of constitutional principle, at least, there are now important limits on the ways in which public schools and other public places can reflect and promote the religious convictions of the powerful. It is not hostility to religion but a greater sense of fairness that justifies curbs on officially sponsored sectarian expression. Public institutions in America are now more truly public—less sectarian—on account of liberal judicial activism.

It is important to recognize that the imposition of these and other basic limits on the curriculum of public schools does not preclude those schools from exploring, studying, and even celebrating the cultural and religious traditions of the citizenry. Celebrating particular identities within society will often be all to the good, so long as they are undertaken in the spirit of equal respect for the dignity of all the groups that participate in civil society. When the religious dimensions of our history and culture are now displayed in public schools and parks and civic buildings, these typically acknowledge the variety of religions and cultures within the nation, those established here only recently and those from long ago. The Christmas crèche set up in a public park is surely more acceptable if accompanied by the menorah and symbols of the holiday observances of other citizens.[8] Liberals should not and typically do not seek to banish all religious expression from the public sphere or from public schools.

It would be hard to miss or deny the fact that school curricula have become centrally concerned with an egalitarian multicultural-ism. Indeed, an oft-heard complaint nowadays is that the concern with cultural variety leaves too little space for learning about shared values and traditions, too little time for learning about any particular traditions deeply rather than superficially, and too little time for in depth study of the best that has been written and produced by human beings across the ages. I believe it is very likely true that, as some charge, more time and energy should be devoted in schools to the study of what can credibly be regarded as truly great works of literature, philosophy, and art that come down to us through the ages. Too much time is spent in many classrooms sampling mediocre writings assembled with an eye toward author demographics, or for the sake of simplistic moralizing, rather than on the basis of enduring excellence. It would be absurd to regard these choices as a matter of "either quality or inclusion." There are difficult tradeoffs to be made here, but taking inclusion seriously does not mean that no time can be made for in depth study of great literary works.[9]

Debates such as these go on within the framework of basic liberal and democratic values: these educational controversies cannot be settled by basic liberal democratic values. All sorts of political failure lie behind failed classrooms. Local school boards, state regulators, textbook writers, and teachers, sometimes, or even often, allow the pursuit of multicultural inclusion to be an excuse for the production and presentation of insipid, boring, but pedantic classroom materials. Parents and taxpayers must not be let off the hook. While reforming the curriculum to pursue both inclusion and the pursuit of excellence is not easy, legitimate causes of dissatisfaction cannot justify turning our backs on the great progress that has been made toward respecting the equal basic dignity of all those cultures and traditions that participate in our collective civil life.

We should not allow a concern with fundamental national values to obscure the fact that most of our politics, most of educational practice and choices, and most of the work of group recognition, takes place at much lower levels of politics: in states and cities and local school boards, in school districts, schools, and classrooms. Educational practices are constrained and shaped by liberal values, but not determined by them. Basic liberal values are consistent with a wide variety of educational regimes.

Liberal values, by creating general conditions of freedom and equality, thereby facilitate all sorts of mundane but important forms of group recognition and affirmation. Much of this focuses on local politics and civil society. Many ordinary forms of group recognition have been woven into public schools and the civic calendars of great cities, so many that we are probably apt to forget them. It was only in the early decades of this century that Irish-Americans entered the mainstream of American politics, but marching in the St. Patrick's Day parade is now mandatory for local politicians in major cities with significant numbers of Irish-Americans. The same goes for participation in Columbus Day celebrations, commemorations for Martin Luther King, Caribbean street festivals, and, increasingly, Gay and Lesbian Pride parades. The proliferation of these symbolic but significant acts of civic recognition of group diversity is all to the good. Groups will continue to jostle and sometimes feel slighted, but there are many weekends on the calendar, the mayor can march in many parades, and the effort at inclusion counts. The dominant Anglo-Euro-Christian inheritance (itself a potpourri from the start) need not be suppressed or denied, but it should be (and it increasingly is) celebrated in the spirit of civic inclusion, and overlain with new forms of assertion and recognition as groups form and reform, and seek to celebrate and gain public recognition of their distinctiveness.

It is worth remembering that basic liberal values—those that inform a just constitutional framework—are a narrow, albeit a fundamental, subset of all political values, so it should not be taken as a criticism or weakness that in important ways our basic liberal values simply permit rather than prescribe educational measures designed to celebrate and sympathetically explore various forms of group identity. As fellow citizens of the nation we are not properly defined by cultural specificity, but rather by our highest political ideals, ideals that should attract allegiance insofar as they live up to their claim to provide justice and a good life for all. But our political and civic lives are multifaceted, and a preoccupation with only overarching and inclusive "liberal" values will of course yield a very narrow view.

Many of these routine forms of civic recognition of diversity are akin to Kymlicka's "polyethnic rights." There are of course dangers in any and all forms of group recognition. Group pride can be obnoxious and silly, and indeed it can distract people from real common interests and perpetuate arbitrary forms of preference and discrimination. Nevertheless, I suspect that Kymlicka is basically right that these sorts of demands for recognition generally amount not to the rejection of a common citizenship, but to a renegotiation of the terms of inclusion. The more local one gets the harder it is to imagine politics without group recognition. What we need to do is to foster cooperation and mingling across group lines, so the differences are not sources of hostility. Ethnic identities persist—as among Irish-Americans—but on St. Patrick's Day, as they say, everyone is Irish. On Martin Luther King Day, many identify with, and take pride in the struggle for, civil rights. And maybe someday, on Gay Pride Day everyone will be gay. It is not crazy to hope that we are heading in that direction. If the proliferation of ethnic festivals and demands for acknowledgment and recognition seems a sign of fragmentation, then work should be done to strengthen common institutions such as political parties, public schools with a strong common ethos, etc. There are many ways of attracting people to the commons, and of empowering overarching civic bonds, and these do not require discouraging more particular identities.

Liberal Worries About Group-based Remedies

Liberal worries about group-based remedies will always exist. One is that, in using racial and ethnic categories to remedy the evil legacy of racial and ethnic discrimination and prejudice, we are perpetuating those arbitrary categories. There are innumerable ways of identifying and sorting people. The salience of certain categories is a consequence of histories of prejudice and discrimination. As David Hollinger notes, we think of Alex Haley as black rather than Irish (in spite of his mixed blood) because racism has made skin color overwhelmingly salient. The fact is that everyone's gene pool is a polyglot mess. Hollinger puts it very nicely: "racism not race is real."[10] Race is a myth, as Anthony Appiah also argues. Racial categories are useful and important because of the long history and deep implications of racism. Racial categories are important because of this unjust past: to identify this species of injustice, measure its effects, and seek to undo it. Jews are no longer regarded as a race, Hollinger argues, because prejudice against them is less severe than it was. Anglo-Saxon, Teutonic, and Gaul used to be important racial categories (into the early decades of the twentieth century). Southern Europeans, Eastern Europeans, and the Irish were all thought to be inferior "races."[11]

These arguments can be overstated. There may be no genetic reality that underlie races as we understand them, and racism is indeed evil. But racial discrimination gave rise to collective identities that have value and significance for people. The resistance to racism was often noble, and rich cultures developed among victims of slavery and discrimination (who were not merely victims). It is hardly surprising that many wish to learn about these cultures, and to celebrate aspects of them.

A somewhat different concern is that racial and other group identities can constitute "scripts" that constrain the freedom of individuals. A consciousness of historical oppression based on a group identity and a desire to resist and overcome it—to claim equal dignity as black, female, or homosexual—is a powerful source of group solidarity. As Anthony Appiah points out, the natural way to defy and revise the negative "scripts" that went along with oppression is to furnish and propagate new positive scripts, whether of "black power", liberated womanhood, or queer identity, and to demand that mainstream society recognize and affirm these scripts. The danger is that the very quest for greater equality will lead some to promulgate mandatory norms of thought and conduct, which can thwart individuality. Struggles to resist and overcome the past often give rise to powerful expectations about how individual blacks or gays should think and behave: firm "party lines" that blacks, women, and gays are expected to adhere to by other blacks, women, and gays. Under the banner of "diversity" there is often no tolerance for intellectual differences. Individuality can be thwarted by shared expectations about the forms of behavior and belief appropriate to authentic members of a group.

Educational institutions need to work to overcome group based stigma and discrimination without fostering false and empty forms of group pride, and without foisting new stereotypes on individuals. Positive stereotypes are still stereotypes that will not suit the aspirations of many individuals. It may be that understanding the varying cultural backgrounds of students can help us understand some of their distinctive problems and aspirations. On the other hand, approaching individuals as members of groups—even with the best of intentions—could lead us to saddle them with cultural baggage that they have no wish to carry.

In his fine book, *Common Schools, Uncommon Identities*, Walter Feinberg argues that public schools should foster educational engagement with cultural differences in order to promote the equal freedom of students to revise or reject their cultural inheritances and to "rewrite" the scripts they have been handed by being born into particular cultural groups. This is unobjectionable so long as the aim is to understand and treat each student as an individual, and so long as educators are alert to the idea that particular students may prefer to largely ignore rather than revise their specific cultural baggage (it is not of course possible to really leave one's particular cultural inheritance altogether behind, but that does not mean that reworking one's particular ethnic or racial or religious inheritance must be one's self-conscious project).

Something bothers me about identifying individual students based on racial and cultural memberships, even when our aim is to reassure them that they are not limited by the life patterns associated with these memberships. Consider Feinberg's remarks:

1. "Multicultural thinking skills ultimately entail students coming to understand the various stories about cultural and national

identity *as scripts* that are presented for them to validate, challenge, negotiate, and rewrite."

2. "Students need to read the scripts not just as means to locate themselves and others in terms of their understanding of the American experience but also as proposals for commitment and action that require careful criticism and reflection, as well as a close reading of different historical possibilities."

3. "Students need ... to be aware that scripts help locate people but do not define them and that people may occupy different roles within the same script at different times."[12]

The liberal element here is obvious and appealing: scripts are open to revision. But I am uneasy with the sense that collective, group-oriented stories allow us to "locate" individuals, even if we mean to empower them to change their location. I am uneasy with the notion that individuality and freedom are best conceived as engagements with investigating (or "interrogating") and seeking to revise the types and stereotypes associated with particular racial, ethnic, religious, or cultural groups. Learning the "scripts" associated with particular cultures is often not the key to understanding individuals. The ideal of liberal education is to make available to as many students as possible the best of the *human* inheritance in all its richness and variety. That means, at some point, not worrying too much about the scripts associated with students' communities of origin.

15.2. Special Exemptions and the Rights of Traditional Communities

Yoder

Generally applicable laws and public policies often impose special burdens on religious minorities. Mandatory Sunday closing laws for businesses impose special burdens on those whose religious obligations fall on Saturday or some other day. When should legislators, school administrators, and other public officials make exceptions and provide special accommodations for minorities whose practices differ from those of the mainstream? This is a vexing area, characterized by complicated political divisions and difficult tradeoffs.

There are all sorts of ordinary and routine forms of accommodations, in public schools and elsewhere: we accommodate religious days of obligation with changes in exam dates, school cafeterias accommodate special dietary restrictions, etc. No doubt accommodations are often too slow in coming, and bureaucrats too often fall back on the ease and apparent fairness of "the same rules for all", even when the special burdens or costs borne by some are unjustified by any substantial collective benefit. Accommodations and exemptions should often be granted when the special burdens are genuine and substantial, when they are not easily avoided, and when the costs of making exceptions are reasonable. Courts should be prepared to intervene when small groups credibly claim to be denied requested exemptions based on prejudice, discrimination, or the simple lack of equal concern and respect.[13] Admittedly, even after every group's interests are taken into account, there are no easy formulas for weighing and comparing the costs and benefits of exceptions to rules.

Hard cases arise when illiberal groups seek accommodations that threaten the basic interests of vulnerable members within the group, including children and women: respect for the group-specific values may compete with what we publicly understand to be the basic interests of individuals within groups. *Wisconsin* v. *Yoder* is a hard case because allowing Amish parents to exempt their children from the last two years of mandatory school attendance laws may compromise the ability of Amish children to make their own decisions about how to lead their lives. There are vexing empirical issues here about how much the exercise of freedom is impaired by the child's early exit from formal schooling. There are vexing principled questions about how far public authorities should go to insure that all children are enabled to make substantially free choices about whether they wish to adhere to, revise, or rebel against the values and beliefs of their parents and neighbors.

At one extreme, some suggest that the authority of the state ends when it protects children from gross abuse and enforces the right of adults to exit from any group or community.[14] Most observers go further, however, and argue that public authorities should provide all children with an education that prepares them to be substantially capable of making reflective and informed choices about how they wish to live. Each commentator on these matters advances a distinctive position. Shelley Burtt argues that it is enough for children to acquire some critical distance on the ways of life of their parents and communities of birth: it is enough that children can shape their cultural inheritance and make it their own. Others go further and insist that in order to be free, all children should be educated about the whole world of options and lifestyles: children should be educated so as to be able not simply to shape their particular inheritance, but to reject it and choose among the wide world of available options.

Susan Okin places a special emphasis on insuring that young women are educated so that they have the same effective freedom as boys to work outside the home, enter public life, and reject traditional roles. Gender based educational differences are as bad as racially disparate opportunities. Okin goes so far as to argue that the "Catholic Church and Orthodox Judaism should be denied tax-exempt status as long as they discriminate against women."[15]

We should neither minimize nor exaggerate the oppressive potential of traditional communities or parents. The Catholic Church does discriminate against women in denying them access to the priesthood, but the fact is that women are important authority figures in traditional Catholic schools. Children educated in Catholic schools may even have more egalitarian gender attitudes than children educated in public schools, at least according to some.[16] While Shelley Burtt, on the other hand, seems to severely diminish public educational authority in favor of parents, she mainly seems concerned with questions of age appropriateness: Burtt would allow parents to choose schools that shield children from sympathetic exposure to the wide variety of lifestyles and value until high school. This would allow children's education to begin, but not end, with a focus on immersion in a particular ethical or religious tradition.[17] Important differences remain among the general positions advanced elsewhere in this volume, though I will not try to sort them out or choose among them.

As I already noted, the Amish parents in *Yoder* sought an exemption from two years of mandatory high school attendance, and it is not easy to say how many children are condemned to subordination or ignorance on account of this exemption. Nevertheless, I am doubtful that the *Yoder* case was decided rightly. A form of accommodation was already available to the Amish, along with any other groups who reject some of the educational values of public high schools: the Amish could have exercised their right to establish and send their children to their own private sectarian high schools, subject of course to public educational requirements and limitations. This is already a concession to educational diversity, and it is widely available rather than available to only one group in society. The pre-*Yoder* status quo seems to me preferable to the special exemption from high school attendance granted by the Supreme Court in *Yoder*.[18]

Christian and Gays on Campus

There is often a real tension between promoting liberal democratic civic values and respecting freedom of association, at least when the association in question reject some shared values. Striking a reasonable balance—in educational settings and elsewhere—is difficult. Freedom of association is a basic value that often requires that we tolerate people's choices to form illiberal associations, but toleration does not mean that we must remain indifferent or neutral toward the aims of such groups.

Consider a recent set of controversies on college campuses involving a national conservative religious group—the InterVarsity Christian Fellowship (IVCF)—which has chapters on over 550 college campuses, involving over 34,000 students and faculty. The group believes that premarital sex is against Biblical teaching, and that homosexual activity is always wrong. Members at several IVCF chapters have been barred from seeking leadership positions after announcing that they had come to reject the IVCF's official position on homosexuality. Some of these students changed their views partly a result of embracing their own same-sex attractions. These IVCF chapters were among the many "recognized" student groups on these campuses, and their "recognized" status permitted them to meet and advertise on campus, and it allowed them to receive a portion of student activities fees. This status also subjected the IVCF chapters to the colleges' antidiscrimination policies, which ban discrimination based on sexual orientation. Should antidiscrimination rules be applied to these religious groups, or should they be exempted?

Complaints were filed against several IVCF chapters. The Tufts Christian Fellowship was in fact "de-recognized", at least for a time.[19] IVCF chapters at Middlebury College in Vermont, Whitman College in Oregon, Grinnell College in Iowa, and Williams College in Massachusetts faced expulsion from campus.

At Tufts, the student who filed the complaint had struggled with her sexuality for years, until finally revealing her feelings to friends in the Tufts Christian Fellowship. She was accepted as a member, and ran Bible study groups as she prayed to God to make her heterosexual.[20] Some months later, while seeking a senior leadership position in the group, she announced a further change of heart, telling her friends that she had decided that homosexuality was not a sin and that she intended to begin dating other women. Shortly thereafter, chapter officers told her that she was not qualified to stand for office because her beliefs ran counter to the Bible's teaching that homosexuality is a sin. She filed a discrimination complaint with campus authorities.

Leaders of the IVCF say that the Tufts student was not singled out because she is gay: they would bar from positions of leadership any member who rejected core Biblical teachings as they understand them (including, presumably, the prohibition on premarital sex). Nevertheless, the Biblical injunction that the student was alleged to have violated was a prohibition on same-sex dating, not the more general prohibition on premarital sex.

At some college campuses, including Williams College, administrators have considered requiring recognized student groups to adopt constitutions clearly stating that the organizations do not discriminate in any of their internal practices (including leadership selection) on a number of grounds including religious belief and sexual orientation. Should campus Christian groups be required to allow non-Christians to stand for leadership positions? If discrimination based on sexual orientation is barred, should gay groups be required to allow straights to run for office? This may seem implausible, but some of the Christian groups cite examples of "hostile takeovers."

First Amendment values are on various sides of this controversy. The Supreme Court has ruled that when public universities collect a student activities fee and make it available to student-initiated groups generally—in order to stimulate campus activity and student intellectual life—they may not single out religious groups and declare them ineligible.[21] It seems reasonable to say that when public universities set up the equivalent of "public forums" for the exchange of ideas, they should respect the expressive viewpoints of students. But what about *private* colleges and universities? They are themselves voluntary associations and it would seem that they have the right to stand for their own distinctive values. Of course, even if private universities have a substantial amount of discretion in deciding what sorts of student groups to officially "recognize" and support, it is difficult to imagine a vigorous intellectual life on campus unless students are free to express themselves, organize, and disagree about important political and cultural matters. The values that private colleges stand for should be subject to debate and contestation by students.

The crucial competing values in the IVCF cases involve opposition to discrimination against gays, on the one side, and freedom of expressive association on the other. How should a college dedicated to liberal educational values balance these competing interests?

If colleges and universities decide to bar discrimination against homosexuals seeking leadership positions in conservative Christian campus organizations like IVCF, this would not necessarily be a matter of Christians being discriminated against or persecuted because of their religious beliefs. If colleges want to take a stand against discrimination based on sexual orientation in any and all student organizations, they are not required to make an exception for religiously based organizations. On the other hand, if campus organizations want to favor the values of freedom of association, then ideological and philosophical student groups should have the same rights as the religious groups.

There is more than one permissible way to settle these disputes. The best way would be to respect freedom to associate and propagate a wide variety of views, while also taking a stand *against* discrimination and *for* other basic liberal values. Colleges should respect the rights of students—subject to certain provisos, including respect for the rules of civility—to form and maintain recognized student groups that propagate the view that homosexual activity is sinful, immoral, and intrinsically inferior to heterosexuality. All of the usual reasons for respecting free speech apply most strongly to college campuses. Bad arguments should be met with better arguments. College is a time when many people are prepared to think critically about their deepest commitments, and students really do change their views. Cultural conservatives need to be engaged intellectually; if liberals have superior reasons and evidence, then we should expect some to change their views. Recognized campus groups should be barred from preaching hatred. I would leave the open forum open in other respects.

It is crucial to remember that universities can accommodate and even facilitate student organizations on both sides of the question of the morality of homosexual conduct, while maintaining and indeed reaffirming a commitment to non-discrimination based on sexual orientation. Colleges and universities should provide health and other spousal benefits to the committed same sex partners of faculty and other employees. Colleges and universities should take a stand for the liberal values—broadly understood—that are essential to the mission of a modern university, or that are important to the just treatment of faculty and other employees, while protecting the rights of students to organize to contest these values.

I would impose additional requirements on recognized student groups. College administrators should not allow groups to exclude from standing for offices members whose views deviate from the group's current ideology. More broadly, a university should require that recognized groups should be student-run: democratically organized, deliberative, and capable of engaging in critical self-examination. Student groups should be required to have regular elections for officers. Qualifications for office might include membership in good standing for a period of time, but not subscription to a particular fixed set of beliefs. Student groups should, at liberal institutions of higher learning, have the right to organize and advocate particular views on questions of politics, sexual morality, gender relations, and the like, but the commitments of groups should be debatable, discussable, contestable in elections, and revisable as a consequence of the group's internal deliberations and elections. Building the freedom to contest and revise opinions into expressive student groups seems to me altogether consistent with the mission of a liberal arts university: and universities should not be neutral with respect to these liberal values.[22]

The "hostile takeover" of a student organization is a danger only when it is the result of infiltration, or takeover from without. When the change takes place from within, it is not a hostile takeover but a revision of what the group stands for on due reflection. If an IVCF member decides that on reflection the Bible's apparent condemnation of homosexuality can and should be reinterpreted, she should have the right to run for office and seek to change what the group stands for. Oligarchic cliques should not be allowed to prevent open debate and contestation within campus groups by keeping dissenters or critics from standing for elections, and this is true whether the clique is composed of current officeholders or those who determine the guidelines of national associations. Churches have a right to organize their affairs that way, but student groups that identify with those churches need not have the same right to do so. Of course, a national association might expel a campus chapter that rejects its orthodoxy, but that is their business and not the concern of university officials.

Some will protest that these rules are not "neutral" with respect to differing religious communities and beliefs. It might suit "liberal" religious denominations to leave basic creedal commitments open to debate and contestation, but this is inappropriate from the point of view of some more conservative and fundamentalist religious organizations: those who believe in fixed truths and those churches which do indeed give "oligarchic cliques" rather than congregants the authority to define doctrine (whether the Pope, mullahs, senior rabbis, or others).

The rules of the game in liberal educational institutions should be determined with an eye to liberal values. While groups of students within the university and adults outside of it are free to reject these liberal rules, it is perfectly permissible to reserve the privileges of campus recognition to groups that are prepared to operate on principles appropriate to the educational environment. Educational institutions dedicated to liberal learning should take the imperatives of civil debate and openness to revision of beliefs even more seriously than the polity at large.

Some might propose a different option. Instead of insisting that dissenters within established groups must be allowed to run for office, let them break off and form their own splinter organizations to compete for members: the "Progressive Christian Fellowship of Tufts University Welcomes Gay Members!" The freedom to form competing organizations is indeed an important aspect of free association. The question is: who should bear the burden of breaking off and founding a new organization? It seems more consistent with liberal intellectual ideals to insist on the right to contest established views *within* organizations: if the losers do not like the outcome, they can consider splitting off. Openness to contestation and revision of beliefs should be fostered within associations on campus, in the name of liberal values. The rules should not be set up to protect established convictions and authorities from criticism and challenge. The last thing a university should do is to set the rules so that the advantage lies with entrenched interests who want to thwart critical re-examination of ideas. There is nothing wrong with tilting the playing field to encourage subgroups to take important liberal and democratic values more seriously.

Colleges and universities can thus protect the freedom of association of conservative students, while taking a stand for the equal treatment of gay and lesbian students and staff. They can support ideological diversity and free association, while favoring the contestation, critical deliberation, and openness to change that are hallmarks of a liberal education. Liberal arts institutions can, in these ways, respect the right of students to oppose some basic values of the institution—including acceptance of homosexuals and openness to criticism and revision of ideas—without adopting a stance of indifference or neutrality with respect to the liberal values that are being contested.

Discrimination Against Gays in Primary and Secondary Schools

Of course, colleges and universities are distinctive educational environments. College students have generally attained "the age of maturity": they are not required by law to attend school, they can enter into contracts, and make a variety of decisions governing their own lives. We believe that they should be able to handle the clash of ideas

on campus without the same level of adult supervision that characterizes lower levels of education.

But what about education at lower levels? How should we feel
about private high schools and grammar schools that teach that
homosexuality is sinful? Should they be allowed to exist? Should
they be eligible for participation in publicly funded voucher
schemes?

There is a range of possible responses open to those who oppose
discrimination against gays and lesbians. Most liberals believe, after
all, that sexual orientation is generally stable and fixed early in life,
and so is part of a person's condition and not alterable. There is,
moreover, nothing wrong with same-sex acts. Discrimination against
gays and lesbians is arbitrary and wrong: it ought to be recognized
as such by the courts. Laws that discriminate on the basis of sexual
orientation (like those that discriminate on grounds of race or religion) ought to be subject to "strict scrutiny", and ought nearly
always to be invalidated. If all this is so, why should schools that
hold that homosexual acts are sinful and morally wrong be allowed
to participate in publicly funded voucher schemes, any more than are
racist schools?

It certainly ought to be permissible for states and localities that
institute voucher schemes to decide that schools that discriminate in
hiring or admissions decisions on grounds of sexual orientation (and
certainly race and gender) ought to be ineligible to participate in a
voucher scheme. There are employment non-discrimination ordin-
ances on the books in some major cities, and these may apply to
government agencies and those who wish to enter into public sector
contracts and spend tax dollars.

It would be possible to go further and say that schools and churches
that teach that homosexual activity is wrong ought not to qualify
for tax-exempt status: institutions that discriminate against gays
(and blacks or women) do not contribute to the public good in the
way that other charities do, and so should not qualify for property
tax exemptions. The IRS ruled in the early 1980s that Bob Jones
University should no longer enjoy tax-exempt status because it did
not allow interracial dating on campus on religious grounds, and the
Supreme Court allowed the IRS to do this in spite of objections
based on religious freedom.[23] Of course, opponents of discrimination could go even further and say that if schools teach that homosexuality is sinful, attendance at them will not qualify as ways of
fulfilling the mandatory school attendance laws. Or the schools
could be closed down. That would be draconian.

Given that many Americans believe that homosexual conduct is sinful and wrong, it would be difficult to maintain that schools that teach this view ought to be closed down. We are far from having arrived, as a nation, at a reasonable consensus with respect to homosexuality. The Supreme Court's jurisprudence still allows states to criminalize same-sex sexual activity.[24]

Even if it could be done in some particular jurisdiction, I would oppose even denying tax exemptions to schools that teach that homosexuality is sinful. For one thing, religious organizations that teach the sinfulness of homosexuality generally have conservative positions on sexual morality as a whole: they do not simply single out homosexuality. The Catholic Church teaches that sex outside of marriage is sinful, and that the use of contraceptives, even within marriage, is sinful. Many of us regard these views as wrong, and even pernicious, but many of our fellow citizens disagree. Moreover, the Catholic Church and many other churches can and generally do teach that homosexual activity is wrong, while denying that people should hate homosexuals. Indeed, Catholic priests and nuns minister to homosexual AIDS patients and many other "sinners." There is really no great paradox in the maxim, "hate the sin, love the sinner."

As a nation, we are very much in the midst of working through our stance toward sexual orientation, and we must work through these issues in our states and cities and school boards and schools and classrooms. Those with liberal attitudes can and should work to change the views of Catholics and others opposed to homosexuality without glib resort to measures that are bound to be antagonistic and unhelpful in current political conditions: such as advocating of the shutting down of Catholic schools or even denying tax exemptions based on the Church's attitude toward homosexuality. The matter would be quite different, of course, if a church or school advocated or expressed hatefulness toward gays and lesbians. Opposition to homosexuality is not a focal point in Catholic education so far as I know. (And while the Catholic Church discriminates against women by disqualifying them for the priesthood, it does not teach that women are inferior to men.) The fact that the Church vigorously opposes hatefulness and violence toward gays, and ministers to the sick and needy of all sexual orientations, makes the reality too complex to allow for simple responses. Churches and private schools need to be engaged in civil society. Insofar as we disagree with the views they express on sexual orientation and some other matters—insofar as we regard their views as unreasonable and un-Christian—we can oppose them civilly, insisting on the avoidance of hatefulness and prohibiting some forms of discrimination in hiring and admissions.

15.3. Conclusion

Liberal educational and political measures will seek to eradicate unfair group-based forms of inequality, and they will support many forms of group-based recognition. Liberals will also protect the freedom of association of those who oppose and seek to overturn many liberal values. But liberals should not try to make life equally easy on liberal and illiberal groups. Indeed, it may be that one reason we can and should respect a broad measure of freedom is that the liberal democratic social environment tilts (in some important ways) in a self-supporting direction.

The values of equal individual freedom, on the one side, and respect for the autonomy and integrity of group values, on the other, do sometimes come into dramatic conflict. Traditionalistic groups, including conservative religious schools and communities, raise some especially difficult and interesting problems for liberal educators. Hard cases are interesting to think about and deliberate on, but they are unrepresentative of the universe of legal conflicts, and even more untypical of human interactions generally, in which conflicts rarely rise to the level of litigation. We are all familiar with the adage that "hard cases make bad law."

Scholars and commentators tend to focus their attention on the most interesting problems, which are often the most dramatic instances of deep value conflict. A danger of this selectivity is that we may forget the far more common experience of ordinary interactions where rules of conduct are mutually observed, where the rules embody reasonable balances and mutual accommodations, and where idiosyncratic revisions and variations can often be worked out on the basis of reasonable consensus.

The ordinary reality of life in a liberal democracy such as America is that, especially at the somewhat unglamorous level of local politics and local schools, group identities are constantly being publicly acknowledged and affirmed in an atmosphere that is markedly more inclusive and accepting of differences than was a few decades ago, let alone a century ago. The liberal spirit of freedom and equality for all is a spirit that is far from hostile to the public expression and acknowledgement of the multiplicitous identities and affiliations of ordinary citizens.

Hard cases do arise, and while different scholars advance competing abstract theories designed to solve a wide range of hard cases, solutions are liable to be tentative and experimental, involving difficult balances, and calling for reasoned judgment rather than the application of abstract formulae.

NOTES

1. In *Voice, Trust, and Memory: Marginalized Groups and the Failings of Liberal Representation* (Princeton University Press, 1998), for example, Melissa S. Williams seems to identify liberalism with hostility toward race-conscious districting (and other group-based remedies for group-based inequalities), as her subtitle indicates, see p. 82, and Chapters 2 and 3. The truth is that opposition to race-based districting, affirmative action, and other race-conscious political measures designed to remedy the current effects of past discrimination, is characteristic of the conservative reaction against "liberal judicial activism."

2. Justice Clarence Thomas, concurring in part, and speaking of federal programs to give incentives for government contractors to award of 10% of highway construction monies to minority owned subcontractors, in *Adarand Constructors, Inc. v. Pena*, 515 US 200 (1995).

3. Justice Antonin Scalia, concurring in part and concurring in the judgment, in *Adarand*, ibid.

4. Justice Harry Blackmun, *Regents of the University of California v. Bakke*, 438 U.S. 265 (1978); and see Ronald Dworkin, *Taking Rights Seriously* (Harvard University Press, Cambridge, Mass., 1977), 227–8.

5. John Rawls, *A Theory of Justice* (Harvard University Press, Cambridge, Mass., 1971), 99, and see p. 73 on fair equality of opportunity.

6. See Justice William Brennan, in *Frontiero v. Richardson*, 411 US 677 (1973), and *Craig v. Boren*, 429 U.S. 190 (1976), justifying "heightened" (or intermediate) judicial scrutiny of sex-based classifications. See also *Plyler v. Doe*, 457 US 202 (1982), extending similar scrutiny to strike down a state law denying the right to a free public education to the children of illegal immigrants; here, Brennan insisted that the purpose of the Fourteenth Amendment's Equal Protection Clause is "nothing less than the abolition of all caste-based and invidious class-based legislation". The Fourteenth Amendment on Brennan's reading issues in a broad positive mandate to dismantle laws and policies that perpetuate group-based disabilities inconsistent with the ideal of equal citizenship. And see Justice Thurgood Marshall's dissent in *San Antonio School District v. Rodriguez*, 411 US 1 (1973), arguing that wealth classifications should be regarded as "suspect." Here, the dispute concerned a state system of education funding that partly reflected local tax contributions, and so channeled more money to wealthier districts. Marshall argued that the scheme should be struck down in part because "the disability of the disadvantaged class in this case extends into the political process." And, finally, see the opinions in *City of Cleburne v. Cleburne Living Center*, 473 US 432 (1985), in which the Court invalidated the application of a municipal zoning ordinance requiring special permits for the construction of homes for the mentally disabled. Justice Byron White insisted that special judicial scrutiny should be exercised when laws disadvantage groups that have experienced a "history of purposeful discrimination", and Justice John Paul Stevens argued that the central question of equal protection law is "What class is harmed by the legislation, and has it been subjected to a 'tradition of disfavor' by our laws?" Or as Justice Marshall put it (joined by Justices Brennan and Blackmun),

"The political powerlessness of a group and the immutability of its defining trait are relevant insofar as they point to a social and cultural isolation that gives the majority little reason to respect or to be concerned with the group's interests and needs...The discreteness and insularity warranting a 'more searching judicial inquiry', *United States v. Carolene Products Co.*, 304 U.S. 144 (1938), must therefore be viewed from a social and cultural perspective as well as a political one. To this task judges are well-suited, for the lessons of history and experience are surely the best guide as to when, and with respect to what interests, society is likely to stigmatize individuals as members of an inferior caste or view them as not belonging to the same community. Because prejudice spawns prejudice, and stereotypes produce limitations that confirm the stereotype on which they are based, a history of unequal treatment requires sensitivity to the prospect that its vestiges endure. In separating those groups that are discrete and insular from those that are not, '...a page of history is worth a volume of logic.' " Marshall concurring and dissenting in part in *Cleburne*, footnote 1. These are the authentic voices of liberalism in American constitutional law.

7. See, for example, conservative versions of this argument in Richard John Neuhaus, *The Naked Public Square: Religion and Democracy in America* (William B. Eerdmans co., Grand Rapids, MI: 1986), and a more politically moderate version, Stephen L. Carter, *Culture of Disbelief: How American Law and Politics Trivialize Religious Devotion* (Basic Books, New York, 1993).
8. See *Engel v. Vitale*, 370 U.S. 421 (1962), *School District of Abington Township v. Schempp*, 374 U.S. 203 (1963), and the Creation Science case, *Edwards v. Aguillard*, 482 US 578 (1987), and *Lee v. Weisman* 505 US 577 (1992), striking down a "non-denominational" prayer at a public high school graduation.
9. David Steiner advances the arresting argument that educational superficiality is built into the standardized testing regimes now being touted as keys to educational reform and improvement, see "High-Stakes Culture," in *Education Next* (formerly Education Matters) http://www.educationnext.org/20013/24steiner.html.
10. K. Anthony Appiah and Amy Gutmann, *Color Conscious: The Political Morality of Race* (Princeton, 1996), 70–4; Hollinger, David, *Post-Ethnic America: Beyond Multiculturalism* (Basic Books, New York, 1995), 39.
11. Hollinger, *Post-Ethnic America*, 37–9.
12. Walter Feinberg, *Common Schools, Uncommon Identities: National Unity and Cultural Difference* (Yale University Press, New Haven, 1998), 154–6. I do not mean to suggest any fundamental problem with Feinberg's argument: he clearly views education as properly aimed at ennabling students to transcend particular cultural or national patterns of life, see 157.
13. Judicial liberals sometimes argue for group-based exceptions and accommodations to such general policies as Sunday closing laws and even the nation's drug laws, see *Braunfield v. Brown*, 366 U.S. 599 (1961), and *Employment Division, Department of Human Resources of Oregon v. Smith*, 494 U.S. 872 (1990). And see my discussion in *Diversity and Distrust: Civic Education in a Multicultural Democracy* (Transaction Books, Cambridge, Mass., 2000), part III.
14. The minimalist position is ably defended by Chandran Kukathas, "Are There Any Cultural Rights?" *Political Theory*, 20 (Feb. 1992), 105–39, and "Cultural Toleration" in Ian Shapiro and Will Kymlicka (eds), *Ethnicity and Group Rights: NOMOS XXXIX* (New York, 1997), 69–104.
15. In this volume, Shelly Burtt's essay in chapter 7; Susan Moller Okin, ch. 12. The Okin quote is from footnote 62.
16. See Andrew M. Greeley, *Catholic High Schools and Minority Students* (Harvard University Press, New Brunswick, NJ, 1982). Greeley speculates that because

women are strong authority figures within Catholic schools, students develop a more positive attitude toward gender equality.

17. See Burtt, ch. 7.
18. I have discussed *Yoder* and related cases in *Diversity and Distrust*, part II.
19. College due process rules were violated and so administrators were required to reconsider the matter.
20. "A Christian Fellowship's Ban on Gay Leaders Splits Two Campuses", *The Chronicle of Higher Education*, May 12, 2000, http://chronicle.com/weekly/v46/i36/36a05101.htm.
21. *Rosenberger* v. *Rectors of the University of Virginia*, 115 S.Ct. 2510 (1995).
22. I do not mean to suggest that this is the only reasonable way of setting up rules for campus organizations. This matter deserves more detailed and careful attention.
23. *Bob Jones University* v. *United States*, 461 U.S. 574 (1983).
24. *Bowers* v. *Hardwick*, 478 U.S. 186 (1986).

INDEX